China and Historical Capitalism

Only recently has it been recognized in th[...]
experience of the world has been as much th[...]
West. The primary subject of this book is the historical relation[...]
that has arisen between the concept of capitalism and the idea of
China. The concept of capitalism was formulated by European
intellectuals to identify the social formation in which they found
themselves. Portraying it either as an ideal system or as its necessary
prelude, they regarded capitalism as unique to Europe and as an
organic outgrowth of Western civilization. In the process, they rejected
China as a model of civilization, considering it merely despotic, feudal,
or stagnant. This Eurocentric judgement has hung over all subsequent
thinking about China, even influencing Chinese perceptions of their
own history. The aim of this collaborative project is to examine how
the experience of capitalism as a European social formation and as a
world-system has shaped knowledge of China. In addition the volume
aims to establish new foundations on which a theory of Chinese society
might be built, in order to perceive and understand Chinese development in less Eurocentric terms.

TIMOTHY BROOK is professor of history at the University of
Toronto, and author of seven books on China. These include *The
Confusions of Pleasure: Commerce and Culture in Ming China* (1998) and,
as co-editor, *Culture and Economy: The Shaping of Capitalism in Eastern
Asia* (1997).

GREGORY BLUE teaches world history at the University of
Victoria. He is the author of numerous articles on Sino-Western
cultural relations and co-editor of *Science and Technology in the
Transformation of the World* (1981).

Studies in Modern Capitalism · Etudes sur le Capitalisme Moderne

This series is devoted to an attempt to comprehend capitalism as a world-system. It will include monographs, collections of essays and colloquia around specific themes, written by historians and social scientists united by a common concern for the study of large-scale long-term social structure and social change.

The series is a joint enterprise of the Maisons des Sciences de l'Homme in Paris and the Fernand Braudel Center for the Study of Economies, Historical Systems, and Civilizations at the State University of New York at Binghamton.

Other books in the series

This book is published as part of the joint publishing agreement established in 1977 between the Fondation de la Maison des Sciences de l'Homme and the Press Syndicate of the University of Cambridge. Titles published under this arrangement may appear in any European language or, in the case of volumes of collected essays, in several languages.

New books will appear either as individual titles or in one of the series which the Maison des Sciences de l'Homme and the Cambridge University Press have jointly agreed to publish. All books published jointly by the Maison des Sciences de l'Homme and the Cambridge University Press will be distributed by the Press throughout the world.

China and Historical Capitalism

Genealogies of Sinological Knowledge

Edited by

Timothy Brook and Gregory Blue

MAISON DES SCIENCES DE L'HOMME

CAMBRIDGE
UNIVERSITY PRESS

PUBLISHED BY THE PRESS SYNDICATE OF THE UNIVERSITY OF CAMBRIDGE
The Pitt Building, Trumpington Street, Cambridge, United Kingdom

CAMBRIDGE UNIVERSITY PRESS
The Edinburgh Building, Cambridge CB2 2RU, UK
40 West 20th Street, New York NY 10011–4211, USA
477 Williamstown Road, Port Melbourne, VIC 3207, Australia
Ruiz de Alarcón 13, 28014 Madrid, Spain
Dock House, The Waterfront, Cape Town 8001, South Africa

http://www.cambridge.org

Kind permission is acknowledged to reprint extracts from R. Bin Hong (1997),
China Transformed: Historical Change and the Limits of European Experience
(Ithaca, NY, Cornell University Press).

First published 1999
First paperback edition 2002

Typeface Plantin 10/12 pt.

A catalogue record for this book is available from the British Library

ISBN 0 521 64029 6 hardback
ISBN 2 7351 0789 2 hardback, France only
ISBN 0 521 52591 8 paperback

In honor and memory of
Joseph Needham
1900–1995

Contents

Preface

This book has had its own long and complex history. The original idea of addressing the formation of European and Chinese interpretations of China in the light of the development of European capitalism we owe to Joseph Needham, who died in 1995 at the age of ninety-four. Needham stood out among Western scholars who have taken China seriously in the sense of using Chinese history to question assumptions about European and world history. He committed his work on the history of Chinese science and technology to the task of recognizing China's contributions to world scientific knowledge and scientific culture. Wanting to understand why Chinese science and technology had been comparatively advanced, only to be eclipsed by "modern" science in Europe after the sixteenth century, he set himself the task of historically reconstructing the Chinese scientific and technical traditions. During the Second World War he formulated his problematic in terms of the negative question of "why modern science had not developed in China but only in Europe," but he soon expanded his inquiries with the more positive formulation of "why was Chinese civilization much *more* efficient than occidental in gaining natural knowledge and in applying it to practical human needs" prior to the sixteenth century. The difference between Chinese superiority until that time and European superiority thereafter Needham credited not to a difference in civilizational genius, as many of his generation and their predecessors had done, but to differences in the historical circumstances shaping the two societies. In Needham's view, Europe underwent the social, economic, and intellectual transformations associated with the full development of capitalism whereas China did not, in large part for reasons of material organization that scholars only now are beginning to identify.[1]

Needham believed that a more profound understanding of the nature of Chinese society would be required to develop a satisfactory explanation for the historical evolution of science in China, and he designated

[1] Needham 1969; Needham and Huang 1974.

ix

volume VII of his *Science and Civilisation in China* (*SCC*) as the place in that series where this issue would be pursued. In his seventies he came to feel that other *SCC* commitments would make it impossible for him to devote his own time to this task, and so engaged collaborators for volume VII to investigate various aspects of the problem of comparing China's development with the emergence of capitalism in Europe, a subject also treated by Francesca Bray in her *SCC* volume on agriculture.[2] In 1977–78 he arranged for Gregory Blue and Timothy Brook to collaborate on volume VII by examining respectively European and Asian interpretations of Chinese society,[3] both of which he acknowledged had exercised great influence on his own thinking. In 1983 he invited Immanuel Wallerstein to examine the conditions of the emergence of capitalism in Europe in order to establish how one might now best understand the specific character of European historical development. Unanticipated difficulties that arose in the course of editing our part of volume VII in the early 1990s led to its cancellation. We decided then, with some regret, to publish our work outside the framework of *Science and Civilisation in China*. To enlarge the scope of the volume, we invited Bin Wong and Francesca Bray to contribute chapters that would help to complete the intellectual trajectory that this book seeks to describe: beginning with the peculiarity of Europe and ending with the specificity of China.

For their comments on sections of this book as it was in progress, we wish to thank Martin Bernal, Joshua Fogel, Dieter Kuhn, Kenneth Pomeranz, and Elinor Shaffer. For their support given during the long gestation of this volume, we are grateful to the successive librarians of the East Asian History of Science Library, Cambridge. The editorial assistance of Ludgard De Decker in the final phase of producing the manuscript and proof reading it is gratefully acknowledged. To Richard

---

[2] She argues there that the technical conditions of production in northern Europe favored the development of large-scale farms capable of economies of scale. They therefore tended to encourage capitalist relations of production in agriculture, while the technical conditions of riziculture, which was labor intensive and skill oriented, did not. See Bray 1984: 6, 134–39, 198–202.

[3] Having previously been struck by the palpable differences between Western sinological scholarship and orthodox Chinese Marxist historiography regarding ancient and imperial Chinese history, the two of us independently came to focus on issues of comparative "pre-capitalist" development prior to our collaboration with Joseph Needham. This we did through separate engagements with Perry Anderson's (1974a) *Lineages of the Absolutist State*, then recently published, particularly the substantial appendix on the Asiatic mode of production, which included a thoughtful appraisal of Needham's notion of "bureaucratic feudalism." (Ray Huang, another collaborator on volume VII, brought this text to Needham's attention.) As it was Bin Wong who first introduced Anderson's work to Brook, we are pleased that he has been able to join us in completing this intellectual odyssey.

Fisher we owe the privilege and pleasure of publishing with Cambridge University Press. In closing, we would like to reserve our final thanks, if we may, for each other. When we set out on our wandering journey to create what this book has become, we had no inkling of the extraordinary length of time it would take to complete the journey, nor of the bonds of friendship that journey would create. We only wish that Joseph were still with us to share, as he would have, in that pleasure.

TIMOTHY BROOK

GREGORY BLUE

9 December 1998

Major dynastic periods in China's history

Shang	1766–1122 BC
Zhou	1122–249
Qin	221–207
Former Han	202–8 AD
Latter Han	25–220
Tang	618–907
Northern Song	960–1127
Southern Song	1127–1279
Yuan (Mongols)	1271–1368
Ming	1368–1644
Qing (Manchus)	1644–1911
Republic	1912–1949
People's Republic	1949–

1   Introduction

Gregory Blue and Timothy Brook

The historical experience of the world has been as much the history of China as of the West.[1] This modest fact has found recognition in the West only recently, and still only in certain circles. The dominance of models of society derived from the European experience in history and the social sciences has served to block this recognition. Too often the generalizations of social science – and this is as true in Asia as in the West – rest on the belief that the West occupies the normative starting position for constructing general knowledge. Almost all our categories – politics and economy, state and society, feudalism and capitalism – have been conceptualized primarily on the basis of Western historical experience. Until recently, China was sometimes taken into account, yet it mattered only to the extent to which it provided corollary proofs for European solutions to European questions. The teleologies of meaning attached to these concepts of analysis in European history have remained intact in spite of the often glaring counterexamples that China and the rest of Asia offer to Western observers. In this volume, we aspire to take account of China's historical experience in a different way: in the first three chapters, to probe the impact that Western genealogies of historical knowledge have had on how China is understood; and in the latter two, to suggest lines of flight from this dead end.

However diminished by Western systems of thought, China since at least the thirteenth century has been an object of intense contemplation for Europeans. Since Marco Polo dictated his account of the prosperity of Khubilai Khan's empire and even before, the West has been fascinated by the scale of this realm at the other end of the Eurasian continent. The dream of profitably trading with the world's most populous market famously inspired Christopher Columbus among many others to search for access routes to China and succeed in soliciting the resources of the expanding European states to back their adventures. The trade was financed by silver extracted from the windfall

---

[1] Or of any other part of the world, for that matter.

1

mines of Potosí in Bolivia, and it was sufficient to compensate for the otherwise unbalanced terms of trade for two centuries. Only thereafter did the balance of trade tilt decisively in favor of the West, and less by trends in the newly industrializing textile trade than by military inter- ventions and the imposition of the British trade in opium. What followed was a combination of coercive measures similar to those imposed on the Ottoman and Persian empires, and for a time on Japan: the opening of ports to foreign commerce, the fixing of tariffs at low rates, the imposi- tion of commercial and banking concessions for foreign enterprises, the provision of residence and evangelization rights for Christian mission- aries and of extra-territorial privileges for Western (and later Japanese) nationals, and the ceding of territories of strategic or economic signifi- cance. The "China trade" continued to grow as this increasingly pervasive free-trade regime was enforced from the 1840s through the 1880s. During that period, China was wracked by major domestic upheavals, most notably the Taiping Rebellion, in which an estimated twenty million people died (approximately the number of total deaths in the First World War), and the famines of the late 1870s, in which nearly another ten million died. Diplomatic entanglements toward the turn of the twentieth century together with a sky-rocketing foreign debt pre- cipitated a dramatic downturn in China's international balance of payments, as well as in its international image.

Filled with a sense of urgency about their nation's weakness, Chinese intellectuals struggled to determine why Chinese society had failed to develop effective, "modern" institutions and standards of living com- mensurate with the West and Japan. This problem had already been posed in the West since the late eighteenth century by social and political theorists, by historians and economists, and by statesmen responsible for defining their governments' policies toward China. By the 1880s this question was absorbing Japanese thinkers as well. Into the second half of the twentieth century it has continued to serve in East and West as the basic intellectual horizon for scholarly research and practical planning with regard to Chinese society and China's place in the world.

A natural explanatory strategy for addressing the problem of China's weakness was to identify China as a discrete civilizational totality and to contrast it with the West, which was conceived as another such totality. The object of this strategy was to discover what was lacking in a Middle Kingdom whose place in the real world, far from being central, appeared more and more peripheral. The "naturalness" of this contrastive ap- proach followed in large degree from the strong and exclusivistic senses of identity to be found both in China and in the West. If there was debate about what the fundamental deficiencies were, most people favorable to reforming China took it for granted that China was poor and backward because it lacked qualities or institutions that Western societies possessed. It was likewise assumed that proper diagnosis of China's deficiencies would make it possible to improve its condition through the implementation of appropriate Western policies and institutions. If today this line of thinking brings to mind Edward Said's persuasive views about how Western imperialism brought about the "Orientalization of the Orient," by 1905 the Japanese example seemed to indicate that a combination of self-Orientalizing and extensive "learning from" the West could be effective in strengthening the state, asserting national sovereignty, and improving economic performance.

The strategy of constructing civilizational contrasts with the West involved several assumptions from which the conclusion seemed to follow that China was intrinsically inferior to the West. The first and most basic of these assumptions was the conviction that the West (or at least the segment of it that one admired) was possessed – whether culturally, socially, economically, or biologically – of a character or of qualities innately superior to those of other peoples. Another assumption was that the historical experience of Western civilization had been a closed process. Together these two ideas buttressed the notion that Western history was primarily a working out of innately superior capacities inherent in some exclusive way in Western society. Thus, in the period since antiquity – perhaps since the Greeks, but especially since the Germanic invasions – Western civilization was seen as having stood above outside influence or interactions with other cultures. While progressive thinkers commonly shared the view that the Western historical experience represented the norm of world-historical progress *per se*, anti-progressives were perfectly happy to depict progress as a dream shared by the lower classes and the "inferior races" alike.[2] Whatever their political orientation, nineteenth-century analysts almost uniformly assumed that Chinese society had remained essentially unchanged in an inferior state since antiquity. Because of these assumptions, the approach of contrasting civilizational totalities seemed to support the conclusion that China's inferiority to the West at that time, rather than being shaped primarily by recent trends in internal socio-political development or in international relations, was instead a long-term consequence of quasi-permanent structural features identifiable as deficient because they differed from features characteristic of the West.

The notion of Chinese changelessness had not always been taken for granted. At the beginning of the seventeenth century, in combatting the

---

[2] Gobineau and some of his followers considered capitalism, like the yearning for progress, as a mark of racial degeneracy; see Blue 1999.

idea that the "starry firmament" was fixed, Galileo used the metaphor of China, with which Europe had recently become better acquainted, to indicate the danger of believing that distance and difficulty of observation justified concluding that an object of investigation was changeless. Later in the century Chinese struggles against the Manchus and the upheavals at the fall of the Ming dynasty were well publicized in the West, and subsequent events and policies were regularly reported to European audiences by Jesuit missionaries resident in China as advisors to the Qing emperors. Though some commentators expressed doubt, the Jesuits reported the impressive fact that the Chinese population more than doubled during the eighteenth century. Yet, by the last quarter of that century, Western thinkers were coming to perceive China in a new light that assumed Western secular as well as religious superiority. Adam Smith still understood that China "had long been one of the richest, that is, one of the most fertile, best cultivated, most industrious, and most populous countries of the world." He nevertheless considered it to have been "long stationary" and to have changed little in terms of "cultivation, industry, and populousness" since the time of Marco Polo.[3] We single out Smith not because his assessment of China was extraordinarily novel or negative – indeed, it was mild compared to those of some of his contemporaries. We cite him because Chinese historical stagnation became a cliché over the following century, a cliché that European social theory mobilized to develop its understanding of capitalism (or, as Smith called it, commercial society). Though the Galilean vision of the universe as a dynamic system was becoming more widely accepted, Western thinkers were increasingly perceiving Asia as a whole, and China as a part of it, as historically static.

For nineteenth-century Western thinkers who identified capitalism as either the ideal economic system or the necessary prelude to an ideal system, capitalism was a unique and organic outgrowth of Western civilization. Curiously, as Bin Wong argues in this volume, the Smithian model of commercial society as involving a multiplicity of small, more or less equal producers realizing efficiency gains through the market seems actually to have been rather apt for describing later imperial Chinese society. However, from the late eighteenth century until the period between the two world wars, the notion of capitalist society was embedded in Eurocentric theories of stages of progress. While capitalism was thought of as standing at or near the pinnacle of historical development, China was thought of as a historically stagnant society that remained naturally near the bottom. Its only hope for economic

---

[3] Smith 1937: 55.

progress was to turn its back on the past and to take lessons from the West. These notions were perpetuated through the Romantic, Hegelian, and positivist traditions of scholarship into the early decades of the twentieth century.

Given the power of the negative identity that "capitalism" conferred on China, almost every attempt to place China in our field of knowledge involves recurrence to a prior recognition of China and capitalism as a contrasting pair. The consequences of this pairing of ideas have been potent: capitalism is credited with having brought China into history, and China is discredited for having failed either to develop capitalism on its own or adopt it compliantly from the outside. Capitalism set the terms by which China had to fail, and China provided the example of failure from which capitalism could assert its civilizational identity and its superiority as an efficient form of political economy.

This book is our collective attempt to consider elements of the relationship between China and Western social theories of capitalism. We do not address the effects that Western capitalism has had on China's political economy, nor do we examine the economic growth currently underway in East Asia. Our interest is rather in how capitalism as it has been conceived as a European social formation and as a world-system has shaped knowledge of China. We aim to identify distortions introduced in the understanding of China under the influence of cultural and ideological trends that took Western capitalist relations and patterns of development to be the norm for the world, and in doing so hope to contribute to devising more adequate understandings of Chinese society. To understand China better we must begin to see past the narrative of modern world history as the "European miracle," and so develop less Eurocentric ways of understanding the world.

Pursuing this inquiry has involved framing three questions. The first is, what is distinctive about the emergence of a capitalist order in Europe? The assumption behind this question is that part of Europe underwent significant social, economic, and political changes between the fourteenth and sixteenth centuries that heightened its capacity to act in the world economy, and that these changes can be understood as constituting the early formation of European capitalism.

The second question is, how has the idea of the capitalist transformation of Europe affected how Europeans and Asians have viewed China? This question assumes that the relative repositioning of Europe and China in the world economy in the wake of Europe's capitalist transformation had profound effects on knowledge in both places. Europeans came to regard their place in the world, and the place of other societies in the world, differently as a result of changes in the sphere of global economic competition. So too, the Chinese assessment of what China was and had been was profoundly affected by the same expansion of Western dominance, not so much when the expansion was first under way, but after it was well advanced at the turn of the twentieth century when China found itself subordinated to the European capitalist world-system.

The third question is this: On the premise that our understanding of China has been distorted by the view that Western capitalism constitutes a universal historical outcome, how might we move beyond such distortions in analyzing Chinese history? As the structures of the Chinese economy and state did not have to approximate European state and society during or after a transition to capitalism, distinct institutional models and models of historical change may be required to capture different dynamics at work at the two ends of the Eurasian continent. A thorough reinvestigation of Chinese history that seeks to go beyond existing categories of historical analysis based primarily on the Western experience may lead to a rethinking of current models of world history, most conspicuously the story of "the rise of the West."

The five chapters of the book proceed in sequence through these questions. Immanuel Wallerstein presents a conjunctural analysis that sees the emergence of capitalism in Europe as resulting from the working out of broad Eurasian trends in the particular conditions of one region of the medieval "Old World" trade ecumene. His analysis strongly challenges the traditions of attributing that transition to any timeless "spirit" of Western civilization or to an institutional miracle unrelated to what was going on elsewhere. Treating the emergence of European capitalism as a specific response to a general crisis that involved the entire Old World trading system, he analyzes the European "break-through" to a capitalist order as resulting from the peculiar breakdown of social and political restrictions that in other predominantly agricultural societies served to limit the growth of production and consumption. In placing the origin of crucial features of European capitalist societies in the late medieval period, this analysis throws light on long-term structural differences between Europe and Asia. It leaves open the issues of when and in which respects Europe achieved superior levels of economic performance.

In the second chapter, Gregory Blue turns to European representations of China from the sixteenth to the early twentieth century. Those representations were spurred by the gradual aggregation of a body of knowledge about a society that loomed distantly as one of Europe's most significant "others." This body of knowledge included a growing number of items of information about China which were bound together with a porous mortar of interpretation that crumbled and was remade over time as the West faced changing political and economic pressures in the capitalist world-system around the globe, including in China. The early contacts through the Jesuit mission produced a generally positive view of Chinese society, but Western depictions became more disdainful from the late eighteenth century as European colonial power in Asia was strikingly extended and consolidated, and as demand for raw materials and markets for the West's newly mechanized industries drove capitalism to exploit the economic potentials of Asia more systematically. The consolidation of colonialism led either to writing a generically inferior past for the non-European world, or to ascribing a feudal past similar to Europe's but lacking the capacity to make the passage from feudalism to capitalism. Within this regime of knowledge China fared badly. Its troubled story of decline was offered to the world as part of the epochal tale of Europe's own successful modernity.

Timothy Brook continues the analysis of China's historiographical subordination to the capitalist West in the third chapter by moving from European narratives to those that Asian intellectuals constructed. By early in the twentieth century, Asian intellectuals were abandoning indigenous approaches to Chinese history in favor of European-derived analyses that focused on the non-development of capitalism in China. Struggling against the political disruptions that followed the incorporation of China and Japan into the capitalist world-system, many Chinese and Japanese subscribed to Western views of China based on the model of the passage from feudalism to capitalism. The European Marxist narrative of the growth and eventual overthrow of capitalism promised an eventual transcendence of China's non-capitalist backwardness and access to modernity without capitalism. In the past two decades, as capitalist modernity has become increasingly established in the Chinese culture area, the discourse of transcending capitalism may have receded, yet Chinese historiography at present remains focused on the development of capitalism more than ever, substituting genealogies of continuity for those of transcendence.

In the final two chapters, Francesca Bray and Bin Wong take our project of interrogating the Western foundations of sinological knowledge further by considering how Chinese and European history might jointly be conceived without simplistic recourse to models constructed around the rise of European capitalism. Bray examines long-term trends in Chinese material civilization to investigate the linkages among culture, economics, and politics that obtained in China. She concentrates on the shift of regional predominance from the north to the south, which occurred during the late Tang and Song dynasties, from the ninth to the thirteenth century. This shift she relates to long-term shifts in the empire's mix of rural products, with northern wheat, millet, and silk as central to state revenues in the early centuries, but with rice and cottons, hailing primarily from south China, becoming the central products from the Song. In turn, she explores how changes in gender roles in farming and textile production heightened the anxieties of the elite and the Confucian state about moral disorder as the rural economy became increasingly commodified in later centuries.

Bin Wong turns our attention to the dynamics of China's internal economic transformations and the changing relation of the Chinese economy to the capitalist world system. Following both sides of this subject through the late Qing and the Republican periods and finally into the era of the People's Republic, he brings the discussion back to the central issue of finding adequate economic and historiographical theoretical tools for explaining the burgeoning commercialization evident in China from the Song, but particularly impressive from the sixteenth century onward. Wong takes up Adam Smith's model of a commercial society in which a multiplicity of small producers compete. While pointing out difficulties in the recent literature that depicts near perfect fluidity in labor and commodity flows across regions, he finds the Smithian model of commercial society useful for analyzing the evidence not only for early modern markets in Western Europe but also for those in late imperial and Republican China. In macroeconomic terms, however, Chinese made decisions about capital concentration, the distribution of economic goods, and the provision of sustenance that differed from the choices of Europeans, and had different consequences with regard to the formation of capital and the character of society. These choices, accordingly, have generated a different agenda for economic growth in China today.

The challenge this volume poses is not simply for China historians to break away from Eurocentric theories, difficult as that is, but for social theorists working within Western historiographic assumptions to recognize the challenge that knowledge of China constitutes to theory, and to reconsider the modern history of the world in this light. The point is to take China seriously in devising theoretical concepts that embrace the diversity of social reality, not just to fix on those elements of the Chinese record that confirm or deny particular aspects of existing Western (or other) social theory, but to treat China as a significant case that must be integrally explained by any theory that is to be considered adequate.

The deepening involvement of the People's Republic of China with the capitalist world-system since the economic reforms of the late 1970s, and the increasing success with which Chinese communities outside the PRC have been able to compete in international markets, intensify the pressure to develop social theory in ways that can take China and all of East Asia into account. Some theorists, like economist Yukio Yoshihara, have sought to distinguish the contemporary historical formation of East Asian economies by characterizing them as "pariah" or "ersatz" capitalism.[4] Others, like anthropologist Ruth McVey, find the dynamics of large-scale commodity trading in contemporary East Asia to be well within the definition of capitalism.[5] Still others, such as world-systems economist Andre Gunder Frank, have taken the historical record of commerce in East Asia as grounds for questioning the validity of capitalism as an analytical category that sets Europe apart from Asia.[6] As the debates on these issues continue, a condition of explanatory success will be a willingness to step back from European models where those models cast shadows rather than throw light. We hope that our consideration of the relationship between China and capitalism in this volume demonstrates the value of taking China seriously, and we encourage others to rethink social theory in the same spirit.

[4] Regarding "ersatz capitalism," see Yoshihara 1988.   [5] McVey 1992.
[6] E.g., Frank 1991: 171–72, 185–86; restated in Frank 1995: 186–90 and now most fully in Frank 1998. See also Bergeson 1995.

2   The West, capitalism, and the modern world-system

Immanuel Wallerstein

> If one wonders what is the "sense" of their endless chase, why [businessmen] are never satisfied with what they have, and thus inevitably seem to act in senseless ways in terms of any purely worldly approach to life, they would occasionally respond, if they knew how to answer at all: "to provide for my children and grandchildren." But, that argument not being peculiar to them but working just as well for the traditionalist, they would be more likely to respond in a simpler, most exact fashion, that business with its constant work had become "indispensable to their life." That is in fact the only accurate explanation and brings out what is so irrational in this lifestyle from the point of view of personal happiness, that a man exists for his business, and not the other way around   (Weber 1947: 54).

The Rise of the West?

The West, capitalism, and the modern world-system are inextricably linked together – historically, systemically, intellectually. But exactly how, and why? This is a question on which there has been little consensus up to now, and there is indeed less and less.

The imbrication of the three concepts (three realities?) reached its apogee in the nineteenth century. But how even do we delimit this nineteenth century? – 1815–1914? or 1789–1917? or 1763–1945? or even 1648–1968? Within any of these time frames, but particularly as we narrow them, there seemed little doubt for most people in most parts of the globe that the "West" (or "Europe") had "risen," and that it was exercising, particularly after 1815, effective political and economic domain over the rest of the world, at least until this dominance began to recede in the twentieth century.

The nineteenth century was also the period during which the historical sciences became institutionalized as formal "disciplines," as arenas (and modes) of knowledge. And, of course, this particular institutionalization occurred originally within "Western" universities, to be imposed subsequently upon the entire world-system. Furthermore, it is scarcely

10

an exaggeration to assert that the central intellectual problem with which the various emerging disciplines concerned themselves was the explanation of this presumed (but seemingly self-evident) "rise of the West" (otherwise known as "the expansion of Europe" or "the transition from feudalism to capitalism" or "the origins of modernity").

Given the dominance of Enlightenment thought in the nineteenth-century world, the explanations that were offered all tended to presume a theory of progress, of the inevitably progressive progression of societal forms, that had reached by some teleological process the particular configuration of the world-system as it was then structured. There existed no doubt a quarrel about the future, a quarrel about whether the modern world-system represented the culminating qualitative level of this progress (essentially the "Whig interpretation of history") or only a penultimate stage in the progression of humanity (essentially the core assertion of Marxist historiography).

The quarrel about the future, however, was fought out primarily in the political arena, and by political means. It was the quarrel about the past that preoccupied the universities. This quarrel revolved around two central questions. First, what was the agent or propelling force or prime mover of this historical trajectory? Was it the development of technology, or the striving for human liberty, or the class struggle, or the secular tendency to an increase of scale, and/or the bureaucratization of the world? And, secondly, whatever the answer given to this first question, why was it that the "West" (or some sub-part thereof) was "first" or furthest "advanced" in this historical trajectory?

It is interesting to note what questions were not asked, or seldom asked, either in the nineteenth century or since. It was not asked why this new phenomenon (whatever it was called) had not occurred much earlier in human history, say a thousand years earlier. It was not asked whether there had existed any plausible historical alternative to this particular "transition" or development. That is to say, was the development of "capitalism" or "modernity" unavoidable, at least at this moment in time? And, since this latter question was not asked, it follows that it was not asked why the alternative paths were not followed. The entire discussion in fact centered around the premiss that whatever had occurred had to have occurred. And, since it had to have occurred, it seems that it was by this very fact to be considered more or less progressive. I should like to turn the question around, to reverse the problematic. Instead of asking why capitalism or modernity or industrial development or intensive growth occurred in the West first, I want to ask the question why did it happen at all anywhere? After all, almost all the standard explanations invoke variables that had been in existence at many times and in many different climes at earlier moments of world history. Yet previously there had been no such transformation. Apparently only circa 1500 (but this dating is subject to much argument) did there occur the particular concatenation of these variables such that – in (Western) Europe – there was this transformation of the world that most people agree today was special in some way and significantly different from anything that had occurred before or elsewhere.

If one uses the physical analogy of an explosion caused by some critical mass or particular assemblage of variables, the question of whether this "explosion" was intrinsically necessary or historically "accidental" becomes a real intellectual question, one that has to be resolved before constructing an entire theoretical scaffolding for the historical social sciences out of an inevitable "transition."

Let us start by reviewing the statements upon which there is a relative consensus in this entire discussion. Most scholars throughout the world, and of many different persuasions, seem to agree on the following minimal descriptions of part of the empirical situation.

1 (Western) Europe, in what is called the Middle Ages, was organized in a system (productive, legal, political) that may be designated as "feudalism." But there is little consensus on what were its crucial or defining characteristics, and on whether this system was unique to Europe or also known elsewhere in the world.

2 European feudalism came to an end, or broke down, and was transformed into or replaced by another system that some call capitalism, some call modernity, and some give still other names. But there is little consensus about the crucial or defining characteristics of the successor system, nor about whether this "transition" occurred only once in history, or repetitively (in the separate "states").

3 This system, which originated in Europe (or in various European states), somehow spread gradually over the whole world. In geographic terms, this can be visualized as an "expansion" of European ideas, power, and authority. But there is little consensus about whether Europe imposed this system upon the rest of the world, or whether the system simply "diffused" as a result of its supposedly patent superiorities, nor is there consensus about the degree to which non-Europeans opposed this spread or the degree of advantage this spread offered to the non-Europeans, if it offered any at all.

4 This new system resulted in an enormous increase in world productive capacity and in world population, but there is little consensus about the ratio of the two (and how to measure it), nor about the degree to which the increase in productive capacity is evenly distributed over the (increased) world population.

In short, a very minimal framework of agreed observations are there, though each is surrounded by important related questions about which even the empirical description is under severe debate.

Finally, there is an enormous confusion about what is to be explained under the heading "rise of the West" (or any of its alternative wordings). There are at least three separate sub-questions about which there is considerable argument. One is the explanation of what caused the so-called "crisis of feudalism," that is, what brought about the decline/ disappearance of a particular existing historical system. The second question, whose relation to the first is unclear in most accounts, is why, at the very time that "feudalism" was declining or disappearing in *Western* Europe, did it seem to be increasing (or even occurring in some areas for the first time) in *Eastern* Europe in the form of the so-called "second serfdom." A third question is whether meaningful distinctions can be made in the patterns among Western European zones, and in particular whether (and why) England became "capitalist" before France (or the Netherlands, or "Germany" or "Italy"). Finally, there is a literature that seeks to explain why other civilizational zones of the world (China, India, the Islamic world) did *not* proceed to become "capitalist" or "modern" at this moment in time, but Europe did. Nevertheless, despite this confusion, I note once again one unifying premise – that some zone had to move "forward" in this way, and at this approximate moment in time.

And since, in virtually everyone's view, the zone that did move forward was in fact Western Europe (or for some, more narrowly, England), it seems clear that there occurred a "rise of the West." Indeed, this has been frequently denoted as "the European miracle." The miracle, it seems, is the realization of the central value of the capitalist system itself: productivism.[1] E. L. Jones states it quite clearly: "The vital question ... is how did a world of static expansion give way to one of *intensive* growth? ... History is to be thought of as repeated, tentative efforts of *intensive* growth to bubble up through the stately rising dough of *extensive* growth."[2] This stark formulation of the nature of the miracle fits well the prevailing mood of the intellectual problem as it had emerged in the nineteenth century. It is to be sure somewhat solipsistic. The West rose. How do we know the West rose? It achieved intensive growth. Why did the West rise? It achieved intensive growth. Why is it that achieving intensive growth is considered to be a "rise"? Because it is a universal value, one however

---

[1] See Jones 1987. Gellner underlines the point by saying: "The phrase should not be read ... the *European* miracle. It must be read ... the European "*miracle*" (1988: 1).

[2] Jones 1988: 31.

that originated in the West – in large part, in fact, after the West had begun to grow intensively. What makes it then a universal value? It was culturally imposed upon (diffused into) the whole of the world, and has its adherents today in all parts of the world, most particularly among the governments of the world.

Once again, we might invert the question. Did the West really rise? or did the West in fact fall? Was it a miracle, or was it a grave malady? Was it an achievement, or a serious failing? Was it the realization of rationality, or of irrationality? Was it an exceptional breakthrough, or an exceptional breakdown? Do we need to explain the limitations of other civilizations and/or historical systems such that they did not produce a transition to modern capitalism, or do we need to explain the limitations of Western civilization or the medieval historical system located in Western Europe such that it did permit the transition to modern capitalism? And was it programmed, or was it a fluke?

I propose to discuss these matters as two successive questions: What is distinctive about the capitalist "modern" historical system that distinguishes it from alternative (and preceding) historical systems? How was the capitalist world-economy in fact historically constructed?

What is distinctive about capitalism?

There have been three approaches to defining the *differentia specifica* of capitalism (or "modernity") as a historical system. One is to delineate the social activities or social phenomena considered to be primary or fundamental. A second is to specify the processes by which these presumed activities or phenomena occur. A third is to describe the structures that account for the processes. In each case it is necessary to argue that these activities or processes or structures can be seen as sufficiently different qualitatively (or quantitatively or in both ways) from those of other historical systems such that they warrant a special designation. This turns out to be a more difficult task intellectually than most analysts have admitted.

There is of course no reason why we should prefer defining an historical system in terms of its activities or in terms of its processes and/or its structures, or vice versa; the three vantage points are clearly linked. But it is not certain that they are linked in such a tight way that defining an historical system from one of the three vantage points immediately and certainly determines its definition from the other vantage points. In any case, various authors have asserted a strong preference for utilizing one or the other of the vantage points.

Let us start by looking at the presumed distinctive activities of the capitalist/"modern" historical system. There seems to be little difference in this regard among analysts of conservative, liberal, or Marxist ideological persuasion. Virtually everyone tends to see capitalism as the system in which humans seek to transform (or "conquer") nature in an eternally expansive way and to amass ever larger residues of this expansion. Whether it is David Landes speaking of "Prometheus unbound," or Carlyle deploring the "cash nexus," or Marx analyzing the search for an endless accumulation of capital, or Keynes's references to the "animal spirits" of (Schumpeter's) entrepreneurs, or, as we have already seen, the description of the achievement of intensive growth as a "miracle," the phenomenon that is being observed takes the form of a hyperbolic curve that knows no *social* limit. To be sure, whether physical limits exist beyond the control of the historical system itself, that is, whether "nature" inherently places limits on humanity is a question that has been increasingly asked in the twentieth century. But that modern capitalism is an historical system without conscious internal social constraints to its systemic activities is widely asserted, and it is this ceaseless accumulation of capital that may be said to be its most central activity and to constitute its *differentia specifica*. No previous historical system seems to have had any comparable *mot d'ordre* of social limit-lessness. Thus, capitalism involves not merely the sale of products for profit or the growth of capital stock (commodities, or machines, or money). It specifically refers to a system based on accumulating such stock endlessly, a system wherein, as the Weber epigraph says, "a man exists for his business, and not the other way around."

A definition at the level of the continuing search for growth, expansion, accumulation without end, whose justification is itself ("we climb Mount Everest because it is there"), has the signal double advantage of not only being consonant with virtually all the explanations of the structures and processes of the capitalist/"modern" world, but also of being a good fit with historical reality. The capitalist world has in fact grown, steadily and for many variables geometrically, for several hundred years, its cyclical downturns all being part of long-term secular linear trends – at least thus far.

Furthermore, it is quite apparent that this description of capitalist activity fits well with the central tendencies of Western "universalist" thought since the late Middle Ages – the Renaissance and the Reformation, Baconian–Newtonian science, the Enlightenment, "modernity" as a cultural expression. We shall see, when we proceed to discuss both the processes and the structures of capitalism, that there are many problems in distinguishing the capitalist/"modern" historical system in these regards from prior non-capitalist ones. But it is quite easy to perceive the distinction at the level of its *Weltanschauung*, at the level of this central defining activity of ceaseless growth, the ceaseless accumulation of capital. In this regard, no other historical system could have been said to have pursued such a mode of social life for more than at most brief moments.

The agreement on the assessment of capitalist reality that exists for the description of its central activity breaks down as soon as one turns to analyzing the processes by which this activity is pursued. Indeed, the analyses we have of the processes of our capitalist/"modern" historical system are doubly confusing. First, we are given virtually opposite descriptions by differing analysts. And secondly, it is not clear that either of the opposing descriptions describes a reality clearly different from that of other historical systems. We may see this in the dissecting of three processes which are referred to in almost all analyses: the freedom of subjects, the distribution of surplus, and the construction of knowledge.

The freedom of subjects to pursue their interests has long been one of the central themes in the analysis of the capitalist/"modern" historical system. What, however, one can mean by the "freedom" of subjects to pursue their interests is far from self-evident. In the evolution of Western universalist philosophy, the emphasis has been placed on the (progressive) elimination of external constraints – external to the subject (or individual) – on the part of both political institutions and collective social institutions (for example, religious structures). This is in part a question of jurisprudence, in part a question of mentalities. The evidence that is usually adduced to demonstrate a decline in constraints is, on the one hand, the possibility of mobility – geographical, occupational, social – and, on the other hand, the absence or minimization of political or social repression.

However, the absence of constraints has been interpreted by other analysts in a directly opposite fashion. The elimination of constraints has been considered to be the elimination of guarantees for reproduction. A "constrained" system offers rights for current reproducton on the basis of past activities – past activities of the present individual or his forebears. When the "constraints" are removed, however, current reproduction becomes dependent on current activity. And current activity depends on current alternatives. If one is "forced to be free," that is, if the alternative of rights deriving from heritage are eliminated, the scope of alternatives may in fact be reduced, not increased. This might be true whether one is comparing a medieval serf to a contemporary proletarian or a medieval seignior to a contemporary middle-class professional.

We find ourselves in what is an unclear debate about the range of effective freedoms that result from ability (rights) to act in the present and ability (rights) to preserve the fruits of past acts. Furthermore, whichever set of factors one emphasizes (the increased range of choice in the "present" or the diminished guarantees deriving from past activity), it is uncertain how great the difference is between the capitalist/"modern" historical system and other (past) systems. For example, the *de facto* mobility of serfs was greater than the comparison usually assumes, and the *de facto* mobility of proletarians less. On the other hand, the *de facto* guarantees of reproduction of serfs was less than the comparison usually assumes, and the *de facto* guarantees of reproduction of proletarians greater.

We encounter similar problems when we look at the process by which surplus is distributed. The unequal distribution of the total social product has presumably been true of all known historical systems. There are however several aspects of the unequal distribution that may vary. One is how large is the produced "surplus" (meaning the value produced by an historical system over and above the amount necessary for simple reproduction). The second is how unequally it is distributed (as measured for example by a Gini curve). But the third and most often cited in the discussion is the process by which the unequal distribution occurs.

Given the ceaseless accumulation of capital, already established as the primary activity of the capitalist/"modern" historical system, it follows that the absolute surplus is large and far larger than that of previous historical systems. But is it more unequally distributed? Here the theoretical (and empirical) positions of contending ideological schools have been directly at odds one with the other. One school contends that our current system is relatively more egalitarian in distribution than previous systems and getting ever more so. The opposing school contends the exact inverse: that the distribution is more unequal (or more polarized) and getting ever more so. One of the sources of this difference is that the two camps take different spatial units to measure. Those who see increasing equality tend to focus on so-called "advanced" industrial countries, alone categorized as fully capitalist/"modern" (on the basis of certain structures, to be discussed below). Those who see increasing polarization tend to focus on the capitalist/"modern" historical system as a whole. It remains difficult, therefore, to take as a defining feature of an historical system one (degree of equality of distributed surplus) about which the empirical evidence is so contentious.

We arrive therefore at the measurement most frequently proposed, the mode or process of distribution. This comes down to a distinction between "rent" and "profit." Both terms are subject to much terminological confusion. The ideal type of "rent" is derived from the model of the seignior who controls ("owns") land whose use he allocates to direct cultivators in some sort of contract, in return for some kind of payment generically called "rent." What makes this payment "rent" is a combination of two factors: a politically secured "right" to exact such payments and the fact that the seignior need put no labor into the arrangement in order to receive the payment. The ideal-type of "profit" is derived from the model of the urban industrial factory in which the capitalist entrepreneur/owner hires wage laborers to utilize his machinery, retaining the "profit" from the sales of the final product, the "profit" being the difference between gross income and total costs. What makes this net income "profit" is that there has been an "investment" of capital by the entrepreneur/owner and some direct management of the economic operation.

One difference between the two modes of distribution of surplus is the form of moral justification offered. In the ideal-typical situation of "rent," the primary moral justification is "tradition." Unequal distribution is somehow God-given (and perhaps in a secondary way a reward for past military activity). In the ideal-typical situation of "profit," the justification offered is quite the opposite. The unequal distribution is precisely not considered God-given but primarily the result of human activity, mostly in the present but partially in the past. To be sure, we are speaking of the moral justifications offered in each system by the beneficiaries of the unequal distribution and those who defend them. Critics, with opposite views, have always existed to contest these moral justifications. But, critics aside, it is important to note the difference of emphasis of the two moral justifications: spiritual versus material, presumably eternal versus continually to be renewed by current activity, serving the public weal through the maintenance of collective order versus serving the public weal by achieving an optimal collective "growth."

But here too, on closer inspection, the two ideal types seem to lose much of their distinctiveness. "Rent" seems to play a central role in the capitalist/"modern" historical system, and we are becoming more and more aware of how many operations in prior historical systems took the form of "profit." Furthermore, for very many economic operations, it is difficult to decide whether the appropriation of surplus is "rent" or "profit."

The difference between capitalism as a mode of production and the multiple varieties of a redistributive or tributary mode of production is surely not, as often asserted, the difference between a mode in which all transfer of surplus is mediated through the market and one in which the transfer is accomplished through "extra-economic coercion." For there is considerable extra-economic coercion in our capitalist/"modern" historical system, and markets of some kind have almost always existed in other historical systems.

The most we can argue is a distinction that is more subtle. In the constant tensions between allocation via market mechanisms and allocation via administrative (or political) mechanisms, and in the contradictory behavior that results from the conflicting pressures, either mode of allocation may prevail in given situations in either kind of historical system in the short run. But in the middle run, the market will play a larger role in the capitalist/"modern" historical system than the political arena. To be sure, the "market" is itself shaped, in the middle run, by the political arena. Nevertheless, once shaped, it has a conjunctural autonomy whose impact is hard to constrain administratively, and which thus forces political redefinitions, from time to time, of the shape of the "market." It is not really the case that in capitalism the market is "free" from political controls, as is asserted by neo-classical economists. It is rather that the market becomes itself an important political mechanism, something not true (or far less true) in redistributive/tributary historical systems.

We can put this in the language of the invisible hand. In redistributive/tributary systems, the methods in which transfers of surplus are accomplished tend to be quite visible: rent, taxation, plunder, ritual payments. In the capitalist/"modern" historical system, some significant portion of the transfer occurs less visibly, via the "market," in the form of "profit." The advantage to the recipient of the larger share is that the losers may be in part unaware of having lost, or less immediately aware, and also less aware of exactly to whom they have lost. They may thus be less able to analyze the operations by which the transfer has occurred, and therefore less able to contest its injustice to them. In any case, a capitalist system operates by trying to convert visible transfers into "invisible" ones. However, since the "invisible hand" is a hand that is politically structured (and constantly restructured), it is difficult to keep it "invisible." Thus the political success of the device is far from perfect; it has nonetheless been reasonably efficacious, in part precisely because it is so complicated.

The third process which is repeatedly offered as a or the *differentia specifica* of the capitalist/"modern" historical system is the construction of knowledge. This is put forward in a number of guises. In general, the emphasis is on the predominance of science, or of a certain form of science and therefore of scientific method, a mode of thought sometimes referred to as Newtonian or Baconian–Newtonian, and which presumes or emphasizes the linearity and universality of physical phenomena. It is less that this mode of science constitutes in some way the essence of the capitalist/"modern" historical system than that it alone, it is argued, could have made possible the remarkable transformation of technology that has historically occurred. In turn it was this transformation of technology that made possible the large-scale substitution of non-human for human energy in productive activities which in turn accounts for the phenomenon of intensive growth.

There are a number of levels at which this thesis can be, and has been, challenged. In the late twentieth century, there has been increasing challenge, from within the community of science itself, of the adequacy or utility of this model of science. The challenge, to the degree that it is correct, raises questions implicitly about the rationality of the technological choices that were historically made on the basis of the Newtonian model. This however amounts to a critique of the practice of the capitalist/"modern" historical system, and not necessarily a questioning of its nominal existence.

A quite different challenge has been to question the singularity of the technological achievements of this historical system. One effort has been to establish a continuous pattern of scientific/technological advance, located in many different world regions (China, India, the Near East, the Mediterranean zone), into which recent Western European scientific efforts have fit themselves, primarily since the sixteenth century. By underlining continuities, this argument reduces the distinctiveness of what occurred in Western Europe. Furthermore, it has been argued that, in this arena as in many others, Western Europe had previously been a "backward" or "marginal" zone, implying therefore that any explanation of significant change could not be accounted for exclusively or even primarily in terms of some West European affinity for or tradition of scientific knowledge.

This rapid survey of processes that may be thought to distinguish the capitalist/"modern" historical system from other systems suggests that the distinctions are difficult to etch clearly, and that it is dubious to erect a theoretical scaffolding of explanation on the basis of these presumedly distinctive processes. Can we do better if we look at the structures of the capitalist/"modern" historical system?

There are three structures that have been established in the capitalist/"modern" historical system which repeatedly have been (separately and collectively) asserted to be its distinguishing features: private property; commodification (of goods, of land, and of labor); and the sovereign "modern" state. Each poses problems in the effort to uncover the *differentia specifica*.

Private or quiritary property rights refers to the assignation of ownership to individuals (real or fictive) of physical phenomena (extended to include so-called intellectual property), who receive legal guarantees that they can retain their property indefinitely, transfer or sell it, and bequeath it. They may also use it (or leave it unused), rent it, or use it up. Furthermore, no one may confiscate it, use it, or dispose of it in their stead or against their will. Finally, all physical phenomena are in principle owned by someone.

There are certain elementary objections to this picture of the institution. Not all phenomena are in fact owned by someone. For example, it is generally agreed that air is not owned, and water seldom is. It is not true that property is exempt from all outside decisions. For example, states retain the right of eminent domain. They may legislate limitations on certain usages to which property may be put. In times of "emergency," they may go even further. Sales of property are subject to various legal limitations. Thus, on the one hand, property rights are far from absolute in the capitalist/"modern" historical system. On the other hand, this system is not the only one to have had such property rights. As frequently noted, ancient Rome, for example, had a similar structure of quiritary rights.

If, however, we leave these objections aside as minor, and agree that property rights are a pervasive phenomenon of the capitalist/"modern" historical system and it alone, there remains the question of how relevant this is. Property is first of all the securing of phenomena that potentially lead, directly or via the market, to some kind of consumption. Against whom, and why, does consumption need to be secured? Obviously, there are generically only two possibilities: against the collectivity of others, and against individual others.

Security of property against the collectivity is of course not absolute. We have already noted the concept of eminent domain, or the rights of the state in an "emergency." But how effective is it, even normally? Can not modern states (and their substructures) tax, more or less at will? If they are restrained in taxation, is it not primarily by political pressures rather than by constitutional fiat? No doubt, there is a point at which "normal" taxation may be thought to be exceeded, and the state is considered to be (illegitimately) confiscatory. But this is hard to define, and harder to enforce legally against the state bureaucracy, and in any case the very definition of the threshold level that constitutes confiscation is subject to constant redefinition and stretching. The real question is the *de facto* difference between the security of so-called private property against the collectivity and the security of other forms of control of physical phenomena in non-capitalist historical systems against the collectivity. In the latter systems, the constraint on the collectivity (or the political ruler) may not be thought of as the illegitimacy of confiscation but rather as the illegitimacy of violating the "moral economy." But in practice, how great is the distinction?

There is of course the second guarantee of security, that against other individuals. This is the guarantee against theft, plunder, fraud. But surely there are no essential differences here, either in law or in practice, between the capitalist/"modern" historical system and other (previous) ones. Perhaps more pertinent is the securing of property rights against those other individuals who are close relatives. Presumably, in the capitalist/"modern" historical system, property rights inhere in designated individuals and not in a "family" or a "community," which is more frequently the case in other systems. But even here, the distinction blurs. There has been a very wide gamut of rules in the capitalist/"modern" system that has ensured "family" rights in property (inheritance rules, spousal or parental responsibility rules, etc.). Conversely, in systems that emphasize the "community" nature of property, often the "leaders" of these communities dispose *de facto* of rights that are very close to those associated with individual private property.

Security of goods is not the only object of property rights. Commodification is a second. Security presumably matters primarily because it acts as an incentive for entrepreneurial risk behavior by ensuring the permanence of the rewards. Entrepreneurial risk behavior is market-oriented behavior, and this requires commodification. Commodification is structured, by law and by custom. It has first of all to be permitted, then socially encouraged.

Of course, the marketing of goods is a phenomenon in no way exclusive to the capitalist/"modern" historical system. To be sure, fifty years ago, there were many scholars who considered it to be rare or exceptional or restricted to special arenas in non-capitalist systems. But all the empirical work of the past fifty years on these other systems has tended to reveal that they had much more extensive commodification than previously suspected, even if globally not quite as extensive as in our present system. The existence of real markets (and merchants) in these other systems is certainly sufficient nonetheless to eliminate a view that the mere commodification of goods is sufficient to distinguish the capitalist/"modern" historical system from other previous systems.

An argument based on commodification therefore has to rest largely on the commodification of two special phenomena: land and labor (or labor power). It is in some ways difficult to know why analysts have always singled out these two phenomena as cases apart. It cannot be that they have been historically the most resistant to commodification. As already noted, air (and even water) have been more resistant to commodification than land. Such special status as land has is clearly related to the fact that agriculture has been the central economic activity of the past 10,000 years, upon which the reproduction of humanity has been fundamentally dependent. It is only in the twentieth century that we have begun to move in any significant way to a situation in which less than the majority of the world's population will be employed in agricultural work. Even so, most of the world's food supply still comes essentially from the land. It is not surprising therefore that various historical systems have developed mechanisms to constrain (even ban) the commodification of land. Has this been undone in the capitalist/ "modern" historical system? To some extent, of course. Most land is today alienable. But it is of course a matter of degree: not all land is alienable, even today. And it was not true in prior times that no land at all was alienable. Indeed, there were some zones, like China, where land was largely alienable. It has been primarily a matter of increasing world-wide in the last few centuries the percentage of land that is alienable.

In addition, we must pose the question of how important it is that land is alienable, and in terms of what? Market transactions are surely not the only way of transferring control of land, and transfers of control have been a frequent and recurring phenomenon of all known historical systems. If consolidation of control is optimal for production (and productivity), there has surely been as much consolidation in the course of non-capitalist systems as in the capitalist/"modern" historical system. If so-called "family-size" units are optimal, once again they have been as frequent in the ones as in the other. In short, it is not clear that the relatively increased alienability of land has resulted in any enormous difference in the essential morphology of landholdings.

What then of the commodification of labor, or of labor power? The key importance of the proletarian wage worker has been stressed in many analyses of capitalism. Here too, we must look first at empirical reality and then at its consequences. Wage work has of course been a central feature of the capitalist/"modern" historical system. But it has never been the only mode of the use of labor power. Indeed, it may be questioned whether it has been even the majority mode within historical capitalism. Conversely, it has seldom (if ever) been entirely absent as one mode of the use of labor power in non-capitalist systems. As with the alienability of land, the alienability of labor power is a matter of degree. There has been no doubt more of it in the capitalist/"modern" historical system, but it is not immediately self-evident that the difference of degree has been qualitatively significant.

This leaves undiscussed what justification there is for distinguishing between the commodification of labor and that of labor power, that is, the difference between the sale and purchase of a human's labor power for a lifetime (slavery) as opposed to its use for a specified period (a year, an hour). It is surely not clear that in the history of the world there has been less slavery within the capitalist/"modern" historical system than in previous ones. One might perhaps make the opposite case.

Finally, however, the question remains, as with the alienability of land, what difference does alienability of labor (and/or labor power) make? If it is argued that, only if labor and/or labor power is alienable, will it be possible to allocate optimally its use, this leaves out of consideration the possibility that "administrative" transfers might achieve the same objective, indeed achieve it better under certain circumstances. If it is argued that commodified labor power is essential to provide a substantial commodity goods market, this leaves out of consideration that collective purchase of goods for reproduction (as by an army intendancy or by a factory/plantation owner) can have substantially the same effect of providing market purchasing power, and indeed has had this effect historically.

We are left therefore with the uncertainty as to whether the degree of commodification achieved under the capitalist/"modern" historical system, while quantitatively greater than other systems, has been *thus far* qualitatively fundamental. And even if it has been so, whether it is in fact true that commodification by itself transforms productivity.

We thus turn to the third structural feature considered specific to the capitalist system – the sovereign "modern" state. What is it about the "modern" state that is different from the political structures of previous historical systems? In the political theory of the capitalist/"modern" historical system itself, the theme that is emphasized is sovereignty. The word itself makes clear its essence. Sovereignty is derived from "sovereign" – a single ruler of a geographically defined area who has comprehensive and exclusive authority within this area. Sovereignty is the unification of political authority, the opposite of the "parcelization" that had marked the political structure of European feudalism.[3]

If sovereignty is often considered essential to the capitalist/"modern" historical system, it is because it is considered the necessary complement to the institution of private property. Private property requires political guarantees, and these guarantees can only be taken seriously if offered by a state that is sovereign and thereby has the necessary authority to make those guarantees.

[3] Anderson 1974a: 19ff.

There are however two problems here. One is, once again, the fit between the theoretical structure and the real structures. Have sovereign states actually been sovereign? Have they had both comprehensive and exclusive authority within their boundaries? Clearly, in the historical reality of the modern world, no state has ever been totally sovereign. In addition, the states have varied widely in terms of the effective authority they have been able to exercise. Many have been quite weak; a very few relatively strong. Secondly, if sovereignty is measured by centralized and unified authority as opposed to parcelized authority, other historical systems have known this condition (or made this claim): for example, the major world empires, although in fact the real power of world empires was for the most part less than that of sovereign states in the modern interstate system.

This leads, then, to the question whether there is some way of distinguishing the "modern" state from the world empires. The whole corpus of Max Weber's political writings may be said to be an attempt to do just this. The two key elements that Weber discerns, closely linked in fact one to the other, are the mode of legitimation of power and the structure of the bureaucracy. Weber (and the Weberians) have emphasized the degree to which the modern state is based on "rational-legal" premises as opposed to being "patrimonial." A rational bureaucracy is said to be technically superior and is directly linked by Weber to the needs of a capitalist market economy "that the official business of public administration be discharged precisely, unambiguously, continuously, and with as much speed as possible."[4] As with the other essential structures, the question is double. What is the empirical reality of the practice, as opposed to the theoretical description? Even if in practice a difference exists, what are the real consequences of this difference?

The operational importance of "rational-legal" legitimation is located in the rationality of the bureaucracy. But how rational have rational bureaucracies been? The limitations on the degree to which bureaucracies of "modern" states have in fact been composed of impersonal and disinterested rational technocrats is indicated by the now very extensive literature on "corruption," which is continuing and pervasive (in one form or another). Indeed may we not consider it an integral element of the operations of the historical system? Just as wage labor turns out to be only one mode of remuneration among several (not residually but constitutively), so disinterestedness turns out to be only one mode of bureaucratic behavior among several (not residually but constitutively). In addition, as the administrative structures of

[4] Weber 1978: 974.

"modern" states have grown in size, far from becoming more "rational," as Weber asserted, they have in fact removed a larger stratum of positions from the direct operations of a system of rational bureaucratic recruitment.

It may also be asked whether bureaucratic public administration is an essential element in the maximization of the ability of entrepreneurs to pursue their profit-oriented interests. Obviously, it has advantages in terms of predictability and objectivity (in terms of the conflicting interests of the competing entrepreneurs). But the interest of particular entrepreneurs, especially the largest among them, might be better served by less predictable, less objective (hence more collusive) public administrations.

There is a third structural feature that distinguishes the "modern" state, one that is least frequently discussed. It is the fact that these "sovereign" states are in fact precisely not politically isolated structures but rather members of an interstate system; indeed, they are defined by their membership in this interstate system. This was not of course true for the multiple antecedent world empires. But what is the significance of this final structural particularity of the capitalist/"modern" historical system? Is it not first that the interstate system constrains the sovereign states in precisely all of the features which presumably distinguish the "modern" states from other forms of states? The interstate system limits the sovereignty of the states, thereby recreating a form of parcelized sovereignty. The interstate system creates the possibility of recourse beyond the boundaries of the state, thereby undermining the permanence of decisions on the security of property rights. The interstate system provides the framework within which trans-state patrimonial systems may flourish (e.g., the existence of "compradore bourgeoisies," subversive networks, paid agents of foreign powers, etc.). Finally, the interstate system subverts the significance of proletarianization within a given state as it reinforces a world-economy-wide division of labor in which the role of non-wage labor remains significantly high.

The one thing that the interstate system does not constrain is the basic activity of the capitalist/"modern" historical system – intensive growth, expansion, the ceaseless accumulation of capital. Quite the contrary! The interstate system has been itself one major expression of this activity. As the world-economy has "grown," so has the interstate system, from its limited boundaries (as codified, say, in the Treaty of Westphalia in 1648) to its global inclusiveness (as recorded in the universal vocation of the United Nations).

We thus return to the question, what is distinctive about capitalism? This rapid review of the standard responses to this question has served to present the case that the presumably specific structures and processes of the capitalist/"modern" historical system all are less distinctive in practice than in theory. And it has raised questions about whether the various processes and structures, to the extent they are in fact different from those of other systems, can be said to account for the economic and scientific-technological development that we see. The one thing that seems unquestionable, and unquestioned, is the hyperbolic growth curves – in production, population, and the accumulation of capital – that have been a continuing reality from the sixteenth century. But hyperbolic growth curves are not per se to be applauded. Cancers too grow hyperbolically.

We must now turn from the outcome – the existence of a capitalist/ "modern" historical system – to the description of the origins. This is often referred to as the question of "the transition from feudalism to capitalism," or how it is that our current system actually came into existence.

The historical construction of a capitalist world

We have tried to specify what we mean by "capitalism" and/or "modernity." Similarly, it is necessary to specify what we mean by "feudalism," at least in Western Europe, if we are to ask how it is that there was a "transition" from one to the other in this specific geographic zone. Furthermore, as Bois reminds us, "a theory of feudalism must take account of its origins as much as of its disappearance."[5]

At one time, it had been argued that "feudalism" was some kind of "natural economy" with a near total absence of markets, money, and manufactures. This has become hard to defend in the light of current scholarship. On the contrary, it seems clear that European feudalism involved a significant growth of markets, money, and manufactures. We must begin with the fact that the instituting of the feudal system in its classical form in the eleventh century was at the time a new solution to the continuing problem of how to exploit agricultural labor by an upper stratum whose primary skill was warfare. Slavery had been an important (perhaps the key) mechanism to accomplish this, not only in the Roman Empire, but in the early Middle Ages as well (fifth to ninth centuries +).[6]

However, the maintenance of slavery, in significant numbers, requires

---

[5] Bois 1976: 261.
[6] Domenico Vera (1989: 32) points out that Marc Bloch's famous article, entitled "Comment et pourquoi finit l'esclavage antique?" (1963), might better have been entitled "How and Why Did Ancient Slavery End in the Middle Ages?" given that this was "the heart of his reflections."

two simultaneous conditions: first, the constant procurement of new slaves by warfare on the edges of (or outside) the zone in which the slaves are used (and consequently the ability of the state, or warriors within the zones, to conduct or benefit from the necessary "razzias"); and, secondly, the maintenance of a high degree of internal order within the zone in which the slaves are used (and consequently the difficulty for slaves to rebel or desert). Dockès summarizes the historical ups and downs of the use of slavery in Western Europe as follows:

There were relatively few rural slaves, and especially prebendal slaves, during the ethnic and social unrest of the third century (Bacaudae, invasions), and later during the "final" crisis of the second half of the fourth and the fifth century. By contrast, the number of slaves increased with the establishment of barbarian kingdoms, which combined repression internally with military forays externally. There may have been a considerable number of both escapes and domicilings in the seventh century (at least in its second half), followed by a resurgence of the slave system with the Pepins beginning in the early eighth century and of course with the empire of Charlemagne. After the collapse of the imperial venture and its associated state organs, and the ensuing social and tribal unrest coupled with the Viking, Saracen, and Hungarian invasions in the second part of the ninth and early tenth century, slavery declined once again.[7]

Slavery was not incompatible with the presence of "free" laborers, as tenants or even proprietors of land adjacent to that being cultivated by slaves. Indeed, the co-presence of the "free" laborers may even have been highly positive for the political reinforcement of the slave system. The creation of this "ethnic" distinction among the work force may have facilitated the maintenance of order. However, such "free" laborers were by no means necessarily joined together in primordial communities whose differentiation would later give rise to feudal land property, although that is how Takahashi had pictured the sequence.[8] This model

---

[7] Dockès 1982: 93.

[8] The *Hufe* (*virgate*) is a total peasant share (*Werteinheit*, Lamprecht calls it) composed of *Hof* (a plot of ground with a house on it), a certain primary parcel of arable land *(Flur)* and a part in the common land (*Allmende*); or, roughly, "land enough to support the peasant and his family" (Waitz). It is the natural object by which the peasant maintains himself (or, labor power reproduces itself). Its economic realization, in the sense of the *Hufe*'s general form, is the community or the communal collective regulations: the *Flurzwang* or *contrainte communautaire* (G. Lefebvre), *servitudes collectives* (Marc Bloch) which go with the *Dreifelderwirtschaft* and the open-field system, or *Gemeingelage* or *vaine pâture collective*. The collective regulations constitute an apparatus of compulsion by which the labor process is mediated. However, the inevitable expansion of productivity arising out of the private property inherent in the *Hufe* led, and could not but lead, to men's "rule over men and land" (Wittich). The relationships of domination and dependence into which this sort of *Hufe* community branched off constituted the feudal lord's private property, i.e., the manor, or feudal land property. In this way we have the sequence of categorical development, *Hufe – Gemeinde – Grundherrschaft*. Conversely, as this sort of domination by the feudal lord took over the village community and the *Hufe*, and the rules of seigneurial land property penetrated them, *Hufe* and village community

not only ignores the existence of the medieval villas and their slaves, but also misses the fact that the rural communities (and their quasi-egalitarian ideologies), far from being primordial, were themselves relatively late products of the inclusion of the tenants in the feudal dependency network. As Guerreau argues: "To see in fourteenth-century communities heroic survivals of primitive communities reaching back to the Bronze Age ... goes counter to the most elementary sense of history."[9]

The manorial system, with its combination of slave labor on the demesne and "free" laborers, collapsed by the end of the tenth century.[10] It is this collapse – Bois calls it a "revolution" – that was "the immediate cause of massive initiatives of the rural population in numerous regions, which led to the famous expansion of the eleventh–twelfth centuries."[11] These initiatives were institutionalized as the "classic" feudal system (serfs bound to their masters, but also bound to each other in communal structures). For most previously "free" laborers, this new system in fact involved a considerable increase in their exploitation, combined with a relative opportunity for some to improve their situation. Johsua explains this increased pressure on two grounds. On the one hand, there was the increasing cost of slave supply. As the near zones for razzia were exhausted, one had to go further afield.[12] On the other hand, the reemergence of an urban network (beginning already in the eighth century) created a demand for increased production.[13] Thus it was that by 1000+, more or less, "the banal seigniory was established virtually everywhere," in part (in large part?) because of the end of the system of "fruitful pillage."[14] And, with the creation of this new exploitative system, there may be said to have begun the "period of dynamism and ascendancy for Christian Europe in general."[15]

Still, despite the economic and geographic expansion of the following two to three centuries, the new system of exploitation was still on quite shaky structural legs. One crucial element was that the principal means of production, arable land, "had itself to be produced" by a process of land clearance.[16] Brenner notes this by arguing that colonization was the "archetypal form of feudal development and feudal improvement."[17] He states this, however, too narrowly, since the colonization of entirely

---

as "natural" objects and their mutual relations were changed into a historical (specifically, the feudal) form and relationships (Takahashi 1976: 73).

[9] Guerreau 1980: 86.
[10] Bois 1989.   [11] Guerreau 1980: 196.   [12] Johsua 1988: 63.
[13] Ibid.: 127. The importance of urban networks in, indeed their centrality for, the feudal system in Europe has been increasingly recognized in recent literature. See Merrington 1976.
[14] Ibid.: 23.   [15] Gimpel 1983: 9.   [16] Johsua 1988: 20.
[17] Brenner 1985b: 237.

"new" areas was only one means of creating arable land. The second was converting land in the vicinity of existing holdings (pasture lands, forests, swamp lands, etc.) into arable lands by "improvement."

The colonization of entirely new lands was not necessarily more profitable than improvement of old lands since colonization often entailed the cost of "conquest." Though the developers, because they were free from the constraints of custom, were sometimes able to impose new and advantageous relations of production on the direct producers, at other times they found that the low labor–land ratio required significant concessions to the direct producers. To be sure, improving "old" land required changing old social patterns and this met with resistance. It also frequently involved the cultivation of less fertile land (since otherwise the land would probably have been cultivated previously). But it had the advantage of utilizing land somehow already in the purview (if not the total control) of the developers, and therefore involving no new obligations to overlords.

In either case, development of land required the political acquiescence, if not the political assistance, of overlords and thus encouraged "the build-up of larger, more effective military organization and/or the construction of stronger surplus-extracting machinery."[18] It is thus appropriate to insist, as does Anderson, that:

The singularity of feudalism was never exhausted merely by the existence of seigneurial and serf classes as such. It was their specific organization in a vertically articulated system of parcellized sovereignty and scalar property that distinguished the feudal mode of production in Europe.[19]

The efficacy of feudalism was precisely located in the tight link between the economic and political powers of the seignior, "the total assimilation of power over the land and power over men."[20] Or, as Hilton puts it, it was "lordship which is specific to feudalism."[21]

On the other hand, the seemingly tight link of economic and political power was precisely undermined by the parcelization of sovereignty and the limited control of the productive process:

These lords, with their armed retainers and their far-reaching private or public jurisdictions, had by no means complete control even over the servile peasantry. In particular, their military and political power was not matched by their power to manage the agrarian economy. This was because of the great distance between them and the productive process. Nor was this simply the contrast between the vast scale of feudal landownership and the small scale of the family enterprise, for these distances applied to the petty lords of single villages as well as to magnates possessing hundreds. It was also because, on the whole, the effective intervention of the lord or his officials in the economy of the peasant

---

[18] Ibid.: 238.   [19] Anderson 1974a: 408.
[20] Guerreau 1980: 180.   [21] Hilton 1985: 124.

holding was very limited. It is true that the lord could affect, usually in a negative sense, the resources of the peasant holding by his demands for rents and services. He could also (though never as much as he hoped) control the movement of the dependent population. But he was not able to determine the application of labour and other resources within the economy of the holding; nor, on the whole, was there much attempt in terms of leases, even when customary tenure began to break down at the end of the middle ages, to specify good husbandry practices.

We therefore have a landowning class whose very existence depended on the transfer to it of the surplus labour and the fruits of surplus labour of a class which was potentially independent of it, over which it exercised political, military and juridical power, but in relation to which it fulfilled no entrepreneurial function.[22]

It is for these reasons that Bois insists on defining feudalism as the "hegemony of individual petty production" combined with, of course, the appropriation of part of the surplus by the seignior, an appropriation that was made possible by political constraint.[23]

This system worked wonderfully well for the seigniors for a time, but then ceased to do so. It was circa 1250+ that the system entered into its "crisis" which is conventionally seen to have lasted until circa 1450+. Hence, we seem to be dealing with an historical system that existed for only 500 years at most, a period that apparently may be said to be composed one-half of a rise or flourishing of the system and one-half of a crisis or fall. This seems a curiously abbreviated and formal schema. Some authors solve this anomaly by stretching the definition of "feudalism" beyond the seignior–serf model to include within it the period of circa 400–500+ up to circa 1000+. But this in turn poses another intellectual dilemma, well stated by Dockès: "What is needed is either to revise the concept of the feudal mode as composed of two successive forms within a single mode of production, or to regard the Middle Ages as a prolonged transitional period between the slave mode and the capitalist mode of production."[24]

---

[22] Ibid.: 125–27.
[23] Bois 1976: 355.
[24] Dockès 1982: 262, fn. 103. See a similar formulation by Harbans Mukhia (1981: 274): "Feudalism, like other social formations before or after it, was a transitional system. As such it stood mid-way in the transition of the west European economy, from a primarily slave-based system of agricultural production to one dominated by the complementary classes of the capitalist farmer and the landless agricultural wage-earner, but in which the free peasantry also formed a significant element."

Guerreau considers the life of the feudal system to be even briefer: "The feudal system was launched in the eleventh century, developed in the twelfth and died before even reaching full growth in the thirteenth at the hands of the royalty. On this point, Guizot had understood the evolution quite perfectly. The fief, as it is described somewhat maliciously in the textbooks, was a form entirely transitory, uncertain, and fluid" (1980, 197–98).

The feudal system in Western Europe seems quite clearly to have operated by a pattern of cycles of expansion and contraction of two lengths: circa 50 years and circa 200–300 years. The two kinds of cycles seem to show parallel characteristics and the shorter ones were ensconced in the longer ones. The evidence for the shorter ones is most clearly presented in the careful reconstruction by Bois for Normandy.[25] The longer ones (or rather the longer one) has received the consensual accord of most economic historians dealing with the late Middle Ages.

It is a curious phenomenon, remaining to have an adequate theoretical explanation, that these 50-year cycles seem to resemble cycles found in the capitalist world-economy (the so-called Kondratieff cycles of the nineteenth and twentieth centuries), which many also think to exist in the sixteenth to eighteenth centuries.[26] As for the cycles of 200 to 300 years in length, they are widely agreed to have existed in the sixteenth to eighteenth centuries,[27] and an argument can be made that they continued in the nineteenth and twentieth centuries as well. Thus, in still one more way, we find an uncomfortable blurring of the distinctiveness of the patterns of the European medieval and modern world.

The pattern of the expansions and contractions is clearly laid out and widely accepted among those writing about the late Middle Ages and early modern times in Europe,[28] although of course the direction of the causality is subject to very intense disagreement.[29] It is generally agreed that the expansion and (relative) contraction of population, total land area under cultivation, nominal prices, total production, and amount of monetary transactions went up and down in parallel. Increasing demand and prices led to an increase in land area devoted to arable production; decreasing demand and prices led to a shift away from arable to either pastoral or viticultural production. Increased demand led to more agricultural innovation, greater use of fertilizers, higher yields, greater concentration on the more expensive grains (wheat, then rye); decreased demand had the inverse effect. Increased land use and population was correlated with increased numbers of farm units, their average size being reduced; decreased demand led to greater concentration of land units. Expansion was correlated with greater rent income to rent receivers; contraction with less total income. Expansion was correlated with more favorable terms of trade of agriculture with industry; contraction with the inverse (the so-called price scissors). Real wages went down with expansion and population increase; up with

---

[25] Bois 1976.   [26] Wallerstein 1984.   [27] Kriedte 1983.
[28] Anderson 1974b: 197–209; Bois 1976: 349–65; Génicot 1966; Slicher van Bath 1977; Wallerstein 1974: chapter 1; 1980: chapter 1.
[29] See Brenner (1985a) and the responses in the same book.

contraction. Industry was more urban in times of expansion, more rural in contraction. Expansion in the feudal system led to more serfdom; contraction to less.

It is the long swing that was crucial. Thus 1050–1250+ was a time of the expansion of Europe (the Crusades; the colonizations in the east and far north, and in Ireland), which were then halted or pushed back. It was the time of flourishing of the urban centers, the construction of the great cathedrals, the strengthening of the state structures (and hence of more internal peace, if more warfare at the edges of the system). The "crisis" or great contraction of 1250–1450+ included the Black Plague, the period of numerous peasant revolts (and the flourishing of "egalitarian" heresies in the Church), the crisis of seigniorial revenues and the greater internecine struggles of the nobility (e.g., the Hundred Years War, the Wars of the Roses), all of which involved violence and disorder that added to the decline in both total production and productivity.

It is because of, or in the wake of, this long contraction of the economy throughout Europe, this "crisis" of the feudal system, that most commentators argue there occurred (or began) a "transition" to capitalism, or to a "modern" commercialized economic system. Some analysts lay emphasis on the rupture this represented. Others prefer to see the picture from 1000+ to today as a relatively steady evolution, but even the latter seem to recognize that a qualitative shift took place circa 1500+. This concept is consecrated in our accepted periodization which sees circa 1500+ as the end of the Middle Ages and the beginning in Europe of "early modern times," or sees the Renaissance plus the Reformation as a critical turning-point.

But what are the explanations normally given as to why this "transformation" occurred? Here the literature is far more murky, since many of the "explanations" are primarily empirical descriptions of what is thought to have changed or evolved, rather than what caused the changes to occur. Why in fact did any fundamental changes occur at all? That is to say, that a particular variant of an agricultural system in which some overclass exploited in some fashion the mass of the rural producers gave way to another variant was nothing new – in Western Europe or elsewhere. This had been the story of mankind ever since the so-called agricultural revolution. All the variants had been unstable, in the sense that any given one had seldom lasted more than 400–500 years. But, when any given one had collapsed, it had been replaced previously via mutation or conquest by another variant which shared certain structural characteristics: (a) the primacy of agricultural production, combined with artisanal activity; (b) the limited global surplus; (c) the sustenance of non-agricultural producers by a politically enforced transfer of surplus to the upper stratum of (usually) warriors, clerics, and merchants; (d) some networks of trade, usually at least one long-distance network, combined with very local ones. Probably the most prosperous of all these historical systems were located in the most fertile agricultural zones, wherein we find the "great civilizations" over the millennia.

Many of these historical systems had what we might call protocapitalist elements. That is, there often was extensive commodity production. There existed producers and traders who sought profit. There was investment of capital. There was wage labor. There were *Weltanschauungen* consonant with capitalism. But none had crossed the threshold of creating a system whose primary driving force was the incessant accumulation of capital. Circa 1400+, when the relatively insignificant, obscure, and short-lived system of European feudalism was in full collapse, there was little reason to presume that anything more than a new variant of a redistributive/tributary system of exploitation would replace it. Instead, there was the genesis of a radically new system. I cannot emphasize too strongly how much I agree with Sweezy when he says that why this should have happened is "a genuinely puzzling question."[30]

Civilizational explanations

Most solutions to the puzzle tend to look for some Western European structural secret, some long-standing "civilizational" characteristic which led inevitably to this development. These structural explanations cross the great ideological divide of liberal and Marxist thought. A few solutions to this puzzle, and only more recently, suggest conjunctural explanations, citing developments that were contingent and therefore not inevitable. Such explanations too do not necessarily correlate with a particular ideology. In fact, the distinction between civilizational and conjunctural explanations is somewhat factitious. The question turns out to be really this: is the something that happened circa 1500+ in the "West" to be explained by phenomena that emerged much earlier, say before 1000+, perhaps millennia before? Or were all these "early" factors only necessary conditions, still lacking the sufficient condition, which however was conjunctural, in the sense that it involved a "conjuncture" of occurrences (during the two centuries immediately preceding the transition to a capitalist/"modern" historical system), a conjuncture that was unlikely, but without which the transition could

---

[30] Sweezy 1976b: 106. Roberto Unger (1987) similarly builds his whole analysis around the normality of "periodic breakdowns" of agrarian-bureaucratic societies and what he calls their "reversion cycles."

never have occurred? That is to say, was it the case that the actual
outcome of the "crisis of feudalism" was only one possibility among
many, and not necessarily the most likely?

Obviously, any historical occurrence has immediate roots whose
derivation can always be traced further back, *ad infinitum*. However, if
we believe that the crucial turning-point was 500–2500 years earlier, we
are coming up with a cultural–genetic explanation which in effect says
that the development of capitalism/"modernity" in the West, and in the
West first, had been rendered "inevitable" by this earlier "civilizational"
system. If, however, we find that as late as 1300+ there was no reason to
expect that the qualitative changes that would occur 200 years later were
built into long-standing historical trajectories, but rather were "conjunctural," we are freer to appraise the wisdom of the historical choices that
were made, and are liberated from the self-fulfilling and self-congratula-
tory qualities of the "civilizational" explanation.

The "civilizational" explanations are well known. Perhaps the most
influential has been that of Max Weber, who made his agenda quite
clear in the very beginning of the analysis:

A product of modern European civilization, studying any problem of universal
history, is bound to ask himself to what combination of circumstances the fact
should be attributed that in Western civilization, and in Western civilization
only, cultural phenomena have appeared which (as we like to think) lie in a line
of development having *universal* significance and value.[31]

We know what Weber found: that the Judeo-Christian tradition (thus
something going back thousands of years) took particular expression in
the sixteenth century, with the Reformation, in something he called the
Protestant ethic; that this ethic provided the normative support for the
activities of capitalist entrepreneurs; that such normative support was a
critically determining variable in the emergence of a capitalist system.

Although Weber's views are supposed to be contra-Marxist views, it
seems clear that a large number of Marxists also give "civilizational"
explanations. Perry Anderson, for example, argues that capitalism could
only have emerged out of a feudal mode of production. This is of course
a standard view among Marxists. To this, however, he adds the insistence that feudalism was not known in all parts of the world, but only in
Europe and Japan. Inveighing against "a colour-blind materialism"
which "inevitably ends in a perverse idealism," he denies that such
"social formations" as the nomadic Tatar confederations, the Byzantine
Empire, or the Ottoman Sultanate, among others, may be described as
feudal at any point in their history. He is aware, of course, that there are

[31] Weber 1930: 13.

respected scholars who have claimed precisely this about these systems, but he asserts that these scholars:

have argued that [the] overt superstructural divergences [of these systems] from Western norms concealed an underlying convergence of infrastructural relations of production. All privilege to Western development is thereby held to disappear, in the multiform process of a world history secretly single from the start. Feudalism, in this version of materialist historiography, becomes an absolving ocean in which virtually any society may receive its baptism.

The scientific invalidity of this theoretical ecumenicism can be demonstrated from the logical paradox in which it results. For if, in effect, the feudal mode of production can be defined independently of the variant juridical and political superstructures which accompany it, such that its presence can be registered throughout the globe wherever primitive and tribal social formations were superseded, the problem then arises: how is the unique dynamism of the European theatre of international feudalism to be explained?[32]

Still, if feudalism explains the "unique dynamism" of Europe, why then did not Japan go forward to capitalism as early as Europe? To answer this question, Anderson must appeal to deep (or at least longer) history; he must give a "civilizational" response:

What, then, was the specificity of European history, which separated it so deeply from Japanese history, despite the common cycle of feudalism which otherwise so closely united the two? The answer surely lies in the perdurable inheritance of classical antiquity. The Roman Empire, its final historical form, was not only itself naturally incapable of a transition to capitalism. The very advance of the classical universe doomed it to a catastrophic regression, of an order for which there is no real other example in the annals of civilization. The far more primitive social world of early feudalism was the result of its collapse, internally prepared and externally completed. Mediaeval Europe then, after a long gestation, released the elements of a slow ulterior transition to the capitalist mode of production, in the early modern epoch. But what rendered the unique passage to capitalism possible in Europe was *the concatenation of antiquity and feudalism*. In other words, to grasp the secret of the emergence of the capitalist mode of production in Europe, it is necessary to discard in the most radical way possible any conception of it as simply an evolutionary subsumption of a lower mode of production by a higher mode of production, the one generated automatically and entirely from within the other by an organic internal succession, and therewith effacing it . . . . The "advantage" of Europe over Japan lay in its classical antecedence, which even after the Dark Ages did not disappear "behind" it, but survived in certain basic respects "in front" of it.[33]

It is thus the Roman heritage – the legal system and in particular the concept of quiritary ownership – that distinguishes Europe in the period 1000–1500+ not only from China, India, and the Islamic world, but from Japan as well.[34]

---

[32] Anderson 1974a: 402–03.   [33] Ibid.: 420–21.

[34] Note in this regard Talcott Parsons' modification of the Weberian thrust. He acknowl-

Yet another version of what I am calling "civilizational" explanations has been given by Michael Mann. He starts with the argument that although, as of 1000+, Europe may have had less "extensive" power than say China, it had nonetheless more intensive power, "especially in agriculture" (Mann, 1986: 378). And this advantage in intensive power was achieved early:

The medieval dynamic was strong, sustained, and pervasive. It may have been implanted as early as A.D. 800. The Domesday Book, with its profusion of water mills, documents its presence in England by 1086. The transition that saw Europe leap forward was not primarily the late-medieval transition from feudalism to capitalism. That process was largely the institutionalization of a leap that had occurred much earlier, in the period that only our lack of documentation leads us to label the Dark Ages. By A.D. 1200 that leap, that dynamic, was already taking western Europe to new heights of collective social power.[35]

For Mann, most of the explanations "start *too late* in history." Christendom was *"necessary* for all that followed," which takes us back at least 1500 years.[36] It was necessary because the "dynamic" required a multiplicity of power networks (a theme common to many analyses), but "these local groups could operate safely within the extensive networks and normative pacification provided by Christendom." The content of this civilizational explanation is a little hard to discern. The Christian norms were spatially extensive, but so were Islamic or Confucian norms. In what sense these Christian norms "pacified" anyone is hard to say, unless norms do so by definition, in which case it is equally true of the norms of other extensive religions. This is all the more true since, as Mann himself notes in the very next phrase: "Christendom was [in the Middle Ages] itself split between being an immanent ideology of ruling-class morale and a more transcendent, classless ideology,"[37] a somewhat pale rendering of the fierce battles between the Dominicans and the

---

edges ancient Israel and Greece as "seed-bed societies" of what he calls "the system of modern societies." But he insists on the crucial role of the Roman Empire in the "institutionalization" of their cultural values. Its dual significance was that, first, "it constituted the principal social environment in which Christianity developed," and, secondly, "the heritage of Roman institutions was incorporated into the foundations of the modern world" (1971: 30).

[35] Mann 1986: 413. Once again we can find parallel shifts backwards of Marxists to those of non-Marxists like Mann. Johsua goes back to the same point in time to see the beginning of the long economic upward thrust of Europe. The key changes for him are to be found not in the towns but in the countryside (a view that Mann shares in his emphasis on agriculture). What Johsua singles out in northern or northwest Europe (locus of later full capitalist development) as opposed to southern Europe is the institution, as of the eighth century, of the "classical manorial regime [which] will turn out to be the antechamber of capital" (1988: 368).

[36] Mann 1986: 501, 507.   [37] Ibid.: 412.

Franciscans, to take but one instance. There is considerable question whether we can in fact talk of a single set of Christian norms in this epoch.

The epitome of the civilizational argument however is to be found in none of these magnificent total explanations. It lies in the "hurrah for England" school, alongside of which exists a less well-known but equally passionate "hurrah for Italy" school. For these schools, it is not *Western* "civilization" that explains all, but the narrower English or Italian model.

That England's nineteenth-century triumphs were extraordinary is a view that has had wide resonance – in England to be sure, but not only. Some find that nineteenth-century triumphs were explained by eighteenth-century wisdom (inventing steam engines, or planting turnips, or giving the gentry their due). Some trace the triumphs to sixteenth- and seventeenth-century wisdom (moving from the elimination of serfs toward the elimination of yeomen, or sustaining the new science, or starting down the road to constitutional monarchy). But, of late, there has been a tendency to move English wisdom further and further back in time, to 1066+ or even further back, when the Lord blessed the Anglo-Saxons. Two recent explanations, one in terms of "culture" by Alan Macfarlane (very much a liberal) and one in terms of "class struggle" by Robert Brenner (very much a Marxist) share this long temporality.[38]

Macfarlane specifically seeks to debunk the standard Marx–Weber view that there was a watershed in the sixteenth century between, on the one hand, a traditional, peasant feudal society and, on the other, a modern, individualist capitalist one. He says this is a false picture because the country in which the industrial revolution occurred "first" (England) did not meet the criteria of being a peasant society – in the sixteenth century, in the fifteenth century, or probably ever. He argues this by drawing up a long list of features of a "model" peasant society (extended household as the basic unit of production and consumption, production for use, multi-generational households, high fertility, early marriage, strong "community" bonds, unilineal descent, patriarchal authority, etc.) and denying that England ever fitted this model. Instead, it was always a "'controlled' fertility society," one that was "orderly, controlled and non-violent," one that was "unusually secure, and over which ordinary people had an unusually developed control," one in which "ordinary people [were] accustomed to a world not of absolutes, but of relative good and evil, where all could be changed by money."

[38] Macfarlane 1977 and 1987; Brenner 1985a and 1985b.

England already had marriages that were "modern" in structure, Mac-farlane says, by the eleventh century and "in all probability [already] between the fourth and ninth centuries." Far from tracing capitalist virtue to Roman heritage, as does Anderson, Macfarlane finds England's distinctive and, he says, critically important pattern of kinship and marriage to be a "Germanic" heritage, one that "never died out in England, whereas in much of Europe it had been largely submerged by old and renovated features of the preceding Roman civilization."[39] England escaped Rome; hence it became capitalist.

To be sure, feudalism did precede capitalism, but England had a "rather unusual form" of feudalism, one that "already contained an implicit separation between economic and political power, between the market and government."[40] Indeed England was probably never really "feudal" at all.[41] If England was the "cradle of civilization"[42] it is because it had Adam Smith in its cultural genes, so to speak.

Robert Brenner is equally concerned to demonstrate that not only was Europe ahead of Asia, and Western Europe ahead of Eastern Europe, but England ahead of France (and to be sure the Low Countries, the Germanies, etc.). In early modern times, France was less capitalist than England because it suffered from "the predominance of petty proprietorship," the consequences of which were manifold: technical barriers to improvement, especially within the common fields; heavy taxation of the monarchical state which discouraged agricultural investment; squeezing of the leaseholders by the landlords; subdivision of holdings by peasants. All of these together "ensured long-term agricultural backwardness" for France.[43]

But the sixteenth-century difference turns out to be explained by a thirteenth-century difference, for England showed: "no sign ... of the crisis of seigneurial revenues evident ... in France and, in turn, there is no tendency to substitute an emergent system of centralized surplus extraction for an eroding decentralized system – no embryonic rise of an absolutist form of rule."[44] If England showed any signs of faltering, it was "only several decades into the fourteenth century, if then"; in any case, the "economic disruption appears to have been significantly less severe in England than in France."[45]

But this thirteenth-century difference, it seems, goes still further back, because the "divergent evolutions" of England and France of the thirteenth century were caused "not so much [by] the backwardness of England's 'economic' evolution relative to that of France, as [Guy] Bois

---

[39] Macfarlane 1987: 6–7 (table I), 50, 55, 94, 121, 133, 138.   [40] Ibid.: 189.
[41] Ibid.: 206.   [42] Ibid.: 184.   [43] Brenner 1985a: 29.
[44] Brenner 1985b: 264.   [45] Ibid.: 270–71.

would have it, but rather [by] England's relative advance in terms of
"'feudal' ruling-class organization."[46] And what accounts for this? Not
quite the doings of the Anglo-Saxons, to whom Macfarlane ultimately
gives the credit. Rather, English feudal centralization "owed its strength
in large part to the level of feudal 'political' organization already
achieved by the Normans in Normandy before the Conquest, which was
probably unparalleled elsewhere in Europe."[47] Fortunately for England,
God had arranged that the Normans did not conquer France.

Ultimately, the explanation of the difference is that the English state
was strong – otherwise known as "the extraordinary intra-class cohesiveness of the English aristocracy" (let us overlook the Wars of the Roses) –
and the French state was weak – otherwise known as "the relatively
extreme disorganization of the French aristocracy." This meant that the
former had a high "capacity to dominate the peasantry" and the latter
"made possible the French peasants' success ... ." In this sense, this
explanation is not "merely political" but is about "the construction of
social-class relations which made possible the most effective 'accumulation' in the economic realm."[48] Aside from whether the description is
empirically correct – "Just as Brenner ... minimizes [the] independence
[of the English peasantry], so he exaggerates the independence of the
French peasantry"[49] – there remains the very pertinent query of Bois:
"By virtue of what specific predisposition would French peasants have
fought better than English peasants?"[50] Furthermore, given Brenner's
insistence on the particular political skills of Norman aristocrats, why
would they not have achieved these same results in Normandy itself, the
exact terrain in which Bois's analysis indicated remarkable peasant
strength?[51]

---

[46] Guy Bois had argued that, in the thirteenth century, "feudalism was most advanced" in
France, consequently most pure in form, and *hence*, there was the strengthening of
small-scale holdings at the expense of domains, leading to the lowest seigniorial levels
(1985: 113).

[47] Brenner 1985b: 254–55.   [48] Ibid.: 257–59.

[49] Croot and Parker 1985: 83.   [50] Bois 1985: 110.

[51] Unger goes further, by arguing that England is the deviant case in Western Europe in
the negative sense, that is, that England represents the case of Western Europe almost
not breaking with his "reversion cycles":

> The fourth thesis of my argument is historiographical. Both Marxist and liberal
> views of European history have been dominated by a stereotyped image of the
> modern English road to worldly success: relentless agrarian concentration and
> the triumphal march from domestic production and the putting-out system,
> through centralized factories, to mass production. The political counterpart to
> this economic picture is the gradual enfranchisement and assimilation of the
> working classes on terms that make possible the reconstitution of a ruling and
> possessing elite. Whatever departs from this English stereotype is made to
> appear a deviation, qualifying or delaying an inexorable developmental
> tendency. But the argument of this essay turns this prejudice upside down. It

And yet, curiously enough, the English aristocracy's stranglehold on the poor peasants (as compared to the French aristocracy's ineptitude) seems not merely to have disappeared by the sixteenth century, but it is now the very opposite equation that is said to explain the English lead: "It was the English lords' inability ever to re-enserf the peasants or to move in the direction of absolutism (as had their French counterparts) which forced them in the long run to seek novel ways out of their revenue crisis," a crisis that had been previously discussed by Brenner as relatively minor in England. "Lacking the ability to reimpose some system of extra-economic levy on the peasantry, the lords were obliged to use their remaining feudal powers to further what in the end turned out to be capitalist development."[52]

The "hurrah for Italy" school is more obscure, for two reasons. In the nineteenth century, Italy did not seem as resplendent as Great Britain (although since the 1970s it may be getting its revenge). And fewer people read Italian. Nonetheless, there has always been a strong voice for this theme, most recently brought up to date by Pellicani.

For Pellicani, as for many others, "the history of capitalism and the history of the limitations on the powers [of the state] are an identical story or, at least, have appeared on the historical stage as two tightly interlinked histories."[53] Macfarlane might not disagree. But for Pellicani, the story started in Italy, not England.

In order to present the case for Italy, Pellicani must deal with the Weber argument on the critical importance of the Protestant ethic. He acknowledges the historical correlation by the sixteenth century of the economic leadership of northern Europe and the predominance of Protestantism, but argues that the key element was not the ethic motivating or justifying entrepreneurship but "the weakening of the spiritual control of hierocratic institutions which are all inspired by an intense antagonism to Mammon" combined with "religious tolerance and openness in relations with foreigners." This the Reformation encouraged, but more importantly this the Counter-Reformation eliminated. This tolerance and openness made possible the distinction between the civil society and the state, born historically, he says (citing Jean Baechler), out of "the inability of either to eliminate the other."[54]

---

suggests that the English stereotype – to the extent that it accurately describes even the English events – represents the least telling and distinctive aspect of the European experience. The English route is the closest Europe could come to Asia – that is, to the situation of the agrarian-bureaucratic empires – without falling back into the Asian cycles. The supposed anomalies were and are the real Western thing (1987: 7–8).

[52] Brenner 1985b: 293.   [53] Pellicani 1988: 178.   [54] Ibid.: 102, 109, 119.

Pellicani argues that capitalism had always previously been thwarted by "megamachines," a term he borrows from Lewis Mumford, which created "insecurity of property," thus paralyzing initiative.[55] The question is why this didn't happen in Western Europe. The answer is that there existed no megamachine because of "the disintegration of the Western Roman Empire," something that we may consider "quasiprovidential" in that, "by liberating European people from the 'iron cage,' it offered them the *opportunity* to construct ... modern industrial society."[56]

This collapse of Rome is thus "the most important" of the factors that accounts for the birth of capitalism in the West.[57] The second was the fact that the medieval struggle between the Papacy and the Holy Roman Emperors was a draw, whose ultimate victor was the "bourgeois commune." Furthermore, at that time, it was in central-northern Italy that "the protobourgeoisie benefited from a particularly favorable historical conjuncture and knew how to take maximal advantage of it."[58] So it is Rome once again, not in this case because it left a legacy (positive for Anderson, negative for Macfarlane, but which the English fortunately escaped) but simply because it collapsed. And once the Italian city-states grabbed the ring (some eight centuries later or so), capitalism could emerge.

The problem with "civilizational" explanations is that they tend to be *post hoc ergo propter hoc*, and they therefore assume that the developments were somehow inevitable. It is always difficult to ascertain in this genre of explanation why the process was so *slow*. Between the deep root (Germanic family patterns or the disintegration of the Roman Empire) and the final product (English capitalism in the nineteenth century or even in the sixteenth century), there is a long interval of time. We are left

---

[55] Ibid.: 130, n. 57. This is a strange usage since Mumford explicitly asserts that the modern world has a "new" megamachine, which has one additional "institutional prerequisite." This prerequisite is "a special kind of economic dynamism based on rapid capital accumulation, repeated turnovers, large profits, working toward the constant acceleration of technology itself. In short, the money economy" (1964: 241).

[56] Pellicani 1988: 153–54. Once again, a curious usage, since this term is that of Max Weber, who used it specifically to express his pessimism about rational capitalism. Weber said that, with its ethic of duty and vocational sense of honor, it had created "that iron cage ... through which economic labor receives its present form and destiny ... a *system* which *inescapably* rules the economy and through it the everyday destiny of man" (cited in Mitzman 1970: 160).

[57] Pellicani 1988: 157, n.24. Hall adds an important footnote to this concept of the disintegration of the Roman Empire leading to a set of weak political entities in Europe. "The fact that *several* sets of barbarians came into Europe at the end of the Roman empire, rather than a single set as was the case with China and Islam, was doubtless an initial condition in favor of a multipolar system" (1985: 134).

[58] Pellicani 1988: 189.

with the impression that the deep root led to the final product by a process of slow maturation, as though it were organically programmed. The least one can say about such a maturational process is that a strong case needs to be offered that such "programming" actually operated. But it is in fact seldom argued, merely presumed, and thus the explanation is not very persuasive. It might be more reasonable to start with a premise that is found in Pellicani himself: "Wherever we look, we find traces of capitalism, but we also find that economic life is somehow 'cooped in' by rigid political, religious and social structures which allow little space for the game of catallactics [the science of commercial exchange]."[59] In other words, all other known systems have "contained" capitalist tendencies, in both senses of the word contain. They have had these tendencies; they have effectively constrained them. If so, the question then becomes what broke down in the historical system located in Western Europe such that the containment barrier was overwhelmed? This pushes us in the direction of exceptional circumstances, a rare coming together of processes, or what was referred to previously as a conjunctural explanation.

Conjunctural explanations

There are strong voices, from differing ideological camps, asking us to recognize how *unlikely* was the emergence of a capitalist/"modern" historical system. Ernest Gellner urges that our model be "the fortuitous, contingent opening of a normally shut gate."[60] Michael Mann speaks of it being "a gigantic set of coincidences," even if he insists there was "also something of a pattern."[61] And Eric Hobsbawm suggests that "it is very doubtful whether we can speak of a *universal* tendency of feudalism to develop into capitalism." Rather, he tells us to look for the "fundamental contradiction in this particular [Western] form of feudal society" which accounts for the outcome, even as he admits that "the nature of this contradiction has not yet been satisfactorily clarified."[62]

We shall therefore discuss four elements of an explanation, emphasizing in each the particular conjunctural "exaggeration" of a longstanding structural factor. We shall formulate each as a collapse, and see what was the effect of the cumulated collapses. The four are the collapse of the seigniors, the collapse of the states, the collapse of the Church, and the collapse of the Mongols.

We have seen already that the relative power of seigniors or aristocrats over "peasants" or at least over small agricultural producers is a

---

[59] Ibid.: 16.   [60] Gellner 1988: 4.
[61] Mann 1988: 16–17.   [62] Hobsbawm 1976: 160, 163.

frequently cited consideration. We are also aware of the vast literature on what Marc Bloch called "the crisis of seigniorial revenues" in the period circa 1250+ to circa 1450+. Everyone agrees there was a demographic collapse in Western Europe resulting primarily from the Black Death. Whether this is to be treated primarily in its role as cause or consequence is an issue that has been much debated, and with passion, but for the purposes of this argument, the resolution of this question matters little. The reality was clear. There were fewer persons to till the land. Ergo revenues from their rents had to fall, even if the seigniors had been able to increase the rates, which in fact they were not able to do. Creating new tenures was by and large out of the question. Indeed, quite the opposite was happening: lands were being "abandoned," that is, left uncultivated.

In this situation, each side utilized what political cards were available. Initially, the feudal lords turned to the states:

The State, which was reviving all over western Europe at this time [fourteenth century], intervened on behalf of the lords by fixing wages at the pre-Black Death level, and by legally restricting peasant mobility. . . .

The peasantry, on the other hand, was so situated as to be able to defend its gain much more forcefully than ever before, for demand for labour was much greater than the available supply. The desolate lands also provided the opportunity to those peasants who had the other necessary means to emerge as free peasants. The peasantry thus responded to the "feudal reaction" by bursting out in a string of rebellions everywhere in western Europe.[63]

The seignior's appeal to the states for their intervention failed because the dramatic demographic collapse gave the peasantry a strong weapon: the ability to bargain with one seignior against another. This led both to a reduction in rents (at a time when the total number of rent-payers was already declining) and the disappearance of various servile restrictions. The two combined "allowed the retention of surplus on the peasant holding," which Hilton calls "the declining exploitability of the peasants."[64]

The peasant revolts did not have to succeed in the sense of achieving state power. Their very occurrence changed the *rapport de force*, which is why Dobb insists that it is on the "revolt among the petty producers" that we must fix our attention in seeking to explain the "dissolution and decline of feudal exploitation."[65] To be sure, the seigniors resisted long and hard. But the multiple modes of loss accumulated: non-cultivation of marginal lands; reduction of rents; reduction of the price of land; increase of arrears in rental payments by tenants in difficulty; increase of

---

[63] Mukhia 1981: 283.   [64] Hilton 1985: 128, 133.   [65] Dobb 1976: 166.

demands by rural communities. Bois sees a long trend which culminated in a major collapse "between 1415 and 1450."[66]

The landlords, in financial trouble, failing to stem the tide of rising retention of the surplus by the peasantry, turned on each other. This started quite early. In his explanation of the crisis of feudalism, Perroy argues:

It is in the decade 1335–1345 that the kingdoms of the West shifted, without being in the least aware of it, from a peacetime economy to a wartime economy, a shift that events would render permanent. They would thus come to suffer the constraints of debilitating taxation, reduction of agricultural and artisanal production as well as of interregional trade, the crisis of credit and of monetary instability.[67]

Perroy lays particular emphasis on the fiscal consequences, but one should not neglect that the wars had two other significant consequences. First of all, the wartime disruptions of production reduced revenues still further, less by killing off small producers than by making it more difficult for them to work or trade in zones directly involved. In addition, however, the wars – particularly the Hundred Years' War and the Wars of the Roses, but not only these – killed off the aristocracy. The severe reduction in their numbers (over and above losses from the plague) further weakened them politically *vis-à-vis* the direct producers.

And if all this were not enough, real wages went up steadily for two centuries, both in the towns and for rural wage workers. Bois notes of Norman peasants, comparing 1320 with 1465:

From one century to the next, their wage (calculated in cereals) more than tripled.... Facing this better-fed man, death retreated and life progressed. He was different as well in the work world: should we not presume a greater aptitude for work? Does not the Renaissance itself find its roots in this marvelous terrain?[68]

Dobb says that it was "the inefficiency of feudalism as a system of production," along with the growing needs for seigniorial revenue, that was "primarily responsible for its decline."[69] Perhaps, although this accounts less for permanent decline than for cyclical downturn. Sweezy insists that the decline was due to "the inability of the ruling class to maintain control over, and hence to overexploit, society's labor power."[70] No doubt this happened, but we must wonder why this inability was so profound at this particular time. In any case, it is surely true, as Bloch puts it, that "at the end of the Middle Ages ... the small producers found that those over them were an enfeebled class, deeply shaken in their fortunes and mentally poorly prepared to make the

[66] Bois 1976: 201.   [67] Perroy 1949: 172.   [68] Bois 1976: 98.
[69] Dobb 1946: 42.   [70] Sweezy 1976a: 46.

adaptations called for by an unprecedented situation."[71] The great victor of this struggle was the yeoman farmer (or *laboureur*), the peasant with the metal plow (*charrue*), the controller of a plot large enough so that he had surplus to market and often needed wage laboring assistance to complete the harvest.

If this were not enough to make the aristocracy tremble, the collapse of the states could only add to their political discomfort, if not to say their political desperation. The states were never strong in Europe throughout the Middle Ages. But they were stronger at some times than at others. The expansion of the economy in Europe between 1000 and 1250 which created new revenue bases for the states and new needs for internal order, on the one hand, and the outward expansion of "Europe" (the Crusades, colonization in the east and far north) which called for some military unification, on the other, combined to create a new life for nascent state machineries. The results were perhaps meager by today's standards, but they mattered. These stronger states began to relapse again into symbolic shells when the great downturn came after 1250.

In explaining the decline of the power of the seigniors, Bois lists two background variables. One is of course "the strengthening of the middling peasantry"; the second is the "hypertrophy of the state (royal absolutism)."[72] One of our difficulties in interpreting what went on between 1250–1300 and 1450 in the political arena is our ideological insistence on interpreting "Western" history as one long, steadily upward striving for democratic political institutions. In the beginning, it is intoned, was the all-powerful monarch, whose power has been steadily reduced ever since. But it was not like that at all. In the beginning (1000–1250), there was a weak monarch seeking to establish some semblance of central authority. These "sovereigns" had severe setbacks in the period 1250–1450. It is true, as we shall discuss, that after 1450, their powers grew again and quite considerably, but this was precisely because the period 1250–1450 revealed the danger that the weakness of the state represented for the seigniors.

What had been accomplished in the period 1000–1300? Some political entities had begun to have an enduring existence, and hence a certain legitimacy. England and France were the foremost examples. Strayer notes that the beginnings of a bureaucracy had been put in place, a chancery coordinating estate-managers, financial agents, local administrators, and judges. This had occurred to some degree everywhere in Western Europe. Then came the great economic depression.

---

[71] Bloch 1976: 122.   [72] Bois 1985: 111.

Strayer concludes that "Europeans had created their state system only in the nick of time," but he himself provides the evidence that the fledgling state system was sorely afflicted by the economic downturn, that "many of the wars of the fourteenth and fifteenth centuries checked, or even set back the process of state-building."[73] There was a resurgence of baronial power. Weakened *vis-à-vis* the peasantry, the seigniors could at least become stronger *vis-à-vis* the kings. Indeed many of the economic factors which enabled the peasants to gain advantage in their dealings with their seignior landlords enabled the latter to gain advantage in their dealings with their sovereign monarchs.

One result was that the internal cohesiveness of the central power was seriously undermined by a now "dangerously wide" gap between the policymakers and their bureaucrats:

The gap between policymakers and bureaucrats had not been serious down to 1300, but in the fourteenth century it was widened by faults of both groups. Policy was made by the king and his Council, a body composed of members of the royal family, royal favorites, heads of baronial factions, and the chief officers of household and government departments. Attendance of princes and nobles was sporadic; often the Council was composed completely of household and administrative officials. Such a Council could deal with routine matters of internal administration and could implement policies already agreed on, for example, the mustering or supply of an army. But when the great (and expensive) questions of peace and war, truces and alliances came up, the princes and baronial leaders had to be consulted. Such men were usually not very well informed, nor did they work very hard to repair the gaps in their information.[74]

Clearly the increased power of the seigniors, their inclusion in policy-making was decisive in this process. This can be verified in the fact that there was a particular "slowness in the development of the departments dealing with defense and foreign affairs," which Strayer regards as a "real puzzle."[75] But it is no puzzle at all. In a period of extensive warfare and state disintegration, these are precisely the arenas in which "heads of baronial factions" would be least willing to see the royal bureaucracy strengthened since it would reduce their own margins of maneuver for upward mobility.

Thus it was that "most governments became bankrupt,"[76] that they were "incapable of controlling their mercenaries, their currency, their judicial system, [that] they were run by cliques and lived badly from day to day." And thus it was that "there was reborn in Europe a series of principalities, micro-states, that were autonomous, even independent, and that this phenomenon eventually undermined the illusion of a kingdom by mutual consent."[77]

[73] Strayer 1970: 35, 57, 59.   [74] Ibid.: 74–75.   [75] Ibid.: 80.
[76] Strayer 1955: 206.   [77] Fossier 1983: 116–17.

No wonder that Strayer could summarize this period by saying that "the movement toward a new type of political authority was checked just as it seemed to be acquiring irresistible momentum. During the fourteenth and early fifteenth centuries, secular governments grew weaker rather than stronger."[78] No wonder Fossier could introduce his discussion of the political situation on this somber note:

What a sad image the State offers us in this period [1250–1520]! Pontiffs who are honorable but contested, becoming dubious and hated; emperors swollen with projects, whose names we cannot recall; Western monarchies in full disarray, old men, minors, madmen (openly acknowledged or probable); and a kaleidoscope of *Podesta*, of princes and captains who have in common only the brevity of their power and the irreality of their projects.[79]

One might think that the seigniors/aristocrats would have been over-joyed with their increased liberation from central authority and basked in the "beautiful privileges" which they "wrenched" from their sovereigns with the emergence of "representative assemblies" in these states that Guenée says became "democracies of the privileged."[80] Not at all, as we shall see.

The collapse of the seigniors and the collapse of the states was accompanied by the collapse of the Church. This is well known; it is not always termed a collapse. But let us reflect on what happened. In the final epoch of the Roman Empire, Christianity had become the state religion. This was normal, in the sense that most world empires had official "churches," that is, a set of religious functionaries who propagated a world view which supported the imperial establishment and which constrained disintegrative forces. A notable example is Confucianism, but it is scarcely the only one. Among other things, these religions constrained capitalist thrusts, in the form of preaching against avarice (to be sure, more the avarice of private persons than the avarice of emperors). The old Roman God system had lost its hold in the Roman Empire for many reasons. One surely was the mistake of beginning to deify living or just deceased emperors, which turned the gods into political figures and ended their necessary minimal distance from material existence. When Christianity surged forth to fill the gap, Constantine moved to co-opt it as the state religion.

Christianity had created an integrated hierarchical structure and thus was able to survive the fall of the Roman Empire. The result was a unique situation, in which a hierarchical world religion became the normative and even institutional cement of a politically disaggregated civilization. For a long time, the Christian Church was therefore strong enough to defend its organizational, economic, and ideological interests

---

[78] Strayer 1955: 197.   [79] Fossier 1983: 110.   [80] Guenée 1971: 405.

against any intrusion of particular political authorities. The "cultural consequences for later intellectual development were to be considerable," says Perry Anderson .[81] Most analysts would agree.

Most would also assume that the consequences were positive. The usual argument goes along the lines that the non-concordance of church and state in the Middle Ages prepared the ground historically for the modern separation of church and state, hence for secularism as the basis of a capitalist, individualist civilization. There is however an alternative way of looking at this evolution. One could argue that the Church's organizational strength *vis-à-vis* the multiple political entities was in fact its fatal flaw. The fact that it was ultimately not subordinate to lay political authority – as in some sense had always been the case with religions hitherto and elsewhere – fatally undercut its ability to serve the political authorities as their constraining force on proto-capitalist elements.

The constraint began to disappear quite early. Nuccio argues that already in the late Middle Ages there occurred a "profound detachment from the religious and ethical attitude in the field of political ideas."[82] And this detachment took place first of all, of course, where the capitalist thrust seemed strongest.

From the twelfth century onwards, Italian entrepreneurs had substantially worked on the basis of a worldly ethic that had been put in the dock and condemned by ecclesiological morality and they had defended it as best they could, at the same time formulating the principles of their autonomy and the "lay" criteria of their economic activity, especially in the city statutes and the mercantile codes.[83]

But why was the Church so weak? For one thing because the Church was a major economic actor itself and was hurt by the economic downturn in the same way that both seigniors (as recipients of rents) and states (as recipients of taxes) were hurt. To defend its own organizational life, the Church became at this time even more involved in economic and financial matters.

The gulf between the Church's spiritual ideals and its members' failure to fulfil them in their daily lives grew evermore paradoxical. What, for example, are we to make of the fact that in Bruges, during this later period, the Collegiate Church of St Donatian licensed several pawnshops on its property? These numbered fourteen in 1380 and they were run, not by Lombards, but by Flemings and Walloons. Because of the ecclesiastical licence, they were free of municipal supervision. Or of the loans by Pope Clement V to Edward II (169,000 florins) for a mortgage on the revenues of Gascony? Or of Nicholas V, who granted the great French merchant Jacques Coeur (1393–1456) a wide licence to trade with the infidels? . . .

The effect of the financial crises was damaging to the papacy. Rightly or

[81] Anderson 1974b: 152.   [82] Nuccio 1983: 121.   [83] Ibid.: 105.

wrongly, a great deal of the criticism directed at the papacy by the heretics, and later by the Protestant reformers, is that it paid lip-service to spiritual values opposed to capitalism, yet was itself deeply immersed in, and concerned with, its fate as a shareholder in capitalism. Or again, if the papacy organized its financial affairs properly, it did so with the aid of the bankers, and in return it protected them by threatening excommunication and interdict. The weapon was used against laity and churchmen alike, but it did not make the papacy any more respected.[84]

The various heretical sects, which received a renewed impulse in this era, were largely egalitarian, anti-authoritarian, and often "communist." In the period of economic tightness, the internecine warfare of the ruling strata for the declining global revenues was reflected in increased conflict between the Church and the temporal rulers, and by great struggles within the Church itself. This was the period of the Great Schism of the West (1378–1417), which involved, among other issues, the assertion of power by cardinals and bishops against the Pope, parallel to the assertion of baronial power against the kings.

Had the Church been subordinate to the temporal rulers, it might actually have had more moral authority. It might have been available for use as the constraining moral force. The Church's very independence transformed the Church into one more secular contender for power and wealth. "So far from Tawney's comment about the Church being unable to compromise with capital being true, it seems only too certain that compromise had been of little difficulty in the accomplishment, and virtually impossible to break."[85] Knowles, in his analysis of the last two centuries of the medieval Church, concludes on this note: "This, then, is the religious climate of the fifteenth century: a church sick, indeed, in head and members, and crying for reform, but with no fear of a catastrophe such as was so soon to occur."[86] The net result was the Sack of Rome in May 1527, "the terminal point of the Medieval Papacy."[87]

Overall, 1250–1450 was a disastrous period for the ruling classes of Western Europe, collectively. Their incomes were squeezed. They were involved in an exceptionally high level of internecine struggle, which negatively affected their wealth, their authority, and their lives. They were faced with popular revolt – peasant rebellions, heretical move-ments. Public disorder was high, as was public intellectual turmoil. What had been solid was melting away. There was a "crisis" in the historical system. Perhaps most threatening to the seigniors, who were the bulk of the ruling strata, was the rise of those "one had begun to call the 'cocks'"[88] – the better-off peasants (yeomen farmers, *laboureurs*), the

---

[84] Gilchrist 1969: 83, 95.   [85] Ibid.: 138.
[86] Knowles and Oblensky 1968: 466.   [87] Binns 1934: 366.
[88] Fossier 1983: 88.

number and size of whose units of production had grown, and who weathered the economic storm better (indeed profited from it). As seen by the aristocrats-landlords, Western Europe was moving in the direction of a paradise of the kulaks. And there seemed no way to slow down this trend.[89]

The collapse of a ruling class is not unusual in history. It happens, if not frequently, at least regularly. Normally, what happened in history was that a collapse allowed for the possibility of external conquest. And such conquest, or invasions, when the dust settled, put in place some new ruling strata who could impose their exploitation effectively upon the direct producers.

This did not occur in Western Europe at this time. We shall discuss this crucial non-event under the symbolic rubric of the collapse of the Mongols. Abu-Lughod argues that 1250–1350 represented the apogee of a "world-system" that connected in a non-hierarchical fashion the Chinese, Indic, Arabo-Persian, and European "subregions" on the basis of long-distance trade. She argues that the inclusion of the Mongols in this system provided a crucial element in its optimal functioning, since it effectively added a "northern" route, reestablishing a link that had previously existed in Roman-Han times:

The simultaneous operation of two different routes across Central Asia (a southern and a northern) and two different routes between the Middle East and Asia via the Indian Ocean (the Red Sea and the Persian Gulf) meant that any blockages developing at specific synapses of the circulatory system could be bypassed. This flexibility not only kept the monopoly protection rent that guarders of individual routes exacted from passing traders within "bearable" limits, but it guaranteed that goods would go through, in spite of localized disturbances.[90]

None of the "subregions" was capitalist in structure. All permitted, however, the functioning of long-distance merchants. The eleventh-century economic upsurge in the West that we have discussed was matched by a new market articulation in China, abetted by the improvements in internal waterways. Both linked up to a Moslem trading ecumene across the Middle East. China's commercialization reinforced this model and, in McNeill's words, "acted like a great bellows, fanning smoldering coals into flame."[91] The Mongol link completed the picture.

What disrupted this vast trading world-system was the pandemic Black Death, itself quite probably a consequence of that very trading

[89] Unger, whose detailed explanation only partially overlaps with the one given here, wishes to argue that what accounts for the rise of capitalism was "the very severity of [the] collapse" of the feudal system. He speaks of the paradox that "the escape from reversion" may be explained by the very severity of the reversion episode (1987: 25).
[90] Abu-Lughod 1989: 336.   [91] McNeill 1982: 53.

network. It hurt everywhere, but it completely eliminated the Mongol link.

The shock appeared in the second third of the fourteenth century with the outbreak of the Black Death, which apparently spread fastest among the most mobile elements of the society, the army. Demographically weakened, the Mongols were less able to exert their control over their domains, which, one by one, began to revolt. Such revolts disturbed the smooth processes of production and appropriation on which the rulers depended, which in turn led to a reduced capacity to suppress the revolts. Once the process began, there was little to prevent its further devolution.

As the plague spread to the rest of the world system, the impulse to conduct long-distance trade was similarly inhibited, although it did not entirely disappear. But when trade revived, the myriad number of small traders sought more secure paths. These were, however, no longer in the forbidding wastes of Central Asia. The lower risks, and therefore lower protective rents along that route, were forever gone.[92]

The Mongol link might have broken down in any case, given the fact that the Mongols faced technical limits they never overcame in sustaining a routinized extensive empire. In any case, the Black Death occurred and its effects were immediate. The negative economic effects occurred throughout the erstwhile trading system. We have already described the impact in Western Europe. It was not so different for China:

As was true in other subregions of that world system, the economic health of China rested primarily on her own ontogenic developments in political organization, technological inventiveness and skill, and commercial sophistication – that is, her ability to harness her local resources. But another part of her economic vitality – a fairly large part by the thirteenth and early fourteenth centuries – came from her ability to extract surplus from the external system. When the external system underwent retrenchment and fragmentation, it was inevitable that all parts formerly linked to it would experience difficulties, including China.[93]

[92]   Abu-Lughod, 1989: 169.
[93]   Ibid.: 326–27. She states her views on how to analyze this period in Chinese economic history even more provocatively in another passage:
> [T]he real question is not why China withdrew from the sea but, rather, why China experienced an economic collapse in the fifteenth century that forced her to scuttle her navy. Even when historians of China abandon the "change of philosophy" argument and examine economic factors, they still tend to look primarily at internal causes – pointing to rampant corruption, political factions, "bad government," and a growing gap between revenues and expenditures under the later Ming dynasty. Although these explanations cannot be discounted entirely, they have to be placed in the context of the rise and fall of the world system traced in this book.
>
> Could the economic difficulties experienced by China have been caused, at least in part, by the fact that the world system had collapsed around it? This is a line of reasoning worth exploring. It is our hypothesis that the foundations of

But what has all this to do with the emergence of capitalism in Western Europe? What Abu-Lughod is calling the "Fall of the East," which she says preceded the "Rise of the West,"[94] had a straightforward politico-military implication. It caused the various "subregions" to pull into themselves. None had the strength at that moment to engage in imperial expansion. Western Europe was unthreatened in the critical period 1350–1450, when it would precisely have been most vulnerable because of the triple collapse it was undergoing. The local West European aristocracy/ruling strata would be neither replaced nor reinvigorated by an outside force. They faced the rising kulak strata alone and weak.

We must now renew the question, why did not capitalism emerge anywhere earlier? It seems unlikely that the answer is an insufficient technological base. It is not clear what kind of base is "essential" in any case. Furthermore, most of the technological base of the capitalist/ "modern" historical system is the consequence of its emergence, scarcely the cause. It is unlikely that the answer is an absence of an entrepreneurial spirit. The history of the world for at least two thousand years prior to 1500+ shows an enormous set of groups, throughout multiple historical systems, who showed an aptitude and inclination for capitalist enterprise – as producers, as merchants, as financiers. "Proto-capitalism" was so widespread that one might consider it to be a constitutive element of all the redistributive/tributary world-empires the world has known. If therefore these proto-capitalist elements were unable to assume the "commanding heights" not only of these various historical systems as systems but even of their productive units, it must be that something was preventing it. For they did have money and energy at their disposition, and we have seen in the modern world how powerful these weapons can be.

Who would have wanted to place limits on the ceaseless accumulation of capital? The answer is obvious: all those who held existing power in any historical system. The ceaseless accumulation of capital inevitably permits new persons to challenge existing power, to undermine it, to become part of it, and does so ceaselessly. Power in redistributive

that system had begun to erode early in the fourteenth century, that they were precipitously weakened by the epidemic deaths in the mid- and later-fourteenth century, and that they were finally undermined completely by the collapse of the Mongol "empire" that, although it allowed the Ming to come to power, also cut China off from its Central Asian hinterland. Thus, what is viewed in Chinese history as a restoration of a legitimate dynasty must be viewed in world system perspective as the final fragmentation of the larger circuit of thirteenth-century world trade in which China had played such an important role (1989: 323–24).

[94] Abu-Lughod 1989: 338.

systems is based on rents, that is, on incomes that are politically assigned and justified. In a capitalist system, profits may be politically obtained, abetted, amplified, but they are never justified politically. Enough profit can therefore lead to the ousting of existing rent receivers.

Of course, in non-capitalist historical systems, existing rent receivers can be ousted militarily. But the military threat is visible, understandable, and acceptable. The insidious threat of market-generated wealth is invisible, capricious, and ultimately totally irrational. It was therefore always unacceptable. To let that genie out of the box one would have to be very desperate indeed. I have tried to indicate the reasons for the desperation of Western Europe's ruling state during the "crisis of feudalism," why it is they saw no way out within the parameters of social organization as they knew it, and why therefore in effect the large majority of the seigniors began to transform themselves into capitalist entrepreneurs.

Remember, capitalist skills and methods were not unknown to them; they had merely previously been rejected for fear of the long-term consequences of utilizing them. Marc Bloch's description of the behavior of the French seigniory at this time may stand as typical of the new thrust:

Faced with the threatened catastrophe brought about by the transformations in the economy, were French seigniors, because they were forbidden by law to engross the land, simply going to give up? To believe this would be seriously to misperceive the state of mind which the most recent entrants into the status of fief-holder, formed as they had been in the school of bourgeois fortunes, had disseminated among the class they had just joined. Their methods merely had to be more insidious, more supple. True seigniorial rights were far from being worthless; but their value had become much reduced. Might it not be possible, by means of tighter management, to obtain a higher return? The system that had made of the seignior less someone whose income came from production and more from rents had turned out to be disastrous. Why not try to reverse the operation and, without using violence, since it was not permitted, work with tenacity and shrewdness to reconstitute the demesne?[95]

As one seignior after another began to do this, it began to pay off, not in more rent but in more profit. But the seignior was neither a philosopher nor a social scientist. After a long crossing of the economic desert, whether "rent" or "profit" the increased income was revenue, increased revenue. Now as burgeoning capitalist and no longer so much a military claimant to honor and rents, the seignior discovered the importance of the state, as guarantor and facilitator of capitalist development. Strayer puts it very well:

[95] Bloch 1976: 134–35.

In short, the people [sic! I would have said the aristocracy] of Western Europe had become convinced that the evil of weak government was worse than the evil of strong government and that undeviating loyalty to the king was the only way to prevent disorder and insecurity. Rebellion seemed more dangerous to society than royal tyranny; it was better for individuals to suffer injustice quietly than for them to make protests which might lead to new civil wars. These ideas were extolled by almost all the political theorists of the period and were accepted by the great majority of the people. In actual fact, the "new monarchies" were rather inefficient despotisms, and left a good deal of room for individual initiative within the framework of the security which they had established.[96]

As Perry Anderson says, "the rule of the Absolutist State was that of the feudal nobility in the epoch of transition to capitalism,"[97] except that he should have added that it was that of the feudal nobility becoming capitalist entrepreneurs.

What let the genie out of the box was the desperation of the ruling classes. What made it possible for the seigniors to overcome their kulak adversaries were the new rules of the game which "disarmed" the latter by distracting them – the more "invisible" exploitation of profits. What sustained the new system and allowed it to consolidate itself was that it worked for the ruling classes, worked that is in the elementary sense that, within 100 to 150 years, all threat to the position of the ruling strata from the emergent kulak strata had disappeared and the seigniorial (now capitalist) share of the absolute and relative surplus had catapulted up once again, to maintain itself at a constantly high level throughout the history of the capitalist world-system.

This is not the place to recount the history of this historical system, something I am trying to do in the successive volumes of *The Modern World-System*. There are however two more questions which should be discussed, if briefly. One is the question of technological progress. The second is the question of rationality.

As Brenner correctly states, the "technologies capable of significantly raising agricultural productivity by means of relatively large-scale investments" were available in medieval Europe, and we should add in many other parts of the world. Furthermore, as he adds, these techniques were even used on occasion. "The question which needs to be asked, therefore, is why they were not *more widely applied*."[98] The answer is surely that there were significant social constraints on these innovations. Ceaseless growth was politically feared and seemed substantively irrational as a social objective. Once however one creates the incentive for technological transformation, there seems little reason to doubt – we see

[96] Strayer 1955: 222.   [97] Anderson 1974a: 42.   [98] Brenner 1985b: 233.

it clearly in retrospect – that humans are ingenious and can develop scientific knowledge and the derived technology.

But is it rational? It was none other than Max Weber, that great protagonist of rationalism, who characterized the businessman's "restless activity" as the leading of an irrational life "where a man exists for his business, and not the other way around." We are used to measuring the gains that the capitalist/"modern" historical system has brought, and to neglecting the fact that the gains have gone to a minority, a large minority perhaps, but still a minority of the world's population. We have been less willing to calculate the costs to the majority – in material terms, in quality of life. And only recently have we begun to measure the costs to the biosphere.

The capitalist world-system has been well established now for some 400 or 500 years. It covers the globe. The history cannot be undone. I have tried to indicate here what were some of the peculiar failings, the conjuncture of circumstances, that made it Western Europe that launched humanity on this irrational adventure. This of course indicates nothing of what might be the substantively rational alternatives possible, given the fact that this historical system now exists and is in turn facing its own "crisis." Just as it was by no means inevitable that the capitalist/ "modern" historical system be born anywhere in the sixteenth century, so there is no inevitable outcome to the current "crisis."

The West invented this curious system where "instead of economy being embedded in social relations, social relations are embedded in the economic system."[99] All other civilizations had sensibly avoided this inversion. Being substantively irrational, this system is ultimately untenable. It remains to be seen however what more fully rational system mankind can invent now, and if it can.

[99] Polanyi 1957: 57.

3   China and Western social thought in the modern period

Gregory Blue

Western interpretations of the nature and significance of Chinese civilization have varied widely over the past eight centuries. At times quite opposing readings have been made of China even within a single period.[1] This diversity of opinions has been documented in a number of detailed surveys on the history of Western ideas about China,[2] and it is not the aim here to elucidate it in detail. In the present chapter, attention will be devoted rather to situating the development of certain key ideas about China in terms of trends in the evolution of Western social thought, especially notions related to what was often termed "the nature" of Chinese society, a concern that underlay and shaped Western discourses about China from the sixteenth till the mid-twentieth century when the bourgeoisies of the leading Western states asserted themselves and then consolidated power in classical fashion both at home and globally. The different phases in the development of ideas about China were linked to broader trends in ideology, political goals, and capitalist economic priorities, though not always in obvious or predictable ways. For present purposes we will not examine the large bodies of literature written by or devoted to authors who over the centuries traveled to China and wrote accounts of it; nor will we consider the corpus of expert works by scholars who devoted themselves primarily to Chinese studies. Instead, we will concentrate on analyses of China by authors and schools of thought that were especially influential in shaping modern Western social thought. Such authors invariably lacked direct or expert knowledge of China, and as a rule drew on sinological writings

[1] The question of periodization is discussed by Lundbaek 1982.

[2] See especially Mackerras 1989, Dawson 1967, and Étiemble 1988–89 for medieval times to the Enlightenment; Barthold 1947 and Lach 1965 for the sixteenth and seventeenth centuries generally; Appleton 1951 for seventeenth-century England; Pinot 1932, Maverick 1946, and Guy 1963 for seventeenth- and eighteenth-century France; Berger 1990 for the Enlightenment in England, France, and Germany; for the nineteenth century, Mason 1939 and Kiernan 1972: chapter 5; for the nineteenth and twentieth century, Decournoy 1970, and on the United States in particular, Isaacs 1980. For bibliographies there is the classic Cordier 1904–08 as well as the more recent Lust 1987, valuable for its annotations on books published before 1850.

for ideas and information about China. Their role lay primarily in bringing such ideas and information together with other intellectual materials in new, more or less credible syntheses that reflected the concerns of their times. Their syntheses in turn shaped the thinking of other writers, including sinologists.

The first part of this chapter attempts to delineate four successive phases that characterized the general evolution of ideas about China in the context of changes in Western intellectual culture and capitalism's global prospects. The second part concentrates on interpretations of the relationship between the structure ascribed to Chinese society and the perceived historical stability of that society.

The wonder of the late Middle Ages and the Renaissance

By the late Middle Ages, European lore about China was attached to three distinct place names, namely the Serica of the ancients and the Cathay and Manzi of the medieval travelers who took advantage of the *pax mongolica* and traveled east. Prominent among the works that made China known to the literate elite in fourteenth- and fifteenth-century Europe were Marco Polo's *Description of the World*, the fictitious *Travels* of Sir John Mandeville and Vincent de Beauvais' learned encyclopaedia, the *Speculum Mundi*. These works advised European readers that China was the world's wealthiest kingdom and that its emperor, the Great Khan, was the world's most powerful ruler. They provided the information that the Chinese people were highly skilled and prosperous, that they had their own writing system, and that they were in possession of the Christian scriptures. The Chinese were also said to adhere faithfully to the constitution on which their kingdom had originally been founded and to prefer to remain aloof from other peoples. That last piece of intelligence seems to have caused no hesitation to the early modern European princes, navigators, and merchants who avidly sought avenues for entry into the famously profitable Asian trade. By the early sixteenth century, European predominance in the carrying trade in the Indian Ocean and South China Sea had been established, and the subjugation of the Americas was in full swing. Christopher Columbus himself had used the wealth of the Great Khan and that of Japan to lure Ferdinand and Isabella into funding his venture.

Imagery relating to the Chinese realms became a conventional part of Renaissance literary culture during the period of European maritime expansion. In the mid-sixteenth century, for example, Boiardo and Ariosto assigned notable roles in their respective *Orlando*s to fictitious "Chinese" characters like the ambitious king of Sericana, Gradasso, and his delicate daughter, Angelica. Such imaginative exoticism was accompanied in the same period by a more distinctly intellectual discourse. Already in the fifteenth century the Renaissance spirit had gone beyond the re-affirmation of ancient Graeco-Roman culture, as can be seen from the wide interests of Cosimo de' Medici. By the middle of the sixteenth century, Guillaume Postel was seeking to integrate all philosophies into an orthodox Catholic framework and thereby to outflank the Church's opponents of various persuasions.[3] Such cosmopolitanism was not without gradations in the degree of respect it accorded other peoples, but the Chinese usually seem to have come out quite well in European estimations. This can be illustrated by Jean Bodin who gave a new extension to the older notion that virtue pertains to the East, when he wrote: "The Spanish have remarked that the Chinese, that most Oriental of peoples, are the most ingenious and the most courteous, and that those of Brasil, the most Occidental, are the most barbarous and cruel."[4] Meanwhile, Montaigne drew on information about diverse societies in order to take distance from Western habits and to suggest new, universal criteria of morality. He too wrote favorably of China and took the opportunity to praise the Imperial censorate in particular:

In China, the civilization and arts of which kingdom, without commerce with and knowledge of ours, surpass our examples in many branches of excellence, and the history of which shows me how much broader and more diverse the world is than either the ancients or we might grasp, the officers delegated by the Prince to inspect the state of his provinces, as they punish those who have abused their responsibilities, so also do they reward most graciously those who have conducted themselves well, beyond the ordinary and beyond what duty requires of them.[5]

Bodin and Montaigne invoked Chinese examples only cursorily, but other writers in the same period went into more detail. One example was the great Portuguese historian of Asia, João de Barros, who wrote glowingly of Chinese social and political institutions, and praised achievements in the arts and sciences such as the invention of printing and artillery. Barros concluded that Chinese civilization was even superior to that of the ancient Greeks and Romans – praise indeed from a Renaissance humanist, as Boxer has noted.[6] Another cache of admiration for the Middle Kingdom is found in the writings of Giovanni Botero, the influential Italian critic of Machiavelli's political doctrines.

[3] Postel 1543 and 1575; see the analyses of Hentsch 1988: 102–07 and Étiemble 1958–61: 1,201. The closeness of Postel's strategy to that adopted by the Jesuits later is clear.
[4] Bodin 1579: 5, 481.
[5] Montaigne 1979: vol. III, 282. See also Lach 1977: 297.
[6] Barros 1563: 2, chapter 7; cited in Boxer 1981: 106–08.

For Botero, China was the model of a prosperous urban culture, its prosperity being based, in his view, on the skill of its artisans, the importance of its internal waterways, and its access to the sea. The political wisdom of the Chinese, he believed, was shown by the fact that unlike certain European states China placed limits on expansion and refrained from pursuing a course of unbridled aggression.[7]

These few examples may serve to illustrate the admiration for China that was widespread in Europe in the sixteenth century. The sources of information available to Western authors about China at this time were very limited,[8] but a consensus of positive opinion seems to have formed on the basis of ideas concerning the economic prosperity of the Empire, its social and political organization, and the ingenuity of its people.

Mixed opinions in the seventeenth century and the early Enlightenment

In the seventeenth and early eighteenth centuries, by contrast, interpretations of Chinese civilization were taken up as weapons in some of the great cultural debates of the age in Europe. This entailed a greater variation in evaluations of China, though not always greater objectivity. As evidence of this, one can refer to the opinions of Francis Bacon. Bacon would seem to have known that many of the most important discoveries and inventions that he thought made modern Europe more learned than antiquity had originated in China,[9] but he nevertheless judged his Chinese contemporaries to be a "curious, ignorant, fearful, foolish nation," and to have been made so by the imperial law that excluded foreigners from entering the kingdom without permission – perhaps not a surprising assessment coming from a leading light in a kingdom with mercantile aspirations in Asia.[10]

To be sure, the aspects of Chinese civilization that commanded European respect in the sixteenth century generally continued still to do so in the next century. In particular, enthusiasm about China's social and political philosophy seems to have become even more widespread. The religious discord and wars that had racked Europe for over a

[7] Waley and Waley 1956: 38, 142, 266–69; Botero 1630: 586, 595–96. Lach (1977: 238–42, 245–49) points out that Botero's later work remained favorable to China, though Jesuit influence probably made him more critical.

[8] Mendoza's (1585) two-volume work, commissioned by Philip II of Spain and available in Spanish in 1585, was the first major European publication devoted solely to China. By 1614 there were twenty-eight editions, and translations in seven major European languages.

[9] See, e.g., Bacon 1905, bk 1: 292, 300, aphorisms 109, 110, 129.

[10] Ibid.: 720.

hundred years made many thinkers well disposed toward the non-sectarian civil order they saw in China. Recommending Chinese example in 1624, Michel Baudier wrote:

Men's care for their persons causes [them] to seek in the Indies, and throughout the Orient, drugs and remedies which purge the body of maladies which afflict it. And this enterprise [also] draws forth from the lore of such oriental regions, lessons which, when exposed to the eyes of the public and imitated, are able to dissipate certain disorders and to heal in the spirits of the age the passions which disturb them.[11]

Not much later François La Mothe le Vayer associated Socrates and Confucius as paragons of natural religion and morality,[12] and brought the theme of the praiseworthy scholar official into the mainstream of skeptical thought in the absolutist era. Yet even such a devout Catholic writer as Athanasius Kircher could speak of the Chinese state as the realization of Plato's Republic.[13] At the behest of Richelieu, La Mothe le Vayer set himself against the Jansenist idea that original sin made it impossible to lead a moral life without the saving grace of Jesus Christ, and he praised the moral doctrines of Buddhism and of contemporary Confucianism. His commitment to rational morality based primarily on human experience and intellectual values rather than on revealed truth and ecclesiastical sanction was something of a challenge to the social and political position of the Church in France.[14] But this was not the only cause in which the image of China was enlisted.

In the second half of the seventeenth century, one of the most important lessons drawn from China was that politics there amounted to nothing more nor less than rational, collective morality. This idea was helpful for those who wished to uphold the mystique of governance and repudiate the Machiavellian separation of politics and morality. Likewise, the example of a civil service whose officials were chosen for distinction in learning, rather than on the basis of hereditary or estate privilege served to legitimate a greater role for the intellectual elite within European state structures. Now the Jesuits were early modern Europe's main purveyors of information about China, and they themselves purported to be such an elite within the Church. Their accounts of China lent ideological support not only to the consolidation of absolutism generally, but also to the political roles they themselves were playing in Bourbon France and the Hapsburg domains. However, such accounts were also to be used somewhat subversively, since Chinese civil order seemed to be based on a "philosophical" moderation free of

[11] Baudier 1624: Préface; Guy 1963: 97–98.
[12] Étiemble 1976: 42.   [13] Kircher 1667: 166.
[14] On La Mothe, see Guy 1963: 118–22, and Étiemble 1966: 48–49.

the religious partisanship in politics that had occasioned so much conflict and bloodshed in Europe.

The Jesuits' near monopoly of the China mission led them, on the one hand, to argue that the Chinese literati, while well disposed to Christian thought, were intelligent and therefore required sophisticated – i.e., Jesuit – missionaries. On the other hand, their conviction that the Chinese should be converted led them to characterize the neo-Confucianism dominant among contemporary officials as atheistic, and to denounce various strands of Chinese thought as materialistic.[15] From such Jesuit descriptions other thinkers drew their own conclusions. In the last three decades of the seventeenth century, the prestige of much of Chinese culture remained high in Europe, and the various components of the Jesuit China-image were taken over by many thinkers including the opponents of the Society. However, the Jesuits were increasingly forced to defend themselves on several fronts in the context of the Chinese Rites Controversy: against other factions of the Roman Church in Europe – particularly the Jansenists and the Société des Missions Étrangères, who objected to allegedly lax Jesuit theology as well as to the Society's political power; against competing missionary Orders which supported a stronger campaign of proselytism in China; and, finally, against a group toward which the Jesuits and their enemies in the Church shared hostility, namely, the Libertines, or Free-thinkers, who argued against the political position of the Church in Europe and used the Chinese example to temper belief in certain Christian doctrines.

One such doctrine was the account of the origins of mankind in the Book of Genesis. This was called into question by means of comparisons with the chronologies of non-Biblical peoples.[16] As Edwin Van Kley has said, "perhaps the most serious challenge to the traditional scheme of world history and the factor most instrumental in changing that scheme was the discovery of ancient Chinese history."[17] In 1659, one year after the publication of the Jesuit Martini's *Decas sinicae historiae*, the Dutch

---

[15] For example, Couplet's introduction to Intorcetta 1687 treated the neo-Confucians as *atheo-politici*, an identification probably related to the seventeenth-century perception of atheism and materialism in the philosophy of Spinoza. Another common association during this period was that of Stoicism and Chinese thought, as in the 1744 quotation from Brücker cited in Needham 1956: 476. The Jesuits, like the other missionary groups, considered Buddhism and Taoism to be idolatrous.

[16] Lach (1977: 414–15) observes that Joseph Scaliger, the father of European historical chronology, was inspired by the study of Asian history and languages. His writings exerted a strong influence on later writers including Hugo Grotius and his associate Gerhard Vossius, Isaac's father.

[17] Van Kley 1971: 362.

historian Isaac Vossius used that work to argue[18] that the Chinese historical annals were superior to the Biblical chronology and that the flood of Noah had not been universal. The views of Vossius and other Libertines were quickly contested by orthodox religious authors keen to re-assert the authority of the Pentateuch and the historical status of the ancient Hebrews. Yet even such figures had to take the Chinese chronology seriously. This was partly because of the antiquity of the events it included (which led John Webb to claim that China had been peopled before Babel[19]), and also because of the Chinese chronology's relative credibility based on datings that were often supported by astronomical observations.[20] Debates on these points concerning the roles of China and the east Mediterranean in world history lasted well into the eighteenth century. In these debates, attempts were made to identify Chinese counterparts with significant Biblical personalities, and three trends developed which would be of importance for later historiography. The first was an increasingly critical, de-sacralizing attitude toward historical sources, whether Biblical or Chinese. The second was a skeptical readiness to treat the fabulous as myth. A third trend, one that came to mark the entire early Enlightenment, was a relativization of Western historical experience and in particular an acceptance of the restricted validity of Judaeo-Christian culture. All three reinforced the broadening of intellectual and cultural horizons typical of the Enlightenment and of the expansion of northern Europe's increasingly global prospects.

In addition to affecting historical conceptions of the world, China inspired secular political theoreticians who were seeking a practical political morality unencumbered by the metaphysical dogmas that had so enflamed the passions of previous generations of Europeans. An example in the late seventeenth century was Gassendi's disciple François Bernier, one-time physician to the Great Moghul and an adviser to Colbert. His negative characterization of the nature of Indian society are well known, not least because of the support Karl Marx later accorded them when developing his idea of an Asiatic mode of production. However, Bernier himself gave vastly different pictures of India and China, for he recommended as a model of virtuous rule the Chinese political order based upon filial piety and mutual respect between ruler and subject. Referring to the durability of Chinese government, he

---

[18] Vossius was influenced by the ideas of La Peyrère who in 1655 had mentioned the Chinese in passing as one of the peoples whose history could be reconciled with Genesis only by recourse to his thesis of a pre-Adamite race; see Guy 1963: 109–12.

[19] Webb 1667: 60–62. On Webb's sinophilia, see Ch'en Shou-Yi 1935–36.

[20] Comparison of dates with the Chinese chronology was a major factor influencing acceptance of the Septuagint instead of the Vulgate as the standard version of Bible history.

maintained in 1688 that the rationality of the Confucian political tradition had enabled the Chinese to surpass all other peoples in "virtue, wisdom, prudence, good faith, sincerity, charity, gentleness, honesty, civility, gravity, modesty and obedience to the Celestial order."[21] Such praise of Confucian doctrines and practice was similarly shared at about the same time in Britain by Sir William Temple, probably the greatest of the English Sinophiles. He wrote in 1690 that:

the kingdom of China seems to be framed and policed with the utmost force and reach of human wisdom, reason and contrivance; and in practice to excel the very speculations of other men, and all those imaginary schemes of the European wits, the institutions of Xenophon, the republic of Plato, the Utopias, or Oceanas, of our modern writers.[22]

In a similar vein, Leibniz drew on China's political reputation in formulating his ideas of accommodation and reconciliation between Protestants and Catholics, just as he drew on its reputation for ancient wisdom in publicizing his version of the calculus.[23]

Leibniz's "maximalist" ecumenical program coincided roughly with John Locke's and Pierre Bayle's advocacy of religious tolerance in the 1680s. Of the three, only Bayle argued that atheists should be allowed civil rights, and long-standing Chinese example provided him with powerful evidence for his argument that religious toleration was a viable principle of government. Conversely, when the Edict of Nantes was revoked, the Kangxi emperor's permission for Catholicism to be practiced enabled Bayle to reproach the French Church and state alike for hypocrisy on the grounds that, while urging toleration of Christianity abroad, they proceeded to repress creeds other than their own at home. Bayle's reflection supported the idea, shared by Locke, that intolerance and fanaticism constituted threats to social harmony and therefore ought not to be tolerated, in China or elsewhere.[24] Later, Bayle cited Chinese "atheism" in rejecting the argument for God's existence based on "universal consent" and in maintaining that morality is logically independent of religious belief in a transcendent God.[25]

Such twists to the Jesuits' depictions of China poured oil on the

---

[21] Bernier 1689.

[22] From "Of Heroic Virtue" in Temple 1720: vol. I, 203; Appleton 1951: 43 notes that the Dutch diplomat Johan Nieuhof was Temple's main source.

[23] On Leibniz' ideas about China, see especially Mungello 1977; Étiemble 1988–89: vol. II, chapters 26–30; and Elster 1975: 239–50, which discusses arguments raised in *SCC*, vol. II concerning a possible transmission of holistic positions in philosophy from China to Europe via Leibniz. Elster argues that Leibniz was as far from neo-Confucianism as he was from European scholasticism.

[24] Bayle 1686a: vol. I, 184; and Berger 1990: 61 on Bayle's depiction of China.

[25] Pinot 1932: 321–28. The relation of Chinese and other extra-European notions to the development of Enlightenment atheism is explored by Kors 1990.

flames of the Chinese Rites Controversy,[26] the vehement polemic in which the Society of Jesus and its ecclesiastical opponents had been engaged since the mid-seventeenth century. The Jesuits' views were linked to their mission strategy; among the most notable of these were the ideas that Confucianism retained elements of an ancient knowledge of the true God, that the Chinese practiced an exemplary morality[27] and that Confucian ceremonies were of a social and political, and not of a religious, nature. The Jesuits lost a major battle in the Rites Controversy in 1700 when the theological faculty of the Sorbonne condemned several of their positions. In the following decades they fought an ideological rear-guard action for the reversal of the condemnations, but the judgments of the Sorbonne were upheld in later papal judgments. Part of the reason why papal authority went against the Society's positions was that by this time the Vatican had become worried about Jesuit gallicanism. Consequently, rituals that were integral to Chinese social life – such as those by which ancestors were remembered and honored – were judged to be pagan and inimical to Christian beliefs and practices. The condemnations were a severe blow to China's reputation in establishment circles in Catholic Europe during the first half of the eighteenth century.

The connection between the attack on Chinese religion and philosophy and that on the Chinese chronology was well summed up by Eusèbe Renaudot, a major protagonist in the Rites Controversy, who had polemicized against both Vossius and the Jesuits. He thought:

What we are taught by Jesus Christ is too well grounded to want the concurrence of Chinese Philosophy; and if any believe it may perfect the mind and reform the manners, though they know nothing thereof but by paraphrases, as obscure as the Text; they are advised to inquire what may be objected to the Antiquity of this Proud Nation, to their History and Philosophy.[28]

In 1733 Renaudot's work was translated in England, where protests had already been registered against the use the Libertines made of Chinese example. In 1694, William Wotton, commissioned by the Royal Society to combat Sir William Temple's praise of "ancient" learning, judged the teachings of Confucius (and Mohammed) pitifully lower than those of Jesus.[29] Wotton's view of the Chinese as grossly deficient

---

[26] On the Rites Controversy see Pinot 1932: 71–140; Rule 1986: 70– 149; Rowbotham 1942: 119–75; Cummins (ed. and tr.) 1962: xxxviii–lxiv.

[27] As stated, for example, in Le Comte 1696: vol. II, 141.

[28] Renaudot 1733: 234.

[29] Wotton 1694: 145. On the "Broad Church" appropriation of the new science see M. Jacob 1976. Adas 1989 documents assessments of the scientific records and capacities of non-European peoples by missionaries and other Western travelers. His argument that such assessments were crucial in the formation of general assessments of

in the natural sciences and medicine partly reflected the Newtonian vision of a complementarity between the "new" science and specifically Christian doctrine. Bolingbroke, after an initial enthusiasm for China, later disapproved of the literati as atheists and of the common people as immersed in Buddhist and Daoist superstition.[30] In early eighteenth-century Britain, such views contrasted sharply with the ideas of the anti-clerical radicals, John Toland and Matthew Tindal. In *Christianity as Old as Creation*, Tindal argued that the natural religion of the original Christians had been corrupted by priests and the introduction of super-stitious beliefs. With a provocative twist of cosmopolitanism, he held that he was "so far from thinking the maxims of Confucius and Jesus Christ differ, that I think the plain and simple maxims of the former, will help to illustrate the more obscure ones of the latter, accommodated to the then way of speaking."[31] Establishment dismissal of the radicals' views showed the continued importance of Christianity in the post-1688 British social and political order based on a coincidence of middle class and aristocratic interests.

In France, the situation was different: political antagonisms remained sharper, and cultural conflict more intense. Voltaire for once defended the Jesuits and sharply criticized the Church's condemnation of the Order over the Chinese Rites Controversy. He himself was willing to argue that the Chinese had quite simply "perfected Moral science,"[32] and he gave a reasonably accurate summary of the importance of China for the early French Enlightenment when he commented: "In all the discoveries of the East, the potentates of Europe and the men of commerce who have enriched them have been in search only of wealth. The *philosophes* have discovered there a new moral and physical universe."[33] One *philosophe* to whom Voltaire might well have been referring was Louis XIV's distinguished minister, Marshal Vauban. In the early eighteenth century he cited Chinese example in support of two of his new policy measures, namely, the first national census to be taken in modern Europe, and his reform of the chaotic French tax system through the institution of a single general tax reminiscent of the Ming single-whip system.[34] Similarly, Louis XV's reformist Controller-General, Étienne Silhouette, was an avid sinophile who praised the standardized Chinese taxation system. Though he was no doubt idealistic in this, as he was in describing Chinese foreign trade, his depiction of Confucian emphasis

such peoples is well taken, but should not obscure the insight that European attitudes toward non-Christian religions also played a crucial role in this respect from the outset.
[30] Bolingbroke 1841: vol. IV, 266–67.   [31] Tindal 1730: 296.
[32] Voltaire 1877–85: vol. XVI, 85.   [33] Ibid., vol. XII, 367.
[34] Vauban 1698: 124.

on agriculture did lend intellectual weight to his policies.[35] After him, from the late 1750s until the 1770s, China served as a model for François Quesnay and other Physiocrats, who in a prelude to the classical capitalist economic analyses of Smith and Ricardo reestablished production, or more specifically (in line with Confucian thought) agricultural production, as the foundation of their economic theory.[36]

The absolutist position of the Physiocrats constituted a late, perhaps extreme, case of the then common trope of taking Chinese and Egyptian inspiration in framing eighteenth-century ideals of enlightened government. At Versailles Louis XV performed the ritual spring plowing that was dictated by tradition as a duty of the emperor of China.[37] In England the mandarinate was contrasted favorably with Robert Walpole's patronage network.[38] Even the *Encyclopédie* observed that:

It is certain that all Nations cultivate Science, though some do so more than others; but there is none in which knowledge is more highly esteemed than with the Chinese. Amongst this people one cannot attain the least [State] position unless one is a scholar, at least in comparison to the ordinary people of the nation. . . . It is not sufficient amongst them to have the reputation of a scholar, it is necessary really to be one in order to achieve dignities and honors.[39]

Among political theorists, Christian Wolff subscribed to the tradition of admiring Chinese statecraft for the importance it accorded to philosophical learning, and held that, despite certain flaws in the Chinese system, no more "illustrious Example" of philosophical government could "anywhere be found."[40] Though Montesquieu firmly parted company with the sinophiles in 1748 when he judged Chinese government to be a form of despotism, China continued to be recommended for its political institutions well into the third quarter of the century. Montesquieu's assessment was contested in France by Voltaire and Quesnay, and in Germany his view was criticized by J. H. G. von Justi who favored a Confucian-style civil service and deemed China a "constitutionally limited monarchy."[41]

Throughout this period the perceived antiquity and continuity of

---

[35] Silhouette 1729; 1764; on which see Maverick 1946: 27–33.
[36] Hudson 1931: 322; M. Bernal 1987b: 42, 174.
[37] The Chinese ceremony had been recounted in du Halde 1735 (vol. II: 72), and was even praised by Montesquieu in *De l'Esprit des Lois* (bk 10: 228). Louis XV undertook the ritual plowing at the suggestion of Quesnay made through La Pompadour; see Reichwein 1925: 106. Joseph II of Austria followed suit and did a similar harvest plowing in 1769. Budde *et al.* (eds.) 1985 describes the spate of late eighteenth-century books recounting the European imitations and the Chinese prototype.
[38] For example, Budgell 1731; see also T. C. Fan 1949; and Appleton 1951: 125–27.
[39] Diderot and D'Alembert 1751–80: vol. II, 232.
[40] Wolff 1726; cited in Lach 1977: 570–73.
[41] Justi 1762: 52.

Chinese institutions remained important pillars of the country's general reputation.[42] As interest in universal history developed in tandem with increases in Europe's economic and political power internationally, three historiographical trends regarding China emerged. Though all were to some extent Eurocentric, they were so to different degrees and in different ways. The first was frankly dismissive, and can be exemplified in the words of Nicolas Lenglet-Dufresnoy, whose insights into the geographically restricted scope of Biblical history went in the right direction, but who found East Asian history to be "a study of mere curiosity which does not contain much profit, because these peoples have never had much connection with any of those whose history is necessary or useful to us."[43] A second, diffusionist school followed the course set by the seventeenth-century Jesuit polymath Athanasius Kircher and argued that Chinese culture was derived historically from Mediterranean and especially from Egyptian civilization.[44] A third trend allotted China an important role of its own in world history, but generally restricted this role to the beginnings of political history. The Comte de Boulainvilliers, a prominent spokesman of the French reformists at the turn of the eighteenth century, followed Libertine convention by starting his world history with a chapter on China.[45] Thereafter, the influential world histories of Pretot, Hase, and Shuckford (published respectively in France, Germany, and England) began by treating China, rather than Assyria or Egypt, as the most ancient State on earth.[46] In 1754 Voltaire made the most thorough attempt so far to integrate China into the global historical process. He gave China pride of place in his *Essai sur les moeurs* by devoting to that country his first and penultimate chapters, as well as bringing it into several intermediate ones.[47] Unfortunately, few authors in the new literature dealing with world history followed him in incorporating Chinese developments into their narratives, though the practice of treating China simply at the beginning of history became more and more conventional.

[42] This was so despite the fact that heavy criticism was being leveled at traditional Chinese astronomy, which had been invoked in attacks on the Biblical chronology and on the priority of the ancient Hebrews.

[43] Lenglet-Dufresnoys 1772: bk 9, 81; see also Pinot 1932: 242–44 and Van Kley 1971: 380.

[44] See Baltrusaitis 1960: 226–32; also Needham 1954: 38.

[45] See R. Simon 1940: 312.

[46] Pretot 1753 and Hase 1743. Samuel Shuckford 1728, originally published 1731–37, went through four editions by 1818.

[47] Voltaire 1963; Fueter 1914: 444 – like many other authors – has deemed this the first truly universal history. Étiemble 1958–61: 61–63 and Boxer 1961: 316 stress the importance of Voltaire's use of Chinese chronology as a landmark in establishing the fallibility of the Bible as an historical source.

Meanwhile, the early eighteenth century witnessed contradictory images of China being publicized in the newly emerging genre of the novel. Daniel Defoe, responsible for penning particularly vitriolic attacks on the country's culture, depicted Chinese religion as "ridiculous folly," the mandarins as intolerably proud, and the masses as living in a poverty more abject than that of native Americans.[48] Defoe's dim view of China would become standard wisdom in the nineteenth century, but in the eighteenth it was out of tune with the mood of the many fictional writers who found it handy to use a Chinese yardstick in order to take critical measure of European manners, a technique which eventually gave birth to the figure of the cosmopolitan Chinese traveler. The prime example of this genre in English is *The Citizen of the World* by Oliver Goldsmith. Goldsmith followed the lead of the Marquis d'Argens' *Lettres Chinoises*, a work that anticipated Diderot's *Les Bijoux Indiscrets* in using Chinese imagery to express an irreverently libertarian attitude toward Christian sexual conventions.[49] Brunetière (1906) long ago cited d'Argens' work as representing the "definitive annexation" of discourse about China to the domain of Orientalism. Seen from one angle, these works might be taken to illustrate Edward Said's point that the reduction of "the Orient" to the passive function of a set of symbols opened it to manipulation according to the changing interests of Western power.[50]

It would nevertheless be simplistic to infer that the only tendency at work throughout the Enlightenment was a manipulative fixation of images, for communication between China and Europe was also effecting a transmission of knowledge about Chinese civilization into European society. This transmission made possible the assimilation of new cultural elements that were to be involved in the remolding of patterns of thought and material culture there. The most tangible examples of such influence are in the realm of material culture. Honour (1961) and Impey (1977) have surveyed the Chinoiserie vogue that culminated in this period when Chinese porcelains, lacquers, textiles, wallpapers, and tea came into style in Portugal, the Netherlands, France, England, Italy, Germany, and the Scandinavian countries. Chinese styles also became fashionable (in adulterated form) about the same time in architecture, furniture, and garden design.[51] Such introductions

[48] Defoe 1868: 547–60; also, on Chinese religion, Defoe 1840–03: 42. For further discussion see Ch'en Shou-Yi 1928: chapter 3, and Appleton 1951: chapter 4.
[49] Étiemble 1964: 63–64; see also Étiemble 1988–89 (vol. II: chapters 5, 6) on Chinese erotic lore as a means of challenging Western sexual conventions; and Berger (1990: 148ff) on d'Argens' overall use of China.
[50] Said 1978.
[51] On gardens, see for example Loehr 1976 and Sirén 1950. A first great admirer of the

played an integral role in the evolution of European tastes during the seventeenth and eighteenth centuries. At the end of the seventeenth, Chinoiserie and Gothic styles were linked in an assault upon the austere symmetry of aesthetic neo-classicism.

The decline of China's cultural reputation from the mid-eighteenth century

By the middle of the eighteenth century, however, tendencies to discount Chinese culture were becoming increasingly predominant. The attacks on the Chinese philosophical and religious traditions in the Rites Controversy and Montesquieu's judgment in *De l'Esprit des Lois* that China's government was essentially despotic had represented important steps in discrediting China in European eyes. Similarly, by the middle of the century the alliance between the Gothic and Chinese styles in the aesthetic field was breaking down. Chinoiserie became increasingly degraded and intermingled with the Baroque. It lost ground, on the one hand, to the Gothic style and, on the other, to a renewed respect for the neo-classical. Horace Walpole, a prominent observer of contemporary English fashion, boasted that in the 1760s he was working conversions from Chinoiserie to Gothic.[52] At about the same time, the German historian and philosopher of art, Johann Winckelmann, praised ancient Greek artistic tradition for having progressed to the point of attaining the true ideal of beauty, unlike those of "Oriental" peoples which had stagnated. He held Chinese forms of art in low regard, on the grounds that they differed substantially from the Greek "ideal" and that Chinese faces, being disagreeable "deviations" from the "standard," provided inferior models for sculpture.[53]

Anyone who studies the evolution of ideas about China is soon struck by the radical reversal of Western judgments about almost all aspects of Chinese culture which took place from the mid-eighteenth to the mid-

Chinese garden was William Temple, whom we have mentioned above; later on, William Chambers (1757 and 1772) advocated the same cause, as well as that of Chinese architecture generally.

In the area of furniture design Thomas Chippendale was perhaps the most distinguished of many who followed the Chinese mode. See Reichwein 1925: 45ff. on wallpapers.

From the late seventeenth- to the mid-nineteenth-century tea drinking seems to have spread in line with the fall of prices and according to a fairly straightforward "trickle down" tendency from the wealthy to the working classes in Holland, England, Germany, and Russia; on the nineteenth-century promotion of tea by the Russian temperance reformers, see Smith and Christian 1984: 228–47.

[52] Walpole 1903–25: vol. XII, 10–11.

[53] Winckelmann 1850: 32, 38. On the lack of progress of the "Orient," see Winckelmann 1766: 29, 132.

ninteenth century. Of course, as we have already seen, quite a number of writers had negative opinions of China in earlier times, and even in the nineteenth century one finds positive assessments. What we are concerned with then is a change in the balance of opinion.[54] This change accompanied a definite shift in emphasis and approach, in the sense that discussion in the earlier period often focused on positive implications of Chinese culture for the West, whereas emphasis in the late eighteenth century moved increasingly to explaining how aspects of China deviated from an alleged Western model. In the period, roughly speaking, from 1600 to 1750, the invocation of China by European writers often involved a belief that Chinese history and civilization, like those of ancient Egypt, might hold certain lessons that could be appreciated and applied for the enhancement of Western culture. In the period from about 1750 until the years between the two world wars, another consensus was increasingly consolidated based on an assumption among social thinkers that Western civilization (as this was variously construed) dated back to ancient Greece and that this alone could be considered as "universally" valid.

It is appropriate to consider some possible reasons for this shift in approaches as it concerned ideas about China. Perhaps because of the tangible nature of Chinoiserie, one argument often adduced for the decline in China's reputation has been an art-historical one, namely, that tastes and fashions are by their nature bound to change and that the Enlightenment vogue for forms of Chinese culture was thus bound to fall into decline.[55] While there may be some truth to this, it is too vague to be fully satisfactory. Another explanation of the shift is that Western knowledge of China changed qualitatively, moving from myth to knowledge. When one examines the history of specialist writings on China, it is difficult on internal disciplinary grounds to sustain the conventional argument that the primary sources – accounts by missionaries, diplomats, and merchants who visited the country, or by scholars who studied it professionally – were "ideological" until the mid-eighteenth century and then became "scientific" in the nineteenth.[56] That argument is further weakened by the fact that between approximately 1750 and 1880 there were dramatic falls in Western estimations not only of the Chinese, but also of the ancient Egyptians and of Semitic peoples generally. Indeed the reputations of most non-Western peoples declined in Western eyes at this time. This coincidence constitutes *prima facie* evidence for doubting that what was at stake was simply a matter of

[54] Compare Dawson 1967: 132–34.
[55] For example, Appleton 1951: 172–73.
[56] This case is made in Blue 1988: chapter 3.

growing objectivity regarding China. It is thus worthwhile to examine the shift in the balance of Western views in more concrete terms related to social and cultural tendencies within Western culture, and in terms of the shifts in European power worldwide.

Among authors who have written on this subject Louis Dermigny attempted to place the shift of views regarding China within the field of social history, and in particular within the development of capitalism.[57] In his view, enthusiasm for China was a typical characteristic of the world view of the bourgeoisie in several European countries when that class was in the ascendent and its prospects were convergent with those of monarchs who were promoting the centralization of their realms and trade, but at a time when the bourgeoisie had not yet established its own social hegemony. However, once bourgeois hegemony came to be established at the national level, enthusiasm for China became increasingly redundant. The limits that the policies of the centralized dynastic state had placed on the growth of commercial profits were then increasingly resented, and the bourgeoisie consequently discarded its earlier admiration for China and began to replace it with sinophobic ideas.[58] There is much to recommend this interpretation, since it provides a context for the main tendencies in attitudes toward China, while allowing one to understand lags in the decline of sinophilia in different countries, a decline manifest rather earlier in the Netherlands and England, and somewhat later in France and Germany. Dermigny's thesis can be strengthened if one revises it so as to take account of two further phenomena. The first is the growing disenchantment felt by European merchants directly engaged in trade with China. This manifested itself from the middle of the seventeenth century as a growing disdain for certain elements of Chinese society, and especially for Chinese merchants and the Manchu government that placed official constraints on trade. To some extent this disenchantment coincided with the assertion of bourgeois hegemony within Europe, and especially in the Netherlands and England. Merchants engaged in trade with China formed only one segment of the European bourgeoisie, however, and it took some time for their views about China to spread to the bulk of that class. Second, it is clear that the strongest expressions of enthusiasm for China during the period 1650–1770 came not from merchants, but rather from intellectuals. This point can be accommodated to Dermigny's interpretation by

---

[57] Hudson 1931: 326–28, and Guy 1963: chapter 8 *passim*, have also considered this question briefly.
[58] Dermigny 1964a: vol. I, 32–43.

means of the conventional distinction between the membership of a class and the spokesmen of that class.

At the same time, this second point seems serious enough to merit another hypothesis, perhaps parallel to Dermigny's, regarding the social significance of the rise and fall of the "China vogue." One might argue that sinophilia was characteristic of those early modern intellectuals who supported limitations on the privileges of the hereditary nobility and/or on those of the Church, and who favored revisions to orthodox Christian doctrine. Such ideas then provoked strong reactions within the churches and among the hereditary nobility. In France, opposition to "Chinese" models of state centralization then emerged among the reformist aristocracy and in the *parlemens*, which retained a Jansenist tint down to the fall of the *ancien régime*. In the Protestant Netherlands and England, on the other hand, where revolutionary crises had eventually resulted in social-political pacts in which the middle classes and the aristocracy were joined together, arguments for deflating the hereditary nobility appeared politically outmoded or impertinent from the elite point of view.

In the long run, the great expansion of Western European productive and scientific forces in the Industrial Revolution provided strong reinforcement to ideas of European superiority. The comparative speed of European progress already in the eighteenth century was so remarkable that it led one writer to exclaim quite accurately: "The peoples of the Orient were formerly quite superior to our Western peoples, in all the arts of the mind and of the hand. But how we have made up for lost time!"[59] When the same author jumped from recent real achievements of the West to the conclusion that the "Oriental peoples" had to be considered only "barbarians, or children, despite their antiquity," he used two clichés that were typical of the superiority complex characteristic of European colonialism and imperialism. It was perhaps hardly surprising that China, a country not yet subordinated to colonial domination, became the object of heavy ideological onslaught as India was being brought under Western control politically and militarily.

The shift in late eighteenth-century evaluations of Chinese society and civilization seems to have resulted not so much from any new empirical knowledge about the country, but rather from changes in Western perspectives. The main shift in the balance of opinion came about during the period from the decline of the Jesuit mission and before the advent of the nineteenth-century missions. The new consensus of European opinion hostile to China seems to have been

---

[59] Diderot and D'Alembert (eds.) 1751–80: vol. VII, 455 ("Japon").

consolidated largely on the basis of the views propounded by social thinkers who were not specialists on China. Such thinkers drew on the negative depictions of the country that were found in the reports of earlier missionaries and merchants,[60] but much of the force of their criticism of Chinese civilization lay in the way they fitted China into their own theories about society and history.

Probably the most important thematic innovation behind the shift toward sinophobia in the late eighteenth and early nineteenth centuries was the new emphasis given to the idea of progress, a notion that was developed in such a manner as to set European nations categorically above others. The notion of the historical stagnation of Chinese society was linked in particular to judgments about the nature of the Chinese language and of Chinese geography. Earlier in the century, Vico had reasoned that China's "monosyllabic" language and "hieroglyphic" writing system implied that the country had never passed beyond the primitive, heroic stage at the infancy of mankind, probably on account of its geographical "isolation."[61] Similarly, David Hume believed that the Chinese had the greatest uniformity of character imaginable, and he accounted for this in terms of their common language and their country's geography. In his view, the natural divisions of Europe, and originally of Greece, had resulted at one level in a variety of political regimes and at another in achievement in the sciences and arts, whereas the lack of geographical divisions in China had led to stagnation in the sciences.[62] Dr Johnson for his part invoked the notion of historical progress to dismiss the Chinese writing system in his elderly years. "They have not an alphabet," he said to Boswell. "They have not been able to form what all other nations have formed."[63] Though Chinese had been spoken well of in earlier linguistic debates, from the late eighteenth century it fell generally afoul of the new philology, a major thrust of which was to demonstrate the spiritual superiority of progressive Indo-Europeans. One examplar of this tendency early in the nineteenth century was Wilhelm von Humboldt, who assigned Chinese an inter-mediate rank between the barbarian and the "most perfect" languages (namely, Greek, Latin and German). He argued in 1826 that the Chinese language "stops at a point where it is given for languages to continue their progressive march, and it is already through this that it

---

[60] Their distaste for China contrasted with the relatively positive assessment of the academic sinologist Abel Rémusat in the early nineteenth century. See, e.g., Rémusat 1825a, 1825b.

[61] Daffino 1957: 10–14.

[62] Hume 1854: 130–31, 225.

[63] Boswell 1887: vol. III, 386. On the evolution of Johnson's ideas about China, T. C. Fan (1945) is the basic reference.

remains, according to my deepest conviction, beneath those languages which have articulate grammatical forms."[64] At about the same time, Shelley too praised the ancient Greeks and maintained that without them modern Europe would be faced with the same "stagnant and miserable state of social institutions as China and Japan."[65]

In addition to the idea of progress, one discerns several other notions developed in the late Enlightenment that were important in bringing about the shift away from admiration for China. For example, many late Enlightenment writers were prone to follow Montesquieu's lead in classifying China as a despotism and consequently in taking a dismissive attitude toward Chinese government and Chinese civilization generally.[66] In addition, Rousseau and Winckelmann can be seen as precursors of Romantic sinophobia in their portrayal of particular aspects of Chinese civilization as "unnatural." Rousseau, for example, cited China as a decisive demonstration of his proposition that civilization corrupts.[67] Furthermore, praise of China wounded Christian pride and continued to provoke an anti-pagan reaction as it had done during the Rites Controversy. "Is not the whole panegyric," asked John Wesley, "a blow at the root of Christianity, insinuating all along that there are no Christians in the world so virtuous as these heathens?"[68] The established notions of despotism, paganism, and the "unnatural" came to be commonly applied to China in the latter half of the eighteenth century, as was the emerging idea of innate racial character that would come into greater prominence in the following century.[69] These notions, in the forms in which they were formulated in the late Enlightenment, were important ideological weapons in the campaign to discredit the China vogue.

One key sinophobe in the late eighteenth century was J. G. Herder[70] whose scornful assessment of the Chinese *Volksgeist* or "racial character" is treated below. Still more intense disdain was expressed by the English essayist Thomas De Quincey, who envisioned a gulf that separated

---

[64] Humboldt 1906: vol. V, 290–91, 294, 299–300.
[65] From the "Preface" to *Hellas* (1821); Shelley 1970: 447.
[66] On Montesquieu's analyses of China, see Étiemble 1988–89: vol. II, chapter 3, with further bibliography.
[67] In the *Discours sur les sciences et les arts* he used the Manchu conquest of China as evidence that the sciences and arts corrupt public morality and patriotism; Rousseau 1971: 42.
[68] Wesley 1909–16: vol. VI, 187.
[69] The genesis of the notion of four or five biologically distinct races can be placed in the late seventeenth century; Olender (ed.) 1981: 39–40. However, it was during the eighteenth century that this idea began to solidly congeal, as geographical determinist explanations of human diversity were called into question.
[70] See Herder 1800: 311 and Hsia (ed.) 1985: 138–39.

Europeans and Chinese: "The mere antiquity of Asiatic things, of their institutions, histories, modes of faith, etc., is so impressive, that to me the vast age of the race and name overpowers the sense of the individual. A young Chinese seems to me an antediluvian man renewed."[71]

Not long thereafter, the rival philosophers Hegel and Schelling shared and passed on to their followers a similar attitude, which they expressed in typically absolute terms. Schelling gave a representative sample of their view when he wrote:

China lies in the beginning of history, [but] only to the extent that it has given up all movement. Indeed, the condition of humankind as we think it was before all history is in the Chinese condition fixed, or rather exists in it only in paralyzed form, and thus in fact is no longer captured in its *original* state. Chinese consciousness is no longer the primitive condition itself, but only a dead copy of it, like its mummy.[72]

Ideas like this were essential to making China a symbol of stagnation for Western thinkers across the political spectrum throughout the nineteenth century.[73] China's alleged non-progressiveness can be considered the dominant component in the Western image of the country at least until the downfall of the Qing. This meant, among other things, that Western writers often treated traditional Chinese culture as fundamentally similar to the cultures of the Egyptians and Romans in antiquity and to that of the Jews.

The stress on the alleged historical stagnation of Chinese society brought into discredit the older idea that Westerners might ever have learnt anything from Chinese social practice.[74] Auguste Comte voiced a typically nineteenth-century feeling of superiority when, in opposing himself explicitly to the *philosophes*, he maintained that a scientific approach to history should restrict itself to the nations of Europe, who constituted the avant-garde of the human race.[75] Similarly in 1856, just four generations after the Physiocrats, Tocqueville dismissed as utopian "ecstasies" their admiration for Chinese policies. He wrote:

it is no exaggeration to say that not one of them [the Physiocrats] fails, in some part of his writings, to voice an enthusiasm for China and all things Chinese. As a matter of fact China was an almost unknown country in those days, and what they wrote about it was absurd to a degree. That unenlightened, barbarian

---

[71] De Quincey 1885: 138, entry for May, 1818.
[72] Hsia (ed.) 1985: 229–30.
[73] The consensus in Germany was documented many years ago in Rose 1951.
[74] Even at this period these barriers were not completely impermeable, for Chinese example seems to have provided the conscious inspiration for one of the major political innovations of the nineteenth century, the introduction in Britain and the United States of the civil service based on competitive examinations. Evidence of Chinese influence has been presented by Teng Ssu-yü (1943) and Y. Z. Chang (1947).
[75] Comte 1864: vol. V, 7–8.

government which lets itself be manipulated by a handful of Europeans was held up as a model to the world.[76]

For Tocqueville to hold against the Physiocrats their ignorance of the fact that China would "let itself be manipulated" by the Western powers in the nineteenth century was hardly fair, though it reflected a broader Western tendency to treat contemporary non-Western weakness as a permanent condition. And whether the general level of knowledge among Western social thinkers about "China" as a historical civilization was higher in the nineteenth century than it had been in the eighteenth, as Tocqueville asserted, is not so easy to say. Certainly more writings were available – but is it right to assume that an equitable synthesis of knowledge had been carried out? What is clear is that the ideas of the nineteenth century were more uniformly chauvinist than those of the early Enlightenment and that they were more directly instrumental in promoting the assertion of Western social and cultural hegemony.

In any case, a range of supremacist attitudes was already in evidence at this time. For example, in England, one can place John Stuart Mill at the intellectualist end of the spectrum. Though conceding that the Chinese people possessed "much talent, and in some respects, even wisdom," he nevertheless cited China as a warning example of what happened when "philanthropists" were allowed to succeed "in making a people all alike." The government corresponding to this social uniformity he likened to those of ancient Egypt, of Russia, and indeed of the Society of Jesus – "a bureaucracy of Mandarins" that inhibited change. Consequently the Chinese had "properly speaking, no history," having for thousands of years remained "stationary," – and "if they are ever to be improved, it must be by foreigners."[77] On the other hand, there were many who supported the more physical approach of Lord Palmerston, who directed British military activities in the Opium Wars. He was of the opinion that backwardness called for an appropriately interventionist pedagogy:

These half-civilised governments such as those in China Portugal and Spanish America all require a Dressing every eight or Ten years to keep them in order. Their minds are too shallow to receive an Impression that will last longer than some such Period and warning is of little use. They care little for words and they must not only see the Stick but actually feel it on their Shoulders before they yield to that only argument which to them brings conviction the argumentum Baculinum.[78]

---

[76] Tocqueville 1974: 183–84.
[77] J. S. Mill 1872a: 129, 200, 247.
[78] Palmerston, autograph note, 29 Sept. 1850 (F. O. 17/173), cited in Costin 1937: 149–50.

In both cases the conviction was clear that the "progressive" peoples of Europe knew best, by definition.

Post-Enlightenment developments in racialist sinophobia

By the nineteenth century, ideas about differences in the genetically determined capacities of different peoples were taking on widespread theoretical importance in European intellectual culture. Many thinkers shared the conviction that the roots of the generally accepted social, cultural, and moral inferiority of non-European peoples could be found at the natural, biological level, in human racial distinctions which could be attested scientifically. From the middle of the nineteenth century especially, theories of Indo-European or Aryan racial superiority, of racial competition, and of the noxious consequences of racial mixture were used systematically to explain past or present social behavior or to justify Western policies. In accord with conventional wisdom, Asians were ranked as better than Africans, but as very much inferior to whites.[79] The Scottish anatomist Robert Knox put it bluntly: "It is not merely the savage races, properly so called, which seem incapable of civilization; the Oriental races have made no progress since Alexander the Great. The ultimate cause of this, no doubt, is race."[80] Knox argued that the differences in the populations of Britain and China meant that the latter's recent military humiliations in the Opium Wars were only comprehensible if one accepted the racialist case for white superiority. He was pleased to think that the Chinese faced inevitable extinction, probably at the hands of the Russians and Anglo-Saxon Australians.[81] Arthur de Gobineau, writing in 1853, drew on the Orientalist scholarship of his day and shifted the chauvinist clichés he found there to an explicitly racialist mode. For him, the "yellow" race was characterized by "an absolute lack of imagination, a concern only with the satisfaction of natural needs, much tenacity and single-mindedness in pursuit of

---

[79] For some the image was of a ladder with Europeans on the top rungs; for others, that of a European golden mean with deviations to either side.

[80] Knox 1862: 599. Knox's notoriety stemmed from public disclosure of the fact that he commissioned the grave-robbers and later murderers, William Burke and William Hare, to supply him with fresh bodies for his dissections; he nevertheless went on to become a successful lecturer on the basis of his ideas about race which were coming into vogue. See Gillespie 1970–80: vol. VII, 414–15, and Bernal 1987a.

[81] Knox 1862: 229–30, 282, 449–50. Already before Knox the idea that the Chinese would be made extinct – after the manner of the Amerindians confronted by Yankee expansion – was current in the United States; see Horsman 1981: 156, 226.

ideas that are humdrum or ridiculous ... little or no activity and no spiritual curiosity."[82]

China marked the highest degree of the yellow race's culture, but its original civilization was the result of ancient immigration by a branch of the "Hindu, Kschattrya, Aryan, white race." Chinese government was a patriarchal despotism, and its civilization had stagnated[83] since taking on its current form during the "revolution of Qin Shi Huangdi, which wiped out the last visible trace of the white race."[84] Gobineau saw the "Aryan" race under siege, and he thus pioneered the idea (though not the phrase) of the "Yellow Peril," a theme which in various versions – genetic, demographic, military and cultural – spread widely during the late nineteenth and twentieth centuries.

To be sure, such racialism was by no means uniformly accepted. In an earlier generation Blumenbach, Herder, and Alexander von Humboldt had denounced the use of the idea of race as a justification for slavery, though they had advanced racialist explanations of other phenomena. Similarly, the Indianist Friedrich Max Müller, who coined the term "Aryan" for a linguistic family, was sometimes loose and chauvinist in his own usage, though he did repudiate any biological connotation to the term[85] that Gobineau had borrowed from him. John Stuart Mill was more lucid in dismissing anti-Irish racialism. He argued that: "Of all the vulgar modes of escaping from the consideration of the effects of social and moral influences on the human mind, the most vulgar is that of attributing the diversities of conduct and character to inherent natural differences."[86]

In fact, Gobineau too acknowledged that social factors were a major concern lurking behind the rhetoric of innate biological antagonism. Speaking of Chinese immigration to Indonesia, California and Australia, he noted that "The Chinaman, though far from his native land, has become the object of horror and fear in all these countries because people do not know how to answer the industry, application, persistence, and, ultimately, the unparalleled cheapness of his labor. These are the concrete reasons why we know the Chinese is to be feared."[87]

In fact, the industriousness of Chinese workers as well as the business

[82] Gobineau 1983: vol. I, 559–60.
[83] Gobineau 1983: vol. I, 602 held that by their inertness China and India constituted the two great proofs that a race left to itself does not change, except in details.
[84] Gobineau 1983: vol. I, 570–71, 585, 595.
[85] Cited in Huxley and Haddon 1935: 149–51 and Chaudhuri 1974: 313–14. Max Müller (1866) described the Chinese language as "the most primitive stage in which we can imagine human language to have existed" (306), yet observed that "there is no shade of thought that cannot be rendered in Chinese" (120–21).
[86] J. S. Mill 1872b: bk 2, 197.
[87] Gobineau 1970: 242 (*mod. auct.*).

sense of Chinese merchants were often much appreciated by Westerners, where they coincided with the promotion of Western economic and political interests. Similarly, a certain esteem for Confucianism as a pillar of social order was manifest in the West from the time of the Taiping upheaval, and from the 1870s the imperial state was accorded a certain degree of respect by the British both because it provided a check on Russian influence in Turkestan, and because British capital became increasingly involved in the lucrative handling of Qing bond issues (as it did with those of the Ottoman state).[88]

The racialist fear referred to by Gobineau undoubtedly existed. As applied to the Chinese, it was played upon in order to promote or defend the interests of Western labor and business groups under circumstances in which other factors, such as purely economic performance, were not sufficient to do so. In general, "Yellow Peril" propaganda served as a ploy that could be used in particular circumstances both to reinforce social cohesion among "white" populations and to justify various forms of oppression of East Asians. Such forms of oppression included both exclusion of Chinese people from various territories, discrimination against Chinese communities within countries other than China, and imperialist projects against China itself.[89] From the 1870s until the Second World War, the "Yellow Peril" idea was important in the USA, Australia, and Canada[90] in mobilizing public opinion in support of legal barriers to immigration and to the practice of particular professions. Its use for the support of imperialist projects against China reached its apogee with the suppression of the Boxer Rebellion.

One of the main legitimating factors that won adherents to racialism was the fact that it was an ideology largely elaborated by natural scientists in the latter half of the nineteenth century and well into the twentieth. In the 1830s and 1840s Samuel George Morton had begun an important new trend when he immersed himself in the comparative craniometry of various human populations. He managed to devise a "racial" ranking according to brain size (Caucasian, Mongolian, Malay, American, Ethiopian,[91] in the then current terminology) which conve-

---

[88] Cain and Hopkins 1993: chapter 13, examines the relationship between British finance and the Qing in the framework of British imperialism's global structure from the first Opium War to World War I. Kasaba (1993) focuses on the parallels in British imperialism's involvement in China and the Ottoman empire respectively.

[89] The best works on "Yellow Peril" ideology are R. A. Thompson 1978; Decournoy 1970; and Gollwitzer 1962.

[90] On the American immigration see S. C. Miller 1969, Saxton 1971 and Sandnemyer 1973; on Canada, P. Roy 1989.

[91] Gould 1981: 54–72 is a refutation of Morton's figures and argument; page 50 cites him for likening the Chinese "to the monkey race, whose attention is constantly changing from one object to another."

niently demonstrated with apparently empirical precision the validity of dominant Anglo-Saxon attitudes. Morton's figures were enthusiastically transformed to literary-historical mode by Gobineau,[92] but Morton's approach and expectations also became part and parcel of the scientific culture of the day. Charles Darwin himself not only saw a serious case for the proposition that various human populations constitute distinct species, but also accepted the idea of the extinction of non-European human races through the struggle for survival.[93] Such ideas reflected the strength of the broader culture of scientific racialism and eventually lent credibility to Social Darwinism.

A period piece of scientific thought entitled "Observations on a Chinese Brain" appeared in 1894 in the prestigious journal *Brain*, the organ of the Neurological Society of London. Its findings were reported almost immediately in the pages of *Nature* and then in the *North China Herald*. This article treated the eighth Chinese brain analyzed by modern scientific methods. The author was not shy about suggesting, on the basis of less than a dozen samples, that the brain of a Chinese was closer to that of a chimpanzee than it was to that of a "normal" human.[94] This account was in turn included in the *Descriptive Sociology* series of Herbert Spencer, who also, elsewhere, wrote of China as a declining society and of the Chinese language as "one of the lowest kinds of human speech."[95] Meanwhile, on the basis of the theory of parallel degeneration in racial and individual pathology, Dr John Down had given to the chromosomal disorder known today as Down's syndrome the designation "Mongolian idiocy,"[96] a label which, though soon contested, remains in current usage. In the eugenicist literature of the 1920s and 1930s, the craniological and the pathological sides of these racialist researches were brought together in the volume, *The Mongol in Our Midst*, which drew parallels between non-Western "races" and various types of ape.[97] In this context the reminder of the one-time medical student Guo Moruo, that the Chinese were neither gods nor monkeys, need not be seen as simply a literary flourish.[98]

[92] Gobineau 1983: 246.
[93] See Darwin 1881. Chapter 7 is significantly entitled 'On the races of man,' a reference probably to the work of Knox, whom he cites not unfavorably along with the standard US racialist textbook, Nott and Gliddon 1854.
[94] C. H. Bond 1894: 39; reported in the issues of *Nature* of May 31, 1894 and in the *North China Herald* of July 20.
[95] Tedder (ed.) 1910: 1; Spencer 1937: 286, 336.
[96] See the brief account of Gould 1981: 134–35.
[97] Crookshank 1931. On eugenicism, see for example Gould 1981: 75ff, passim; on its manifestations in the 1920s, confer Barkan, chapters 3–5, and Werskey 1974: 30–37.
[98] Guo 1955: 1; cited by Timothy Brook, p. 135 below.

New vistas in the wake of the First World War

The First World War and the years that followed it, with their imminent sense of crisis and transformation, marked the beginning of a new period of Western attitudes toward China, one in which the consensus about Chinese inferiority and the superiority of the West began to fragment. To be sure, this fragmentation was to come but slowly. The Versailles Treaty itself was a far-reaching example of the victorious Great Powers acting together in blatant disregard for Chinese aspirations. Moreover, various types of fundamentally anti-Chinese thought remained clearly in evidence during the interwar period. Racialist ideas and the various forms of "Yellow Peril" ideology exerted significant social influence and in certain quarters became even more intensely anti-Chinese than previously. At the same time, even among authors who were not strongly committed to biological doctrines of racialism many continued to write in thoroughly dismissive ways of Chinese culture. An eminent example was the French anthropologist Lucien Lévy-Bruhl, who treated China as an ossified culture in *Les fonctions mentales dans les sociétés inférieures*. According to him, "those best acquainted" with "the Chinese mentality . . . almost despair of seeing it free itself from its shackles and cease running around in circles. Its habits of thought have become too inveterate, the needs it has created too imperious."[99] On the other hand, Oswald Spengler as a philosophical pessimist might have abandoned belief in the West's innate progressiveness, but he did so without giving a hint of any positive appraisal of China's prospects. He restricted the creative "inner history" of China to the Zhou and Han dynasties, and further maintained that Chinese civilization had been "gradually returning to the biological order" since antiquity.[100]

Nevertheless, certain authors in post-First World War Europe also manifested a new appreciation of China's importance in the world, and a broader realization that neither China's present nor its past could be summarily dismissed. We can distinguish two levels at which re-evaluation took place. The first was that of China's political prospects, and the second that of the significance of its cultural tradition. The predominant role of progressives in initiating a better understanding of China's political prospects has been well portrayed by Jerome Chen when he reflects that:

[99] Lévy-Bruhl 1926: 380–81.
[100] Spengler 1928: vol. II, 49–50, where the author also argued that "a Japanese culture in the genuine sense there has never been," on the stereotyped grounds that the Japanese could only imitate.

in the century of East-West intercourse before 1937 there had been two choruses – a Western chorus denigrating China and a Chinese chorus lauding the West. The few discordant voices in each seem to have come from singers who were following a different score."[101] In the 1920s and 1930s, only the left-wing liberals of the West, who had enough suppleness of mind to see the serious defects in their own civilization and the merits of the Chinese radical movement, and the Marxists (including Russian communists), were prepared to accept the proposition that there was hope and a future for China. Consequently they could both by instinct and by intellectual conviction treat the Chinese masses as their equals.[102]

Significant among such figures was Lenin himself.[103] He shared with Marx not only certain negative assessments about traditional social relations in Asia, but also the conviction of the inevitable growth of progressive, democratic movements throughout the continent. He condemned the imperialist powers for suppressing the Boxer uprising and later for violating Chinese integrity at Versailles, and after the First World War he was particularly hopeful about prospects for social change in China. At a time when some spokesmen of the European and North American right were combining racialist and anti-socialist ideas and warning of an impending "Red-Yellow Peril,"[104] Lenin proposed a joint anti-imperialist alliance between the Soviet Union and progressive forces in China and India. The Sun-Joffe Accord then inaugurated Soviet organizational and military support for the Guomindang and set the stage for the first Nationalist–Communist united front. From that time Soviet-oriented Marxists of various leanings involved themselves in analysis of Chinese history and society, though in the mid- and late 1920s the question of which strategy the Chinese revolution should adopt within a global anti-capitalist program was a major bone of contention dividing the Bolshevik leadership.[105]

In Britain too, a number of influential progressives began to rate China's indigenous human and cultural resources highly. In 1919 H. M. Hyndman recognized that Europe had learnt much from Asia in the past. He even felt that European interference in Asia over the centuries had been "almost wholly harmful." It was his view that "the China of the past is rapidly fading, and the Chinese of the present are

---

[101] One such discordant voice was that of the Russian novelist and populist Tolstoy, whose pacifistic attraction to Chinese philosophy has been documented admirably by Bodde 1950.

[102] J. Chen 1979: 88.

[103] Behring (1959) is a useful anthology of Lenin's views on China. For analyses of these, see Nikiforov 1970: chapter 2, and D. M. Lowe 1966: chapter 3.

[104] Decournoy 1970: chapters 7–8.

[105] Stalin (1974) and Trotsky (1966) set out the political analyses of the main contenders in the mid-twenties.

taking up the line of their own historic achievements and will play a great, possibly the greatest, part in the future of humanity."[106] The evaluation of R. H. Tawney was similar: "though a nation may borrow its tools from abroad, for the energy to handle them it must look within. . . . It is in herself alone, in her historical culture, rediscovered and reinterpreted in the light of modern requirements, that China will find the dynamic which she needs."[107]

If it was especially the left that came to appreciate China's political potential in the inter-war years, the growth of interest in Chinese culture and history was more widely diffused. In the literary arena the Confucian Classics were appreciatively reinterpreted by Ezra Pound, whose sympathies were well to the right, while Bertoldt Brecht made regular use of Chinese motifs in his revolutionary theater and poetry.[108] From the 1920s down to recent times, authors of the most diverse political persuasions have enthused over the perceived merits of Daoist philosophy.[109] The crises and transformations of capitalism might thus be said to have broken the nineteenth-century monotonal disparagement and fostered a wider variety of appropriations of what "China" is and means.

In the fields of history and sociology, two theoretical approaches forged in the first forty years of the century have greatly influenced the way later scholars have interpreted Chinese history within the context of world history. In the second decade of the century, Max Weber gave detailed attention to the historical sociology of traditional China as part of his systematic comparative study of the economic ethics of diverse Old World civilizations. Though the contrasts he drew between China and the West were in many cases too stark, some of his analyses continue to command respect still. After his death, Marxist scholars in the Soviet Union and elsewhere concerned themselves during the 1920s and early 1930s with elaborating a materialist framework for world history. This task was intimately linked with the practical need to define revolutionary policies, and it consequently gave rise to heated debates over the analysis of the type of social formation found historically in China and other Asian societies. At one stage the debates focused on whether one should speak of a distinct and special Asiatic mode of production proper to such societies. The universalist model of five successive stages of

[106] Hyndman 1919: vi–vii, 30.
[107] Tawney 1966: 194–95.
[108] For example, in *Der Gute Mensch von Sezuan* (Brecht 1953). Tatlow 1973: 163ff analyses Brecht's relationship to Chinese poetry. Hermann Hesse's interpretations of China are examined by Adrian Hsia (1974).
[109] This is documented nicely by Étiemble 1964: 97–113, to whose examples on the right we can add the relatively early H.S. Chamberlain 1911: 350–51fn.

historical development that became dominant in Soviet Marxist histor-
ical writings in the 1930s incorporated a preference toward treating
Chinese and Western histories in uniform theoretical terms, though this
left the model open to charges of reductionism. The Weberian and the
Soviet Marxism approaches both eschewed explanations formulated in
terms of biological racialism, as did the historical anthropology of
Marcel Granet who developed a Durkheimian analysis of ancient
Chinese society.

Political sympathy for China grew greatly as a result of Japanese
aggression and occupation during the thirties and the years of the
Second World War, and the atrocities that resulted from Nazi racialism
marked a crucial step in discrediting biological racialism as a form of
scholarly and scientific discourse.[110] After the Communist victory in
China in 1949, a certain amount of anti-Chinese literature written along
"Yellow Peril" lines again appeared. However, the importance of China
in the twentieth-century world had by this time become obvious
enough, and the "hearts and minds" of Chinese populations outside of
the People's Republic were deemed important enough, to ensure that
most serious writers in the West would no longer simply dismiss Chinese
culture and social history in blanket fashion. It is perhaps only in the last
three decades that Chinese studies have once more begun to have an
important theoretical impact on Western social scientific thought as a
whole. However, the general period since the First World War can be
described as one in which a degree of competition among interpretations
of Chinese society has been the order of the day, though many of the
older molds for representing China are still in use.

Social structure and historical stability

The preceding discussion has indicated some of the intellectual and
cultural contexts in which historical stability came to be imputed to
Chinese society as one of the latter's more notable characteristics. From
what has been said so far one might justly conclude that from the
seventeenth until the early twentieth century Western social thinkers
generally emphasized the continuity of Chinese history and took it for
granted that Chinese society had remained essentially unchanged for
thousands of years. Agreement on this point did not exclude recognition
of a certain degree of variability. For example, the fact that successive
dynasties had introduced their own specific legal codes was well under-

[110] Barkan (1992) traces the development of refutations of racialism among British and
American anthropologists and biologists in the interwar years.

stood. However, China's constancy in respect of its fundamental political constitution and national character was a basic assumption that tended to characterize analyses of Chinese society throughout this period. Indeed, it is striking how this assumption was shared by authors whose world views and ideologies were otherwise radically different. In the pages that follow, we shall examine the ways in which some of the major Western social thinkers developed this idea of China's historical stability, and in doing so we shall focus on how they related it to their analyses of the structure of Chinese society.

The maintenance of social order and stability was one of the major concerns of European thinkers in the seventeenth century, a period when, as we have seen, China's social and political reputation was at a high point. This concern was manifested, for instance, in François Bernier's reflections on "the principal cause of the decline of the states of Asia." His observations on Moghul India, Turkey, and Persia, recorded in the 1660s, gave him occasion to consider "whether it were not more expedient, not only for the subjects, but for the state itself, and for the Sovereign, not to have the Prince such a Proprietor of the Lands of the kingdom, as to take away the *Meum* and *Tuum* amongst private persons; as 'tis with us?"[111]

His view was that the main cause of the impoverished condition of these countries was the suppression of private property and the greed of their rulers. This led directly to the degradation of labor, the absence of a middle class, the decay of cities, and the decline of agriculture and manufactures. As the officials followed the unpaternal example of the ruler, oppression and widespread corruption were the natural result, and political authority could be maintained only through "the cudgel." These factors in turn gave rise to the political instability characteristic of the "despotic" system of government found in these Asian countries.[112] Bernier wrote:

take away the right of private property in land, and you introduce, as a sure and necessary consequence, tyranny, slavery, injustice, beggary, and barbarism; the ground will cease to be cultivated and become a dreary wilderness; in a word, the road will be opened to the ruin of Kings and the destruction of Nations. It is the hope by which a man is animated, that he shall retain the fruits of his industry, and transmit them to his descendants, that forms the main foundation of everything excellent and beneficial in this sublunary state.[113]

In opposition to the system of government headed by an unrestrained individual despot, which he had experienced as the physician to the Great Moghul Aurangzeb, Bernier in 1688 contrasted the exemplary

---

[111] Bernier 1671: 68–69.
[112] Bernier 1914: 226–27, 237, 253, 256.   [113] Ibid.: 238.

Chinese form of rule which he knew from the reports of the Jesuit missionaries. As we have seen, China was known at this time for its wealthy cities and its abundant population, as well as for the thriving state of its manufactures and its system of government based on the deliberations of numerous state councils. The reasonably secure condition of property was implicit in the Jesuits' accounts of their own commercial transactions there. To Bernier, the durability of the Chinese mode of government over four thousand years was evidence of the wisdom of the Confucian political tradition. It was this tradition that enabled the Chinese to surpass all other peoples in "virtue, wisdom, prudence, good faith, sincerity, charity, gentleness, honesty, civility, gravity, modesty, and obedience to the Celestial order."[114] In his view Chinese government was based on virtue rather than greed, and this secured the stability and happiness of the social order. This virtue was inculcated especially through the family, by means of respect for the natural principles of "paternal piety," i.e., of love and respect between parents and children, as well as through the cultivation of the goodness and generosity of the ruler, which provided an example to the officials and the entire nation. Bernier's question, "What more could one ask for people who had no other principles than those of nature?"[115] was a significant one in the cultural atmosphere of the 1680s, and the image of China as an exemplary model seems to have appealed to his philosophical libertinism.

Two generations later Montesquieu echoed Bernier's depictions of Asian societies in several ways. In his early *Lettres persanes*, published in 1721, Montesquieu made use of the format of the traditional travel account, of which Bernier's writings were an important example, but created fictional Asian travelers who reflected critically on European manners. The main work in which Montesquieu treated China, however, was his immensely influential *De l'esprit des lois*, published in 1748, a theoretical and historical treatise that set out the characteristics of legitimate government. His political aim in this was to reform the French monarchy. As a leading spokesman for the *parlemens*, Montesquieu was opposed to absolutism, and he argued that a balance of powers was essential to political stability and legitimacy. He classified states into three fundamental types, namely, the monarchical, the republican, and the despotic. The monarchical and the republican types were politically stable, whereas despotic government was politically unstable, as it had been for Bernier. One reason why the former two types of state were stable was that they each incorporated a distinct

---

[114] Bernier 1689: 37 (*tr. auct.*); Guy 1963: 136.   [115] Bernier 1689: 37 (*tr. auct.*).

balance of power. Under despotism all power rested with the despot, who ruled through fear, and there was no place for a hereditary aristocracy. Since there were no fundamental rights other than those of the ruler and no institutional mechanism for the expression of diverse opinions, the people could assert their interests only through corruption or rebellion. Political instability was thus constitutionally determined by despotic government itself. Montesquieu saw the political stability of monarchies and republics and the instability of despotism as a result of the geographical conditions prevalent in the regions where the different regimes were typical. In his view moderate governments were typical of the medium- and small-sized states found in the variegated and temperate environment of Europe, while the uniform topography and hot climates of Asia, Africa, and America gave rise to large empires lacking a balance of power and political liberties. Such factors accounted for the remarkable endurance of despotic government in various parts of the world.

Montesquieu differed from Bernier and most previous political theorists in classifying China as a despotism along with the rest of Asia. He opposed the image of a virtuous government based on Confucian philosophy with the proposition that in China people acted only out of fear of being "bastinadoed."[116] His geographical determinism made it possible for him to portray an allegedly inherent tendency toward political instability as compatible with the persistence of the same form of constitution, i.e. despotism, over two millennia. At the same time, he also accounted for the historical persistence of despotism by reference to what he saw as a political characteristic of despotic states, namely that the instability engendered by the nature of the government made it expedient for the ruler never to change the customs of his empire. Since customs were the only means by which the harshness of a despotic regime was mitigated, a change in them would lead immediately to a revolution.[117] For Montesquieu, this general characteristic of despotism was most prominently manifest in China, where the primary aim of the laws was to ensure public tranquility. His view that "customs govern China" and that they could "never be changed" there[118] gave a new slant to the image of Chinese historical continuity that had been put forward by the Jesuits[119] and by Libertine thinkers like Bernier.

It was with some difficulty that Montesquieu made China fit this model of despotism. He did so partly by ignoring various aspects of Chinese society, including the institutions of the imperial civil service, which were well attested in contemporary literature, and attitudes

---

[116] Montesquieu 1949: vol. I, 123.   [117] Ibid.: 297.
[118] Ibid.: 294, 298, 303.   [119] To whom he was politically opposed.

toward land tenure, which were more sporadically discussed.[120] On the other hand, he also gave new interpretations to a number of well-known characteristics of Chinese society. He explained Chinese industriousness as determined by the precariousness of subsistence there, which in turn inspired "an excessive desire of gain." Indeed, far from being virtuous, the Chinese were "the greatest cheats on earth."[121] The "rites" for which they were famous were to Montesquieu's mind merely exterior habits and had nothing spiritual about them, and his account of the paternalist nature of Confucian ideology tied in with his idea that despotism was not so much a political as a domestic form of government.[122] This position accorded with his aim of reforming the Bourbon monarchy from a pro-aristocratic point of view.

Montesquieu's interpretation of China was soon contested by thinkers who belonged to the "administrative" faction of reformists, for example, Voltaire and François Quesnay, the leader of the Physiocrats, both of whom continued the earlier tradition of Enlightenment sinophilia. Unlike Montesquieu, Voltaire did not believe that the existence of a hereditary aristocracy was important for distinguishing a moderate monarchy from a despotism.[123] Instead he valued the contribution that a civil service afforded to the reasonable conduct of government and argued that "if ever there has been a state in which the life, the honor and the welfare of men has been protected by the law, it is the empire of China. The more great bodies there are which are depositories of the laws, the less is administration arbitrary."[124]

Voltaire depicted imperial China as a model of civilized government. As far as social mores were concerned, he recognized that the Chinese, like all peoples, had their vices, but in his view the uniformity of the laws throughout the empire meant that vice could be checked more efficiently there than in other places.[125] He also contrasted the policy of religious tolerance traditionally adopted by Chinese rulers with the intolerance of Christian rulers, and in particular with the frame of mind that led Louis XIV to revoke the Edict of Nantes in 1685.[126] Voltaire went further than previous historians in integrating China into a comparative historical perspective. For him the comparatively reasonable nature of Chinese government was due to the fact that China, unlike other countries, had never been subject to theocratic rule. Its pure, original institutions had

---

[120] Le Comte 1698: 248 had noted that in China "every one is the perfect Master of his estate, and enjoys his lands free from disturbance and molestation." In addition, he noted that the Chinese political system made popular remonstration against unjust officials legitimate (260–61).

[121] Montesquieu 1949: vol. I, 297, 304.   [122] Ibid.: 301–03.

[123] Voltaire 1877–85: vol. XIII, 179–80.   [124] Voltaire 1963: vol. II, 285–86.

[125] Ibid.: vol. 1, 217.   [126] Voltaire 1877–85: vol. IX, 76, 178.

thus been preserved and had not undergone the mystical and metaphysical distortions which developed elsewhere.[127] For Voltaire, the essence of China's ancient religion was humane rationality and justice,[128] and its ancient doctrines, transmitted to posterity by Confucius, had since his time remained in practice throughout the empire. China's admirable civilization[129] had thus continued unchanged for four thousand years. He understood the spirit of Chinese government as being virtuous and public spirited because it was based on respect for parents and ancestors. However, this respect, though a virtue, also proved to be a hindrance to progress, for it led the Chinese to rest content with the achievements of the past.[130]

Quesnay too took China as a model for the social and political reforms he favored in France. In his view human society had originally been in accord with nature, but as it developed later in various places disparities had crept in between the natural order and the social order. The task of the Physiocrats as reformers was to restore society to its original natural harmony. In his general philosophy, he depicted the world of Nature as regulated by physical laws, which strictly determined the "natural" moral law. This natural moral law in turn provided the standard with which any humanly enacted "positive" laws ought to be in conformity. A state in which the positive laws accorded with the natural order was in his view obliged to enforce those laws as strictly as possible. Quesnay therefore termed such a state as a "legitimate" despotism, to distinguish it from one that enforced laws which were contrary to the laws of nature. In his opinion, Montesquieu was thus very much mistaken to have confused the two types of despotism.[131] Quesnay believed it was only in China that the properly harmonious and rational social system had been preserved since "primitive" times, and it was precisely because of China's adherence to the "natural" order that its system of government had remained "permanent" and "immutable."[132] China therefore served as "a model" to all states, and its constitution could thus be considered universal.[133] Among the characteristics the Physiocrats cited as demonstrating China's accord with the natural order were the government's encouragement of agriculture as the chief economic activity, the absence of servile status for agricultural laborers, and the freedom to hold personal property.[134]

Quesnay's conflation of the "primitive" and "natural" states of society

---

[127] Ibid.: 165–67.   [128] Ibid.: 176.   [129] Ibid.: vol. XV, 76.
[130] Voltaire 1877–85: vol. 9, 173; vol. 12, 433.
[131] Quesnay 1965: 564.   [132] Ibid.: 605.
[133] Ibid.: 636; Quesnay 1768: lxv–lxvi.
[134] Quesnay 1965: 580–82, 599, 631.

lived on as a historiographical convention and may be seen in later discussions of why centralized states were to be considered "typical" for the dawn of history. However, sinophile theorists were not the only ones to be disseminating the idea that the Chinese social system was more or less historically fixed and unchanging. This is clear, for example, from the work of Nicholas Boulanger, a royal engineer and notable contributor to the *Encyclopédie*, who analyzed Asian social structures in his *Recherches sur l'origine du despotisme oriental* (1761). Attempting to build up a universal model of social development, he maintained, contrary to the view of Voltaire, that China had originally been a theocratic despotism, and he followed Montesquieu in maintaining that its institutions were based only on custom, which meant that China was bound to fall ever further behind progressive Western nations.[135] Similar ideas are found in the writings of Adam Ferguson, one of the chief social theorists of the Scottish Enlightenment. Ferguson was an early proponent of the notion of successive stages of historical progress and social organization. He saw India and China as exceptions in human history because they had not passed on from one stage to another, but had continued to reproduce their ancient constitutions into contemporary times.[136] During the years of the French Revolution, the notion of stages of historical progress was given general currency by the revolution's main historical theorist, the Marquis de Condorcet. In his *Esquisse d'un tableau historique des progrès de l'esprit humain* (1793–94), Condorcet classified China as pertaining only to the third "epoch" of human history, that in which settled agriculture became the foundation of society, but when the alphabet had not yet been invented. In his view the Chinese were condemned to a "shameful immobility" and "eternal mediocrity."[137] Theories about the structural immobility, or the extreme stability, of Chinese society were by this time becoming bound up with notions about national and racial character. The general notion of racial types can be traced back to Bernier, and Voltaire too had used it to explain why different forms of society existed in different parts of the world. One of the most important writers to develop this line of thought in the late eighteenth century was Johann Gottfried Herder. As a Christian, Herder held that all peoples had derived from a single, common source, but had in the course of time dispersed. He believed their genetic stock had then been fixed in accord with the natural environment that each had come to inhabit. That Chinese culture had stood still in its infancy and had been unable to progress since

---

[135] Boulanger 1761: 251, 255, 260.
[136] Ferguson 1966: 111.   [137] Condorcet 1988: 120.

antiquity[138] was the result of the "Mongol" nature of the Chinese and the physical conditions of their country. These factors were also responsible for their form of government, a "semi-tatarian despotism" based on a "feudal" constitution. The fickleness of their "Mongol" genetic character was expressed in China's lack of hereditary social orders; and their general stagnation was due to the fact that they lacked the spirit of improvement.[139] From the views of the authors treated so far, one might conclude that by the end of the eighteenth century social theorists of both "sinophile" and "sinophobic" persuasions tended to emphasize the continuity of Chinese civilization and to contrast China categorically with the West.

These tendencies continued to be pronounced in the nineteenth century. One of the main vehicles by which the ideas of earlier writers were brought together and then transmitted to others was the philosophy of G. W. F. Hegel. In constructing his philosophy of history and his interpretation of China, Hegel drew on the ideas of Montesquieu, Herder, and Condorcet. Although his ideas reflected the spirit of the early nineteenth century, they continued to exert considerable intellectual influence among social thinkers well into the present century. Progressive movement, from unity and simplicity to differentiation and sophistication, was a common theme in Hegel's system of thought. He subordinated China to this theme when he took over the conventional idea that its civilization belonged to the early history of mankind. In his view Chinese civilization marked the lowest level of "world-historical" development. Its failure to reach higher levels was determined by the country's geographical conditions and the racial characteristics of its people.[140] As the embodiment of the principle of unity, China rather than India or Turkey came to serve as the model of a semi-primitive Oriental despotism for Hegel. Under this despotic system the government of the country was dominated by a single all-powerful personality, who ruled with reference only to his own will and to ancient maxims. The government was a "theocratic despotism"; and Chinese society, which was constructed on the principle of the family, had never been able to transcend that principle.[141] It had therefore developed neither a true state (in the European sense) nor a true political life based on the interaction of free individuals.[142] In line with his views of the undifferentiated character of Chinese society, Hegel maintained that all land in China was owned by the ruler and that the entire population was held in a uniform state of serfdom.[143]

[138] Herder 1800: 292, 298.
[139] Ibid.: 293–96, 313.   [140] Hegel 1956: 103.
[141] Ibid.: 112–13, 121–23, 127.   [142] Ibid.: 124, 138.   [143] Ibid.: 130.

Karl Marx and Friedrich Engels were of course heavily influenced by Hegel in their youth, and on issues like the theoretical importance of dialectics they remained in his debt throughout their later careers. In other areas, however, they set themselves the task of forging materialist alternatives to Hegelian philosophy. Historical analysis was one of the areas in which they pushed their research program furthest and made their most far-reaching and original contributions. Yet their mature views in this area continued in certain regards to be marked by earlier doctrines. This was clearly the case with some of their interpretations of the nature and significance of Asian societies in world history. For instance, they generally agreed with Hegel, and with British economists such as J. S. Mills and Richard Jones, in considering socio-economic conditions in Asia to have remained fundamentally the same since the beginnings of social history. They did nevertheless develop innovative ideas on the occasions when they applied their materialist conception to the history of Asia. One of their more stimulating, if always rather cryptically expressed, ideas on this subject was that of the Asiatic mode of production. It should be observed that the part of Asia they studied most carefully in constructing this was not China, but the Indian subcontinent, which they were interested in because of its importance for the British empire, and hence the world economy. It can also be pointed out that in their eyes the key to understanding any society was the analysis of the mode of production dominant in that society, i.e., the characteristic combination of productive forces (including natural resources, skills, technologies and materials) and relations of production and exchange (including relations between producers and their means of production, ownership relations, relations between producers, etc.). For Marx and Engels the notion of modes of production provided the key to assessing a society's level of historical development, since the various modes of production could be seen as representing successive levels of historical progress. As Marx once put it,[144] "In broad outline, the Asiatic, ancient, feudal and modern bourgeois modes of production may be designated as epochs marking progress in the economic development of society."

In the writings of the founders of Marxism there were several features characteristic of the "Oriental" type of society and the Asiatic mode of production.[145] The basic economic units of such societies were self-

---

[144] Marx 1971: 21.

[145] Krader (1974; 1975) has argued that Marx shifted from the rather Hegelian inspired model of "Oriental society" found in his earlier writings to the more concrete category of an "Asiatic" mode of production. Since there were nevertheless important overlaps between the two notions for Marx and Engels as well as for later Marxists, we need for present purposes simply to mention some of the characteristics Marx and Engels frequently ascribed to Asian societies.

sufficient village communities, whose members occupied themselves in agricultural production and simple domestic industries, and there were few real cities. The communities and society at large had only an elementary and fixed division of labor, and commodity production remained embryonic. Geographic features of the environment, including hydraulic conditions, made a centralized authority necessary to the economic life of the society. The state served as such an authority and constituted a social institution that bound the isolated villages together. Despotic in form, the state supported itself on the surplus extracted from the villages, and it was the sole owner of the land. Because of this, there was no distinction between tax and rent. Marx and Engels saw in the lack of such a distinction an indication of the primitive level of Asian social development. Following Bernier and Hegel, they thus thought that an absence of private property was typical of "Asia"; and like Hegel, but unlike Bernier, they took this alleged lack as characteristic of a rudimentary level of development.[146] Theoretically speaking, historical stagnation and a weakness of socio-economic differentiation were two aspects of the same fundamental Asian reality, and they resulted concretely in poverty and overall backwardness.

The extent to which Marx and Engels understood imperial China as approximating their model of Oriental society or an Asiatic mode of production remains, however, open to question. This is partly due to the unsystematic nature of their definitions of an Asiatic mode and partly to ambiguities about how the various "abstract" modes of production are to be related to the analysis of particular historical societies. It is also due to the fact that Marx wrote about China in different ways at different times. For instance, in his articles analyzing the Anglo-Chinese Opium War, he invoked the vocabulary of essential Asiatic stagnation and referred to "Old China" as the "rotting semi-civilization of the oldest State in the world."[147] He also wrote of small-scale agriculture and domestic manufacture as the pivots of the contemporary Chinese economy,[148] a form of words that fits squarely with the characteristics of the Asiatic mode of production. In general he would thus seem to have assimilated China to the model of the Asiatic mode of production. On the other hand, he elsewhere contrasted contemporary China with India, his prototype for the Asiatic mode of production, when he wrote that in China communal property in land had been the *original* form of

---

[146] For detailed critical analysis of Marx and Engels's idea on the Asiatic mode of production see Krader 1975: 19–79, Anderson 1974a: 462–72, and Draper 1977: 629–64. For recent Chinese understandings, see below, pp. 144–45.

[147] Ibid.: 4, 45.   [148] Torr (ed.) 1951: 64.

ownership.[149] This implied that such property was no longer the form currently predominant in China, though he did not go on to indicate what was.[150]

In any case, it is evident that analyzing Chinese society was not a priority for Marx and Engels. While placing emphasis on the economic structure of Asian societies was a coherent theoretical strategy in principle, they showed little sign of appreciating the complexity of property forms in China or the extent to which private property existed. Nor did they examine the richness of Chinese urban life, the nature of agrarian relations, the extent of landlordism in the countryside, or the extent to which the Chinese economy had historically been developed. These oversights reflected the fact that their primary concern was with the analysis of modern capitalist societies in the West, where they foresaw the imminent possibility of working-class revolutions. The gaps in their analysis of China and the ambiguities in their theoretical treatment of pre-capitalist societies left room for major differences in interpretation among their disciples in later generations. We shall consider some of these differences below when we turn to the early Soviet debates on these subjects. Before doing so, it is necessary first to examine briefly the ideas of Max Weber.

Weber carried out his detailed studies of traditional Chinese society in the second decade of the twentieth century. In these, as in most of his later works, his ultimate aim was to specify the features that define Western civilization in general and modern capitalism in particular and to identify those that were responsible for the emergence, in the West alone, of cultural phenomena he thought of as having universal validity. One of his characteristic techniques for analyzing social structures and forms of culture was to contrast broadly similar phenomena found in different civilizations in order ultimately to highlight what was unique in the West. Unfortunately this consistently led him to represent China and the West as polar opposites and to overlook or underestimate what they had in common. It also frequently led him to interpret Chinese culture as deficient in the capacity for innovative historical development.[151] His idea that China was an archetypical case of a bureaucratic society and his belief that bureaucracy was the major obstacle to creative social change gave theoretical justification to his tendency to depict

[149] Marx 1954–59: vol. III, 333–34.
[150] In this, his view may be seen as paralleling that of G. T. Staunton who considered the question of whether the land in China belonged to the emperor or rested in freehold with individuals, and who gave the opinion that the truth lay somewhere between the two extremes; Staunton (ed. and trans.) 1810: appendix, cited in O. Franke 1903: 5.
[151] Weber developed a great many lines of inquiry into comparative history and what he said in one place was not always consistent with arguments he developed elsewhere.

Chinese history as essentially static since at least the beginning of the imperial era.

Like many nineteenth-century writers, Weber stressed that in China, as in "the Orient" generally, large-scale hydraulic works played a great part in the early development of society.[152] This fact was important for distinguishing China's later development from that of the West, since in China the ruler's power was exercised from the beginning through a centralized staff of officials. Chinese cities were administrative and military centers lacking political autonomy, and the notion of the free citizen thus never developed.[153] Since the state took on both civil and ecclesiastical functions, the distinction between spiritual and secular domains did not develop either, and no creative tension between them emerged.[154] Similarly, at the level of ideology, China lacked the tradition of ethical prophecy grounded in a monotheistic conception of a Deity.[155] The Chinese character therefore never developed the creative inner tension with the world that would be an essential factor in the eventual emergence of modern forms of rationality in the West. During the Zhou dynasty, society was organized according to a particular variant of feudalism. Weber termed this variant "prebendal" feudalism, to indicate a form of organization in which officials were endowed with fiefs, in contrast to later Western feudalism, in which aristocrats held hereditary fiefs in return for military service.[156] The widespread use of money during the Warring States period led him to speak of a "political capitalism" that emerged in coexistence with the prebendal feudal system at that time. However, unification under the Qin and Han dynasties meant the suppression of both feudal and capitalist relations, and the definitive imposition of a social system which Weber called "bureaucratic patrimonialism."[157] In his view the imposition of this system marked the decisive turn toward "traditionalism"[158] and away from the possibility of fundamental historical change.

Unlike many nineteenth-century authors, Weber did not see Chinese social structure as undifferentiated and entirely lacking in tensions. He saw it rather as having generated different types of social structure from those found in the West. However, he consistently portrayed social contradictions in China as inherently static, and he depicted the opposed social forces there as existing in a state of permanent equilibrium. This approach provided a structural explanation for China's historical stagnation. In this regard he identified three such types of

[152] See, for example, Weber 1951: 31, 51.   [153] Weber 1984: 320–21.
[154] Weber 1951: 110–11.   [155] Ibid.: 229–30.
[156] Weber 1978: vol. I, 259.   [157] Ibid.: 1051.
[158] Weber 1951: 112–13.

static opposition. The first was that between the emperor and his personal entourage, on the one hand, and the bureaucracy, on the other. The imperial bureaucracy functioned as a permanent check on the emperor's power, but the emperor was able, by means of the examination system, to restrict the extent to which the literati could form an autonomous status group.[159] At the same time, the rules defining the duration of official appointments and proscribing placement of an official in his native place effectively prevented attempts by officials to build up individual power bases, e.g., along feudal lines. A second fundamental opposition was that between the State and the clans, or lineage associations. While in most of Europe lineage associations had in Weber's view lost their pervasive social significance by the Middle Ages, in China they remained the basic form of economic organization into the twentieth century. As such they served as a constant obstacle to the emergence of modern economic rationality.[160] They also functioned as the basic form of political organization in the countryside and constituted an essential counterbalance to the imperial power represented by officials based in the county seats and provincial capitals. Although the civil service developed administrative rationalism to a high degree, the state and the clans had a symbiotic relationship ideologically just as they did institutionally, and the mentalities of both were basically grounded in magic.[161] Any thoroughgoing technical rationalization of the economy was thus impossible, for the clans opposed economic innovation in itself, and the bureaucracy stood opposed to rationalism of the technical or "instrumental" type that proved crucially important in the emergence of modern European culture. A third static opposition, or at least apparent opposition, was that between the traditionalist social order and the growth of a money economy. Weber did not give a completely clear account of the evolution of the various types of property in China, but he at least appreciated the complexity of this subject.[162] He also realized that over the centuries there had been recurring cycles in which taxation had been extracted at one moment in kind and at another in money. Finally in the eighteenth century, the monetary form won out. The eventual predominance of money taxes corresponded to the long-term growth of a monetarized economy which might, according to Western example, have been expected to undermine the old social order dominated by the literati. However, in Weber's view,

[159] Ibid.: 122.
[160] Weber 1971: 86ff; Weber 1958: 137, 176, 339.
[161] Weber 1951: 30–31, 110–11.
[162] Ibid.: 73–74, 80. Otto Franke (1903) had argued that almost all forms of property known historically in the West, including private property, had also been established in China, where many were still extant.

such a subversion of the social order did not occur in China, or in the "Orient" generally, because of the bureaucratic nature of the state, since the growth of the money economy was effectively subordinated to the prebendal system through which the state allocated income to its officials.[163] Rather than devoting themselves to "rational" forms of enterprise, members of the dominant stratum devoted themselves to acquiring public offices and to using such offices for the acquisition of landed property.[164] Though Weber did accept that all traditional forms of society included obstacles to rationalism and modernism, in his view it was only in the West that there was sufficient cultural dynamism to overcome such obstacles. In contrast to Marxist materialist explanations of historical change, his thought stressed the importance of religious motivations as factors influencing the evolution of different societies. For example, in analyzing the development of early capitalism in Europe, he stressed the importance of God-centered ascetic Puritanism based on a feeling of tremendous tension between God and "the world." He saw in China no similar spiritual or ethical force for moving people to act to rationalize the world as instruments of a greater power, since Confucianism and Daoism were "this-worldly" religions which accepted the world as it was, while Buddhism represented a "flight from the world," without a vision to remake it.[165]

Writers like Marx and Weber who reflected on the structure of Chinese society in the period from the first Opium War till the end of the First World War could hardly fail to be impressed by the way modest-sized nations like Britain and France were able to impose their political will on the great civilizations of Asia and by the fact that China, despite its geographical size and large population, had been repeatedly forced to yield to their demands. There was little doubt among Western theorists, or indeed among Chinese policymakers, that the material reasons for China's comparative weakness lay in its relative technological inferiority, the backward state of its industry relative to Europe, and the comparatively inefficient organization of its economy. An obvious way to explain such disparities between China and the West was to focus on original institutions, relationships, and other cultural elements in each civilization, to depict Chinese society as historically continuous and structurally stable, and to highlight dynamic aspects of Western cultures. This type of explanation nevertheless had the drawback of obscuring the fact that imperial China had in various periods manifested remarkable dynamism in virtually all domains of social life. Weber was well

---

[163] Weber 1951: 60–62.
[164] Ibid.: 85–86.
[165] See de Bary (ed.) 1975 and Metzger 1977 on creative tensions in Confucian thought.

acquainted with the sinological literature of his day, and he wrote with considerable insight on many aspects of traditional Chinese society including in particular the workings of the bureaucracy. There can also be no doubt that his systematic efforts to integrate Chinese historical sociology into a comparative world-historical perspective proved most stimulating to later generations of social theorists and sinologists. In retrospect, it is nevertheless clear that he underestimated the richness and complexity of traditional Chinese ethical thought, and the degree of dynamism and achievements of traditional Chinese science and technology. His analysis of "the" Chinese city as an essentially administrative and military unit, though it found many advocates among later Western sinologists, failed to recognize the diversity of different types of Chinese cities as they developed over time. It also covered up the fact that the economic functions of cities within Chinese society became more important than their political functions from the Song dynasty onwards.[166] In general, it is difficult to avoid the impression that his underestimation of China's social and cultural resources followed from his propensity to treat China and the West as two fundamentally different types of society.

A different approach, one that sought to identify patterns of development that were common to China and the West, came into play during the 1920s and 1930s in the early Soviet controversies about the nature of traditional Chinese society. Most writers who engaged in these controversies in the 1920s were working with the Comintern and were motivated by the urgent practical need to find a strategy for successfully leading the revolutionary movement in China. As Marxists they sought to understand the role of various social forces in contemporary China by having recourse to a comparative historical analysis of the structure and development of Chinese society. Two of their most important concerns were promoting the anti-imperialist struggle and directing the peasant struggle for the transformation of agrarian relations in the countryside. Chinese and Western communists shared the vision of a common struggle against the capitalist world system which had subordinated colonial and "semi-colonial" societies in Asia, Africa, and Latin America and had reinforced traditional pre-capitalist conditions within them. They also tended to share the idea that the same revolutionary strategies and tactics developed by Western revolutionary movements, and especially by the Bolshevik revolution in Russia, could be taken over and, when suitably tailored to local conditions, used with success in other countries. An important interpretative technique, adapted from

[166] Rowe 1984: 1–11 criticizes Weber's ideas in the light of recent work on Chinese urban history, including G. W. Skinner 1977 and Gilbert Rozman 1973.

Bolshevism, was that of using Marxist historical theory to define the targets, objectives, and tasks of other revolutionary movements. This involved identifying correspondences between the types of social structure found in different countries and the stages of historical development defined in the Marxist classics. From the tradition of European revolutionary thought, liberal as well as socialist, Communist thinkers took over the concept of a feudal order as the target of the agrarian revolution. Feudalism in this sense was interpreted broadly and vaguely as a type of society in which the productive forces were backward, agriculture was the predominant economic activity, and the peasants were subject to heavy exploitation. The notion of "Oriental" societies as typically "bureaucratic" was adopted from Marx and from the broader tradition of comparative historiography. In 1920 the Second Congress of the Communist International characterized Asian societies as examples of a feudal or "patriarchal" social order.[167] Nikolai Bukharin drew on the work of Max Weber to give theoretical and historical support to the notion of a "land-owning bureaucratic" social structure with a "peculiarly constructed state authority" in his influential book on historical materialism published in 1921.[168] The "Theses on the Eastern Question" adopted by the Fourth Comintern Congress in 1922 spoke of "feudal bureaucratic" elements in Asian societies.[169] What distinction, if any, there might have been between such a feudal social structure and Marx's notion of an Asiatic mode of production remained unclear. The conceptual problems involved in analyzing the Chinese case were brought to light, however, in 1925–26 through fieldwork done in South China by M. Volin and E. S. Iolk.[170] This made it clear that private property in land was widespread and that the "communal" or clan property, which was central to the Asiatic mode of production, was not even necessarily the predominant type. It also drew attention to the fact that there was no class of great feudal lords of the European sort, but that instead ownership of the land rested either with individual peasant families, or, in the case of large- or medium-sized holdings, with members of the peculiar gentry class. Two problems thus arose. One was how to understand the gentry as a class. The other was how to interpret the course of Chinese history, for the existence of private property implied some degree of social development, and not simple stagnation. Consideration of these problems contributed to political debates in the following years.

During the period 1925–27 social struggles in China intensified, and antagonism between the Nationalist and the Communist parties

---

[167] Degras (ed.) 1956–59, vol. I: 143.   [168] Bukharin 1921: 174.
[169] Degras (ed.) 1956–59, vol. I: 784–85.   [170] Nikiforov 1970: 134–35.

became increasingly sharper. With the development of different assessments of the current political situation by various groups within the Comintern, there also emerged a variety of positions as to the stage of historical development Chinese society had reached. Those concerned with this question invariably referred back to the stages of social development identified by Marx and Engels; but, as the Marxist classics were by no means decisive on the question of the nature of Chinese society, certain authors placed China at one stage of development while others placed it at another. Such differences of opinion revolved to a large extent around the question of the historical role of the Chinese bourgeoisie in the revolution and the attitude to be adopted toward this class. According to the dominant opinion in the Comintern, the social structure of China was basically feudal, and the bourgeoisie could thus be seen as still having a progressive role to play, especially to the extent that it opposed imperialism. Another line of thought was developed by the economist Yevgeni Varga, who drew on Weber as well as Marx. In his view, China had a specifically "Asiatic" social structure in which the gentry typically formed the ruling class and class conflict of the European type had not yet been fully articulated.[171] The political implication of Varga's analysis was similar to that of the feudal interpretation, since both supported the idea of a positive role for the Chinese bourgeoisie in the progressive national movement. There was a reaction against this political assessment from within the Left group in the Comintern in 1926 and 1927. Historical arguments for the Left opposition were supplied by the Polish Communist Karl Radek, the President of Sun Yatsen University in Moscow. Drawing on the ideas of the historian of early modern Russia, M. N. Pokrovski, Radek emphasized the growth of the money economy in China during the later dynasties. He held that China's social system had originally been feudal, but that it had been dominated by commercial capital in recent centuries.[172] The main target of the revolution was therefore the bourgeoisie. Radek's ideas aroused heated controversy, in the course of which the Comintern secretariat dominated by Bukharin and Stalin reasserted the feudal interpretation of contemporary Chinese society by stressing the comparatively backward condition of Chinese society and the predominance of traditional agriculture in its economy. Also arguing against Radek was the Hungarian communist known as John Pepper who maintained that, far from having passed beyond feudalism, Chinese society was still at the level of the Asiatic mode of production. The notion of Asiatic mode was

[171] Varga 1928.
[172] Radek 1927 unpublished, summarized in Nikiforov 1970: 209–10 and in Barber 1981: 52.

also invoked by Besso Lominadze, the Comintern representative in China after the massacre of the Communists by the Nationalists in May 1927. Lominadze explained the Nationalists' behavior as a result of the fact that Chinese society had been dominated by the Asiatic mode of production, and that therefore the native bourgeoisie had known such an extremely feeble development that it was unfit to take on the historical role of overthrowing the traditional social order.[173] By 1928 political objections were raised amongst Comintern officials not only against Radek's "Leftist" reading of China as a capitalist society, but also against Lominadze's use of the idea of the Asiatic mode of production for interpreting contemporary Chinese society.

Nevertheless, an important controversy regarding the historical development of Chinese society developed during the years from 1928 till 1931. The two contending parties in this controversy were those who considered Chinese social structure as feudal since the earliest emergence of classes and those who thought that the notion of the Asiatic mode of production was suitable for analyzing China during part or all of its history. One of the most prominent spokesmen of the latter group was known as L. I. Mad'iar.[174] Mad'iar's works were chiefly devoted to the analysis of the contemporary Chinese economy, but he held that the specific structure and development of Chinese society was partially determined by the existence of remnants of the Asiatic mode of production which had been dominant in the country's earlier history. He maintained in 1928 that not only capitalist but also feudal notions of property had been introduced from the West, and he sought to confirm that the Asiatic mode of production had constituted the basic form of society until the coming of the European powers to Asia.[175] Representatives of the other group, however, sought the origins of Chinese property in ancient China. A marginal member of this group, Gyorgi Safarov, argued, also in 1928, that feudalism and private property had emerged during the Zhou dynasty. Increasing property differentiation led to the growth of slavery, which eventually became widespread. Contradictions in the social and political system deepened into a crisis that was resolved at the beginning of the imperial era by the introduction of the "feudal-bureaucratic" state.[176] During the Han dynasty this state corresponded to a "feudal slave-owning" social structure. In later centuries the system evolved into "state-feudalism." In 1929, S. M. Dubrovskii attempted to

---

[173] Nikiforov 1970: 211–15, and Barber 1981: 52–53.
[174] As with many Communists at the time, this was a pseudonym. Nikiforov (1970) gives his real surname as Milgorf. See below, p. 142.
[175] Mad'iar 1928: 12, cited in Nikiforov 1970: 215.
[176] Safarov 1928: 44, cited in Volin 1929: 22.

undermine Radek's views on the nature of Chinese society theoretically by mounting an attack on Pokrovsky's analysis of the historical importance of commercial capitalism. At the same time he also reinterpreted the Asiatic mode of production as a specifically Asian variant of feudalism. Dubrovskii's article initiated a major movement to systematize Marxist historical theory about modes of production and to conceive these modes as distinct stages of historical development. This movement led to attention being focused especially on two phenomena as the defining elements of different modes of production, namely relations between producers and their means of production, and specific mechanisms of exploitation or of the appropriation of the surplus product. This narrowing of focus in turn implied a tendency toward formalization of historical analysis. A notable example of this tendency is found in Volin's introduction to a long essay on slavery in ancient China published by M. G. Andreev in 1929. Volin rejected Safarov's analysis of a mixture of feudalism and slavery under the Han as theoretically incoherent. Interpreting the Marxist classics in the light of the ideas of the famous German classicist Edward Meier, Volin argued that slavery had never been a major component of social production in Asia and that feudalism had dominated the social order there since the first emergence of classes. According to Andreev, Zhou dynasty society had been characterized by the conflict of tribes and clans. He argued that slavery in the Han had been normally limited to a domestic institution and that the basic relations of social production then were feudal.[177] In the following year E. S. Iolk published an influential article, also in the sinological journal *Problemyi Kitaya*, on the "fundamental social structure" of ancient China. In this he drew on a range of ancient Chinese sources and characterized the social and political structure of the early Zhou as feudal on the grounds that the surplus was typically appropriated from the peasant producers (*nongfu*) by large landowners.[178]

Among the supporters of the notion of the Asiatic mode of production, we can also detect differences of interpretation, in particular on the question of the place of this form of society in the development of world history. Mad'iar and his associates seem to have followed Plekhanov in seeing the Asiatic mode as developing out of primitive society and thus as a form of development parallel to slavery in the West. Mad'iar's colleagues M. Kokin and G. Papayan used the notion of the Asiatic mode of production in 1930 in order to throw light on the discussion of the well-field (*jingtian*) system given in the *Zhou li* and *Mencius*, and in

---

[177] Andreev 1929: 306.   [178] Iolk 1930: 112–13.

order to clarify the transition from primitive communalism to the later Chinese forms of class society. T. D. Berin, on the other hand, saw the Asiatic mode as developing out of feudal society.[179] This view was shared by the German communist expert on China, Karl Wittfogel, who wrote in 1931 of a "military feudal" epoch being superseded by the period in which the "hydraulic-bureaucratic" class became dominant.[180] Unlike many of his Communist colleagues, Wittfogel does not seem to have been affected by the intense competition between tendencies within Soviet historical circles. His *Wirtschaft und Gesellschaft Chinas* differed from their works in its emphasis on such things as the natural conditions of the Chinese environment, their influences on particular types of production from the beginning of Chinese history down till the Qing dynasty, and the characteristics of different productive processes. Despite differences among the proponents of the Asiatic mode of production, these authors tended to agree that this form of social organization had several key traits: in particular, agriculture was the basic type of productive activity; it was carried out by peasant communities and was typically made possible by the use of a system of artificial irrigation, which required an over-arching despotic state to maintain it; and the ruling class which ran the state appropriated the surplus labor and surplus products of the peasant communities through a tax-rent collected directly by the state.[181]

Between 1929 and 1931 a series of meetings took place in the Soviet Union in which the defenders of the Asiatic mode of production were confronted by advocates of the position that Asian societies had been feudal since the first appearance of classes and the state. These debates were not purely sinological events for they brought together specialists in the history of various "Oriental" countries. The last of these debates was held in Leningrad in February 1931, organized as a discussion of the recent work by Kokin and Papayan mentioned above. The chairman of the meeting was Mikhail Godes, a well-known proponent of the "constant feudalism" position.[182] Objections to Kokin and Papayan's work were of three types: political, theoretical, and historical. Several of these are relevant to the present discussion. On the theoretical front, Godes and Iolk argued that the tax-rent form of surplus appropriation was not sufficiently unique to distinguish the Asiatic mode from feudalism. They also followed Dubrovskii in criticizing advocates of the

---

[179] Nikiforov 1970: 226–27.
[180] Wittfogel 1931: 501. Wittfogel made this position clearer still in his article, "The Foundations and Stages of Chinese Economic History," published in 1935.
[181] Mad'iar 1930b: xlviii–lvi.
[182] Nikiforov 1970: 226.

Asiatic mode of production for being distracted by secondary considerations such as geographical conditions and the form of government and for neglecting the essential question of ownership.[183] On these points Kokin and Papayan defended themselves ably enough. Mad'iar had specified that the basic mechanism of surplus extraction under the Asiatic mode was the appropriation of products and labor from the peasantry by the state in the form of a general rent-tax. Kokin and Papayan argued that this appropriation was made possible because of the state's control of water resources.[184] The empirical criticisms of their work were, however, more telling. For example, P. I. Osipov observed that large-scale irrigation works became a major phenomenon only after the Zhou.[185] Similarly damaging was the evidence brought forward by V. M. Stein, drawing on Wittfogel, and by A. S. Polyakov, to the effect that large-scale landed property and a feudal social structure had existed during the Zhou period.[186] However, if the idea of a special "Asiatic" structure in the Zhou was thus placed in difficulty, the idea that "Oriental" societies could be classified as "feudal" throughout their history was firmly criticized by two historians of the ancient Near East, namely S. I. Kovalev and V. V. Struve. While accepting that Asian societies conformed to the broad definition of feudalism since the end of the ancient period, Struve and Kovalev argued that the structures of such societies in antiquity had differed fundamentally from feudalism. They therefore supported the analysis of the ancient period of such societies in terms of the Asiatic mode of production. Struve presented detailed evidence from Pharaonic Egypt in support of this position, and Godes admitted in his concluding address that Struve and Kovalev had raised serious problems for the notion of a uniformly feudal "Orient." Of the speakers who are on record as having addressed the Leningrad conference, half favored the concept of an Asiatic mode of production and half opposed it. However, by October 1931 political concern about the theoretical implications of the various historical controversies then raging became so acute that the Soviet Communist Party leadership decided to establish direct political control over intellectual life.[187] After this, the notion of a distinct Asiatic mode of production was not to be openly upheld again in Soviet historiography until the 1960s.[188]

For several years afterwards the advocates of the view that feudalism

---

[183] Godes and Iolk's addresses are to be found in Godes (ed.) 1931: 5–34 and 59–74 respectively.

[184] Godes (ed.) 1931: 35–54, 145–53.

[185] Ibid.: 103–11.   [186] Ibid.: 82–93.   [187] Barber 1981: viii.

[188] While it is widely agreed that the notion of the Asiatic mode of production was suppressed politically, the precise reasons for its suppression have been the subject of much speculation, but still remain obscure. I have tried to bring together and

had characterized Asian societies throughout their history[189] seemed
to be victorious. This, for example, was the point of view of
A. G. Prigozhin, a well-known writer on Marxist historical theory, and a
champion of the feudal positions, who in 1933 summed up the controversy over the Asiatic mode of production.[190] In the same year, the
sinologist A. S. Polyakov, following Prigozhin's approach to world
history, divided the history of feudalism in China into six periods
starting in the twelfth century BC and extending down to the beginning
of the twentieth.[191] Historical criticism of the notion of a special Asiatic
mode of production corresponded to the desire among many Soviet
Marxists for a unified theoretical framework that would explain all
history in terms of the same historical stages and would depict struggles
between clearly defined classes as the basic motive force behind historical change. However, the theory of "constant feudalism" in Asia was
open to the objections that it could neither accommodate the evidence
that there had been qualitative social changes in that part of the world
over the last three to five thousand years, nor could it indicate the nature
of the social contradictions that had induced such changes. Consequently, the notion of "constant" Asian feudalism came under attack,
though not in the first instance with reference to China, as it might have
done. Instead the challenge came again from V. V. Struve in his work on
the ancient Near East. Struve continued to stress the qualitative change
which affected the social structure of this region in the centuries just
prior to the common era, and in 1933 he began bringing forth documentary evidence in support of his contention that ancient Sumer had
been a slave society. On the basis of this and other evidence, he and
Kovalev elaborated the idea that Asian societies, like Graeco-Roman
civilization, had developed from primitive communalism to slave society
and then from slave society to feudalism. Their definition of slavery, like
the accepted definition of feudalism, was broad: it included not only
chattel slavery, but also a range of statuses in which laborers were
unfree; and they defined the nature of a "social formation" according to
the type of productive relations found in its most important types of
production. In 1934 Kovalev used this model to solve the "problem" of
Marx's theory of the Asiatic mode of production. He wrote:

In this way the problem of the Asiatic mode of production in the writings of
Marx and Engels finds a solution. I by no means intend to discuss all the aspects

---

   compare the various types of explanation for the suppression of the Asiatic mode in
   Blue 1989.
[189] That is, since the dissolution of the primitive communalism of "prehistoric" times.
[190] Prigozhin 1934.
[191] Polyakov cited in Nikiforov 1970: 238.

of this complex question. But from what has been said above it follows that the "Asiatic mode of production" in Marx and Engels manifests itself in two forms. For the ancient, i.e. "slave-owning", Orient, it is the specific variety of slavery that is the concrete form of the slave-owning formation in countries of irrigated agriculture. For the Orient of the Middle Ages, it is the variety of feudalism in those same countries. Really, the specific feature of the "Asiatic mode of production" appears to be, as is well known, the subsumption of communal relations into a system of pure class forms of exploitation.[192]

This new model of an Asian variant of slave society was not immediately accepted by the majority of Soviet sinologists. However, already in 1935 Osipov wrote a substantial article in which he drew on Struve's approach and on the ideas of Guo Moruo in order to give a new interpretation of the Zhou dynasty as a primitive form of slave society. The interpretative element in his work was, however, ostensible in that he translated as "slave" the Chinese term *nongfu* which Iolk had earlier rendered as "peasant." He also criticized the earlier monograph by Andreev which had argued that slavery in the Han was predominantly domestic in form. This marked the beginning of one of the major divergences between Soviet and Chinese sinologists and their colleagues in North America and Western Europe, for the latter have tended to follow the conclusions of an important study published in 1934 by C. Martin Wilbur, who arrived at conclusions similar to those of Meier and Andreev. In the five years following Osipov's article, a more thorough adaptation of the model of an Asian variant of slave-holding society to China before the third century was carried through by L. I. Duman.[193] Meanwhile, the interpretation of imperial Chinese society as "feudal" and of its state as a "feudal bureaucracy" remained firmly established, and indeed unchallenged, within Soviet sinology.[194] The analysis of the gentry as a class, however, continued to be a matter of some dispute. In dealing with the gentry and with the general problem of the stability of the Chinese feudal order, Soviet sinologists in ensuing decades had recourse once again to components of the Asiatic mode theory such as the importance of irrigation and water control and the bureaucratic nature of the State.[195]

In retrospect, one can discern two distinct approaches within the Marxist historiography of pre-capitalist societies in the early Soviet period. The first focused attention on material conditions of production

---

[192] Kovalev 1934: 79.
[193] Nikiforov 1970: 256.
[194] See, e.g., the long analysis of P. Grinevich affirming it in 1935.
[195] On the surreptitious "resurrection" of the Asiatic mode of production as a way for explaining the specificities of Asian history in Soviet historiography after Stalin, see Dunn 1982.

and on social relations generally. The second asserted the primary importance of class contradictions within any given social formation. Both approaches gave rise to new questions about the nature of traditional Chinese society and served as stimuli to new thinking in this field. One of their most important innovations was that they placed priority on identifying social and economic forces for change that were imminent to pre-modern non-European societies. In this sense they marked a theoretical break with the assumption that traditional China was historically stagnant. Though the two approaches were not necessarily exclusive, the one that insisted on universal types of class contradiction and hence on an "orthogenetic" pattern of social evolution[196] came to be established as orthodoxy in the 1930s. By the end of 1931, Chinese history was no longer being referred to by Soviet Marxist theoreticians as a source that might be tapped to challenge and enrich the general theory of historical materialism. Instead it was increasingly treated, in accord with the general shift towards orthodoxy, as a field to which "correct" ideas were to be applied and from which "deviationist" ones were to be eradicated. By 1938, it had become official doctrine that there were five universal stages of historical development (primitive communalism, ancient slave society, feudalism, capitalism, and socialism). In this orthodox approach, types of production and ownership were defined broadly in a way that made it legitimate to seek dynamic models of social contradiction in "the Orient" similar to those found in the West. On the other hand, the interpretation of the relationship between social stability and historical change in pre-modern Chinese history remained highly problematic, because of the difficulty in relating the historical stages to the facts and trends in the Chinese historical record. This difficulty may be seen as a direct result of imposing on China analytical categories constructed on the basis of historical data from other societies, and it was one that was largely eschewed by Marxists who followed the approach of seeking primarily to clarify the relations linking material conditions of production and social relations generally.

Reprise

One of the general aims of modern Western social theory has been to explain the specific nature of various human societies in terms of

---

[196] Franz Boas identified anthropological/sociological "orthogenesis" as the notion that all societies follow a single universal path and must pass through the same stages of development. Identifying this view with such formative nineteenth-century anthropologists as E. B. Tylor and L. H. Morgan (upon whom writers like Marx and Spencer drew), Boas and his followers rejected "orthogenesis" in favor of their notion of "historical evolution." See Lesser 1985: 29–31.

universal principles and categories. In pursuing this goal, social thinkers have taken over ideas and preoccupations current in the societies in which they live. They have also had recourse to writers with specialist experience on other societies,[197] and they have in turn influenced such specialists. The ideas of Marx and of Max Weber, for example, have exerted profound and enduring influence on twentieth-century sinology. One might thus speak of an enduring interaction between social theory and specialist research in Chinese studies. It is however clear that one of the major problems with Western analyses of Chinese society over the last three hundred years has been that principles and categories stemming from the Western tradition of social theory have often distorted that which they were meant to clarify. One of the most important reasons for this has been a tendency to rest content with narrow models of social development and social structure and to avoid accepting various types of evidence from Chinese history and sociology, or indeed from other sources, that might serve as challenges to one's theoretical approach to the study of history and society in general. Part of the narrowness of such models has understandably been due to the fact that they have been primarily based (more or less faithfully) on Western historical experience. Yet such a basis was not sufficient to allow social and historical theory to attain its professed goal of universality. To do so, it would have had to be thoroughly comparative, in the sense that it needed to succeed in systematically taking into account and integrating evidence from the widest possible range of sources. Admittedly this is what Western social theorists including Montesquieu and Hegel claimed to be doing since the Enlightenment, but in fact they failed to take the Chinese historical tradition seriously. From the late eighteenth century until the beginning of the twentieth, any possibility of genuine interaction between social theory and the study of China remained largely suppressed. In this particular sense the nineteenth-century Western approach to China seems to have marked a regression from the more cosmopolitan attitudes of Bernier and Voltaire. Since the Second World War, much has been done to restore that tension between social theory and the study of China and to make it a fruitful one. The chapter that follows will make evident some of the ways in which that tension has been both suppressed and articulated by Chinese and Japanese historians in the twentieth century.

[197] The most prominent types of such writers were missionaries, diplomatic personnel, merchants, and academic sinologists. Discussion of such works and of the relevant secondary literature has been precluded here by the theoretical focus of the present volume, but can be found in Mackerras (1989) and Blue (1988).

4   Capitalism and the writing of modern history in China

Timothy Brook

This chapter probes the historical relationship between China and the concept of capitalism. It is not about how capitalist relations emerged in China, nor about how foreign capitalism affected China; rather, it is about how the concept of capitalism affected Chinese and Japanese intellectuals of the twentieth century, what it meant to them, and how they variously used and resisted it to theorize the totality of Chinese history. This process of theorization took place within a particular set of historical conjunctures: engagement with radical social and political thought from the West at the point of dissolution of the system of rule by emperor; peripheralization in a world economic system dominated by Europe; active participation in the great anti-colonial movements before and after 1945. This set of conjunctures impelled Asian intellectuals to sustain a prolonged and unsettled interaction with capitalist theory and the cultural form of capitalist modernity. This interaction shaped how modern history has been written in China, and is not yet over.

Much of the intellectual production that has come out of this engagement tends now to be regarded as quaintly historical rather than substantively historiographical. It is both. How Chinese intellectuals through the twentieth century chose to think about where they were in the sweep of world history has certainly been an intimate part of this century's history; and, insofar as it guided the thinking of Mao Zedong and other political leaders, it has even helped to shape it. At the same time, the evolving Chinese understanding of the past, though regarded with contempt by most Western historians, constitutes an authentic contribution to the task of reorganizing knowledge of the past in such a way as to understand power and expose the inequities that power makes possible. That Chinese historians imported ill-fitting concepts from the Western discourse on capitalism to write their own history was neither a simple artifact of Western colonialism nor a testimonial to Chinese intellectual insecurity; it was the outcome of their experience as intellectuals at the periphery of the capitalist world-system.

The place of capitalism in Chinese historical theory is a tiny pane in

China's multifaceted relationship with capitalism, one that reflects the intellectual effects of China's exposure to capitalism more than it opens onto the extensive real-world interactions between them. Yet reconstructing some of the initiatives and controversies that engaged some Chinese and Japanese scholars of Chinese history in the twentieth century can contribute to recovering knowledge of what these intellectuals achieved in relation to the international ideological context in which they conceived of China's position. It also provides an opportunity for introducing their intellectual struggles with capitalism, and with the idea of capitalism, into the larger history of capitalism as a world-system.

"Capitalism" and "modernity"

"Capitalism" (Ch. *zibenzhuyi*, J. *shihonshugi*) is a neologism in both Chinese and Japanese. There was no obvious correlative for the notion of investment capital within existing terminology. The term used (Ch. *ziben*, J. *shihon*,) was itself a neologism, combining *zi/shi* meaning "wealth" or "resource" and *ben/hon*, "root" or "trunk," which could be used in a specific sense to designate loan funds generating interest. To this combination was attached the standard suffix for "-ism" (Ch. *zhuyi*, J. *shugi*). Although China had a well-developed tradition of market exchange, the word for "merchant" (*shang*) was reserved to mean "commerce" (Ch. *shangye*, J. *shōgyō*, literally "commercial occupation" or "undertaking") and not extended to designate capitalism. The concept had been neither thought of nor named prior to the arrival of European social science toward the end of the nineteenth century. Chinese Marxist historians would later argue in mid-century that periodic upsurges in commercial activity in China since the twelfth century should be understood as an incipient or "sprouting" capitalism that contained within itself the potential to become "real" capitalism, and would have actualized itself were it not for the distorting effect of Western imperialism. But this is a counterfactual outcome that did not happen, built on an expectation derived from reading European history and phrased in a discourse that was not available until transferred from the West.

Not only was the term of foreign origin, but so too of course were those who brought it to China as part of the justification of their right to pursue their financial interests. Although China was not extensively colonized, those areas of eastern China that were incorporated into the European capitalist world-system early in the twentieth century suffered a shock far out of proportion to the actual foreign presence.[1] So too, the

[1] Pomeranz 1993: 280.

intellectual shock of imperialism was enormous, and again quite beyond the modest scale of the foreign presence. Under these conditions, the Chinese assessment of capitalism could not be anything but ambivalent at best. Intellectuals quickly recognized the enormous productive capacity and military power that capitalism has been able to generate, but they experienced the effects of that capacity and power not from within the capitalist core, where the dream of empire was raised, but in the periphery in the forms of imperialism and colonialism. Encountering capitalism in this guise, Chinese intellectuals felt compelled to resist. To resist required not simply dismissing capitalism, however, but thinking through China's relationship to it. This process of assessment was directed most immediately to the economic and political inequalities with which they felt imperialism burdened China, but also more abstractly to the cultural gap that they perceived between a strong capitalist West and a weak non-capitalist China. The drama that loomed before them was less between systems than between nations. One of the most significant intellectual effects of this assessment was therefore to think about China as a nation, more particularly about the nation's past, in an attempt to understand how China had come to find itself in this disadvantageous position, which is the subject of this chapter.

Capitalism thus served as the point of reference from which Chinese intellectuals early in the twentieth century strove to understand China. Rarely, though, did capitalism serve as the term around which that understanding was structured, inasmuch as few desired that China become capitalist. The goal of this understanding, rather, was to see China become "modern." Thinking through China's relationship to capitalism was thus more usually expressed in terms of its relationship to modernity, capitalism's cultural formation.

Like "capitalism," "modernity" appeared in the Chinese and Japanese languages as neologisms. In Chinese, the standard term is *xiandai*, meaning "the present generation." "Modernization" is *xiandaihua*, literally "undergoing the change of becoming modern." In Japanese, "modern" is *kindai*, meaning "the recent generation." This formulation implies a longer time frame than *xiandai*. *Xiandai* can be rendered into Japanese as *gendai*, but that term is used more restrictively to mean the contemporary present rather than to denote the modern era. "Modernization" is spoken of in Japanese as *kindaika* rather than *gendaika*, which signifies a process of shallower change closer to "updating." Moving in the other direction, the Japanese term *kindai* can be rendered into Chinese as *jindai*, but that term is not widely used and appears only in technical expressions such as *jindaishi*, "modern history," which in the conventional periodization covers the period from the Opium War in

1840 to the Communist Revolution in 1949. One does not speak of "modernization" in Chinese as *jindaihua* (to render *kindaika* from Japanese), for that would mean undergoing change to become as China was before 1949. Modernization is to become modern in the present.

Regardless of how these neologisms vary in their connotations, modernity in Chinese and Japanese is compounded with notions of progress, improvement, and inevitable transcendence over the pre-modern. These ideas were new to the intellectual environment into which they came toward the end of the nineteenth century. There was no notion of modernity. Up until that time, the Chinese conception of time distinguished the "present" (*jin*) from the "past" (*gu*) in such a way that the present was insignificant and inferior to the past, which meant that conventional history was an account of decline from a golden age. Taking on the European notion of modernity was as foreign as taking on the notion of capitalism. Capitalism, however, was an abstract concept whereas modernity had the tangibility of the everyday. The shock of imperialism gave the feel of living in the present a distinctive quality. Young intellectuals felt themselves to be alive in an age unlike anything their ancestors had experienced, and they dramatized that difference through the language of modernity.

Capitalism they would resist, but not capitalism's cultural formation, modernity. As the expression of the modes of social, political, and cultural life under developed capitalism, modernity as that term came to be understood took form in Europe only shortly before it arrived in China. As late as the eighteenth century, the word "modern" connoted in English something unfavorable, or at least sufficiently odd to require justification; in the nineteenth it came to mean something desirable.[2] Having emerged to designate the style of capitalism's cultural formation in Europe, modernity traveled overseas in the guise of something universally desirable that all cultures should aspire to. Becoming modern at the turn of the twentieth century was coded to mean adopting the forms and habits of the West, but with these displaced at a distance from capitalism. So powerful was the ideology of the modern that one could hope to be modern without becoming capitalist. The opponent of capitalism could embrace the overt ideal that modernity expressed: of transcending or breaking with the past and remaking the present according to modernity's institutional signature, the nation-state. By the time of the May Fourth Movement in 1919, the achievement of modernity was regarded as the summit of the struggle to make China a nation equal to nations of the West.

[2] Williams 1983: 208–09.

Central to modernity was this conception of the past that must be transcended. Modernity thus rested on a system of knowledge that codified the superiority of the West in historical terms, setting Europe's recent ascendancy against the ancient backwardness of non-Europe. Chinese intellectuals who desired to take up the task of overcoming the backwardness that knowledge of the modern forced on China thus framed their method as part of the "modern history" that Europeans had been writing since the middle of the nineteenth century, as we shall see. This modern history told capitalism's story with vigor, and Asian intellectuals felt bound to write Asia either into or out of it. In the Chinese case this meant casting the history of China in relation to an absence of capitalism or a lack of modernity, largely without reference to the concepts and cognitive maps that had dominated the thinking of their predecessors. Taking on the European frame of reference was not a matter of slavishly accepting foreign ways as better, however, for just as opponents of foreign imperialism sought to fend off Europeans by learning their methods through "self-strengthening," so too Asian intellectuals adopted models and methods of the triumphant West to institute a "new culture" or "new thought" designed to overcome the backwardness that European capitalism had imposed on China.

Their choice determined not necessarily an access to new freedom, but a complicity in a system of knowledge that located China at the periphery of more important places and events elsewhere. For those in the periphery tended to agree with those in the center that solutions to the problems they faced as a result of Europe's expansion into Asia were not to be found at home. Intransigent cultural traditions they came to regard as resisting the modernist project, and indigenous modes of social and political organization as barriers to transformation. Europeans marked off the "traditional" from the "modern" in order to establish a schedule for what had to be transformed, but Asian intellectuals were to complete the task of rejecting what was derided as tradition for modernity in their search to disrupt their dependent relationships with the West. The capitalist modernity they embraced was self-conscious in its rupture with its own traditions, fiercely committed to the forward motion of civilization and largely contemptuous of the non-European world which it had depended on, then overcome, to achieve world hegemony.

The intellectual choice that Third World modernizing elites faced was thus rarely between an indigenous mode of life and an exogenous modernity, but between a liberal modernity that accepted the capitalist reformation of Asian society and a socialist modernity that conceived of resisting it. Even though liberalism and socialism took opposing stances of the desirability of capitalism, both found Western modernity desirable in some form. The urge to grasp what the West appeared to have achieved was as strong for Marxists as it was for non-Marxists. With regard to Japanese Marxists, as John Hall noted over three decades ago, their intellectual allegiance to Marxism was as much a way of entering into Western-defined modernity as of resisting it. "Despite the popularity of the Western liberal ideal," Hall observed, "for the Japanese intellectual, Marxism has seemed the most useful key to the discovery of the essentials of Western civilization and of the long range changes affecting the modern world."[3]

As modernity – whether formally tagged as capitalist or socialist – became the desirable end point in a grand teleology, the culmination and completion of all previous history, the writing of history became a pressing task. A new history was needed to demonstrate the inevitability of modernity, which meant showing that China's subordination within the world-system was not a permanent condition, although its membership was. This new history was required to construct universal inventories of stages, developments, and innovations: all of which were identified as leading up to the formation of the modern, were shown as being universal in order to rescue China from peculiarity, and were applied to the particular facts of the national history. The purpose of modern history, not just in China but in the West as well, was to celebrate modernity (or capitalism, if the ideological environment permitted or required this) as the legitimate and necessary outcome of the past.

Writing the European capitalist world-system as modern history demanded that what lay outside or before it be organized in ways that confirmed the rhetorical trope of the rise of the West. A "pre-modern" was needed to provide discontinuities that marked the emergence of modernity as a necessary transcendence. Since rupture from the past was the key discursive moment in telling the history of the modern, the pre-modern had to be conceived of as being of a different essence than the modern world, incompatible with the modern but still providing a bed from which the modern could grow to overcome it.[4] As it separated modern from pre-modern, modern history discredited the pre-modern as a source of contemporary value or meaning. Vestiges of cultural greatness or ethnic distinctiveness might be salvaged from the premodern and reproduced as cultural anecdotes or museological artifacts (what Chinese refer to as *wenwu*, "objects signifying culture"), but this salvaging was part of the necessary task of engulfing, and trivializing, the

[3] Hall 1965: 13.   [4] Zhang Shichu 1986: 37.

pre-modern world to give it a place in, and so make it disappear into, the teleology that celebrated modernization.

Pre-modernizing the Chinese past proved to be a troubling project for Asians because of the European assumption that non-Europe not only had been pre-modern, but still was. For Europeans, the modern was not only now, it was also only here. In 1822 Hegel summed up the European notion of non-Europe's failed historical development in *The Philosophy of History*, in which he charted a hierarchy of receding pre-moderns stretching back from northern Europe (the fully self-conscious imperial center in the present) through classical Greece and Rome, to China and India, with Africa relegated to the distant rank of prehistoric. China was thus a pre-modern place in a modern world, and not just in terms of its place in time but as a civilization. Although they were daunted by what appeared to be the universal progress of capitalist expansion, Chinese and Japanese historians accepted European explanations of world history but strove at the same time to rewrite it in ways that could include China and thus redeem China's allegedly deficient national history. The search for modernity was on. Chinese tended to fix the present as the moment of transition to the modern (*xiandai*), whereas some Japanese redefined the terms of modernity and projected China's transition to an Asian modernity (*kindai*) centuries into the past.

An interesting attempt in the 1920s to parry the impulse to embrace the modern in the process of reconceiving China's place in the course of history was made by Liang Shuming. Liang adopted the Hegelian trope of isolating the core essences of the major world civilizations: spiritualism for India, humanism for China, and rationalism for Europe. He did so not to praise West over East, however, but to argue that only Chinese culture offered a promising path to the future. To Hu Shi (1891–1962), the proponent of social science in the American pragmatist vein, Liang's characterizations merely replicated the racist categories of European imperialism. He dismissed Liang as an "Orientalist."[5] It is not surprising that Hu Shi did not appreciate Liang's attempt to give China a positive identity in the world system. Hu was committed to arguing China's case in terms of its capability to make the transformation to European rationalism, not its enduring and allegedly non-rational essence.

Liang Shuming remained an exception among Asian scholars early in the twentieth century, who found intellectual incorporation into models celebrating the West difficult to resist. Indian intellectuals have proven

[5] The rupture of the pre-modern from the modern in the writing of national history in China and India is discussed in Duara 1993.

more conscious of the costs of collaborating with European models that affirm the tyranny of the modern than Chinese, undoubtedly because of India's long experience with direct colonialism. Political philosopher Partha Chatterjee has objected to the Western theory of the modern that "casts every other culture of the world into the darkness of unscientific traditionalism," all the while claiming freedom from ethnocentric bias. Such a view "sanctions the assertion of cultural supremacy while assiduously denying at the same time that it has anything to do with cultural evaluations."[6] Yet most Chinese in the twentieth century, as also most intellectuals elsewhere in the Third World, have absorbed the rationalist ideology of the European Enlightenment with its commitment to universalized values of historical progress and economic well-being. The absorption inadvertently confirms the intellectual hold of European capitalism: desiring modernity, and yet falling short of its standards.

Joseph Levenson in the 1960s expressed this conundrum in the form of a question:[7]

How can the thinker scrap Chinese ideas which the Western impact has made to seem inadequate, while he preserves his confidence of Chinese equivalence with the West? How shall he see himself as modern man and modern Chinese together?

Moving from the crisis of consciousness to the crisis of development strategies, Chatterjee two decades later rephrased the question:[8]

Why is it that non-European colonial countries have no historical alternative but to try to approximate the given attributes of modernity when that very process of approximation means their continued subjection under a world order which only sets their tasks for them and over which they have no control?

For Chatterjee, the only alternative – an alternative that history has not generously endowed – is to undertake a radical critique of Asia's commitment to material and historical progress, to universalism, and to teleology. He goes so far as to argue that "it is not just military might or industrial strength, but thought itself, which can dominate and subjugate." To break the control of Western imperialism requires that those who seek to challenge the hegemony of the capitalist world-system must "approach the field of discourse, historical, philosophical and scientific, as a battleground of political power."

Chinese and Japanese intellectuals in the twentieth century wrote their accounts of Chinese history to understand China's relationship to capitalism. At the time they worried far less about complicity in colonial discourse than Chatterjee does, yet their object was the same: to

---

[6] Chatterjee 1986: 17.   [7] Levenson 1968: xxxiii.   [8] Chatterjee 1986: 10–11.

empower China and break the hold of Western imperialism. Most chose consciously against capitalism while confirming their commitment to modernity; thus they read Chinese pre-modernity in such a way as to prove that China could achieve modernity without capitalism. Within the last decade or so, however, Chinese intellectuals in the cultural mainstream have begun to develop a new assessment of China's relationship to capitalism as China's own position in the world economy improves. The shift has not been to the critical stance of Chatterjee, but to an accommodationist position that accepts modernity as an international standard that China can now attain, and capitalism as an international fact of life. The long passage from resistance to accommodation parallels China's larger journey in from the periphery.

The first "modern" histories of China

The coming of Western imperialism to China marked a historical watershed in Chinese conceptions of history. The rivers on the far side of this watershed flowed back into well-established patterns of historiographical thought and analysis that emphasize the moral imperative of having to act in accordance with one's social obligations: to act humanely to those of equal social status, loyally to superiors, and charitably to inferiors. History praised individuals whose actions exemplified Confucian moral conduct as *junzi* (gentleman) or *zhongchen* (loyal subject). Underlying this historiography was a closed epistemological rationalism that regarded social reality as properly knowable through a limited number of Confucian moral concepts such as *ren* (benevolence), *yi* (righteousness), and *xiao* (filial piety).

In contrast, the rivers on this side have been channeled by conventions of thought about material progress and the march of history that took shape in the European Enlightenment and drew from the springs of the Augustinian inclination to interpret Christian theology historically, as a progressive process moving toward its eventual negation in human perfection. This teleological urge animates the work of all the great intellectual innovators of the late eighteenth and nineteenth centuries: Adam Smith (1723–90) in economics, Georg Friedrich Hegel (1770–1831) in philosophy, Charles Darwin (1809–82) in biology, and Karl Marx (1818–83) in political economy.

The ideas of Darwin and Marx arrived in China and Japan in the late nineteenth and early twentieth centuries respectively. Transformed as Social Darwinism and Marxism, they provided teleologies from which it became possible to interrogate the new relationships of power that imperialism was introducing into China in ways that the Confucian world view could not conceive. What changed was less the methodology of history (although historians came to regard certain topics as more fruitful for research than others) than the overarching vision of the world as a place where change must prevail over stability. Although "Western learning" (*xixue*), or "Dutch learning" (*rangaku*) as it was called in Japan, had been quietly interacting with indigenous thought ever since Jesuit missionaries introduced Europe to China in the seventeenth century,[9] it was only with the material incursion of European colonial powers in the nineteenth century that Western ideas appealed as a language to interrogate this challenge. The process began in the 1860s in the wake of a series of defeats suffered by the Qing government at the hands of both the foreigners and the Taiping rebels. Faced with the need to enable the dynasty to withstand Western military might, government leaders initiated a series of gradualist reforms in the 1870s and 1880s to set China unsteadily on the course of learning Western science and technology. In the course of trying to understand natural science, Chinese intellectuals encountered social science. Through the language schools and translation bureaux attached to the arsenals that were built to carry out self-strengthening, some knowledge of Western theories about social and political institutions and the course of world history became available.

The first scientific translation to stimulate new thinking about the nature of human history was the sixth edition of Charles Lyell's pathbreaking textbook, *The Elements of Geology*. It was produced at the Jiangnan Arsenal's translation bureau in 1873, two years before Lyell's death. In addition to first mentioning in Chinese the name of Darwin (Darwin regarded Lyell's work as a turning point in geology), the book introduced Chinese readers to such novel ideas as fossils, extinction, and geological ages stretching far back beyond human history.[10] Just as these scientific discoveries had helped erode the authority of Biblical chronology and open a path for the social sciences in the West, so also they prepared the way in China for more powerful theories, especially evolution. The initial response was to absorb the teleology into existing conceptions. Late nineteenth-century intellectuals like Kang Youwei (1858–1927) read *The Elements of Geology* and incorporated evolutionist ideas to redeem the Chinese past. In his most visionary work, *Datong shu* (Book of the Great Harmony), Kang "made Confucius the prophet of progress to a utopian Confucian future, toward which the West, with its modern values, was also on its way."[11] The marriage was not viable,

---

[9] Zhu Weizheng 1990: 113–42.   [10] Pusey 1983: 26.   [11] Levenson 1968: 81.

however, and would end among the next generation of reformist intellectuals in divorce and the harsh rejection of Confucian models.

The reception of the Western teleology of rational progress in Japan was initially more straightforward. Tokugawa Japan had been better able to protect itself from the direct impositions of imperialism that affected other Asian countries in the nineteenth century. The new elites that came to power through the Meiji Restoration in 1868 abandoned the Tokugawa model of social cohesion and opened the country to foreign trade and capitalist enterprise, in the process absorbing the ideal of progress toward modernity. As Stefan Tanaka has observed, "Those elites leading the regeneration of society found the notions of rationality and progress, rooted in science, particularly attractive." The idea of progress was powerfully persuasive because it "held out hope that less advanced cultures could also evolve" in the same direction as the capitalist West. The early Meiji elite also understood that the best way to demonstrate that hope was to write modern history. Writing Japan into modern history thus became a means of validating Japan's strategy to become a nation-state in the Western image. History writing was "the way by which the new nation-state, Japan, could become part of 'world' civilization, eradicate arbitrary (archaic) social hierarchy or relations, determine what was best for society, and establish a sense of order and sequence."[12] History was the discipline most suited to the task, and Japanese historians of the early Meiji era adopted Western historiography and its claim to scientific method to construct a modern history of the forward-moving nation.

The European writer through whom Japanese intellectuals came into touch with what was then known as "scientific history" was the English historian Henry Buckle (1821–62). His highly original *History of Civilisation*, which appeared in two volumes in 1857 and 1861, generated – first in England, then throughout Europe, and finally in Japan where it was widely read – a sensation quite as great as Darwin's *The Origin of Species*. In the opening methodological chapters, Buckle argues that the advance of civilization through time demonstrates a universal logic. The purpose of history is to discover the underlying regularity of events leading to the civilized state, just as natural scientists discover order in nature. As Raymond Williams observed, "civilization" by Buckle's time had come to represent both the process and the universal goal of all human societies from the European point of view:[13]

It expressed two senses which were historically linked: an achieved state, which could be contrasted with "barbarism", but now also an achieved state of *development*, which implied historical process and progress. This was the new historical rationality of the Enlightenment, in fact combined with a self-referring

---

[12] Tanaka 1993: 36, 40.   [13] Williams 1983: 13–14.

celebration of an achieved condition of refinement and order. The developmental perspective of the characteristic eighteenth-century Universal History was of course a significant advance. It was the crucial step beyond the relatively static ("timeless") conception of history which had depended on religious or metaphysical assumptions. Men had made their own history, in this special sense: that they (or some of them) had achieved "civilization". This process was secular and developmental, and in that sense historical. But at the same time it was a history that had culminated in an achieved state: in practice the metropolitan civilization of England and France. The insistent rationality which explored and informed all the stages and difficulties of this process came to an effective stop at the point where civilization could be said to have been achieved.

Buckle believed that he, and the England of his age, occupied that state of achievement, standing at the pinnacle of a civilizing process by which every society developed in accordance with immanent laws of the sort that also governed natural phenomena. The physical conditions of society created the means for accumulating wealth, which was in turn the basis for the accumulation of knowledge. The progress of knowledge signified the degree to which a civilization had advanced.[14] Other nations, and all of Asia, were relegated to lower stages on the ladder of progress, although not without the capacity to move up. "Civilization" in nineteenth-century discourse meant roughly what "modernization" would mean in the twentieth.

The assumption that every civilization was obliged to tread the same path of historical development up to the pinnacle occupied by the West can be found in other European authors translated into Japanese at this time. François Guizot (1787–1874), whose *History of Civilization* was as widely read as Buckle's, contrasted Europe with the relative backwardness of non-European civilizations and saw the latter as laggard on the same track of development, rather than following a different track altogether. Ernest Gellner has described this way of thinking:[15]

Global change was endowed with a systematic direction, and it was underwritten by some persistent mechanism or force which guaranteed that this overall direction should remain beneficial and operative. Basically there was but one principle and one mechanism of change. It manifested itself, in its most striking and best developed form, in European or Western history.... The rest of the world exemplified the same principles, the same mechanisms, the same destiny as the West. But these other cultures or races or civilizations exemplified them in feebler, slower and retarded forms. They could see their future in us. We could see our barbarous past in them.

Meiji historians of what became known as the *bunmei* (enlightenment or civilization) group were not deterred by the inferiority that the new

---

[14] Buckle 1908: 2, 23, 163. The influence of Buckle and Guizot on Meiji historiography is discussed in Tanaka 1993: 39–44.
[15] Gellner 1988: 2.

modern history assigned to Japan. They regarded Japan as only temporarily backward in the march of civilization and moving to the same laws governing the progress of all. These laws confidently predicted Japan's ascent.

The effect of Enlightenment historiography on Japanese views of China was harsh, and is most distinctly visible in the writings of the group's intellectual leader, Fukuzawa Yukichi (1834–1901). Rather than challenge the contempt for Asia that was intrinsic to European history's account of the rise of capitalism, Fukuzawa accepted Europe's assertion of superiority over Asia. Having done so, however, he distinguished Japan from the rest of Asia and placed it in the same category as the European nations. Japan was to be "a Western country in the East," willing to "adopt contemporary Western civilization in all things, official and private, across the entire land" and not be bound by the old customs chaining the rest of Asia to its unenlightened past. Fukuzawa expressed this view in a famous essay published in 1885 in which he appealed for Japan to *datsu-A*, or "dissociate from Asia."[16] Fukuzawa's call to dissociate from Asia and associate with the West was a declaration not that Japan should have nothing to do with Asia, but that it should embrace the universal truths that European development embodied and abandon the partial knowledge endowed by its Asian heritage. Fukuzawa's adoption of "Ajia" (Asia, shortened for sloganeering to "A") was itself a capitulation to the European division of the world between a civilized Europe in the West and a less civilized Asia in the East.

The "Westernization" of Japan expressed by *datsu-A* was ambiguous, however. First of all, Japan could not escape its geocultural location within Asia, however it argued the lineages of its identity. Secondly, there was no evidence at the time that the imperial center in Europe was willing to view Japan as equivalent with Europe or as anything other than Asian: the best of the Asian nations, perhaps, but still Asian. The Orientalism inherent in Europe's partialistic historiography of the modern blocked the possibility that Japan might escape from being viewed as other than "a perpetually incomplete version of the West."[17] Japan could at best become Westernized, but not Western. Nor, thirdly, is becoming Western what was wanted. Japan faced the challenge of embracing modernity while retaining a distinct identity. Fukuzawa's own uneasiness with the formulation – his sense that it could not achieve what it appeared to call for – is expressed in his essay on *datsu-A* when he describes the spread of Western civilization throughout the world using the image of measles. He desired that Japan partake of universal

---

[16] Fukuzawa 1966; Hashikawa 1980; Vinh 1986.   [17] Tanaka 1993: 45.

history, but was sufficiently ambivalent about the West that he yearned to dissociate from Europe as well: to provide for Japan its own pure embodiment of the modern.

Both dissociations began to be realized in the 1890s as historians moved away from the Europe-centered Enlightenment approach to a more Japan-centered history. They continued to narrate modernist values of progressive development, but did so in relation to Asian history. The modern history of the Europeans was gradually reduced to the status of "Western history" (*seiyōshi*), now nothing more than a particular manifestation of universal knowledge, and supplemented with "Oriental history" (*tōyōshi*). The history of Asia thus became the field of knowledge within which Japan could represent itself as the most highly developed entity. Writing modern history as *tōyōshi* meant that Japan could assert a sense of superiority over the rest of Asia, giving *tōyōshi* the status of an imperialist ideology not unlike modern history in Europe. This ideology proved beneficial in mobilizing Japanese public opinion in favor of the sort of interventions on the Asian continent in the twentieth century that European nations had inflicted in the nineteenth.

The passage from Enlightenment history to Oriental history in Japan had implications for how Japanese would write China into modern history. As Tanaka has noted, the new historiography "established Japan's equivalence – as the most advanced nation of Asia – with Europe, and also the distinction from, and cultural, intellectual, and structural superiority over, China."[18] A sense of this superiority can be gleaned from *Shina tsūshi* (Comprehensive history of China), published between 1888 and 1890 by Naka Michiyo (1851–1908). Naka's book was the first "modern" comprehensive history of China in any Asian language. (It was immediately followed by a host of similar works by Japanese, and within a decade was circulating in China.[19]) One of the translators of Buckle, Naka accepted his concept of progress but also desired to eliminate the Eurocentric bias in Buckle's application of the concept and endow Japan with a historical narrative that was just as heroic. His proposal in 1894 that world history be separated into Occidental and Oriental history in middle school (a curricular arrangement adopted by the Ministry of Education two years later) is regarded as the beginning of *tōyōshi*. Naka's history of China appeared slightly ahead of the establishment of Oriental history in Japan, but it reflects the intention of the *tōyōshi* approach to locate Japan in relation to Asian rather than European history. It is concerned less with writing China's

---

[18] Ibid.: 12.
[19] Fogel 1984: 6–9, 95. The analysis of Naka that follows draws heavily on the interpretation in Tanaka 1993: 17, 46–48.

history than with understanding the roots of Japan's ascendency in Asia, and hence with Japan's distinctiveness from China.

Japan's defeat of China in the war of 1894–95 appeared only to confirm the authority of Japan's emerging account of its neighbor as the embodiment of what Japan had successfully left behind. By having built an effective modern navy through mastering the heavy industrial technologies of capitalist Europe, Japan had proved that it was a modern nation; it also demonstrated that China was not. China's defeat effectively precluded the possibility of working up a modern history of China along the lines of *tōyōshi* in Japan. To rescue China from being nothing but Europe's Other, and now Japan's Other as well, Chinese intellectuals needed a device to work out an independent place for China according to a universal pattern of progress that presented China with the same possibility for forward motion as Japan. The device was Social Darwinism, introduced to Chinese readers in 1896 in Yan Fu's (1854–1921) celebrated translation of Thomas Huxley's *Evolution and Ethics*.[20] Kang Youwei's younger associate, Liang Qichao (1873–1929), mobilized Social Darwinist thinking in a 1902 essay entitled "The New Historiography."[21] Liang argues that history is progressive and evolutionary and calls for a new "scientific" historiography to show that China was developing along the same course observed in other parts of the world. He presents the evolutionary principle in a racialist fashion, white Europeans being the only "world-historical race" in the sense that they alone have struggled in competition with other races to attain world dominance. Of the other races, all except the Mongoloid are "non-historical," having not progressed at all along the evolutionary path toward the great goal of civilization. As a Mongoloid race, Chinese had a place within the charmed circle of the "historical races," inferior to Caucasians but still capable of moving into the "world-historical" class.

Liang Qichao had already tried to meet his own challenge before 1902 by adapting a model of historical stages from Kang Youwei. Kang had pictured China's path as proceeding in three phases from disorder to approaching peace to great peace, arranged along a Western-style ascent from barbarism to civilization. Liang elaborated his mentor's model by picturing the age of disorder as the age of rule by many, proceeding from tribal chieftanship to feudalism and hereditary aristocracy; the age of approaching peace as the age of rule by one, which happened also to be

[20] Schwartz 1964: 100–03, points out that Huxley was actually writing against Spencerian evolutionism, but that Yan reworked Huxley's book of lectures into a pro-Spencerian text.

[21] This article is analyzed in detail in Pusey 1983: 193–98 and Tang 1996: chapter 2. For his elaboration of the "scientific" principles of the new historiography, see Liang 1922.

Hegel's view of China, though Liang imparted to this stage positive movement from monarchy to constitutional monarchy; and the age of great peace as the age of rule by all, which for Liang predicted a movement from republicanism to anarchism.[22] Liang abandoned this model in his 1902 essay in favor of a simpler European periodization framework: "ancient" (prior to Qin unification), "medieval" (up to the end of the Qianlong reign, 1795), and "modern" (since 1795). This way of staging the Chinese pre-modern asserted that China had already abandoned pre-modernity and was well into the terrain of modernity.

A strain in Japanese historiography postulated China's transcendence of the pre-modern more aggressively in the work of the great Kyoto historian, Naito Konan (1866–1934). In 1914, Naito argued that China entered its modern period not at the turn of the nineteenth century, as Liang Qichao assumed, but in the later part of the Tang dynasty, sometime between the eighth and tenth centuries. The intervening ten centuries he called China's "modern age" (*kinsei*, literally, the recent age). Naito based his analysis on many social and cultural factors, of which the most important was the replacement of aristocracy by autocracy. Whereas the bureaucracy up to the Tang had been dominated by aristocrats with independent bases of power, from the Song forward it was staffed by officials without such bases. As the old aristocracy disappeared, the position of the emperor was immensely elevated; at the same time, peasants were freed from servile status and could enter more open, contractually limited tenurial relationships. These features, combined with the growing vitality of the market, created the outlines of modernity.[23]

Naito concentrated his scholarly work on China, but his principal concern was to explicate China's relationship to the Orient (*tōyō*), and hence to Japan. The center of Oriental culture had been in China through the "modern age," but it had gradually moved from the cradle of antique Oriental civilization in China's northwest in a southeasterly direction. The impulse for change, in survival-of-the-fittest logic, came from nomadic invasions. The "modern age" scheme acknowledged China's high cultural development, but it also rendered that status

---

[22] Pusey 1983: 120.
[23] Miyakawa 1955; Fogel 1984; Tam 1980. Xia Zengyou, roughly contemporary with Naito, also saw the transition from Tang to Song as a major turning point, though for him it was a negative development, marking a falling off from the cultural vitality of Tang civilization rather than the eruption of modernity. Naito's position was echoed in European sinology by Étienne Balazs, who regarded the Song as "marking the beginning of modern times in China" when the growth of commerce led to "the birth of capitalism," although it was a capitalism that could not develop further into the competitive industrial capitalism of Europe (Balazs 1964: 53).

conditional on recurring penetration from Inner Asia, for without it, "modern" Chinese society stagnated and Chinese politics sank into corruption. China had become modern too early. The decay of contemporary China was proof to Naito that the center of Oriental culture had now passed ineluctably to Japan, which was better able to resist the conservatism and pacifism that overwhelmed China – and by implication was in a position now to penetrate the feminized body of China and integrate it thoroughly into Japan's historical course.[24] As he gave Japan its own modern history, Naito restricted China's to the pre-modern. Even though China could claim a kind of Oriental modernity since the Song dynasty, its proximity to modernity led downward to a profound distancing between rulers and people. This proximate modernity could not generate the sort of political unity and mobilization that Japan had been able to muster to embrace the modern. Writing China into the modern as Japan's transcended pre-modern rescued Japan from being an incomplete version of Europe, but it consigned China to being an incomplete version of Japan.[25]

Locating China in Asia was not a defensive strategy that Chinese intellectuals wanted to adopt, as it did not present any obvious resolutions to China's relationship to European capitalism. They turned away from civilizational explanations, which too readily collapsed back into Confucian arguments about China as the center of the world, and moved instead toward an idea of China based on another concept coming out of the capitalist West, the nation.[26] As they felt their way

[24] Tanaka 1993: 195.

[25] Although Naito predicted in 1933, a year before his death, that Japanese military intervention in China would lead to disastrous consequences for Japan (Fogel 1984: 260), the Kyoto school interpretation served an ideology that gave Japan the right to intervene in Chinese affairs. Some of Naito's intellectual associates in 1941–43 joined discussions promoting the view that Japan's mission in Asia was to negate the Eurocentric construction of modern history. Japan was not merely to achieve modernity, but to "overcome" or "transcend modernity" (*kindai o chōkoku*). This popular late-war phrase, which built on the *datsu-A* notion of Fukuzawa Yukichi, called for Japan to situate itself at the center of a new East Asian world order grand enough to resist the material and philosophical power of the West. Chinese were supposed to understand "transcending the modern" as surmounting the narrow, Western-derived nationalism that inhibited them from accepting Japan's mission for revitalizing and liberating Asia. See Takeuchi 1980 (he makes the connection to *datsu-A* on p. 66); also Dower 1986: 226–27; Olson 1992: 63–66.

[26] Partha Chatterjee has questioned the value of the nation as the conceptual framework for resisting Western capitalism. He concedes that nationalism "administered a check on a specific political form of metropolitan capitalist dominance. In the process, it dealt a death blow (or so at least one hopes) to such blatantly ethnic slogans of dominance as the civilizing mission of the West, the white man's burden, etc." But he points out that "nowhere in the world has nationalism *qua* nationalism challenged the legitimacy of the marriage between Reason and capital" (1986: 168). Such qualms did not occur to Chinese intellectuals, whose self-identification with China's cause was automatic.

toward the concept of China as a nation, Chinese intellectuals were drawn to the idea of "modern" history as the history of the people, not the throne. Yan Fu had already touched on the importance of the people in the political process by recounting Western ideas about democracy and popular rights, but one of the first to enunciate the concept of the modern nation-state as a nation of all the people, and to apply it historiographically, was Xu Renzhu, provincial director of education in Hunan and a partisan of the reform movement there. Xu posed the problem by contrasting Chinese dynastic history with modern history in the West:[27]

The histories of the Westerners all record both state policies and affairs among the people so that the reader can examine [the character of] the age. The dynastic histories of China simply record the means through which one family controlled the realm and protected its territory, along with praise for the deeds of those in its service. Life among the people is left entirely unrecorded, which means that [the Chinese historical record] amounts to nothing but the genealogies of seventeen imperial families. How can this be called history?

The first to write a history of the nation in this fashion was Xia Zengyou (1863–1924), a junior official in the Qing government and a close intellectual associate of Yan Fu. Appearing serially in three volumes under the title *Zuixin zhongxue Zhongguo lishi jiaoke shu* (The newest textbook of Chinese history for middle school) between 1904 and 1906, Xia's history abandoned the Confucian narrative of a cyclical dynastic past and adopted instead an evolutionary approach (he cites Darwin and *The Origin of Species* in the opening section of the book). Both Yan Fu and Liang Qichao were enthusiastic.[28]

The collapse of the monarchy in 1911 (Xia Zengyou was active in the constitutional movement that led to its fall) seemed to verify the forward motion of the world-historical races, and China's place as a nation. Yet the new republic proved difficult to establish, a setback that had as great an impact on Chinese intellectuals as the revolution itself. Believing that Western institutions and ideologies could not be successfully introduced into an environment still firmly shaped by indigenous ideology and practices, some argued that Chinese civilization itself was the problem and had to be superseded by a Western model of modernity. In what came to be known as the New Culture Movement, younger scholars like Hu Shi, Chen Duxiu (1879–1942), and Lu Xun (1881–1936) spoke with eloquence about the new ways of thought that the new age

[27] Xu Renzhu, *Youxuan jinyu*, quoted in Yin Da 1987: 407.
[28] Yin Da 1987: 432–37. The three volumes of 1904–06 were posthumously combined into one and published in 1933 under the title *Zhongguo gudai shi*. After the 1911 Revolution, Xia worked in the Ministry of Education for four years, then became head of the Beijing Library.

demanded, although none as yet was ready to take up the task of rewriting Chinese history.[29] Nationalism enlarged the New Culture movement into the much broader mass mobilization of May 4, 1919, when students from Beijing University protested the decision of the Versailles Peace Conference to hand over Germany's Chinese possessions to Japan. In politicizing the younger generation, May 4 inspired a thorough rejection of Chinese traditions. The movement targeted imperialism but promoted modernity, the foreignness of which quickly came to be overwritten as "cosmopolitan."[30] The ability to interact openly with other cultures and traditions became the virtue of working to higher standards rather than the vice of capitulating to the superior power of the capitalist West. Embracing capitalist modernity was reevaluated as a positive way of dragging China out of the mess that May 4 had shown it to be in.

Not all were prepared to reject the past. A nativist position emerged in reaction, arguing that selective aspects of Chinese culture be retained as a body onto which some "modern" elements could be grafted. The Society for the Preservation of National Essence, a radical organization founded in 1904 to overthrow the Manchus, advocated this position. The society's goal was to retrieve the best components of Chinese culture, China's "national essence" (*guocui*), that both foreign cultural penetration and Manchu control threatened. The quest of National Essence scholars for an authentically Chinese cultural identity was anti-imperialist, but to some degree anti-modernist as well, channeling the task of cultural revision away from the direct absorption of Western ideas.[31] One of the more notable converts was none other than Liang Qichao, who regarded the recently concluded world war as evidence of Europe's moral weakness and turned with renewed fervor to the Chinese tradition. Liang rejected cosmopolitanism in favor of an extreme nativism that opposed the importation of Western cultural forms into China. He hit cosmopolitanism's political Achilles heel of

---

[29] Looking back several decades later, Hu Shi (1934: 44) felt that the two most significant influences of the New Culture Movement on historiography were that the past came to be viewed critically, and that the tools for this reexamination drew almost entirely on Western methodologies.

[30] Regarding the nativist–cosmopolitan dichotomy, see Cheek 1984.

[31] The National Essence position moved to the political right and found itself under ridicule by the next generation of cosmopolitans, who preferred to embrace the new culture of the modern West rather than preserve the Chinese tradition against that challenge. Lu Xun (1973: 24–25) argued in 1918 that the National Essence reversion to tradition would doom China to permanent exile in the past. The National Essence view had the advantage of projecting a familiar image for Chinese identity that was narrowly nationalistic and congruent with conservative nation building, and for this reason became Guomindang policy in the 1920s. For a positive evaluation of the National Essence position, see Yü 1993: 129–30.

praising foreign ideas and values at a time when Western imperialism was the leading issue among progressives.

The appeal of cosmopolitanism was nonetheless strong among many within the younger generation of 1920s intellectuals. Their "liberalism," for want of a better term, was cosmopolitan in its willingness to accept Western intellectual discourse and methodology, yet was also sympathetic to recognizing continuities between Chinese culture and the culture of modern Western construction. Liberal intellectuals hoped to preserve something of the inner spirit of Chinese civilization as they remade China's past in ways congruent with the new ideas from the West. Unlike National Essence supporters, they interpreted continuity as change rather than preservation and looked to history as a means to forge new culture out of old by recovering the best of the past and integrating it with the present.

The leading representative of this view was Hu Shi. Like other intellectuals of the May Fourth era, Hu drew on ideas expressed by National Essence thinkers like Liang Qichao, but he did not regard the past as inviolable. As a Social Darwinist and Deweyan pragmatist, he was convinced that history was progressive, moving gradually and with the purpose of revealing the individual's capacity for rational thought and civilization's capacity for improvement. History did not, however, unfold according to suprahistorical laws. Hu approached history not to reveal "natural laws" that had previously been derived theoretically, but to ascertain the specific causes of historical facts in ways congruent with "modern" ideals. He first applied this approach, which he called "objective criticism," in his *Zhongguo zhexueshi dagang* (An outline of the history of Chinese philosophy) published in 1919. His method was to gather up all the relevant facts about a subject, in this case Chinese philosophy, and from those facts reevaluate the subject in a process he termed "reorganization" (*zhengli*).[32] Reorganization was not value-free. In Hu Shi's introduction to his own attempt to "reorganize" the writings of the Warring States philosopher Mo Zi, he identified his principal problem as how to "best assimilate modern civilization in such a manner as to make it congenial and congruous and continuous with the civilization of our own making." He turned to Mo Zi's logical methods because, as he put it, "I have the strongest desire to make my own people see that these methods of the West are not totally alien to the Chinese mind, and that on the contrary they are instruments by means of which much of the lost treasures of Chinese philosophy can be recovered."[33] He believed that some roots of European modernity were

[32] Hu Shi 1919: 4, 29.
[33] Hu Shi 1922: 9. Mo Zi was an appropriate subject for carrying out "scientific" research

available for recovery in the Chinese past, and that this recovery would facilitate China's transformation into a "modern" nation, preserving its integrity while meeting the standards of Western modernity.

The "modernization" of China's past was enthusiastically taken up by younger scholars like Gu Jiegang (1893–1980), who dramatizes the liberating impact of the new "reorganization" of history in his autobiography:[34]

Our eyes have been opened to a new world of hitherto uninvestigated and unorganized materials; questions which were once believed to have no significance have now taken on entirely new meaning. Our position to-day is like that of a prisoner, who has long been confined within walls beyond which his eyes could not penetrate; while he was there he felt reasonably satisfied, but the walls have hardly opened and the shackles fallen from him before a thousand new sights meet his vision – an unending succession of strange-looking houses, exotic flowers and queer animals. In a world so new, he hardly knows how to organize his existence; the excitement and perplexity of his environment bring grief and joy in equal proportions.

Gu's study of ancient legends, completed in 1922, led him to suspect the authenticity of most of China's earliest written records and to argue that China's history had been "manufactured by accretion." There followed a spate of articles by Gu Jiegang and others challenging the authority of received interpretations by attacking the reliability of the classics.[35]

The formulation of a Marxist historiography: feudalism

Liang Qichao was the first Chinese writer to mention Marxism in the Chinese press, in 1902. He became aware of Marxism while he was in exile in Japan, where a Marxist literature was just developing. Chinese students at that time in Japan were being drawn to Marxism through such books as Fukui Junzo's *Kinsei shakaishugi* (Modern socialism) and Kotoku Shusui's *Shakaishugi shinzui* (The essence of socialism). Both were immediately translated into Chinese, Fukui's little book introdu-

---

into China's past, for in Mo Zi's philosophy Hu found much that could be regarded as anticipating European scientific method.

[34] Ku Chieh-kang [Gu Jiegang] 1931: 161. Gu's conversion to "modern" historiography is examined in Schneider 1971.

[35] Another leader in this critical movement was Qian Xuantong. Pleased with the results of the new skepticism, Qian in 1925 adopted a catchword of the Tang historiographer Liu Zhiji, *yigu* ("doubting antiquity"), as his pen name. In doing so he mocked Liang Qichao, who criticized Hu Shi's historical writings as excessively "doubting of antiquity." Qian and Gu in 1926 published their essays, together with those of like-minded historians including Hu Shi, in the first of a series of four volumes entitled *Gushi bian* (Critiques of ancient history), claiming for the first time to uncover the "real" meaning of ancient texts.

cing Chinese readers to some basic principles of Marxist history, and Kotoku's providing an outline of historical materialism. By 1903, original Chinese commentaries on Marxism began to appear, including one by Ma Junwu, the translator of Darwin's *The Origin of Species*.[36] Marxist thought did not gain significant ground in China, however, until the Russian Revolution in 1917 publicized the revolutionary potential of Marxist theory. The Bolshevik success did far more than any reasoned appeal could have done to draw Chinese intellectuals to historical materialism.

The scholar principally responsible for introducing historical materialism to Chinese intellectuals was Li Dazhao (1888–1927). Head librarian at Beijing University, Li began his conversion to Marxism during the winter of 1918–19. Historical materialism would be his main intellectual preoccupation from 1920 until his execution in 1927 by the warlord Zhang Zuolin. The idea that historical change proceeds on the basis of contradictions between the ever-expanding material forces of production and the social relations of production was appealing because it was wedded to a revolutionary strategy. By arguing that "the history of all hitherto existing society is the history of class struggles," and that the development of modern industry empowers the workers in new ways and renders inevitable the fall of capitalism, as Marx and Engels had done in *The Communist Manifesto* (first translated into Chinese in 1920), they offered the historical evolution of capitalism as proof that the proletariat would one day be able to cast off their chains. Li Dazhao recognized the enormous power of history as ideology when yoked to this kind of revolutionary conception. As he wrote late in 1918, "If one can write the history of billions of people, then one can have the authority to move the minds of billions of people."[37]

Li Dazhao published only one book, *Shixue yaolun* (Essentials of historical study), in 1924. He wrote it to promote the materialist conception of history. The book says almost nothing about Chinese

---

[36] Zhu Weizheng 1987: 321–23. The first appearance of Marx's name in the Chinese press was actually in 1899, in an American missionary journal; it appears to have attracted no notice. Kotoku's book was published in 1903. Kotoku (1871–1911), an anarchist, was executed eight years later for treason; Hoston 1986: 19–20. On Chinese scholarly interest in evolution and the adoption of Marxism, see Zhu Weizheng 1990: 180–87. For the early history of Chinese translations of Marxist classics, see Dirlik 1978: 22–24. Incomplete Chinese editions of the first volume of *Capital* translated by Hou Wailu and others were published between 1930 and 1936. The first full translation appeared in 1938, by Guo Dali (1905–76) and Wang Yanan (1901–69); the modern standard translation was published in 1972. For a full history of the reception of *Capital* in China, see Hu Peizhao and Lin Pu 1985. Guo Moruo's translation of *A Contribution to the Critique of Political Economy* was published in 1931.

[37] Quoted in Meisner 1967: 155.

history but concentrates instead on the approach Li judged to be essential for rewriting history. Reviewing European historiography, Li mentions Marx and Engels only in passing to avoid attracting the notice of censors, but the work is shot through with a materialist spirit that is unmistakably Marxist. It stresses the need for viewing the past developmentally according to a universal scheme applicable equally to Europe and China, and strongly advocates a comparative approach for building the kind of theoretical structure needed to bring what he calls the dead facts of history to life. Conceding that Hu Shi-style "reorganization" of historical facts is one part of the historian's job, he insists that the more significant part is to develop a theory of society in which to locate those phenomena:[38]

The historian's job is most certainly not exhausted by just examining and establishing characteristic historical facts. He must go further and search out the inner logic within the facts ... to gather up all manner of facts and categorize each as part of the comparative study of all historical phenomena, past as well as present, Eastern as well as Western, in order to develop a general understanding and elucidate their common inner logic. This is the responsibility of the historian.

Li Dazhao set a high standard: the history of the world he wanted was not one that wrote China into a Western narrative, but one that relied on the history of China as much as of Europe to construct a new narrative. Yet he had no interest in writing Asia or China into a history that differed from Europe's. His goal, rather, was to see China in a universal pattern that linked its future to the same leap over capitalism that Russia appeared to have just experienced. The appeal that historical materialism had for Chinese intellectuals in the 1920s was not just as a political weapon to resist imperialism, but a means to probe, even embrace, modernity.

Marxist perspectives found entry into Chinese historical discourse toward the end of the 1920s. They did so through an intense and convoluted controversy, beginning in 1928 and lasting until the Japanese invasion of China in 1937, about the nature of Chinese society and the character of its historical development.[39] The debates that arose around these issues were dubbed the Social History Controversy (*shehuishi lunzhan*) in 1931 by Wang Lixi, the editor of *Dushu zazhi* (The readers' magazine). *Dushu zazhi* served as the main forum for the debate, sponsoring the publication of three volumes of essays entitled *Zhongguo shehuishi lunzhan* (The Chinese social history controversy). The essays

---

[38] Li Dazhao 1926 [1924]: 20–21.
[39] He Ganzhi 1939; Schwartz 1954; Dirlik 1978; Ye Guisheng and Liu Maolin 1983.

were of varying quality, but they represented the main positions among left-wing historians at the time. The interchange of views that occurred during the controversy produced the main contours of the Marxist historiography that was practiced in China down to the 1980s.

The Social History Controversy involved both historical issues and present questions, and arguments for one entailed positions on the other. Out of the debates emerged three positions. The key issue dividing them was China's relationship with capitalism, which in turn depended on how one interpreted what was emerging as Marxist orthodoxy in the Soviet Union: the five-stage model of development through which all societies had to pass. Marx in the 1840s had conceptualized a stadial process of historical change in relation to four forms of property: tribal, ancient, feudal, and capitalist.[40] In the decade following the completion of *The German Ideology* in 1846, he had turned his attention to Asia in search of comparative material for understanding the evolution of property prior to capitalism.[41] The results of this research is summarized in his 1859 Preface to *A Contribution to the Critique of Political Economy*, in which he periodizes the history of human civilization as sequential modes of production: "In broad outline, the Asiatic, ancient, feudal and modern bourgeois modes of production may be designated as epochs marking progress in the economic development of society."[42] These and other casual references in Marx's writings were formalized by Soviet Marxists into a unitary formula of five stages: primitive communism, ancient slavery, feudalism, capitalism, and socialism. To undertake a Marxist analysis of Chinese history meant having to specify a relationship to capitalism in these terms.

The left-wing Guomindang position, represented by Tao Xisheng, argued that Chinese society had been feudal in the past, but that in the 1920s it was "neither feudal nor capitalist but a society where the ambiguity of the class structure had enabled parasitic political forces of a feudal nature to retain their power, with these forces, at the same time, serving the cause of imperialists."[43] The solution for China was to develop its forces of production and build an industrial economy that could serve as the sort of base China needed to banish the feudal remnants and build socialism. The "Trotskyist" position argued that China was already a capitalist society, with a native bourgeoisie (allegedly represented by Chiang Kaishek) in league with foreign capitalism. This

---

[40] Marx and Engels 1970: 43–45.

[41] This exploration is recorded in the *Grundrisse*, of which the section on precapitalist forms of property was separately published in Chinese in 1963 (translated by Ri Zhi) and in English in 1964 under the title *Pre-Capitalist Economic Formations* (Marx 1965).

[42] Marx 1971: 21, to recite a key passage quoted above, p. 93

[43] Dirlik 1978: 72.

position called for a peasant and worker alliance to struggle against international and domestic capitalism in the cities and to foment revolution in the countryside. The "Asiatic" interpretation of the Chinese premodern (to be discussed below) became linked to this position, in part for ideological reasons.

The third position, adopted by the Communist Party at its Sixth Congress in 1928 and favored by Soviet Marxism, identified China as semi-feudal, semi-colonial.[44] According to this interpretation, China had been a feudal society until the advent of imperialism distorted its original character, generating a unique hybrid. Merchant capital had existed in Chinese feudal society, but rather than undermine feudalism or fuel capitalism, as capital accumulation had in Europe, it had colluded with landlord and later imperialist power to reinforce feudal exploitation. The solution to the "China problem" was to turn the revolution against both the imperialists and the landlords, uniting temporarily with native capitalists until socialism could be achieved.

This third interpretation was the one that would triumph within Chinese Marxism. In the Social History Controversy it was most ably presented by the writer Guo Moruo (1892–1978). Guo was a writer of fiction and drama who had been a keen participant in the earlier "reorganization" movement, but whose politics obliged him to flee to exile in Japan. With the publication of his impressive *Zhongguo gudai shehui yanjiu* (Studies in ancient Chinese society) in 1930, Guo replaced Tao Xisheng as the central figure in the Social History Controversy. In this collection of essays, Guo established what would become the dominant model for a Marxist interpretation of China's history for the next half-century. The book is noteworthy in two respects. First of all, it was the first book to apply the five-stage historical framework without exception to all of China's history. A Marxist model of five stages had been aired in the Chinese translation of Kotoku Shusui's 1903 primer on Marxism, but Guo was the first to align all of Chinese history with this framework. Secondly, it was the first book to apply the analysis back to Shang and Zhou society. Using the newly discovered oracle bones as evidence, Guo offered them as proof that China had had a slave society, just as Europe had had Greece and Rome.[45] This conclusion had the remarkable effect of making ancient history the most contentious subject of serious study among radical historians and social

---

[44] The polemics of attributing colonial status to China and withholding it are examined in Barlow 1993.

[45] Other Marxist scholars, like Lü Zhenyu, would turn to the same body of evidence to build their analyses, and use it, as Lü did, to criticize Guo as still under the influence of Hu Shi's "reorganization." Li Ji 1936: 14 levels the same criticism at Guo Moruo.

theorists in the early 1930s. No participant in the Social History Controversy could avoid referring to Guo's theses. By the time the controversy died out in the mid 1930s, his interpretation of China's early history, with minor revisions by Lü Zhenyu, prevailed as Marxist orthodoxy.

Guo Moruo identified China with the five-stage model on the strength of his belief in the universality of human history. To analyze Chinese history into the five stages Marx had identified in the history of the West (though Marx himself was never categorical on this point) was to confirm that China was not exceptional:[46]

As long as you have a human being, then – whether he be red, yellow, black, or white – his growth will generally be the same. Human society is just like this. The Chinese have a saying which goes: "Our national character is different." But this kind of national prejudice is found in almost every race. We Chinese are not gods, nor are we monkeys, and society as the Chinese people organize it should be no exception [to universal patterns].

By this logic, capitalism was not foreign to Chinese history, even though it happened to be foreign in 1930. Since feudalism applied equally to China and Europe, capitalism was not a social formation unique to Europe. There was no European genius at work that justified condemning China to second-class status in world history. Both shared the same world-historical process. Guo Moruo doubted that either the "national character" arguments of the National Essence school or Hu Shi's "congenial, congruous, and continuous" assimilating of the pre-modern to the modern[47] was sufficient to grant China its full, rightful place in the history of the world. Placing China in Europe's historical narrative meant relegating it to the status of precapitalist, but this did not disturb Guo, whose first concern was to affirm that China was subject to the same historical trajectory that had led Europe to capitalism. With Japan's invasion of China in 1937, the outpouring of critical essays on social theory ceased. Essayists turned to writing anti-Japanese propaganda, and professional historians turned to producing popular general histories in a Marxist vein to inspire patriotic resistance.[48] The

---

[46] Guo Moruo 1955: preface, 1. Lü Zhenyu quotes this passage approvingly in his 1934 work on ancient history; Lü Zhenyu 1943:

[47] Lü Zhenyu (1943: 3) similarly charged Hu Shi with having simply tacked foreign technical terms onto traditional categories of explanation in his history of Chinese philosophy, a superficial strategy that did not establish real correspondence between Chinese and Western history.

[48] Most of the journals carrying the Social History articles were forced to close in 1937 for political or economic reasons, and those who had thrown themselves into the Social History Controversy turned to more pressing tasks. Professional Marxist historians concentrated on writing general histories to mobilize anti-Japanese sentiment. The most prominent was *Zhongguo tongshi jianbian* (A concise comprehensive history of

period of experimentation was over. With limited exceptions, no important new insights would appear subsequently in Marxist Chinese historiography.

Feudalism was the model that Chinese Marxists, as well as postwar
Japanese (Tokyo school) historians, chose to identify China's recent
pre-modernity. The term was neologized from the outside using the
ancient Chinese concept of parcelized sovereignty (*fengjian*), a term
that designated the multi-state system under the Zhou dynasty in the
first millennium BC that was eradicated by Qin unification in 221. The
first application of this European model of pre-capitalist feudal society
was attempted in Japan in 1887. In the first volume of his *Shina kaika
shoshi* (A short history of Chinese civilization), Taguchi Ukichi
(1855–1905) simply treated the *fengjian* period before Qin unification
as feudal in the European sense of the word.[49] Taguchi's interpretation
gained ground with Chinese intellectuals after the turn of the century.
In 1923, Liang Qichao used the term "true feudalism" to describe the
period of parcelized sovereignty during the millennium prior to Qin
unification.[50]

Identifying a feudal period in the Chinese pre-modern posed conceptual problems. The European model supposed the necessary transcendence of feudalism by capitalism, whereas Chinese feudalism had failed
to produce capitalism after 221 BC. Taguchi resolved this problem by
arguing that China had stagnated through a long "despotic" period: a
feudalism that should have become capitalism was prevented from
doing so because of its political structure. Most Chinese intellectuals

China), which Fan Wenlan (1893–1969) produced in Yan'an (Fan 1942–1943).
Commissioned by the Communist Party, the book was compiled by a group of
researchers under Fan's direction at the History Research Institute of the College of
Marxism-Leninism in Yan'an during the period 1939–41, and published serially there
in three volumes over the following two years. Fan completely revised this work and
published it in three volumes sequentially in 1953, 1958, and 1965. Fan also produced
a history of modern China in 1945, reissued in revised editions in 1947, 1949, 1951,
and 1954 under the title *Zhongguo jindai shi* (Fan 1945). Unlike the Social History
debaters, Fan was a trained historian, a graduate of Beijing University who had
originally worked within a more traditional historiographical framework. He used that
training to refashion Chinese history according to the Soviet five-stage theory of
historical development, producing what within China has been called the first truly
Marxist history of China (Pan Ruxuan 1979: 15). Fan's book was enthusiastically
received by the Communist Party, and Fan himself was regarded by the Party as a
model of the loyal intellectual. Also prominent among the general histories of the war
period is *Zhongguo shigang* (An outline of Chinese history), which Jian Bozan
(1898–1968) published in Chongqing. In the preface dated 1943, Jian acknowledges
the influences of both Guo Moruo and Lü Zhenyu (Jian Bozan 1944: 5). Other
significant general histories were Deng Chumin 1942 and Tao Xisheng 1944.

[49] Fogel 1984: 9. Naka Michiyo expressed roughly the same view in 1888 in his *Shina
tsūshi*.
[50] Liang Qichao 1959: 156.

found it more compelling to identify imperial, rather than pre-imperial, society as feudal: to make feudalism not a distant stage far in the past, but the stage that brought China directly up to the modern. Feudalism was more attractive as the proximately pre-modern – out of which capitalism would have had to grow through natural teleology – rather than the ancient (and by implication permanent) pre-modern.

When Taguchi Ukichi and Liang Qichao invoked the concept of feudalism to describe China prior to imperial unification, they were doing so within a European, but not a Marxist, framework. Finding in Chinese history a society in which sovereignty was distributed among feudal lords, they deemed it to be the same as the feudalism of medieval Europe. The neologism they used for feudalism, *fengjianzhuyi*, drew on the traditional term *fengjian*, which referred to precisely this arrangement in the Warring States period. Significantly, the term was being revived at the time not so much to build arguments about the pre-modern, but to construct an indigenous argument for local self-government. Liang Qichao and Kang Youwei invoked the *fengjian* concept as a defense against centralized autocracy and as an indigenous model for reforming the constitution and empowering local elites.[51] Marxist historians used *fengjian* in a different sense, however, to describe a more general economic relationship between rural landlords and peasants. Their feudalism had no necessary tie to political structures like enfeoffment and was therefore not bound to the Warring States period.

Replacing the neutral definition of feudalism as a form of political sovereignty with a class-based economic definition appealed to some Asian historians because it resolved their backwardness in two ways. It placed Asia along the same developmental track as Europe, which had also experienced feudalism on the way to capitalism, representing their backwardness as temporary; and by locating Asia in terms of Europe's pre-modern it provided an account of why Asian societies had not yet assimilated the capitalism that modern Europe had brought. Feudalism was something of a category by default in its application, however. China in the Qing dynasty was clearly not a primitive or slave society, nor had it developed into capitalism: therefore it must be feudal. But Marxists who used the concept chose not to see this as a problem. Their purpose in embracing the model was to show a logic that would relate the Chinese pre-modern to capitalism.

Tao Xisheng was the first Chinese scholar to apply an economic definition of feudalism to China. Toward the end of the 1920s, Tao argued that feudalism was a socio-economic system of class opposition

[51] Min 1989: 137.

based on land, not a political system of enfeoffment, and that China in the twentieth century, though not feudal, was still dominated by "feudal forces." These forces were remnants of a feudalism that had existed in various forms in China from early in the Zhou dynasty. Despite his rejection of political criteria for distinguishing feudalism, Tao followed Liang Qichao in describing the Zhou dynasty as China's period of pure feudalism. Thereafter, China from the Qin to the Qing had been dominated by what Tao called "transformed feudalism," in which "post-feudal" or "pre-capitalist" elements (he used the terms interchangeably, because they were logically so) were present but incapable of over-powering the feudal elements in the economic system. The ascendancy of a money economy over a barter economy in the Southern Song indicated the presence and strength of the pre-capitalist element.[52]

The most unambiguous early application of the Marxist concept of feudalism, without any implication of making it correspond to enfeoff-ment under the Zhou house, was presented by Guo Moruo in his *Zhongguo gudai shehui yanjiu* in 1930. In Guo's view, feudal economic relations began with the onset of iron technology in the Spring and Autumn period. Once feudal relations of production were established as a consequence of this change in the means of production, China evolved out of the political system of enfeoffment in the direction of centralized power. But enfeoffment *per se* had nothing to do with feudalism. In another influential Marxist study of early history published four years later, Lü Zhenyu sustained one part of the feudalism-equals-enfeoff-ment equation by arguing that Chinese society in the Zhou period was "early feudalism," and from the Qin to the Qing, "later feudalism."[53] The Japanese Marxist Moritani Katsumi (1904–64) preferred to distin-guish "early feudalism" from "bureaucratic feudalism," adding a further label of "developed bureaucratic feudalism" for Chinese society from the Tang forward.[54]

By the time of the Social History Controversy, most participants

---

[52] Tao Xisheng 1944: 28, 195; 1933: 7–8, 26. The historian Zhou Gucheng experimented with a similar application of feudalism to the Chinese pre-modern in a book he published in 1930, in which he argued that China in the Zhou dynasty was purely feudal, followed by two millennia of monarchy when "feudal forces" continued to influence Chinese society. This long imperial phase he regarded as the period of feudalism's gradual dissolution (Zhou Gucheng 1935: 31–46). In his comprehensive textbook published nine years later, Zhou laid more emphasis on the development of private landholding in accounting for changes in political form in the Zhou. Feudalism only began to wane in the Song dynasty, timing closely with the onset of Naitō's "modern age" (Zhou 1940: 145, 289).

[53] Lü Zhenyu 1943: 29–30.

[54] Moritani Katsumi's *Shina shakai keizai shi* was published in Tokyo in 1934 and appeared in two Chinese translations in 1936. The revised edition by Wang Yudun has been consulted here.

worked from the assumption that imperial China had been in some economic sense feudal, and that the feudal backwardness had lingered on to threaten the development of Chinese society.[55] Although some preferred other labels, such as "despotic," for the long stretch from Qin to Qing, almost every discussant treated this vast expanse of time as a single historical epoch. By a process of negative logic, the absence of major alteration in the structure of power was taken to indicate a static social constitution. This willingness to think of the circular ebb and flow of the imperial dynasties as only superficial sound and fury meant that historians were still captive to the imperial model, one that, paradoxically, harmonized with Marx's assumption that Asia was a stagnant society.[56]

Equating feudalism with the imperial period generated the further question of how to characterize China before feudalism during the original pre-Qin *fengjian* era. The European model provided the category of slave society. Guo Moruo was the first Chinese scholar to apply the Marxist concept of a slave mode of production to China and to argue that China moved from slavery to feudalism in the Spring and Autumn period.[57] The interpretation was controversial outside and inside Marxist circles. Some initally disagreed that China had experienced slavery,[58] though the debate quickly shifted from slavery's existence to its dating.[59] Lü Zhenyu argued for an earlier beginning in the

[55] The periodization disputes are reviewed in Lin Ganquan *et al.* 1982; Ye Guisheng and Liu Maolin 1983; see also Dirlik 1978: 99–102, 187–90. The despotism label was applied by Wang Lixi and Hu Qiuyuan.

[56] On Marx's reading of China, see above pp. 93–5 and Lowe 1966: 1–29.

[57] Guo argued in his 1930 book that the transition between slavery and feudalism had come about in the Spring and Autumn period as a result of the diffusion of iron technology, which led to an upsurge in the means of production. To support his assertion, Guo engaged in close textual study of references to humans in bronze inscriptions and ancient classics like the *Book of Changes*. Both sources, he argued, provided evidence of the widespread existence of slavery in the Western Zhou (Guo 1955: 11–16, 267–69, 281–82).

[58] In the same year Guo's book appeared, Zhou Gucheng in his *Zhongguo shehui zhi jiegou* (The structure of Chinese society) (Zhou 1935) adapted the ideas of Marx and Engels to Chinese history without positing a slave period. Zhou argued that classes and the state developed slowly during the long tribal phase before the Zhou dynasty, leading directly to the emergence of feudal society at the beginning of the Zhou. The formation of ethnic identity, the growth of population, the improvement of tools, and the expansion of surplus product led to this transformation of tribal society into feudal (Zhou Gucheng 1935: 19–28). Japanese historians, like Moritani Katsumi, were similarly skeptical of the claim, postulating instead, as did Zhou Gucheng, a direct transition from tribalism to feudalism (Moritani 1936: 19–21). The first thorough critical examination of the textual basis for the claim of Zhou slavery is Pulleyblank 1958, an essay written in response to the Chinese Marxist search for a slave period.

[59] Wang Yichang, for example, argued that the transition from slavery to feudalism did not occur until 317, when the Eastern Jin dynasty replaced the Western Jin. Wang was a member of the China Economy school, named after the journal, *Zhongguo jingji*, that

Shang dynasty, and a consensus gradually emerged combining the Guo and Lü positions.[60] Before the debate about the dating of the slave period could get to more difficult questions, it was cut short by the Japanese invasion in 1937, leaving a periodization of the pre-modern that Arif Dirlik has called a "consensus by default."[61]

Weberian influences: Asiaticism

East Asian Marxists in the 1920s and 1930s had little of Marx to consult, and so drew much of their theoretical framework for a Marxist analysis of Chinese society from interpretations within Soviet circles. The Chinese in particular were unaware of the extent to which Soviet Marxism had been influenced by the work of Max Weber and his students, as that influence had been energetically repudiated in the 1920s before they could have become aware of it. But an unrecognized Weberian strain runs through Chinese Marxist historiography. Although it requires some digression away from the work of Chinese scholars, the topic deserves our attention in the light of the role that Weberian scholarship would play in elaborating hypotheses connected with Marx's notion of an Asiatic mode of production, a notion that, though dead-ended early on, has kept resurfacing in Chinese and Japanese historiography.

Like Marx, Weber was motivated in his research by the desire to understand how capitalism had come about, and only in Europe. In pursuit of this question, he undertook sociological investigations of the pre-modern history not just of Europe, but of major cultures throughout

represented its views. The school advocated a more restricted concept of feudalism, arguing that China was fully capitalist in the twentieth century and no longer semifeudal or under feudal influence (He Ganzhi 1939: 123). Lü Zhenyu, on the other hand, insisted that slave society be pushed back, not brought forward. He posited that China's slave society, which remained relatively underdeveloped, existed in the latter half of the Shang dynasty, and was already being replaced by feudalism at the beginning of the Western Zhou. Chinese feudal society in turn was not fully developed until the end of the Western Zhou, making that period a long transition from slavery to feudalism (1943: 22, 28).

[60] Guo Moruo concedes this dating in the postscript to the 1947 edition of his book (1955: 344). During the Yan'an period, Yin Da sought to restore Guo's original dating of the onset of the slave period to the end of the Shang on the strength of archeological fieldwork he had done at Yangshao sites in the 1930s; Lin Ganquan and Ye Guisheng 1985: 1652–53.

[61] Dirlik 1978: 229. After 1937, Deng Chumin, Fan Wenlan, and Jian Bozan all adapted the combined Guo/Lü dating of slavery and feudalism in their textbooks. Tao Xisheng took a different position in *Zhongguo shehui shi* (A history of Chinese society): he acknowledged that the "primitive feudal" period of the Eastern Zhou included the operation of a slave economy, but argued that slavery, rather than feudalism, followed in the Qin dynasty, and that feudalism did not arise until the Han-Tang interregnum (Tao 1944).

the world, including China.[62] Unlike Marx, who focused his attention
on differences in economic relations in Europe compared with elsewhere, Weber trained his attention on pre-modern political and cultural
structures. Weber contrasted the emergence of the "aristocratic city
state" in Rome with what he called the "bureaucratic city kingdom" of
the Near East. In the latter he found an administrative rationality that
challenged the conventional wisdom that such rationality was the
unique attribute of modern Europe – which had after all emerged not
from feudal kingdoms in which bureaucracy had been important, but
from underbureaucratized city states.[63]

In later work on China, Weber found bureaucratic rationality even
further developed there. He looked for a reason for this development
and, following Marx, who had in turn simply echoed his predecessors,
found it in water. Weber attributed the origin of the Chinese bureaucracy to the state's need to manage complex engineering projects to
control water. But why, he was forced to ask, had China created a
reasonably rational bureaucracy that had not ushered in economic
rationality's highest expression, capitalism? He hypothesized that the
political system was responsible for this. The feudal state in Europe
blocked merchants from getting into office, and so they directed their
wealth to bourgeois uses, establishing their independence as a class. The
bureaucratic state in China, on the other hand, tolerated social mobility
and the acquisition of wealth to a degree that prevented independent
economic and social power from turning to activities outside the ruler's
purview. Thus, while the late-feudal aristocracy and the new bourgeoisie
in Europe struggled against each other for supremacy, the Chinese state
prevented the autonomy of either group.[64] The Chinese pre-modern
thus provided an important contrasting case in Weber's larger study of
the rule of bureaucracy, a question he raised to the level of universal
history.[65]

Weber's analysis of the impact of bureaucratic administration on
Chinese society did much to draw European attention to this aspect of
Chinese civilization. Soviet scholars in the years immediately following
Weber's death took up this characterization. Nikolai Bukharin in 1921
drew on Weber's *Gesammelte Aufsätze zur Religionsphilosophie* to describe
ancient China as "a peculiarly constructed feudal state authority" ruled

[62] Weber's work on China, which appears in most concentrated form in his *Religion of
China* (1951), was intended to establish negative verification of the uniqueness of
European capitalism as described in his most widely known book, *The Protestant Ethic
and the Spirit of Capitalism* (1958). His influence on Western sinology is sketched in
Brook 1993: 6–13.
[63] Weber 1976: 74.   [64] Weber 1984: 1102, 1107.   [65] Mommsen 1984: 166.

by a "feudal-bureaucratic stratum."[66] Bukharin accepted the Marxist assumption that pre-capitalism meant feudalism, but he chose to qualify China's feudal identity with the concept of bureaucratism, following Weber. In 1925, Jenö Varga (1879–1964), a Hungarian Marxist who served as a member of Josef Stalin's personal secretariat, further enlarged Weber's indirect influence within Soviet circles by citing him as his major source to argue that state power arose in China not out of the class struggle, but from the imperative for building large irrigation works (though Marx himself had made the same point). The state that resulted was not feudal.[67] As Bukharin's authority came under challenge within Soviet Marxist circles, so too did the authority of Weber's ideas. Among the critics, Karl Radek in 1927 published an essay against the "hydraulic" theory of Chinese society, vigorously opposing the idea that the need for flood-control on a vast scale impelled the early emergence of a bureaucratic state that came to dominate and stifle China's development.[68] Radek, like Varga, singled out Weber as the author of this view, though by tarring Weber he was clearly intent on obscuring Marx's association with the hydraulic interpretation.

The most creative elaboration of Weber's insights within a Marxist framework came from the Hungarian activist and intellectual Lajos Milgorf (1891–1938), best known by his alias, Liudvig Mad'iar.[69] Mad'iar worked in China in 1926–27 for the Communist International and in the year following his return to Comintern headquarters in Moscow published one of the first major sociological studies of the Chinese economy. He did not accept the formalistic equivalence of China's and Europe's societies as feudal but stressed the considerable differences in their political and social organization. In this study, which became widely influential in China through its 1930 translation, Mad'iar formally analyzed China in Marxist terms, but the Weberian influences are striking. Together, Weber and Marx led Mad'iar to identify Chinese society as "feudal bureaucratism."[70]

The Weberian influence on early self-styled Marxist analyses of China

---

66 Bukharin 1925: 159.
67 Sawer 1977: 81. Varga Russianized his first name as Yevgeni in his Russian publications. See above, p. 101.
68 Barber 1981: 51–53; see also chapter 3, pp. 101–102.
69 Mad'iar 1930c: 87. Sawer 1977: 88 argues that Mad'iar over time became less Weberian in his analysis, eventually preferring Marx's village-based model of Asian society to Weber's kinship-based model. Elements in Mad'iar's later analysis, however, continue to betray Weberian influences. A clear example is his contrast in the role of cities in Europe and China, formulated in his second book, which was published in Russian in 1930 and in Chinese in 1933; Mad'iar 1933: 381–84.
70 In Western sinology, the analysis of China in terms of "feudal bureaucratism" has been continued by Joseph Needham, e.g., Needham 1969: 150, 193; see also Brook 1996.

is visible as well in the work of Mad'iar's better-known contemporary, Karl Wittfogel. Obscuring the extent of his debt by criticizing Weber in the 1920s as an epistemological nihilist,[71] Wittfogel nonetheless chose to entitle his 1931 study of Chinese society *Wirtschaft und Gesellschaft Chinas*, echoing the title of Weber's great work, *Wirtschaft und Gesellschaft*. Wittfogel insisted in the introduction that the title was intended to mirror the Marxist conception of economic structure, "economy" corresponding to means of production and "society" to relations of production. He makes no mention of Weber in the book, except to cite some "methodological errors."[72] Yet as Wittfogel's biographer has pointed out, his concern with pre-capitalist political power and bureaucracy – elements that did not greatly attract Marx's attention – came directly from Weber. The theoretical significance of Wittfogel's work was in combining Marx's concern with class relations and Weber's with power into a unified sociology.[73] And it is to Weber that Wittfogel owes both his dominant question – why did industrial capitalism not emerge independently in China? – and his overriding preoccupation with bureaucratism as a negative force (a preoccupation that would eventually lead him to become a crusader against state socialism in the 1950s, and a more sympathetic reader of Weber).

Weber understood bureaucratism in the context of the rationalizing influence of capitalist management, but he also regarded it as a threat to individual freedom under advanced capitalism. These ideas were not directly available to Chinese scholars in the 1930s, although fragments were available through the writings of Bukharin, Mad'iar, and Wittfogel, among others.[74] The first attempt to bring together something like a Weberian critique of bureaucratism with a historical analysis of the role of bureaucracy in imperial China was a book of essays on Chinese bureaucratism published in 1948 by Wang Yanan (1901–69). Wang wrote it at the suggestion of his friend, Joseph Needham, who also approached China from a Weberian–Marxist position.[75] Wang knew

---

[71] Weiss 1986: 19 (also 97, 165–66).

[72] E.g., Wittfogel 1931: 101, 396, 495. Wittfogel met Mad'iar in Frankfurt in July 1929 at the Second Congress of the League Against Imperialism; Ulmen 1978: 105.

[73] Ulmen 1978: 38, 108.

[74] Wang Lixi and Hu Qiuyuan mention Weber in essays published in 1932, but do so only because they are repeating comments made by S. M. Dubrovskii in his 1929 critique of the concept of the Asiatic mode of production; Dirlik 1978: 207. They had no independent access to Weber's work. In Japan, Hani Gorō drew on Weberian elements in the Asiatic concept for his analysis of Japanese capitalism, though he did so again at second-hand via Weber's Soviet critics; Hoston 1986: 176.

[75] Wang Yanan 1981: 14. Needham was introduced to Wang by Wu Dakun, who became a visible proponent of the Asiatic mode of production; Needham and Needham 1948: 224.

nothing about Weber, but he was familiar with Mad'iar and Wittfogel and could draw on their work for the Weberian concerns that drove his study. The uneasy linking of Weberian with Marxist insights did not produce a creative breakthrough, however. Wang's theoretical solution to the problem of bureaucratic influence in Chinese history was to subordinate Weberian insights to the Marxist model and conclude that bureaucracy was simply a particular political form of Chinese feudalism, its rationality contributing to feudalism's excessively long survival in China.[76]

Questioning bureaucracy was not the task on which the Weberian influence exerted itself most strongly. It was, rather, reviving and giving substance to the awkward topic of the Asiatic mode of production. The Asiatic mode was not a Weberian concept. It comes from Marx, listed in *A Contribution to the Critique of Political Economy* among the "epochs marking progress in the economic development of society." The concept became awkward in part because Marx never properly defined it; in part because Soviet Marxism in the early 1930s banned it from their model of historical development; and in part because its relationship with capitalism was ambiguous.

Marx's ideas on the Asiatic mode may best be gleaned from comments on Asiatic forms of property in the *Grundrisse*, and various descriptive accounts of Asia elsewhere in his writings. Seven main features of this model of pre-modern society have been distinguished:[77] Asiatic society is not marked by a division of labor between agriculture and handicraft production, their unity being due to the virtual absence of commerce. Water is the key resource for agriculture and is distributed through large irrigation projects that require a strong state. The basic unit of Asiatic society, the village community, is not internally divided by class exploitation. Land is owned communally, though the state enjoys formal ownership in the absence of private property. Exploitation nonetheless occurs in Asiatic society, not between property-based classes but between the village members and a parasitic class that serves the state. The form it takes is tax rather than rent, unlike feudal society. Finally, despite violent dynastic overthrows at the political level, Asiatic society undergoes no significant change at its base; in historical terms it has no necessary preceding stage and it never progresses beyond itself. As such, it is outside the history of capitalism. It may have been Asia's apparent

[76] Wang Yanan 1981: 318. In the 1950s and 1960s, Chinese scholars outside China like C. K. Yang and Chung-li Chang used Weber's insights on the bureaucratic organization of Chinese society in path-breaking studies on mobility, social control, and the gentry. Only late in the 1980s did scholars in China begin to consider Weberian methodology.

[77] Brook 1989: 10–11, drawing on the analysis of Wang Dunshu and Yu Ke.

exceptionalism to the European notion of forward motion, where people appeared to pursue what Marx called an "undignified, stagnatory, and vegetative life,"[78] that prompted him to shape this vague formulation of a type of society not reducible to capitalist Europe's prehistory.

The Chinese Communist Party briefly considered employing the Asiatic mode of production in 1927 to formulate an analysis of the problems facing China's modern transformation, only to reject it at the Sixth Party Congress the following year on the grounds that it implied an absence of private property in contemporary China, a position in conflict with the policy of struggling against landlords. But the topic attracted the attention of scholars. The journal *Xin shengming* (New life) in August 1929 carried essays on the concept by Wittfogel and Mad'iar. Both characterized imperial China as Asiatic. Wittfogel dated the beginning of the Asiatic period to political centralization under the Qin, which is when he felt feudalism ended. Mad'iar dated Asiatic society back to the Spring and Autumn period, when it superseded the system of clan patriarchy. In his first book, translated into Chinese the following year, Mad'iar expanded his theory of Asiatic constraints on China's development, drawing on the insights of both Marx and Weber. His interpretation found little support within Soviet Marxist circles. Following the Leningrad conference in 1931, from which Wittfogel and Mad'iar were excluded, the Asiatic mode of production was repudiated.[79] The Chinese pre-modern could be slave and feudal, but not Asiatic. Asiaticism was incompatible with capitalism, and hence with a Marxist revolution.

The Asiatic mode of production nonetheless continued to excite interest among Chinese and Japanese historians. The German-trained socialist Li Ji (not the prominent archaeologist of the same name) was among the most enthusiastic. He regarded the Asiatic mode as a theoretically coherent concept and applied it to Chinese society prior to the Zhou dynasty; after unification, China entered a long transitional phase he called "pre-capitalist."[80] Most scholars preferred to deal with the Asiatic concept by equating it with one of the standard five stages.

---

[78] Marx 1972: 41.

[79] Refer to the preceding chapter for an account of the Leningrad conference. In Mad'iar's second book, published in Russian in 1930, in Chinese in 1933, and in Japanese in 1936, he distances his analysis from the Asiatic mode, calling China simply "pre-capitalist." Mad'iar was arrested in 1934 and executed in 1938. His only work to appear in English is a partial translation of his introduction to a 1930 study of the *jingtian* (well-field) system published by M. Kokin and G. Papayan, portions of which are included in Bailey and Llobera 1981: 76–94. A full Japanese translation appeared in 1934 in *Mantetsu chōsa geppō* (South Manchurian Railway research monthly) 14: 2–3.

[80] Li Ji 1936: 22.

Guo Moruo wrote in 1929 that "what Marx means by Asiatic society is the primitive communal society of ancient times,"[81] although this interpretation, as contemporaries pointed out, neglected the role Marx attributed to the state in Asiatic society.[82] A second interpretation, proposed in the Soviet Union by Sergei Kovalev and echoed by Lü Zhenyu, regarded Asiatic society as an Asian version of slavery. This reduction became popular among orthodox Marxists.[83] The notion that Asiatic society was simply a local variant of the universal category of slave society, rather than being a category apart, preserved Soviet orthodoxy.

Japanese Marxists remained more sympathetic, possibly because the notion of a stagnant Asiatic China conformed to certain condescensions in Oriental History. Asiaticism, after all, was a civilizational state from which contemporary Japan had excluded itself: the pre-modern that China was still embroiled in but which Japan had transcended to achieve modernity.[84] Hayakawa Jirō, who sponsored a complete Japanese translation of the Leningrad papers in 1933, did not directly embrace the Asiatic mode but thought that a class system similar to the Asiatic mode of production, which he called a "tributary system," appeared in Japan at its point of transition out of primitive communalism. Japan did not proceed directly from primitive society to a slave society of the Greek or Roman sort but evolved into a tributary state system that incorporated aspects of slavery without maturing into a fully developed slave society. The tributary phase had enabled Japan to leap over mature slavery and proceed directly to feudalism.[85] Others found this association between the Asiatic model and Japanese history uncomfortable, though not so between the Asiatic model and China. Hirano Yoshitarō (1897–1980) in an essay published in 1934 disagreed that Japan had ever gone through an Asiatic phase but allowed for China an Asiatic character that prevented it from developing proper feudalism.[86] Akizawa Shōji went further in his *Shina shakai kōsei* (The formation of Chinese society) of 1938 to declare that China was a classic Asiatic society, which gave modern Japan the historic role of overcoming a pre-modern stagnation

[81] Guo Moruo 1930: 165.
[82] E.g., Lü Zhenyu 1954: 35.
[83] Deng Chumin used slavery to rebut those who favored an Asiatic interpretation for China. In his 1942 textbook on Chinese history, he reviewed the characteristics associated with Asiatic society – means of production in the hands of the state, large-scale hydraulic engineering, stagnant village communities, despotism, and non-differentiation of rent and tax – and concluded that these were the main components of Chinese slave society (Deng Chumin 1942: 78).
[84] Tanaka 1994: 38.
[85] Fogel 1988: 71; Hoston 1986: 152–60.
[86] Tanaka 1993: 253–56.

that China on its own could not escape.[87] Such formulations convinced most Chinese intellectuals that an Asiatic interpretation was a sentence of exile from world history.

Embedding capitalism in the Chinese pre-modern

The inability of Asiaticism to generate capitalism – confining Asia to a state of permanent pre-modernity – prejudiced most Asian intellectuals against the concept in any case. Feudalism was much preferred because it implied a necessary relationship between China and capitalism. As what was presented in China under this category had the capacity to look unlike anything feudal found in Europe, notions associated with the Asiatic model had got attached to Chinese feudalism to account for its differences from the West.[88] In the post-war era, however, most Chinese and Japanese historians preferred not only to eschew quasi-Asiatic reshapings of Chinese feudalism, but to assert with full confidence that China's history ran steadily along the stadial tracks laid down by Marx via Stalin, tracks that ran across capitalist terrain from feudalism to socialism. In China, the Guo Moruo/Lü Zhenyu model remained intact after the founding of the People's Republic in 1949.[89] What was open to debate was not the periodization scheme itself, nor the analysis of the Chinese pre-modern that underlay it, but the details:

---

[87] Akizawa was severely criticized for his view by Lü Zhenyu (1954). Regarding Akizawa's formulation in 1935 of a transitional community-based Asiatic phase in Japanese history, see Fogel 1988: 73. Controversies in Japan between feudal and Asiatic interpretations of China faded out during the war, although wartime studies of China often mention Wittfogel as a negative example of how to analyze Chinese society, though the denunciations often have an ambivalent ring. For example, Tokyo's Tōa kenkyūjo (East Asia Institute) in 1939 compiled an entire collection of essays by its members for internal circulation devoted to denying Wittfogel's "materialist" analysis of Chinese society, notably his reliance on geographical factors; yet the contributors repeat many classic Asiatic formulations, such as that state and society in China are not integrally linked, and that Chinese society has no classes but is composed of kin collectivities. Tōa kenkyūjo 1939: 2, 33–35, 46–50, 112–14; for critiques of Mad'iar and Godes see 119, 122.

[88] Moritani Katsumi, for instance, allowed the concept of feudalism for imperial China, but he emphasized the prolonged stagnation of Chinese society and freely borrowed the Asiatic (and Weberian) notion that this stagnation arose because a superstructure of bureaucratic centralization overlay a hydraulic society. He even went so far as to identify large-scale waterworks as the material base of feudalism in China, a view that would have baffled both Marx and Weber (Moritani 1936: 25). Regarding Moritani's views on the Asiatic mode, see Hoston 1986: 148–50.

[89] When Jian Bozan was invited to address Japanese colleagues in Toyko in 1955, he indicated that Chinese historians continued to debate minor aspects of the Guo/Lü periodization, but he located these debates securely within a shared commitment to "the objective laws of the historical process" (Jian Bozan 1957: 61).

the dissolution of slave society leading up to feudalism,[90] the nature of feudal landownership,[91] and the role of peasant rebellions as a dynamic element in Chinese feudalism[92] were three topics open for discussion. These discussions constituted, as Joseph Levenson noted:[93]

a refreshment, not a threat, to Marxism as "grand theory." ... Intellectuals were allowed "freedom" within the maze. They should never emerge, but they could roam, in tonic exercise. It was hardly serious but a kind of sport, vital in the constraining Marxist framework. But if flexible boundaries of historical periods helped make Marxism viable in China, the rigorous order of periods ("Oriental despotism," a disturbing joker, omitted) gave Marxism much of its explicitly Chinese appeal.

"Oriental despotism" was not entirely omitted from discussion. The joker appeared in the form of two dozen essays on the Asiatic mode published between 1951 and 1964, but it was dismissed as a misconceptualization. The only point of controversy was which period the Asiatic mode restated, primitive society or slave society, rather than what alternative it might pose to feudalism.[94] Political economist Wu Dakun was prominent in the 1950s in arguing that the Asiatic mode represented Asian slavery. When genuine historiographical debate recommenced in 1978, the Asiatic mode was at the top of the list and Wu Dakun led the way in arguing for an expanded concept of the Asiatic mode to account for the obstacles in the way of China's modernization program, such as despotism and bureaucratism.[95] Asiaticism provided a relatively "safe" platform from which to argue that modernity was still compromised by the pre-modern, that the pre-modern had not yet been

---

[90] The debate revolved around whether the Han dynasty was a slave society: Jian Bozan (1954) opposed the idea while Wang Sizhi *et al.* (1954) and Wang Zhongluo (1957) supported it. Wang defended Han slavery on the grounds that, as he quotes Marx, "the class struggles of the ancient world took the form chiefly of a contest between debtors and creditors" (Marx 1975, vol. I: 135). The only attempt to question the existence of a slave period was the prominent 1950s historian Tong Shuye, who argued for a direct transition from primitive to feudal society in the late Shang dynasty; see Lin Ganquan *et al.* 1982: 216–17.

[91] Hou Wailu (1955) regarded feudal state landownership as the highest expression of state sovereignty, effectively precluding the possibility of real private property in land. He Changqun (1964) preferred to think of it as simply a form of feudal landownership by which the state appeared as one landowner among many, with no implications as to the character of its ultimate rights over land. This debate is studied in Caprasse 1975.

[92] The key question was whether peasant rebellions were anti-feudal: that is, whether they manifested the basic underlying contradiction between landlord and peasant, or whether they were directed against not the landlords but the state and its oppressive systems, including taxation. This debate is reviewed in Rong Sheng 1979; see also Harrison 1969.

[93] Levenson 1968, vol. III: 50.

[94] For a review of some aspects of the debate, see Tian Changwu 1989; Tian Renlong 1981: 147–50.

[95] Wu Dakun 1989: 43–45.

transcended. By indirection, it offered a theoretical explanation as to why "feudal" China had not become capitalist.[96]

Whereas the Revolution in 1949 brought the Guo/Lü model to the status of orthodoxy in China, in Japan it discredited pre-war sinology. In his study of Takeuchi Yoshimi (1910–77), a prominent post-war essayist and commentator on modern Chinese history, Lawrence Olson has described this impact by observing, "Where many scholars in the older tradition had approached China convinced of the superiority of Western civilization and its rule of reason, in the post-war era fewer had confidence in a standardized model of the West as the non-West's universal goal; many were reluctant to look for Asia's future in the West's past." Takeuchi was among those who regarded China as a new civilization qualitatively different from both Japan and the West, a position that "implied a criticism of the whole idea of modernization conceived primarily as a quantifiable process through which all societies undertaking it perforce must pass."[97]

The academic world of post-war China studies, particularly the Tokyo school, was dominated by Marxists critical both of the imperialistic assumptions of pre-war Oriental History as well as of Western models of modernization. They abandoned what they regarded as the imperialist presumptions of the Kyoto school of Naito Konan and moved closer to the Chinese model of feudalism. Yet the two Marxist historiographies still did not converge, for the Japanese came to the conclusion that feudalism began in China not with early centralization, but in the Tang-Song transition in the tenth century, a dating that kept alive in altered form Naito's "modern age." What had been for Naito the point of passage from medievality to Asian modernity became, in the post-war period, the transition from ancient slavery (*kodai doreisei*) to medieval feudalism (*chūsei hōkensei*).[98] Thus both Japanese and Chinese detected feudalism

---

[96] For some of the theoretical difficulties of formulating an Asiatic mode of production, see Hindess and Hirst 1975: chapter 4; also Krader 1975. Some scholars have sought to replace the Asiatic with a tributary mode of production, in which the state exacts tribute from the agricultural communities under its control and maintains a ruling class through this form of surplus extraction; e.g., Amin 1976. Hayakawa Jirō and He Ganzhi experimented with the notion of a tributary state in the 1930s. Fragments of this idea can be found in Marx's writings on late medieval Eastern Europe, particularly Romania; e.g., Marx 1975, vol. I, 227. Wickham 1984 has developed the concept in relation to an analysis of the ancient Mediterranean world, which he sees as a subtype of tributary society in which the slave mode interacted with the tributary mode. In 1980, Zhou Gucheng proposed a similar interpretation in an essay tracing the evolution of the ancient empires of Greece, China, Egypt, and Persia, though he cleaved to safe ground by using the term "ancient feudalism."

[97] Olson 1992: 45.

[98] This feudalism, based on serfdom, constituted its own unique "type," of which Japanese and European feudalisms were other "types"; Niida Noboru 1981: 98–100.

in the Chinese pre-modern but did so in the context of fundamentally disagreeing over the long-term trajectory of historical change in China.

An interest that post-war Chinese and Japanese Marxists held in common was the role of commerce within Chinese feudalism, although here too their interpretations diverged. The European model of capitalism recognized commerce as a contributor to the transition from feudalism to capitalism. Merchants engaged in trade and accumulation at the margins of the pre-capitalist social order were seen to have developed capitalist practices that undercut feudalism once its hegemony came under attack from other quarters. Chinese and Japanese historians in the 1950s began to focus their research on commercial development in certain periods when commerce was widespread, notably the late Song, the late Ming, and the Qing dynasties. They appealed to scattered references in Marx's writings concerning changes in commercial and industrial organization in Europe in defense of the concept, and identified similar phenomena in the Chinese record, which they called "sprouts of capitalism" (*zibenzhuyi mengya*).[99] These signs of capitalistic developments were taken to confirm that protocapitalist elements had existed within Chinese feudalism. Even though Chinese feudalism did not generate an indigenous capitalism, the sprouts discussion bolstered the assertion that China was on the track toward capitalism, and elided the historical non-formation of capitalism in Chinese history. The absence of capitalism was now turned to symbolize its potential presence.

The argument was not new. Tao Xisheng had pointed out as early as the 1920s that commercial capital had the potential to undermine a parcelized feudal structure. He argued that it would not automatically replace it with capitalism, for commercial capital could exist in harmony with the feudal economy so long as there were adequate opportunities for profit through usury and speculation.[100] The Communist Party

---

Chinese historians have tended to see serfdom as one form of feudal labor relations; see, e.g., Wang Yanan 1981: 5.

[99] The Chinese literature on the sprouts of capitalism was collected into two volumes entitled *Zhongguo zibenzhuyi mengya taolun ji* (Essays on the debate on the sprouts of capitalism in China) published in 1957 and 1960. The sprouts debate has been reviewed, with unnecessary scorn, in Feuerwerker 1958 and 1968; far more interesting are the commentaries by Nishijima Sadao 1957, and Tanaka Masatoshi 1957. Aspects of the sprouts analysis are touched on in Brook 1981: 178–81.

[100] Tao Xisheng 1944: 212–15. For a similar argument regarding the role of commerce in feudal Europe, see Dobb 1946: 38–42. Dobb uses the term "adolescent capitalism" for Europe's transitional phase in the fourteenth century between the decline of feudalism and the rise of capitalism, without assuming, however, that the economic forms of the fourteenth century had to lead necessarily to full capitalism.

preferred to emphasize the revolutionary potential of commercial capital. This idea is outlined in a textbook entitled *The Chinese Revolution and the Chinese Communist Party*, which was written in Yanan in the winter of 1939 under Mao's editorial scrutiny. The textbook asserted that "China's feudal society had developed a commodity economy, and so carried within itself the seeds of capitalism." From this was drawn the conclusion that "China would of herself have developed slowly into a capitalist society even without the impact of foreign capitalism."[101] The sprouts discussion of the 1950s was thus pursued to demonstrate the plausibility of this hypothesis. Scholars like Shang Yue were confident that the sprouts of capitalism developed in the Ming-Qing period to such a degree that a proto-bourgeoisie was emerging and engaging in the primitive accumulation of capital that would have led in time to capitalism. But not everyone was blithe about capitalism's prospects in the Chinese socio-economy. Wu Dakun argued that the sprouts were too weak to exercise any influence against the entrenched feudal economy and the control of the feudal state.[102] Wang Yanan, writing in 1957, expanded this idea to suggest that the early sprouts of capitalism in the Tang and Song encouraged the formation of close ties between merchants and the landlord elite, creating a relationship that neutralized the mutual antagonism that in Europe had impelled merchants to challenge the feudal order.[103] Fu Yiling, who produced the finest empirical work during the sprouts controversy, eventually concluded that the integration of agriculture and handicraft industry strengthened the natural economy and thus posed a barrier to the full development of a commodity economy, short of which the emergence of capitalism was unlikely.[104]

Tokyo school historians in Japan pursued parallel research on this question during the same decade, producing some of the best post-war scholarship on China.[105] But it led them toward a different conclusion. They accepted the Chinese hypothesis that the appearance of incipient capitalistic elements in the feudal economy marked the beginning of a major structural shift in Chinese society, yet they were dubious about the ultimate direction of that shift, pointing out that a feudal social formation was capable of absorbing a high degree of both urban and

[101] Mao Zedong 1965, vol. II, 305, 309.
[102] This view of the weakness of the commercial economy was first argued in 1937 in Deng Tuo 1979: 148–66. I am grateful to Timothy Cheek for this reference.
[103] Wang Yanan 1957: 7.
[104] Fu's interpretation became standard in the early 1980s, when he continued to publish on the topic; see, e.g., Fu 1982.
[105] For a brief review of Japanese studies relating to the sprouts of capitalism, see Yamane 1980: 115–18.

rural commercialization without compromising the dominance of the feudal mode of production. Opinions were divided between those such as Nishijima Sadao who doubted that indigenous capitalism could arise from commercialized industries in a feudal setting, and those such as Tanaka Masatoshi who allowed the possibility of a transition, however gradual, from feudal to capitalist relations of production in the country-side once the rural labor force had begun the process of internal differentiation. This differentiation might proceed in an extremely gradual and heterogeneous fashion, producing not just the wealthy kulak and the landless laborer but a range of strata. Once the process had begun, enabling some peasants to exploit the labor of others in a systematic way, at least one of the important preconditions for the rise of capitalism would have been in place.

But this was all in theory, inasmuch as a capitalist transformation (at least in the terms defined by the European experience) never took place. Accordingly, in the opinion of the late-Ming historian Mori Masao, Japanese research on the sprouts of capitalism "failed to produce satisfactory theoretical results, though it uncovered a wealth of historical facts which had hitherto been unknown."[106] The effect of this stalemate was to induce Japanese historians in the 1970s to expand their research interests away from commercialization to basic structures of Chinese society that might have inhibited the kinds of social changes that the sprouts theory anticipated, particularly the structure of gentry control in the local setting and the role of the state. A Weberian orientation quietly overtook the Marxist focus of the earlier generation as younger scholars abandoned the search for an indigenous Chinese relationship to capitalism.

Mori's summation could be applied even more surely to the work of Chinese historians between 1949 and 1979: three decades of writing that produced few satisfactory theoretical results. It is too difficult yet to judge whether Chinese historiography since 1979 has made greater strides in developing appropriate social theory for China. But certainly the old historiography has been eroded in the cultural environment created by the country's expanded participation in the capitalist world system, giving way to new theoretical initiatives. One of these initiatives involved revalorizing capitalism and China's incorporation into the European-capitalist world-system, such as praising nineteenth-century compradores as heralds of China's "modernization" instead of "running dogs" of foreign imperialism. The sprouts of capitalism proved accordingly to be a resilient historical topic in the 1980s, as capitalist practices

[106] Mori 1980: 32.

were being introduced into China and reevaluated for what they could contribute to China's economic development.[107] Puzzlement over the failure of feudalism to lead to capitalism led to a broader discussion through the 1980s on the factors causing the "underdevelopment" of Chinese feudalism and the "prolongation" of the feudal period.[108] Various contradictory qualifiers were attached to Chinese feudalism to make it work – "transformed," "deformed," "ancient," "incomplete," "mature" – though the instability of these attributions signalled the difficulty of continuing to conceive China in terms of European models.[109]

The most aggressive reconceptualization of the history of capitalist elements in China came not from within the ranks of historians in China, but from the Chinese–American scholars Yü Ying-shih and Tu Wei-ming. At the heart of their concerns was the reevaluation of Confucianism, an important component of which was "vulgar" Confucianism, meaning the assemblage of values and habits in popular Chinese culture that ordinary people considered "Confucian." Beginning in 1984, Yü Ying-shih produced a series of publications examining the work ethic and moral attitudes expressed in the writings of merchants. His purpose was to take the conundrum of the non-development of capitalism that Soviet Marxist theory had bequeathed to Chinese social theory and rework it from a Weberian perspective. Yü based his

[107] For example, Liu Yongcheng (1979, 1982) shifted discussion from commodity production to hired labor, as some Japanese scholars had done, arguing that the differentiation of the peasants into wealthy and landless – a process well advanced by the mid-Qing – signalled that Chinese feudalism was in its last stage when Western imperialism arrived. New empirical work on the emergence of hired rural labor under wealthy peasant management from the mid-Ming forward appeared to support his argument (Li Wenzhi et al. 1983). On the other hand, Fu Yiling (1982) argued that Chinese feudalism prior to the Opium War was not in serious decline. The Qing commodity economy had not developed to the point of breaking the dominance of the natural economy in the countryside; merchants and producers were hampered by guild and clan organizations; and landlords were exhibiting even more control over rural labor processes than they had before the Qing. Fu Zhufu (1980, 1983) went further in expressing caution on this issue, arguing that the presence of sprouts in feudal society is no guarantee that capitalism will emerge.

[108] In a book-length study of the historical background to the concept of the prolonged feudalism, Bai Gang (1984) traces the origin of the question to Adam Smith's characterization of Chinese society. Regarding attempts to identify "special characteristics" that led in China to "deformed" or "underdeveloped feudalism," see Fu Zhufu 1980; Zhao Lisheng 1984; Wang Zhongluo 1985.

[109] As post-Mao historiography began to develop, some historians felt themselves freed from the burden of comparative analysis. Pang Zhuoheng (1981: 144) even asserted categorically that "the historical world in China has never accepted European models." Pang made this comment parenthetical to a critique of Marc Bloch's method of comparative history and the use of such comparisons by Soviet historians. It says far more about where he hoped history in China would go than where it had been.

approach on Weber's assertion that the emergence of capitalism in Europe be understood as a question not "of the origin of capital sums which were available for capitalistic uses, but, above all, of the development of the spirit of capitalism."[110] Yü applied this spirit-of-capitalism logic to Ming-Qing China, where he found that Chinese merchants in their writings invoked the core values ("spirit") of Confucianism to justify profitable commercial activity and to discipline themselves and their heirs to accumulate wealth rather than spend it. Confucianism was not only not an obstacle to commerce, as elite scholars had so long insisted, but actually an incentive to it. Yü argued further that this reworking of Confucianism as a commercial ethic did not remain sequestered within their social group but acted upon the larger value system in Chinese society, thus preparing the Chinese for participation in the capitalist world-system as, for Weber, Protestant Christianity had Europeans. The analysis was intended to demonstrate that Chinese commercial practices operated according to the full economic rationality associated with capitalism, the proof of which was the economic success of Taiwan and Singapore. In other words, Western values were not unique in encouraging modernization, and where Chinese succeeded as capitalists they did so because of, not in spite of, their cultural Chinese roots.[111] What this interpretation was made to mean at a more general level was that China's development in the late imperial period, while still pictured in terms of Western capitalism, was no longer an account of stagnation but a history of progressive development. This reconstruction was precisely what the sprouts of capitalism discussion had hoped to achieve, but could only do so more through assertion than proof. By constructing what I have elsewhere referred to as a "history of capitalism" for contemporary China,[112] Yü rescued late imperial China from the stagnationist implications of the Marxist perspective of the transition from feudalism to capitalism and relocated it in a more hopeful social theory. His reworked Weberianism grounded change in the active reimagining by the Chinese themselves of the potentialities inherent in their own Confucian tradition, rather than displacing historical agency to an inevitable, but permanently postponed, teleology.

This new history of capitalism was one important initiative in the historiography of the post-Mao period. A different initiative, which ran in a contrary direction, was to declare a misfit between the Chinese experience of non-capitalism and the European model of pre-capitalism

---

[110] Weber 1958: 68.
[111] Brook 1995: 90–92. For a critique of analogous attempts to read Tokugawa Confucianism for a Protestant work ethic, see Kawakatsu 1994: 4–5.
[112] Brook 1995: 79.

and consider ways of dismantling the feudalism/capitalism paradigm altogether. One way to launch this contrary initiative was to agree that China had, as Marx said, "vegetated in the teeth of time." This proposition became the basis for a revival early in the 1980s of the debate over the Asiatic mode of production, which in turn led more ambitious theorists to suggest that social development is not unilinear, that there may be many routes to modernity, not all of which pass through feudalism, and that China and Europe may simply have developed by different paths.[113] As multilinearity gained respectability, Chinese historians, as Zhao Lisheng put it quoting the old adage, could stop "cutting the foot to fit the shoe."[114] As early as 1983, some historians were declaring that no advantage was gained by trading the peculiarities of Chinese history for universal patterns. To continue making that trade was to bind historians to writing Chinese history as monochromatic variations on a single theme.[115] Official ideology in the 1980s continued to declare that China up to the nineteenth century was "feudal," just as it continued unproductively in other spheres to hold on to what Carol Hamrin has dismissed as "nineteenth-century Marxist–Leninist terminology."[116]

As China continues to expand its involvement in the capitalist world-system in the 1990s and political rhetoric within the Communist Party drains "socialism" of all anti-capitalist meaning,[117] the compulsion to define Chinese history in terms of the non-development of capitalism in the 1990s is fading. The old scholarly debates over periodization, feudalism, and the Asiatic mode of production no longer appear in academic journals. Even the 1980s notion of "special characteristics," which made room for Chinese exceptionalism while retaining the basically uninflected absolute scheme of historical development, has fallen from sight.

Paradoxically, as "capitalist" modernity triumphs in China, the West is becoming no longer *the* place where History happened but simply another historical place. How this reformulation of the relationship between China and capitalism in the present day will affect historical research and social theory remains to be seen. It may confirm the value

---

[113] Brook 1989: 25–27.
[114] Zhao Lisheng 1989: 77.
[115] Ning Ke and Zou Zhaochen 1984: 24–25.
[116] Hamrin 1986: 91. She suggests that China will escape from the "archaic language" of "outmoded orthodoxy" as a result of embracing modernization theory. The ahistoricity of modernization theory may not, however, provide a fruitful point of departure for reconceptualizing the Chinese past.
[117] A shift in political rhetoric occurred during the brief "surname" controversy in 1991 ("whether something is surnamed capitalist or surnamed socialist"), which succeeded in deflating the distinction between the two; see Miles 1996: 81–84, also 117–18.

of a mid-level comparative analysis that avoids labeling the Chinese pre-modern as pre-capitalist. Or it may go further and induce an entirely China-based construction that refuses to call up the logic of pre-capitalism to explain the Chinese past. Capitalism may come to be regarded as a local development, albeit with larger historical effects, that need no longer dictate the construction of history elsewhere in the world. In either (or neither) case, the future of social theory in China will be determined less by the logical or ideological claims that can be made on behalf of any of these procedures than by China's position in the world economy. In the mid-1990s, most urban Chinese regarded that position as increasingly secure. Accordingly, they saw their relationship to modernity as unproblematic, involving primarily catch-up. They agreed with the Communist Party that modernization was what China needed and they experienced the transition to a globally linked market economy as that very process. Incorporation rather than transcendence – either of capitalism as Chinese Marxism earlier in the century called for, or of modernity as Japanese wartime capitalism once announced[118] or as Western post-modernism currently implies[119] – was the current concern.

Chinese socialism asserted that it was possible to be modern without being capitalist. This claim sought to disrupt a teleology of the modern constructed exclusively around capitalism. It ended up confirming it, and historical research provided some of that confirmation. Scholars working on the sprouts of capitalism, by locating the ghost of capitalism back in the historical process, made the Chinese pre-modern pre-capitalist, thereby implicitly (and unwittingly, I think) contributing to the ultimate incoherence of a stadial model that could make sense of the Communist leap from semi-feudalism to socialism on the basis of European history. For if China had been feudal in the sense of pre-capitalist, capitalism must follow. And if capitalism rather than socialism should follow feudalism, then socialism can be exposed as an ideological imaginary or a political intervention rather than a genuine historical stage. The alternative of granting Asia a separate historical process, that is, of casting China's past in terms of an Oriental or Asiatic formulation, may also no longer be available. It rescues China from the conundrum

---

[118] See note 25 above.

[119] Liu (1993: 389–91) has observed that although Orientalism was a significant element in the Western modernist strategy, Edward Said's critique (1979) has not been popular in China. She suggests that this is because Chinese historical thinking is used to the dichotomy of East and West. To this suggestion should be added the unshakable appeal of modernity, which rests on the conviction that accepts China as backward but believes that that backwardness will eventually be overcome.

of failed historical capitalism, but cannot construct a logic for installing capitalist modernity in the present.

Modernity continues to exert a powerful appeal within popular culture as well as among academics in the search for a mode of transcending the present. In the mid-1980s, with the ideology of the socialist transcendence of capitalism in full retreat in favor of a capitalist transcendence of pre-modernity, a senior scholar could predict with confidence a time "when modernization has reached such a stage that class distinctions are eliminated and all people are perfectly equal in status" in China.[120] The progressive transformation of the old socialist system since the 1980s seems only to have confirmed this Hegelian conviction in modernity as the "end of history," ironically turning decades of training in Hegelian Marxism to capitalist advantage. As it has throughout the twentieth century, the concept of Western capitalism will continue to dominate how Chinese construct ways of knowing their past into the start of the twenty-first century. Chinese intellectuals may shift away from this perspective only when the "rise of the West" begins with time to look more like a local phenomenon rather than a global destiny.

[120] Li Shu 1985: 62.

5   Towards a critical history of non-Western technology

Francesca Bray

Scientific progress and technological development play star roles in the master narrative of "the rise of the West." The emergence of capitalist social formations and Enlightenment thought in Europe coincided with an unprecedented, exponential phase of growth in scientific knowledge and in technical creativity and expertise. How these elements interacted to produce the peculiarly European "miracle" is a puzzle that continues to preoccupy the authors of comparative, grand-sweep history of technology and science.[1] Conversely, the failure to generate a similar miracle has largely dictated the terms of history of science and technology as it is practiced in and on China. But is explanation of failure the most we can get out of the history of non-Western technology, or can we reformulate our enquiries along more rewarding lines? If the task of the historian is to recreate worlds we have lost, then surely it is more helpful to reflect carefully on what did happen in these worlds, than to ask why something did not happen that did happen elsewhere.

The social theory of the capitalist era treats technology as one of the most significant of human activities. Modern technology, most obviously perhaps in the form of industrial machinery design, incorporates productivity-raising knowledge and is thus the very embodiment of capitalist rationality. In the models of stages of human development proposed by nineteenth-century evolutionary thinkers like Morgan and Marx (and still extremely influential with the general public today), the level of technological development a society had achieved defined its position on the evolutionary ladder. At the bottom were primitives like the hunter bands of Tierra del Fuego, who scorned material possessions, had not even learned to make huts, and apparently saw no need for leaders. At the top were the modern Western nations, whose professional engineers designed ever more efficient and profitable machinery, generating a profusion of material wealth and goods, which in turn supported a civically responsible middle class whose existence under-

---

[1] For instance Jones 1981; Mokyr 1990; Huff 1993.

158

pinned the full institutional apparatus of the rational nation-state. While opinion varied among the intelligentsia of the colonial powers as to whether "more advanced" necessarily meant "morally superior," the builders of empire entertained few doubts on this score, and a society's material backwardness offered ample moral justification for conquest.[2]

At the end of the twentieth century a nation's rank in the league table of development still depends on factors such as levels of energy consumption and the monetary value of industrial production per capita.[3] Meanwhile the history of technology continues to reproduce a parallel league table.[4] More perhaps than any other branch of the historical discipline, the history of technology retains a colonialist mentality. "The 'master narrative' is the Whig reading of Western technological evolution as inevitable and autonomous," writes Staudenmeier, referring to Joan Wallach Scott's definition of master narrative, or historical received opinion, as an account of the past "based on the forcible exclusion of others' stories."[5] Even if the Western path is not treated as inevitable but rather as a miracle, the epistemological framework remains one in which Western technology stands as the symbol of a structured hierarchy opposing modern to traditional, active to passive, progress to stagnation, science to ignorance, male to female, and West to rest. Just as female is not-male, a looking-glass which sets off the male image to advantage, so other societies and their technologies are not-West, a flattering mirror in which the West can contemplate its virtues.[6] By definition negatives of

---

[2] Adas 1989.

[3] Dolores Greenberg documents the gradual emergence among nineteenth-century British and American economists and social thinkers of an *energy ideal* that linked energy consumption to the creation of wealth and social progress: given "the right arrangement of political and economic power, increased physical power would lead to the elimination of drudgery, a source of abundant goods, [and] an improved standard of living" (Greenberg 1990: 714, quoted Staudenmeier 1990: 717). This ideal continues to exert a powerful influence on national governments, international financial organizations, and the general public (Boserup 1981: 12–13; Waring 1988). Despite recent assaults by proponents of appropriate technology, environmentalists, and other groups critical of the presumption that an increase in energy supplies necessarily contributes to social progress, the World Bank and the British government continue to fund contentious dam projects, and the nuclear industry still finds ready clients around the world.

[4] As does economic history. As Bin Wong argues in his essay, Eurocentric models of analysis fail to give proper weight to different forms of economic complexity or patterns of integration into a world system.

[5] Staudenmeier 1990: 725; Scott 1989: 690. See also the granted slightly caricatural high-school textbook "Standard View of Technology" formulated by Pfaffenberger (1992: 494–95), which he characterizes as "a pillar of Modernity."

[6] Until very recently the history of technology was almost exclusively male. The divisions of labor and gender ideals that emerged in the era of industrial capital associated technical creativity and entrepreneurial drive with men; it was presumed that women's links to technology were either as consumers of products or as a class of labor presumed (often erroneously) to be more biddable and tolerant of alienating industrial conditions

the original, the features of such mirror images can by and large be deduced: there is no need to accord them the same painstaking attention that the history of Western technology commands.

Historians of technology hail from a range of disciplinary perspectives: they include engineers, historians of science, economic historians, and general social historians; in the case of China and other non-Western civilizations we might add comparative historians and sociologists.[7] As a field, until very recently the history of technology focused predominantly on the intellectual and social factors that shape the development of scientific and technical knowledge and the processes of technological invention, development, and innovation.[8] Most of the key areas of interest in the discipline reflect our modern understanding of what an economy is and how it is articulated; they include the production or conversion of energy, mechanical design, and the production of key economic commodities (which vary according to period or place but

than men. It is only recently that the discipline has recognized the value of gender theory (see Staudenmeier 1990: 723). In the case of pre-modern China, I do not know of any work on technology other than my own (Bray 1997) that looks systematically at women and at gender.

[7] See Pursell 1984 and Staudenmeier 1990 on the composition of the profession. The best-known Western-language works that address the history of technology in pre-modern China (before its enforced exposure to Western knowledge starting with the Opium Wars) include *Science and Civilisation in China* (see below) by Joseph Needham, a scientist, and *The Pattern of the Chinese Past* by Mark Elvin, a social historian (Elvin 1973). But China also frequently enters into comparative studies such as those by Jones (1981) and Mokyr (1990). China is an important case study for Mokyr in his exploration of why technological change occurs in some societies and not others. In *Technology in World Civilization* (1990), Arnold Pacey (whose intellectual politics are much closer to Needham's) offers an example of what one might call a world history approach, in which he emphasizes the technical pre-eminence of different domains in different societies over time, treating technology as a cumulative world endeavor.

[8] Historians of technology distinguish between *invention* (finding a new solution to a technical problem), *development* (translating this new knowledge into a working and reproducible prototype), and *innovation* (the processes by which a new product gains public acceptance).

Invention and development can be studied from a purely *internalist* perspective, focusing on the internal logic of the development of knowledge and skills, and/or from a *contextualist* perspective, which attempts to integrate technical trends in the specific socio-historical environment in which they occur. Because innovation studies deal essentially with selling a new product, they necessarily require a contextualist approach. Any of these aspects of technology can also be studied from an *externalist* perspective, exploring the cultural context of the production of knowledge, skills, and markets (or desires).

The distinctions drawn here between internalist, contextualist, and externalist approaches borrow the definitions and distinctions made by John S. Staudenmeier (the current editor of *Technology and Culture*) in a recently published survey of the field (Staudenmeier 1990: 716), but other scholars have drawn the epistemological boundaries somewhat differently (see Staudenmeier 1985: 202–09 on the taxonomies of history of technology).

generally include iron and steel, textiles, and weaponry).[9] Technology is treated, on the one hand, as a sign of scientific capability,[10] on the other, as a factor of production,[11] and technical efficiency is computed in terms of returns to capital, returns to labor, speed of production, or efficiency in the use of raw materials.

This perspective offers a celebration rather than a critique of capitalism and its epistemologies, including the negative assessment of and lack of interest in stable social systems discussed earlier by Immanuel Wallerstein: technological development is by its very nature both socially desirable, because it takes us a stage further in human understanding and mastery of nature, and socially destabilizing, because it produces tensions in the relations of production. The history of technology thus written is a history of economic development and of social ruptures. In the absence of such development and ruptures there is no history – stability or continuity are read at best as marking time, at worst as stagnation or decline.

Of course, Europe itself counts frequent and often long periods of technical lull in its genealogy – but from the telos of the Industrial Revolution they must be viewed as marking time, for eventually progress resumes. As Fernand Braudel puts it in *Civilization and Capitalism*:

First the accelerator, then the brake: the history of technology seems to consist of both processes, sometimes in quick succession: it propels human life onward, gradually reaches new forms of equilibrium on higher levels than in the past, only to remain there for a long time, since technology often stagnates, or

---

[9] Staudenmeier distinguishes nine key subject areas among the members of SHOT (the Society for the History of Technology, founded in 1957). Four "have dominated the field for many years: technological creativity; the science-technology relationship; the American system of manufacturing; and electricity. Two are attracting renewed interest: the military history of technology, and technology from a capitalist perspective. Finally, a new generation of scholars is increasingly concerned with issues of work and gender, as well as the symbolic construction of technology" (Staudenmeier 1990: 717).

[10] The linking of science and technology is again a product of our modern industrial world, rooted in the late eighteenth- and early nineteenth-century professionalization and mathematization of engineering, and the somewhat later development of industrial research laboratories, particularly in the German chemical industry. Early historians of science and technology alike tended to retroject on to pre-industrial societies the notion that technology was applied science. Recent studies of how science and technology are produced have done much to undermine this view, even as it might apply in the industrial world. White (1984) justly criticizes Needham for using such reasoning in his interpretation of pre-modern China, presuming or at least suggesting that the undeniable evidence of technological sophistication supposed an equal level of systematic scientific thought.

[11] "No category of scholars has given more attention to the history of technology than the economic historian. Technology (or technological knowledge) is clearly a factor of production, and can no more be ignored in a comprehensive study than can capital, labor, or raw materials" (Pursell 1984: 71).

advances only imperceptibly between one "revolution" or innovation and another.... [The role of technology] was a vital one.... As long as daily life proceeded without too much difficulty in its appointed pathway, within the framework of its inherited structures, as long as society was content with its material surroundings and felt at ease, *there was no economic motive for change....* It was only when things went wrong, when society came up against the ceiling of the possible that people *turned of necessity to technology.*[12]

Yet as Braudel remarks, even in the case of pre-modern Europe "it often seems as if the brakes are on all the time." However, societies that produced undeniably sophisticated technical repertoires but failed to follow the European path to the same conclusion – such as the medieval Islamic world, the Inca empire, or imperial China – are not seen as marking time, rather they have reached a stage where the brakes have locked; in the phrase of Bertrand Gille they are *blocked systems.*[13]

It is ironic but not surprising that Joseph Needham, who so success-fully reinserted China into the history of science and technology, should be famous for formulating a "question" that in many ways subverts his fundamentally humanist enterprise of writing a non-exclusionary history of science and technology. Needham's explicit purpose in devising his multi-volume series *Science and Civilisation in China* was to demonstrate that real science and technology were not the unique products of European minds – that the history of modern science and technology was in fact a world history. His strategy was to divide Chinese knowledge into the disciplinary branches of modern Western science, pure and applied. Technologies were among the applied sciences. Thus astronomy was classified as applied mathematics, en-gineering as applied physics, alchemy as applied chemistry, and agricul-ture was classified as applied botany. Himself a distinguished scientist, Needham was able to demonstrate that China had preceded Europe in a number of important discoveries and inventions – including docu-menting three Chinese inventions that Francis Bacon associated with the birth of the modern world: printing, the magnetic compass, and gunpowder.[14] Furthermore, Needham was able to construct convincing

---

[12] Braudel 1981, vol. I: 430, 435; emphases added.

[13] Gille (1978) lists China, the Muslim world, and pre-Columbian America under his heading of "blocked systems." The Muslim world has perhaps suffered most explicitly from Orientalist gendered contrasts. It is commonly depicted as a *passive* repository of Greek learning rather than a realm with many outstanding centers of learning that actively advanced scholarship.

[14] In fact Needham's claim that the magnetic compass was introduced from China to Europe is only circumstantial. Nor is it clear that Chinese woodblock printing was the direct inspiration for Gutenberg's moveable type. But even if the precision of these claims has subsequently been called into question, there is no doubt that it was a brilliant move to invoke Bacon in this way.

historical narratives of intellectual progress in all the scientific and technological categories covered in *Science and Civilisation in China*. However, he felt that the extraordinary creativity and inventiveness of the Song dynasty (960–1279) declined in succeeding centuries, to be followed by a long period (from about 1400 or 1500 up to the nineteenth-century confrontations with the Western powers) during which China contributed little or nothing to the growth of world scientific knowledge or technological advance.

Needham's project and its methods have been extremely influential both within and beyond the profession of the history of science and technology. It was warmly welcomed in China, and also in India, as a means of restoring national self-respect; both countries have now established institutions to study the history of indigenous science and technology and their contributions to modern knowledge, while in the West children now learn from their high-school text-books that the Chinese first invented gunpowder, fireworks, and printing. However, the teleology inherent in Needham's project raises two serious problems for the history of technology. First, accepting the evolutionary model of a family tree of knowledge whose branches correspond to the disciplines of modern science allows Needham to identify Chinese forebears as precursors of modern science and technology, but at the price of disembedding them from their cultural and historical context. One could caricature this as a Jack Horner approach to history, picking out the plums and ignoring the rest of the pie. It foregrounds "discoveries" and "innovations" in a way that retrojects modern values and understandings on to the past, and distorts understanding of the broader system of skills and knowledge of the period – what one might call its technological culture.

Secondly, arguing back from the telos of Western modernity straitjackets our understanding of what technology is and what roles it serves in different societies. It becomes difficult to imagine alternative trajectories of technical development, trajectories that might have emphasized other criteria than engineering sophistication, scale economies, or increased output. Any deviation from this narrow path then has to be explained in terms of failure, of history grinding to a halt. The "Needham question," which follows a problematic elaborated in somewhat different terms by both Marx and Weber, remains the guiding theme for the treatment of non-Western societies in most local and comparative histories of technology; it asks why societies like imperial China or medieval Islam lost momentum and therefore failed to generate indigenous forms of modernity. What went wrong? What was missing? What were the institutional, intellectual or character failings of that culture? As in the case of contemporary societies that do not adopt Western technology as fast and completely as it is felt they should, the "brakes" are the focus of the investigation, overshadowing the work that technologies actually performed.

Even when they give a prominent role to non-Western societies as world leaders at earlier periods, in comparative histories the heart of the enterprise remains classical interpretations of weaponry, energy conversion, transport, and the production of commodities.[15] The same is true of most history of Chinese technology, which moreover seems recently, like the object of its study, to have ground to a halt.[16]

It is unfair to fault Needham for failing to develop radical new methods to assess the history of Chinese technology, given how slow such methods have been to emerge within the mainstream discipline. Until very recently the internalist and contextualist approaches to technology that predominated within the field explicitly or tacitly accepted the capitalist model of historical progress even when the subject was a pre-industrial or non-Western society. Some scholars did acknowledge the need to break this intellectual mold. Lynn White believed that medieval technology could not be adequately studied using conventional methods; he therefore drew on Alfred Kroeber's cultural anthropology for inspiration.[17] Lewis Mumford's more subversive agenda was to show that the material effects of technology are merely secondary; man engages in technical activities "less for the purpose of increasing food supply or controlling nature than for utilizing his own immense organic resources . . . to fulfil more adequately his superorganic

[15] E.g., Pacey 1990.
[16] Although studies of nineteenth- and twentieth-century Chinese technology have burgeoned in the last ten years, book-length studies of the history of imperial technology are conspicuous by their absence. Archeological finds, whether from the prehistoric or the historic period, continue to stimulate reconsiderations of the state of a particular technology in a certain period, and of its lineages, and during the last decade the archeological journals have offered the richest source for publications relating to pre-modern technology. Otherwise one might mention the field of metallurgical history, which is thriving (see bibliography in Wagner 1993); the continued effort to add detail and breadth to our understanding of agricultural technology and thought in China, exemplified by the work of Guo Wentao and his Nanjing colleagues (Guo *et al.* 1986; Guo 1988); or Pan Jixing's studies of Song Yingxing's *Tiangong kaiwu* [The exploitation of the works of nature] of 1637 (Pan 1989). None of these works has however required any radical rethinking of classical models.
[17] White 1975, cited in Pursell 1984: 82. Trained in the Germanic tradition of cultural ethnography, imported to the United States by Franz Boas, Kroeber treated a society's material culture as a significant expression of its world view; his concept of "styles" presumed a non-hierarchical, non-evolutionary relationship between cultures (e.g., Kroeber 1957).

demands and aspirations."[18] Mumford's philosophical goal was to distinguish between those technics that generated social relations which were not in accord with human nature, and technics which allowed human societies to fulfill their identities as self-creative beings. His work was widely read but had a greater impact outside than within the history of technology. And it was a long while before most historians in the field were prepared to accept the relevance of work by philosophers of technology like Ellul, Heidegger, and Habermas, who like Mumford were deeply critical of the images and experiences of the human condition that a world built by capitalist technology engenders.[19] At last, however, even this bastion of modernist values could hold out no longer in an academic world where critiques of capitalism and modernity had become mainstream. The last fifteen years have seen the gates open to feminists and Foucauldians, to semioticians and labor historians, whose work explores how technology contributes to the ideologies and power structures of capitalism, to modern aesthetics, desires, gratification, and suffering.[20]

In its current state, history of technology both illuminates and questions the capitalist experience, yet so far has done little to develop new approaches to other histories. As an indication of how serious the neglect of non-Western societies remains within the discipline, Staudenmeier points to *Technology and Culture*, the official journal of the Society for the History of Technology. Of the articles published between 1958 (when it was founded) and 1980, only 6 percent dealt with non-Western societies; after 1980 the figure dropped to 3 percent.[21] As another example, reading the program for a four-day international conference, held in Oxford in 1994 and entitled "Technological Change," I noticed that of about a hundred papers, two or three dealt with some form of West-to-East technology transfer and there was a theoretical session on evolutionary models of technological development; otherwise there were no papers dealing with non-Western technologies, and very few on pre-industrial technologies in the West. It is interesting that the new, more cultural history of technology has produced many critiques of capitalist models but as yet few alternatives.

[18] Mumford 1967: 8–9, quoted in Mitcham 1984: 294. In *Technics and Civilization*, published three decades earlier, Mumford had already applied this idealist analysis to the material cultures of technology at different epochs (Mumford 1934).

[19] On the various schools of critical philosophy of technology, see Mitcham 1984.

[20] For example, Ruth Schwartz Cowan 1983, Dolores Hayden 1986, and Mike Davis (1990) on material constructions and political implications of modern American domesticity; Cockburn and Ormrod 1993 on how the design, production, and retailing of household appliances mold gender identities; and Sachs 1992 on our dreams of the pleasures offered by the car.

[21] Staudenmeier 1990: 724.

James Clifford has noted how ethnographic museums put together exhibits by selecting artifacts according to categories that fulfill Western expectations of a "primitive" or "traditional" society, thus creating an *illusion of adequate representation.*[22] Until one questions the underlying master narrative, the conventional history of technology – and the economic history and comparative sociology that still draw upon it for material grounding – succeeds in creating an illusion of adequate representation of the technological histories of non-Western societies, in depicting them as faltering steps along a natural path of progress that only the West has trodden boldly to the end.

How might we devise a critical history of technology that would explore the local meanings of technological systems, not in order to construct comparative hierarchies (and perpetuate ethnocentric judgments), but seriously to study alternative constructions of the world? And how can we move beyond the concept of "blocked systems" to analyze not just the energy that technologies generate in a particular society, but their capacity to channel and absorb these potentially destructive forces – their contribution to continuity, to social reproduction? To this end I propose that we look more closely at the social and symbolic meanings of the material worlds that technology builds. For my purposes a *technique* can be defined as an action performed on some form of inanimate or animate matter (including oneself), as in the actions of plowing or weaving, and designed to produce an object with human meaning. A *technology* is the technique exercised in its social context, and it is this social context that imparts meaning, both to the objects produced, and to the persons producing them.[23] The social meaning of a field of rice depends in part upon whether the harvest will be divided between family subsistence and taxes or sold on the market, and so too does the social identity of the farmer who plows the field.

Technologies in this definition are specific to a society, embodiments of its visions of the world and of its struggles over social order. In this sense the most important work that technologies do is to produce people: the makers are shaped by the making, and the users shaped by

[22] Clifford 1988: 220.

[23] Marcel Mauss described a technique as "an action which is *effective* and *traditional* (and in this it is no different from a magical, religious, or symbolic action) felt by the [actor] to be mechanical, physical, or physico-chemical ... and pursued with this aim in view" (1979 [1935]: 104). Lemonnier prefers to distinguish the technological from the magical or religious by confining techniques to processes that "lead to a real transformation of matter, in terms of current scientific laws of the physical world" (1992: 5). But that drastically reduces both the scope of what constitutes technology, and the criteria by which we judge its efficacity. For my purposes the emic understanding of what constitutes the material world and its transformations proposed by Mauss is more appropriate; see also Pfaffenberger (1992) on "sociotechnical systems."

the using. I have proposed that we think in terms of "technological cultures," with the proviso that "culture" indicates, not a homogeneous set of ideas shared by all members of a society, but a continual dialogue or argument between different groups and individuals about significance and values. I argue that technical activities and artifacts are at one level to be understood as symbols, and like all symbols they are polysemic – they mean different things to different people, and sometimes the ambiguities they embody serve to defuse conflict, at other times they provoke it.[24]

Other material worlds were made in other ways from ours, and embodied different values. How did past societies see their worlds and their place in them, what were their needs and desires, what role did technology play in creating and fulfilling those desires, in maintaining and reshaping the social fabric? Such questions, it seems to me, provide a more creative framework for exploring the technologies of non-Western or non-industrial societies, challenging the illusion of adequate representation. Perhaps the key lies in a recasting of our epistemological mold. If technology, as is generally agreed, performs ideological work, then we need to examine how it might stabilize as well as transform or develop a social order. This approach requires a new materialism, a conceptualization of technological efficiency in which we reconstrue the factors of production and the processes of reproduction in an analysis that includes social and symbolic as well as monetary capital.[25]

To suggest the possibilities of this cultural approach I recast one of the central questions in the history of Chinese technology. As has correctly been pointed out, during the later Ming and the early Qing dynasties (c. 1500–1750) neither agriculture nor textile production benefitted from significant technological development in the sense of new mechanical inventions, although (as I shall describe) significant changes occurred in the volume of output and organization of production. Because it is considered a period of involution or stagnation, historians of technology have usually thought more carefully about the background of this era, the involutionary characteristics of the farming and textile

---

[24] Bayly (1986) gives a marvellous illustration of such ambiguities in his discussion of the conflicting symbolisms, liberatory and oppressive, of cloth production in pre-independence India. In my own work I have suggested that the gendered segregation of domestic space in late imperial China could be experienced by women either negatively, as a spatial embodiment of their subordination to men, or positively, as a symbol of social respectability available to families of any class (Bray 1997: chapters 2 and 3).

[25] The concepts of social and symbolic capital were first proposed by Pierre Bourdieu in *Outline of a Theory of Practice* (1977). My contention that modernity hinders us from understanding the technological cultures of the past parallels Pfaffenberger's: "sociotechnical systems are all but invisible through the lenses provided by Western economic, political and social theory" (1992: 500).

technologies, the social institutions, or cultural mindsets, that are considered to have led to the halt in development, than about how technology might have figured in the ideology of the period itself.

One striking feature of the late Ming and early Qing, however, is the prominence in official discourse of schemes for encouraging agriculture and textile production, most of which, given the prevailing economic realities of a thoroughly commercialized society in which patterns of production had been profoundly reshaped by market forces, seem in retrospect hopelessly outmoded and unrealistic.

I argue that late imperial official discourse and policies about farming and weaving make perfect sense if we set aside the criteria of modern rationalities and materialism to look in the terms of the period at what technologies produced. For late imperial Chinese officials, agriculture and the textile industry were a symbolic pair, inseparably bound together as "correct" male and female work. From this perspective farming and weaving were the activities that constituted at once the moral and the material foundation of a proper social order, they were technologies that produced subjects as well as material goods. This was a concept of the material bases of social reproduction that rested on wholly non-capitalist understandings of materialism, efficiency, and instrumentality. Although the goals and values embodied in this vision of work were at sharp odds with the everyday exigencies of the time, the ruling elite believed it was possible to devise policies that would reform work in such a way as to restore Confucian values.

The production of grain and cloth

I will begin with a historical sketch of agricultural and textile technology and their uses in China, to indicate in terms of the conventional social history of technology how the development of the means of production affected the social formation. I give somewhat more space to textiles than to agriculture, because for the purposes of my subsequent analysis it is necessary to highlight the complex shifts that took place in divisions of labor, and most particularly in the gendering of textile work.

Early Chinese political thinkers were committed to an ideal of a ruler whose officials directly governed and protected the people, *min*, a quasi-sacred category envisioned as an undifferentiated population of subsistence peasants. The *min*, in their turn, contributed labor, armed service, and the essential goods necessary to maintain the social order. The imperial period began in 221 BC. The fiscal regime on which the early empire was founded had its roots in the Warring States period, and it endured largely unchanged until the end of the sixteenth century, despite significant changes in the systems of production on which it was founded.[26] Peasant families paid taxes in kind; the men's work was taxed in grain, the women's work in cloth – *nangeng nüzhi* (men plow, women weave) was the classic formulation of this complementarity of gender roles. The state redistributed the grain and cloth thus procured: some served the needs of the imperial court, a great deal was used to support the army, and officials' emoluments were also paid in kind.

At the period of the foundation of the empire, the northern plains constituted China's economic center. The main cereal crops were millet and wheat; hemp was grown for the coarse cloth worn by peasants (and by the elite during periods of mourning), mulberry trees were grown and silkworms raised to produce silk. In the southern regions of China, which at the time played only a minor role in the national economy, rice was the staple cereal and ramie often replaced hemp; sericulture was underdeveloped. Cotton at that time was a rare exotic. When the central state opened up new tracts of arable land to support troops or displaced persons, or when it redistributed land to peasants, as it commonly did up until about the eighth century in order to break up large estates, the land allotted to a household included allowances both for cereal and textile production – each family received a unit of "hemp fields" or "mulberry fields" as well as of land for grain.[27]

The state's commitment to a direct relationship between ruler and

---

[26] According to Paul J. Smith (1991), the early Song state was a unique exception. Because of the extreme military threats it faced, statesmen of the period sought unprecedented methods to raise revenues. The Song state practiced economic activism at a level unknown before or later, at least until the late nineteenth century. It participated in a burgeoning commercial economy directly (through state enterprises and monopolies) and indirectly (through taxation of commercial activity). Song financial specialists were an elite within the bureaucracy. They elaborated a complex and powerful network of specialized fiscal institutions which regulated increasing proportions of the nation's activities. Commercial taxes provided an ever-growing proportion of state revenues and drain on the economy. The new economic policies, which operated from 1068 till 1085, "extend[ed] state control to new regions and industries and directly challenge[d] private commercial industries for the profits of foreign and domestic trade, in order to finance an aggressive new policy of territorial expansion and national defense" (Smith 1991: 9). As an example, the Sichuan tea industry was converted to a state monopoly in 1074 to finance the purchase of Tibetan warhorses. But these policies contained the seeds of their own destruction, leading to severe exploitation of the peasantry, an increasing state dependence upon merchant middlemen or agents and – inevitably – corruption. The strategy of increasing state revenues through developing a commercial tax base was repealed in the mid Song, after which it fell into permanent disrepute, particularly among orthodox neo-Confucians, who in large part considered it to embody an immoral view of the world order.

[27] Note that the hereditary rights offered under this system were only usufructuary, not rights of ownership; the land remained the property of the state. So interestingly (although the heirs are sons and their wives, not daughters) we could say that land here *is* being allocated for the use of women.

min, unmediated by feudal-style obligations, often required active intervention to reestablish a suitable system of production. The history of
farming technology in medieval North China offers an interesting case
study of state efforts to control potentially disruptive changes in the
relations of production, made possible by technological development.
During the first thousand years of imperial rule (from about 200 BC to
about 850 AD), the northern plains were the central economic region of
China. This was a low rainfall area, and the main grain crops were
millets, wheat, and barley. Farming techniques in the north developed
moisture conservation to a very fine art. Crop rotation, the use of animal
and green manures, drilling the seed in rows, repeated shallow plowings,
harrowing, raking, and weeding were all known by the first century BC
and had been brought to a high degree of perfection by the sixth
century.[28] They were only viable, however, if the farmer had a fairly
large farm, animals for draft and manure, and sufficient capital for
animals and animal-powered equipment; that is to say, if the technical
system presented significant economies of scale. During these centuries
landed aristocrats (and Buddhist temples) were able to increase their
wealth by practicing estate farming, adding to their centrally managed
domains the land of small peasants unable to survive alone. The
proportion of land concentrated in these feudal estates varied over the
period, but when uncontrolled it always increased rapidly.[29]

Such concentration of land management represented a serious threat
to the power of the central state: small farms each paid an individual
land tax, but even when aristocratic (or religious or warlord) holdings
were not exempt from the land tax, such powerful figures were able to
evade many of their obligations. As a result, there was a continual
oscillation: when a new dynasty came to power it would institute radical
land reforms, some variant on what was generally referred to as an
"equal field" (*juntian*) system by which big estates were broken up and
individual peasant households were allotted an amount of land depending on the fertility of the soil and perhaps the number of household
members. But small peasants were seldom able to live profitably under
this regime for long, since they lacked the capital resources to practice
the best farming methods. Meanwhile the aristocracy, given lands in
perpetuity by the ruler as a reward for their support, or allotted estates
in return for service in the bureaucracy, hastened to buy up land from

[28] They are mentioned in fragments of agricultural treatises surviving from the second
century BC, and described in great detail in the *Qimin yaoshu* [Essential techniques for
the peasantry], written by Jia Sixie in 535 AD; fuller descriptions of the techniques and
implements are given in Bray (1984), as well as a more detailed account of the *Qimin
yaoshu* and its significance.
[29] Bray 1979; Hsü Cho-yun 1980.

bankrupt peasants, for they were well able to practice the best methods and could therefore add to their incomes by increasing their estates. So as the dynasty wore on, the rivals of the state became richer as its own income from taxes declined. Had northern China remained the economic and political center of the Chinese polity, it seems quite likely that at some point the state would have lost the power to intervene effectively to restore peasant farmings, and would have definitely lost control to its rivals.

However, the cycle of power shifts was broken when the rice-growing regions of the Yangzi region started to rival the northern plains in gross output, some time around the ninth century AD.[30] Wet-rice cultivation allows almost infinite intensification of land-use, as Clifford Geertz famously noted in his study entitled *Agricultural Involution*.[31] In the twentieth century this has generally been achieved by an enormous increase in capital inputs: specially designed farm machinery, fertilizers, herbicides, and other chemicals.[32] In imperial China it was achieved largely through improvements that required little in the way of capital.

The most striking period of development of wet-rice agriculture in China began in the Song dynasty (960–1279), when the state initiated a series of development policies so sweeping in scope and result that they may well be compared to the so-called "Green Revolution" of the 1960s and 1970s.[33] Fear of the Khitan and other nomadic invaders drove

[30] Li Bozhong 1990; Lamouroux 1995.
[31] Geertz (1963) based his arguments on the contrast he perceived between the trajectories of colonial Java (c. 1880–1940) and Meiji Japan (1868–1912). In the case of Java, he argued, the requirement of the Dutch colonial government that the best land be devoted to sugar plantations forced the Javanese peasantry to produce more and more rice from less and less land, with no resources except their own labor. In Meiji Japan, by contrast, in order to sustain rapid industrialization the state supplied capital resources in the form of chemical fertilizers and mechanized irrigation technology, effecting a qualitative leap in labor productivity characteristic of the passage to modernity. Geertz's analysis of the technical capacities of wet-rice systems is generally accepted. But the social homology he proposes, namely that the intensification of rice production through increased labor inputs leads to an involution of social relations and to general impoverishment, has been forcefully challenged by historians of Java as a misplaced technological determinism (e.g., Elson 1978, Alexander and Alexander 1982). Others have argued that certain types of non-capital investment in rice farming do increase labor productivity significantly (e.g. Smith 1959 on Tokugawa Japan [1600–1868], and Bray 1986: 147–66). In the case of Japan, Akira Hayami has argued that the economic and psychological basis for the Meiji modernization was what he calls "the laborious revolution" – a shift in levels of production and work habits effected by the very processes of rice intensification that Geertz argued stood in the way of indigenous transitions to modernity (Hayami 1990).
[32] The environmental and social problems that this capital-based development strategy generates are now widely recognized; see for instance Shiva 1991 on India, Bray 1986, Moore 1990 and Tweeten *et al.* 1993 on Japan.
[33] Elvin 1973; Bray 1986; Lamouroux 1995.

millions of peasants to abandon their land in the north; by the later part of the Song, the greater part of the population lived in the southern provinces, and the state was faced with the double problem of feeding an increased population over a greatly reduced area, and of maintaining large armies to protect its borders. The state therefore promoted a series of measures to improve farming methods and yields. One of the most famous was the introduction to the Yangzi Delta in 1012 of new varieties of quick-ripening rices from Champa in present-day Vietnam. This transformed production patterns, allowing double-cropping of rice or (more commonly) the alternation of summer rice and winter wheat. Local magistrates disseminated new varieties and information on cultivation techniques. Subsequent improvements during the Yuan, Ming, and Qing included the extension of the irrigated area,[34] refinements in irrigation methods and in cultivation techniques, selective plant breeding, multi-cropping, and the use of small quantities of commercial fertilizers like treated nightsoil or beancake.[35]

In the absence of modern technology like laser leveling, irrigated fields had to be kept small for efficient water control. There was little scope for the use of labor-saving equipment, except for irrigation which generally operated not at the level of the individual farm but of the community. The tasks of transplanting, weeding, regulating water flow, deciding on how to interplant, or how much fertilizer to use required detailed skills and were not easy to supervise on a large scale. Under such conditions the optimal unit of management was very small: a typical example is the Yangzi Delta landlord of the later seventeenth century who says that a household like his own can at most cope with 10 *mu* (0.7 ha) of rice land.[36] Rather than managing a large and well-

[34] Irrigation extends the area that can be planted with rice, increases crop yields, and extends the cropping season. I describe the origins and spread of various forms of irrigation (including dyked fields, terraces, and land reclaimed from the sea) in Bray 1986: chapters 2 and 3, where I also discuss the relative importance of a central state and of local organizations in constructing and maintaining irrigation systems. In premodern societies the main input for such constructions was human labor; the equipment required consisted principally of shovels, buckets, and ropes (for a nice illustration see Needham 1971: 233, figure 865). The capital required went almost wholly to wages or food for the workers; if the state or local government commanded *corvée* labor, or if members of a community contributed their labor to construct their own local system, then the monetary costs of irrigation works was low in proportion to the increase in the value of crops produced.

[35] Elvin 1973; Bray 1984: 477–510. Beancake was the name for the large fibrous disks that were the by-product of crushing soybeans for sauce or bean-curd; the extraction of various vegetable oils also produced cakes that were sold as fertilizer. Silkworm droppings and lime were other forms of fertilizer that were commonly purchased. One beancake was apparently sufficient to fertilize the rice seedlings for a whole family farm (Bray 1984: 289–98).

[36] Zhang Lixiang 1983: 151.

equipped home-farm themselves, landlords rented out most of their land, seeking not yeomen tenants with capital to invest (as in eighteenth-century England) but peasants with experience. As rice farming intensified it offered access to land, either as owners or as tenants, to high densities of population.[37]

The Song state's efforts to increase output were remarkable but by no means unprecedented. The Chinese state continually intervened in the domain of agricultural production. All through the two millennia of the empire the state would undertake to open up new lands for cultivation; to loan tools, seed, and animals to settlers on the lands; to develop irrigation projects; and to disseminate improved methods or equipment and encourage the cultivation of new crops. One of the responsibilities of local magistrates was to encourage agricultural improvement in the region under their jurisdiction, and many farming manuals were written with this form of transmission of knowledge in mind. But although the ubiquitous exhortation to "encourage agriculture" was taken seriously by almost everyone with official responsibilities, it would be mistaken to imagine that the Chinese state ever tried – except possibly for a brief period during the Song dynasty – to promote agricultural *development* in the sense that we use the word today.[38]

As conventionally used by economists, the term development implies improvement in the efficiency (defined usually in terms of labor productivity) of a technical and economic system, resulting eventually in some kind of "qualitative" change, such as a mechanical innovation that allows a quantum leap in labor productivity, and stimulating a transformation of the relations of production (see the discussion by Bin Wong, below). Economic historians of China, correctly noting the absence of this kind of change, speak of agriculture in late imperial China in terms of stagnation, involution, or "growth without development." They hold that although improvements in the micro-management of farming continued to produce small increases in crop yield, this was at the expense of the productivity of labor.[39]

With its favorable reponses to low-capital inputs and micro-management, pre-modern wet-rice farming constitutes what I have called a "skill-oriented" technology, one that tends toward the development and intensive use of human skills, as opposed to a "mechanical" technology that favors the development of labor-substituting, capital intensive equipment and machinery.[40] In conventional economic terms "mechan-

---

[37] Bray 1986: 115–16.   [38] Will 1994.
[39] See for instance Elvin 1973 on "involution," Huang 1990 on "growth without development."
[40] Bray 1986: 113–16.

ical" technologies have the potential for true development. It should of course be noted that by substituting for human labor, such technologies drive labor off the land.[41] Meanwhile labor-absorbing "skill-oriented" technologies are indeed prone to involute, not least because they tie labor to the land and into a diversified set of economic activities. This does not necessarily imply impoverishment: it can be associated with a growth in prosperity and local markets. In the case of China, Perkins believes that food production per capita kept pace with population increase until about 1800; furthermore it was not infrequent during the late imperial period to find the introduction of labor-intensive yet short-term techniques coinciding with diversification of the rural economy and the growth of household manufactures, indicating that many improvements in rice farming increased overall labor productivity as well as crop yields.[42]

Depending as it did on capital inputs and economies of scale, the estate agriculture of early North China had the potential for development in conventional terms. However, the state repeatedly blocked this development by breaking up the large estates, which it saw as threats both to the political ideal of relations between ruler and subject, and to the fiscal regime. Land was periodically redistributed to poor peasants, who could not afford to farm productively, and were economically very vulnerable despite the efforts of the state to protect them.[43] In the wet-

---

[41] The agrarian history of Britain, the cradle of both the "Agricultural Revolution" and the "Industrial Revolution," is a story of steady displacement of labor from the land. Sometimes agricultural workers were displaced not by machines but by sheep, as in the period of the enclosures, and there were some periods when new methods actually increased demand for labor – as when three-course crop rotations increased the need for hands at weeding and at harvest time. But the secular trend that began with the dismantling of feudal domains was a classic case of capitalist rationalization, toward larger farms with higher profit margins.

In the New World scarcity of labor encouraged a parallel process from the period of colonization, and we owe the concept of the reaper-binder and many other now indispensable farm machines to the inspiration of American and Australian engineers. Terry Byres distinguishes between "English," "American," and "Prussian" variants of this pattern of rationalization (Byres 1991), and of course the economies of scale inherent in this model represent a vision of universal modernity that appealed beyond capitalist states: the agrarian policies of the Soviet Union and other communist states were based on large-scale mechanization.

The ultimate farming rationality according to this technological logic is large-scale monoculture run by international agribusiness; for the effects of monoculture on rural populations in the United States see Friedmann 1990; Tweeten *et al.* 1993.

[42] Perkins 1969; Bray 1986: 147–66.

[43] After the Song the North became something of an economic backwater, and peasant farming became the norm until the advent of capitalist industry to regional cities in the early twentieth century (Huang 1985). The introduction of the examination system in the late Tang marked the beginning of the downfall of the Chinese aristocracy and the rise of a meritocracy based on education, not on blood. Moreover the shift of the

rice regions of China economies of scale did not operate and very little capital was needed to farm well. Although the ownership of land tended to concentrate in the hands of the gentry, the most efficient units of management were small and the countryside remained thickly populated by peasants working as independent or as tenant farmers. The technological system of wet-rice farming was sufficiently productive to allow for a double level of extraction, so that in this case landlordism was not perceived by the state as a threat to its revenues – even though tenants often experienced severe exploitation. Modern social scientists have emphasized the involutionary aspects of this logic of development, but from the perspective of the Chinese state the high population-carrying capacity of rice regions was a source of social stability.

However, the rice regimes by no means conformed to the subsistence ideal of *min* activities that I shall discuss later. They formed the basis for a highly diversified rural economy. Irrigated rice requires intensive inputs of labor at transplanting and harvesting, but in other periods household labor can be spared for other activities. Sometimes this diversification generated widespread prosperity, at others it was a response to desperate conditions, but the fact that most households had direct access to land, either as owners or tenants, gave the socio-economic system flexibility and resilience. In lean times farming families could withdraw from commercial activities and fall back on subsistence production; when markets for specialized crops or products arose, they had land and labor to reallocate accordingly.[44] In many areas of South China by the mid-Ming peasant households grew rice almost as a sideline, investing most of their labor in commercial cropping or other forms of household commodity production.[45] Along the lower Yangzi summer crops of rice alternated in the fields with winter wheat. In the seventeenth century the semi-tropical regions of the far south grew two crops of rice a year, with a third crop of rape for oil, indigo for dyeing, barley, or sweet potatoes. Their surplus rice was exported to Canton. In the region around Shanghai late Ming officials fought a losing battle to persuade farmers not to give up most of their rice land to cotton; in other areas farmers turned over their fields to sugar or citrus. Farming households produced the bulk of the processed foods and handicrafts sold on China's thriving markets, and of the huge volume of cotton cloth.[46]

economic center to the Yangzi regions meant that control of land in the northern plains was no longer so profitable.

[44] A fascinating account of modern Sumatran rice-farmers' strategies for participation in a fluctuating national commercial economy is given by Kahn (1980).

[45] Bray 1986: chapter 4.

[46] Bray 1984: 509 on the Canton rice trade; on sugar, Sabban 1994 and Daniels 1996.

Let me turn now to textile production, which was traditionally taxed by the state as one of two fundamental and inseparable peasant activities – producing food and producing clothes. Although men worked outside the home and women inside, both were equally productive members of society performing complementary labor. Women's work in China was classically defined as the making of textiles; the inner quarters were identified not as a zone of dependence but as a site of essential productive activity, tying the household into the polity. As weavers and tax contributors, women were subjects of the state, contributing goods that were indispensable to the maintenance of the social order.

From the Han to the Song there were four main types of establishment producing textiles: (i) peasant households which relied essentially on family labor; (ii) large elite households, rural or urban, in which the mistress organized the production of textiles by family members, servants, and hired female workers; (iii) state manufactures, run by officials, using permanent or temporary conscripted workers, male and female; and (iv) urban workshops of various kinds. State manufactures and urban workshops owned complex looms or draw-looms on which fancy weaves and designs (damasks, brocades, satins, or gauzes) could be produced.[47] They specialized in the production of high-value textiles, mostly complex silk weaves; they did not produce their own raw materials but acquired them from tax goods or on the open market. Peasant and manorial households produced their own raw materials, both silk and plant fibres (hemp in the north, the finer ramie in the south), which in peasant households were all made up into simple weaves (tabbies or twills) using cheap and simple looms; manorial households frequently owned draw-looms as well as simple looms and produced complex silk weaves too.[48]

Up to the Song redistribution of grain and cloth was almost exclusively the prerogative of the state. The taxation system required that all peasants everywhere produce grain, yarn and textiles for tax. Changes in

Both stress the important point that sugar was never an estate crop or a factory product in China.

[47] When the draw loom was first used in China is a matter of controversy. Kuhn (1995) believes the Chinese draw loom was an indigenous development and that it was first used in some state workshops during the Han dynasty. In this he agrees with Chinese scholars, who argue that the ancient Chinese could not have woven figured silks such as those discovered in Latter Han tombs (25–220 AD) without a draw mechanism. Most Western scholars believe that the techniques of weft-faced weaving developed in Central Asia between the fourth and fifth centuries AD were at the origin of the draw loom. (On the difficulties of analyzing complex silk weaves and attributing them to different loom forms, see Desrosiers 1994.)

[48] For a good basic introduction to the development of Chinese textile machinery and technology, as well as to modern Chinese conventions of weave terminology, see Chen Weiji 1992.

regional impositions helped redefine the map of textile production and specialization. Up till the Song, the northern regions were taxed in silk and hemp, the southern provinces chiefly in ramie and other bast fibres.[49] But with the loss of the sericultural regions to invading nomadic rulers in the tenth century, the state fostered the development of a sericultural industry in the Lower Yangzi provinces – encouraging it by providing information and credit, imposing it by levying heavy taxes in silk.[50] It was not possible for individual households to opt out of producing silk if they lived in an area with a sericultural tax, or for individual households, whole villages or even districts to give up subsistence production and specialize in commodity production as many did in the Ming and Qing, buying their food on the open market.

Peasant men were obliged by tax requirements to grow hemp or ramie or mulberries, but in pre-Song times they were not involved in producing yarn or cloth. Women were responsible for every stage of cloth processing, from hatching silkworm eggs and twisting the ends of ramie fibers together, to weaving the cloth and making up the clothes. The following equipment was required: each household needed the basic flat loom used to make tax cloth; it also served for subsistence needs. If they raised silkworms, they needed trays and mats and a room or shed to keep the silkworms, as well as a basic reel for reeling the raw silk off the cocoons, and a spindle-wheel for spooling and quilling – twisting and combining the threads into yarn. The spindle-wheel could also be used for spinning hemp and ramie. This equipment was almost entirely made of cheap materials – ordinary wood, bamboo, hemp cords – and could be made and maintained at home or purchased from a village carpenter.

Peasant households could not afford the capital or the space for the elaborate looms needed to make complex cloth (even though peasant women might have acquired the skills to use them working in a nearby manorial household).[51] But well into the Song the plain tabby silks made in rural households remained an essential element of high Chinese culture. Given the rarity and extremely high cost of luxury weaves, most

[49] The fibres taken from hemp, ramie, kudzu vine, and other native Chinese plants are of the kind technically called *bast-fibres*: they are long and must be spliced together by hand before being twisted into weavable yarn. Cotton has very short fibres which, like wool, require true spinning.

[50] The Northern Song quota for just the ten most important sericultural provinces, representing 65 percent of the total, was almost 3 million bolts of silk and 9.1 million ounces of floss. The total tax in bast-fibre cloth was much lower, around 1.5 million bolts. Between 1131 and 1162, the annual silk quota for the Liangzhe region alone (the two provinces of the Yangzi Delta) was 1.17 million bolts of tabby (Kuhn 1987: 170ff).

[51] On the materials used for basic textile equipment, see Kuhn 1988: 4. A draw loom could be as much as sixteen feet long, with a tower as high as fifteen feet, as depicted in *Tiangong kaiwu* (Song 1637).

well-to-do people's everyday clothing was made from silk tabbies, and fine garments were often also made from plain silks embroidered, painted, or decorated with borders of fancy silk.[52] Before the advent of cotton, tabbies had no competitors in the lower range of the luxury market. The needs of officials and their families were partly provided for by state distribution of tax cloth, but there were also markets, local and inter-regional, for silks. In pre-Song times sericulture was typical of the north, and tabbies were widely produced in peasant households all along the Yellow River.[53] But the demand for silks was great throughout China, not least in the luxurious courts of the southern dynasties, and prices in the south were very high.[54] Through all this period the demand on the open market for plain silks such as peasant households could produce seems almost always to have exceeded supply.

Elite women were also involved in silk production, often very profitably, in urban mansions and on rural manors. The involvement of city ladies in textiles seems to have been most marked in the period from Han to Tang;[55] thereafter they were steadily displaced by the ever-increasing number of private workshops. Unlike the peasantry, some rural manorial households could afford the considerable investment for complex looms and were thus able to produce fancy silks commanding higher prices than tabby, although not the very finest kinds, all of which were produced in city manufactures and workshops by professional weavers.[56] The state ran the manufactures that produced the most elaborate and valuable silks. The raw materials came from the silk yarn or raw silk levied in taxes. The looms and much other equipment used in state manufactures were very specialized and expensive, constructed by skilled carpenters. Xue Jingshi's handbook on loom construction, the *Ziren yishi* [Traditions of the joiner's craft] prefaced 1264, describes the construction of various looms: draw-looms, standing looms, gauze looms, and combination looms. It makes clear the high cost of construction, the need for skilled maintenance, and the complexity of setting up the loom for weaving. A rather later text says a draw-loom included *eighteen hundred* components of water-milled bamboo.[57] The state

[52] Kuhn 1987: 351.

[53] During the Tianbao period (742–56), for example, roughly 3.7 million households out of a national total of 8.2 million were taxed in silk cloth; this represented a substantial proportion of the population of north China.

[54] Texts of the period note that southern officials made efforts to encourage the establishment of silk production, for instance by sending southern soldiers to find skilled brides from sericultural regions in the north (*Guoshi bu* 2, quoted Tong 1981: 109).

[55] See the range of examples cited in Tong 1981.

[56] Kuhn 1988: 387.

[57] According to Kuhn (1977; 1987: 376–86) there were no very significant changes in

manufactures were divided into separate workshops for different stages of production (dyeing, reeling, quilling, weaving), and the workforce, which included male and female conscripted artisans, was correspondingly specialized. Private workshops varied in size from family-size establishments to the occasional huge enterprise with more looms than a state manufacture. One rich Tang merchant specialized in lined garments; his workshop had five hundred looms, more than the Song imperial manufacture in the capital, which had only four hundred.[58] In his historical survey of handicrafts, Tong Shuye hypothesizes that the majority of pre-Song private workshops were much smaller, relying principally on family members and one or two hired workers for labor. Since respectable women worked only in their own or in some other family's inner quarters, urban hired workers were almost invariably men, and many craftsmen had received their training in government service.[59] However, as late as the Song, complex weaves made on drawlooms formed only 4 percent of total production even in the most urbanized and advanced silk-weaving regions of Sichuan and the Lower Yangzi.[60] This changed dramatically in the late imperial period, as did the regional and gendered organization of textile production, and the pattern of demand for silks after the development of the cotton industry.

During the Northern Song the state made great efforts to encourage the growth of sericulture in the southern provinces. Various handbooks to help officials improve peasant sericulture were written and circulated in the Song, but the real triggers for change were the loss of the north in 1126, the mass migration of northern peasants and craftsmen to the Yangzi provinces and further south, and the establishment of the Southern Song capital in Hangzhou. With imperial manufactures and a myriad of private workshops producing luxury silks for a growing market of literati and wealthy merchant families, Hangzhou and the other Lower Yangzi cities became the nucleus of a regional and eventually a national economy, buying up raw materials and processing them into high-quality silk goods that were sold all over the empire.

As the supply of fancy silk fabrics made in urban workshops increased, so too did the demand for raw silk. At the same time there is some

loom-construction after the *Ziren yishi* was written, so we may assume that Song drawlooms were comparable in complexity and value to the 1800–piece loom described by Song Yingxing in the *Tiangong kaiwu* of 1637 (pp. 31 ff). It has been suggested to me that perhaps Song, who was keen to display the sophistication and complexity of all the crafts and manufactures he described, exaggerated the number of pieces required for the draw loom. However, his account tallies with other late imperial references to the cost and complexity of specialized looms.

[58]   *Taiping guangji* 243, quoted in Tong 1981: 103.
[59]   Tong 1981: 104–09.
[60]   Kuhn 1987: 378.

evidence to indicate that a change in fashion affected elite demand for the plain tabbies that peasant households could produce. The total demand for silk luxury fabrics increased and changed in the Song as the literati class consolidated their control over an increasingly elaborate bureaucracy, and the numbers of well-off urbanites with high living standards increased. It seems likely that the Song fashion for silk gauzes (made on a loom with a double warp-beam, beyond the means and the skills of most peasant weavers) diminished the elite market for plain tabbies. Meanwhile the growing number of urban workshops increased demand for silk yarn. When the Yuan state shifted from taxes in silk cloth to taxes levied only in raw silk and yarn, many rural households must have decided once and for all to abandon weaving tabbies and concentrate on sericulture and reeling, especially since a number of technical improvements disseminated during the Song and Yuan allowed sericultural households to increase their output of silk floss and yarn.[61]

Another good reason for many rural households to abandon the slow and painstaking weaving of silk tabbies, indeed to give up the exacting tasks of sericulture altogether, was the advent of cotton. Cotton cloth was an exotic luxury in China during the early dynasties. Perennial varieties were grown in the southern provinces in medieval times, and it is thought that annual varieties were developed from perennials as cultivation spread northwards, becoming established in the Lower Yangzi perhaps as early as the twelfth century, and reaching the Huai and Sichuan by the Yuan. Annual cottons grew in a wide range of soils

---

[61] The Yuan state, avid to have as many craftsmen as possible working under its control to produce luxury goods to order, shifted the silk tax from tabbies to raw silk for use in its own workshops. It also conscripted almost all the craftsmen in China: 720,000 craft households were called up in 1236, and the Eastern Weaving and Dyeing Bureau controlled 3006 households, with 154 looms, producing a quota of 4527 bolts of cloth and 1152.8 pounds of wild silk (Tong 1981: 192, 198).

Improved sericultural methods available to rural households of the period included better breeding methods and the development of several types of reel that improved the quality of the thread or increased the speed with which it could be reeled off; there were also improved techniques for killing the moths inside the cocoon, so that reeling could be postponed or spread out over a longer period (Kuhn 1988: 318, 340–43, citing among other texts Wang Zhen's *Nong shu* [Agricultural treatise] of 1313).

One Song woman who was important in these innovations was Xu Wenmei, the wife of the poet-official Qin Guan (1049–1100) who wrote the *Can shu* [Book of sericulture] in or just before 1090. The *Can shu* is one of the key documents describing improvements and innovation in silk production during the Song. It is a very short work of just ten paragraphs: half treat silk-reeling, half other sericultural equipment and machinery. The details are precise, and the text depicts the Shandong methods which Qin prefers to those of the south. In the preface he indicates that his knowledge came from his wife, whom he married in 1067, and who was trained in Shandong methods as a girl.

and climates, and in the process of acclimatization the length of the staple and quantity of lint were improved, increasing yields, making processing easier, and improving the quality of the cloth, so that cotton really became competitive with native Chinese textiles.[62] Cotton is mentioned here and there in economic documents from the Song, but the industry was really established under the Yuan and expanded extremely rapidly, till by the late Ming cotton was worn by everyone and was cultivated all over China. Late Ming texts tell us that by the Wanli era (1573–1620) it was planted on half the best land in Hebei and Henan; of 2 million *mu* (roughly 130,000 hectares) of land reclaimed by the state and army in the Songjiang region of the Lower Yangzi, over half was planted with cotton, and it was replacing rice in upland regions of the Lower Yangzi.[63]

Once again it was the taxation system, in conjunction with technical innovations, that stimulated the growth of the industry. The Mongols who established the Yuan dynasty were familiar with cotton from India and the Middle East. Sericulture had been severely damaged by the wars of invasion, especially in the north. Yuan taxes on silk producers were very high, but the amount of silk brought in was still inadequate to the state's wants. The incentives to the state to encourage cotton production, and to peasants to switch (if they could) from silk to cotton, were equally compelling. State-commissioned agricultural works like the *Nongsang jiyao* [Fundamentals of agriculture and sericulture] (edited by Hang Qi in 1273) included detailed sections on cotton cultivation. In 1289 cotton bureaux were established in various provinces (Fujian, the Lower and Middle Yangzi) to provide local farmers with the technical information they needed to cultivate the new crop. Then in 1296 cotton was incorporated into the tax system at very favorable rates compared to other textiles.

No sooner did cotton become available than it became indispensable. The cloth was strong and durable, cheap, warmer than ramie or hemp in the winter, and it made padded garments almost as warm and much less expensive than silk; for summer wear it was absorbent and cool and made fine, light cloths that could be dyed in rich colors and calendered to a shine approaching the gloss of silk. A bolt of plain weave could be woven on a simple loom such as most peasant households owned in a single day.[64] The equipment for ginning, bowing, and spinning cotton, said to have been introduced from Hainan to Shanghai by an elderly woman named Auntie Huang (Huang Daopo) in the late thirteenth

[62] Chao 1977: chapter 1.   [63] Song 1637: 41; see also Nishijima 1984.
[64] Fang Guancheng 1808: 2/9–10.

century, spread so rapidly through the central provinces that it was known all over China by the early Ming.[65]

The Ming government, which used as much as 15 to 20 million bolts of cotton a year, continued to promote cotton cultivation through taxation.[66] An edict of 1365 made cotton cultivation compulsory for all farmers with holdings over 5 *mu* (roughly a third of a hectare), but this proved unworkable and it was soon replaced by another stipulating that all farmers must pay part of their tax in cotton, which could also be substituted for grain in other quotas.[67] The demands of court and state were not diminished by the tax reforms of the late Ming, but the role of private entrepreneurs in procuring and distributing cloth was boosted, and the cloth industry continued to grow and develop, the largest in the empire until well into the twentieth century. By the time that taxes in kind were abolished in 1581, cotton was grown and made into cloth in every corner of China. "In every ten houses there will be at least one cotton loom, so there is no need to illustrate it," wrote Song Yingxing in 1637.[68]

The cultivation of cotton, however, spread much faster than its processing, and one of the earlier effects of its adoption was to create a regional division of labor (see also the discussion in Bin Wong's essay). The regionalization of the cotton industry was paralleled by the increasing fragmentation and commercialization of textile production in general; meanwhile agriculture was also becoming increasingly specialized, and the proportion of the population who were no longer primary producers but earned their livings by craft or trade increased. Cash commutations of basic taxes in kind became increasingly numerous and complex, and eventually in 1581 the Single Whip tax reforms did away with the traditional taxes in kind altogether.[69] This consolidated the trend whereby women gave up weaving if more profitable occupations were available; conversely, where home weaving was more profitable than grain farming, peasant men might join their wives and daughters at the loom.

One of the roots from which the regional division of labor in textiles sprang was a simple environmental factor. To spin good quality cotton thread the air must be humid, as it is throughout southern China in the summer. But summers are extremely dry in the north, and thread spun

---

[65] Kuhn 1988: 212.

[66] At 40 Chinese feet to the bolt, 20 million bolts would be the equivalent of some 260 million metres of cotton; compare this to the thousand or more million yards of cotton goods exported annually by the Manchester warehouses *to British India alone* from the 1870s up to the First World War (China was also an important market, but not as big as India) (Kidd 1993: 104).

[67] Chao 1977: 19.   [68] Song 1637: 41.   [69] Huang 1974.

there was brittle and uneven. On the other hand, as long as well-water or river-water was available, cotton grew extremely well in the north, where there was also a great demand for cotton cloth. Very quickly we see the development of a regional division of labor. The southern provinces grew cotton, but had the capacity to process much more than they grew. The northern provinces could produce raw cotton but could not process it. Commercial capital seized the opportunity. Brokers and merchants bought raw cotton from peasants in the north and transported it to the Lower Yangzi and the Huai, where it was put out through local markets to peasant women to be spun and woven. The merchants returned to the north with finished cloth which they sold in the same markets where they bought the raw cotton. Big merchants controlled every stage of production. They bought up raw cotton, put it out at local markets for peasant women to spin and to weave, had the cloth dyed and calendered in town or city workshops, and then exported it all over China for sale. What is striking about this is that the northern producers were in no position to strike any bargains, since it was impossible for them to process the raw cotton on the spot.

The regional division of labor in cotton production consolidated the role of the Lower Yangzi as the manufacturing center of China, and reduced the northern provinces to the status of an underdeveloped periphery that exported raw materials and imported finished goods. By the Wanli reign (1573–1620) Songjiang prefecture, near modern Shanghai, had become the proto-industrial heart of China, the center of cotton-cloth production, and the hub of a complex network of national trade. Songjiang households wove a wide range of cotton goods, mostly plain, but including patterned cloth and twills, as well as bolts that were narrower and longer than usual and went to the inland regions of the south, and other special types that went to the northwest and Beijing. Cloth from Changshu went to Shandong for peasants' clothes. Throughout the Lower Yangzi, villages produced cotton cloth which was said to "pay for their taxes, their food and clothing, their equipment, their entertainments and ceremonies, all the costs of living and dying."[70]

The terms of trade were so unequal during the Ming that the Lower Yangzi provinces were buying northern cotton and exporting some of their own to Jiangxi and Fujian. "Raw cotton is cheap in the north and cloth is dear, while in the south the contrary is true," wrote Xu Guangqi in 1639. But at the beginning of the seventeenth century the peasants of Suning in Hebei discovered that cotton could be spun and woven during the northern summer if it was done in underground cellars where

[70] Jiading gazetteer (1605), quoted in Tong 1981: 223.

humidity could be conserved. The situation changed rapidly. Xu added: "A few years ago the cloth made in Suning was not a tenth as good as that of the Lower Yangzi. At first it was dreadfully coarse, but now it is very fine, almost up to the Lower Yangzi quality." He goes on to say that the northern provinces still produce 20 percent less cloth than the East, and it fetches only 60–70 percent of the price: nevertheless this was quite an achievement for a region that just two or three decades previously produced no cloth at all.[71] At roughly the same date the (Lower Yangzi) Jiading gazetteer is already complaining that the northern market for Yangzi cloth has dried up, and the early Qing *Mianhua pu* [Treatise on Cotton] says Jiangnan now has to import raw cotton from the south since it gets none from the north.[72]

With the dissemination of the Suning cellars, peasant families in the north became essentially self-sufficient in cloth. The men planted the cotton, their wives and daughters thinned out the bolls, picked them, processed them into yarn and wove a sturdy homespun that lasted two or three years: "Whole peasant families assemble, young and old: the mother-in-law leads her sons' wives, the mother supervises her daughters; when the wicker lantern is lit and the starlight and moonlight come slanting down, still the clack-clack of the spindle-wheels comes from the house."[73] Any surplus was sold in the local shop or market, and went from there to nearby towns or to the riverboats. By the later Qing the trade in northern cottons had reached considerable proportions – a governor of Zhili province remarked in the eighteenth century that more cotton was now woven there than in the lower Yangzi, and large quantities were exported to Korea.[74]

In the northern provinces peasant women continued to produce cotton homespuns through into the twentieth century. Although it was not uncommon to purchase the raw cotton, there was no separation of spinning and weaving, both of which remained female tasks. In other parts of China commercialization and specialization meant that different components of the production process often took place in different households or even different regions, and new gender divisions of labor emerged. Cotton cultivation had been profitable in Fujian, but by the Qing most farmers had given it up in favor of sugar, which was exported throughout China and overseas. Local merchants would pay for part of the sugar with raw cotton from the Lower Yangzi, which the sugar

[71] Xu Guangqi 1979: 35.
[72] Quoted in Tong 1981: 237.
[73] Ninghe gazetteer (1779), quoted in Tong 1981: 306.
[74] Chao 1977: 34. Philip Huang remarks that the initial development of cotton cloth markets in the North depended on access to river transport (1985: 118–20).

farmers' wives spun and wove mostly for family use. As markets grew not just for Fujianese sugar but also for its excellent teas, it became more advantageous for peasant women to give up weaving, buy cloth, and use their time processing the sugar grown on their farms, and tending, harvesting, and curing tea. Fujian started to import cotton cloth, as did neighboring Guangdong. In the nineteenth century, Sichuan and Shanxi peasants started growing opium on their cotton land. But opium did not require female labor, and so these provinces imported raw cotton from Hebei, not finished cloth from the Lower Yangzi.[75]

In regions like the Lower Yangzi we increasingly find whole households involved in the production of textiles, with men sitting at the loom while their wives and daughters spin and reel the yarn. The prefectural gazetteer for Songjiang of 1663 says: "In the weaving villages they make very fine cottons; during the agricultural off-seasons they produce some ten thousand bolts daily. The women work hard to supplement farming income by weaving."[76] But the high figures given for the agricultural off-seasons imply that men took over at the looms when they were not busy in the fields. In other villages men were also involved, part or full time, often abandoning agriculture altogether in places where the land was poor. Huang Ang's early Qing monograph on the Wuxi region tells us that in Wuxi "farming only suffices to feed the village people for the three winter months; they begin weaving in the spring, exchanging the cloth for the rice they eat.... Even if there is a bad [rice] harvest, as long as the cotton ripens elsewhere the Wuxi villagers do not suffer too badly.... In villages where the soil is very poor, both men and women work exclusively at spinning and weaving."[77]

Since cotton competed favorably with silk, its development had important repercussions on the evolution of the silk industry. During the Ming and Qing the rural production of silk tabbies almost disappeared except in Huzhou prefecture in the Lower Yangzi. The balance of products shifted markedly from plain to fancy silks, which were mostly woven in workshops concentrated in the cities and suburbs of the main economic centers in the south. Raw silk was still produced in rural households, again largely concentrated in the Lower Yangzi: sericulture died out in regions which could not produce thread of a quality high enough for weaving fancy silks.

One reason for the shift out of rural production of silk cloth was that silk tabbies, which had been made both in peasant and in manorial

[75] Chao 1977: 23.   [76] Tong 1981: 348.
[77] Huang Ang, [Wu]xi Jin[kui] zhi xiao lu; quoted in Tong 1981: 348.

households, suffered badly from the competition from cotton, especially after 1581 when taxes in kind were abolished, so that the state no longer provided any direct demand for silk tabbies even in traditional silk-weaving regions. Another was that the fancy silks made in manorial households or even in certain long-established urban centers were no longer able to compare with the price of fine cottons or the sophistication of the highly specialized silks of the southern conurbations. Even rural production of raw silk and yarn was affected, because all the best Jiangnan businesses preferred to use local raw silk from Huzhou, which was of exceptionally high quality.

During the later Ming silk tabbies were still produced in Zhili and Jiangxi for sale in the central markets such as Hangzhou, but the quantity was insignificant compared to what was produced by urban workshops run with hired labor in Hangzhou and Suzhou, the Lower Yangzi centers of fine silk weaving.[78] Sichuan, Guangdong, and Fujian also continued to produce some homemade tabbies, but mostly they exported raw silk to the Lower Yangzi. The Sichuan monopoly of the finest brocades was now a thing of the past, and the silk industries of Hebei, Henan, and Shandong had also fallen into decline, in part because of the effects of war, in part because of shifts in regional economic balance.[79]

A typical case was Luzhou in Shanxi, which had produced famous tabbies for centuries: "The gentry all wear Lu tabbies," according to Lü Kun who served in the region in the sixteenth century. The tabbies were produced not in peasant households, however, but in workshops in small towns, and in much of the countryside women had apparently lost the skills of textile production. Governor Lü Kun "ordered all female adults *without occupation* in certain districts of the province to learn spinning and weaving." The women's involvement in silk-making lasted no longer than Lü's tenure.[80]

Sericultural skills died out completely in whole provinces. Pierre-Étienne Will tells us that by the time Chen Hongmou served as Governor of Shaanxi, on and off between 1743 and 1758, a local tradition of sericulture stretching back to the Zhou dynasty had been completely forgotten, except for a handful of places where officials or gentry had made efforts to revive the lost skills. A Silk Bureau was established in Xi'an in the 1740s after an official named Yang Shen had spent some years promoting mulberry cultivation, and Chen coordinated his efforts with the Bureau: "the trees became productive just one

---

[78] Hangzhou gazetteer (1579), *juan* 53, quoted in Chen 1958: 7.
[79] Tong 1981: 231.
[80] Chao 1977: 21, my emphasis.

or two years after the shoots had been planted, and once silkworm eggs
had been imported and the breeding techniques had been taught to
volunteer farmers, the problem was to import the skills and install the
machinery and infrastructure for textile production."[81]

The intention was not to reestablish Shaanxi as a national center of
silk weaving. Chen's policies of resuscitation, like many others of the
time, were intended to "enhance local self-sufficiency" so that local
people did not have to sell scarce food grain to buy imported cloth.
Peasant households were to be educated to see that mulberries,
cocoons, and raw silk were all sources of income, and the silk cloth was
initially to be woven in urban workshops, though Chen hoped that
eventually peasants (presumably "females without occupation" as in the
case of Lü) would learn to weave tabbies again at home. Like Lü Kun's,
Chen's project did not long outlive his tenure in the district.

The rural districts around the Taihu Lake, near the great silk-weaving
centers of Suzhou and Hangzhou, produced the best raw silk in all
China, the famous Huzhou silk. Given the ever-expanding demand for
raw silk from the workshops of Hangzhou and Suzhou, it is surprising to
observe the vitality of rural tabby production in Huzhou in the seventeenth century. Perhaps it was the high quality of the locally produced
yarn which kept these tabbies competitive.

The *Shenshi nongshu* [Agricultural treatise of Master Shen], composed
in about 1640 just before the fall of the Ming, describes sericulture in a
landlord household in Huzhou:

Men till and women weave: these are the basic tasks of a farming household.
And especially in my area, every household weaves. Some are extraordinarily
skilled and work from early morning till late at night, and they produce an
incalculable amount. Two women will weave 120 bolts of tabby a year. Each
ounce of tabby is usually worth 1 string of cash [one-tenth of an ounce of silver],
so for 120 bolts, after paying for 700 ounces of warp thread worth 50 ounces of
silver and 500 of weft worth 27, plus the cost of reels and other equipment and
wax for the yarn at 5 ounces, and 10 ounces for the women's food – altogether

---

[81] Will 1991: 12. Susan Mann reminds us that such proposals took as their model an
essay by the seventeenth-century scholar Gu Yanwu, whose essay entitled "The
Profitability of Weaving" advised the state to promote silk weaving in households on
border areas (Mann 1992a: 83). Both Gu and Chen suggest that "master weavers" and
skilled craftsmen able to construct looms should be brought in to transmit their skills to
the local people. It would be interesting to know whether such plans to teach women
new skills were thwarted by the reluctance of families to let their women go outside the
home to be taught by strange men. There is a paradox here, for "in the minds of Qing
statecraft writers, those regions in China where 'women wove' were culturally and even
morally superior to those areas where women had no specialized home crafts" (Mann
1992a: 86). But at the same time morally and culturally superior women were not
supposed to leave their own quarters, nor were they supposed to consort with strange
men. Perhaps the husbands went to the weaving classes for them?

something over 90 ounces of silver – there remain 30 ounces in profit. If you breed your own silkworms, the gain will be that amount more.[82]

Shen is describing a landlord household which purchases its silk thread, already made up into warp or weft yarns. From the figures he gives, we can calculate that weaving tabby added 50 percent to the purchase price of warp thread, and almost double to weft. If we compare Shen's figures with those given by Chen Fu for sericulture in the Yangzi Delta in the mid twelfth century, we find that profits have dropped enormously. Chen says that a family of ten, raising ten trays of silk-worms, would have enough raw silk to weave 31.2 bolts of tabby at a profit of 1.4 bushels of hulled grain per bolt.[83] Even so, and despite the high demand for raw silk, five centuries later it still seems to have been considered worthwhile for sericultural households in Huzhou to invest in weaving tabbies, but obviously the intervention of brokers, providing raw silk on credit and buying back the cloth at their own prices, greatly reduced the profits of any family that was short of capital.

The market for raw silk or even cocoons continued to expand as the number of urban workshops and the amount of fancy silks they produced grew. Huzhou, where Shen came from, produced the best raw silk in all China, and in the Wanli period (1573–1620) "even a plot the size of a handkerchief will be planted with mulberries ... the rich have mere patches of rice field but thousands of acres of mulberry land." Huzhou continued to export raw silk right though the Qing, in fact it almost monopolized the market. At the end of the Ming the weavers of Fujian and Guangdong as well as Hangzhou and Suzhou depended on Huzhou silk; only the silkweavers of Luzhou (soon to become extinct) bought raw silk from Langzhou in Sichuan. Luzhou produced only tabbies, but Fuzhou made satins both for internal markets and for export; Guangzhou (Canton) produced "satins of a fine, even texture and fresh, bright and rich color, while its gauzes and monochrome patterned silks outshine even those of Suzhou and Hangzhou, so that the gauzes are bought all over China and the satins almost as much." Since southern yarns lacked lustre, Fujian and Guangdong were both dependent on the Lower Yangzi for the raw materials to make their luxury products.

Meanwhile in Huzhou and nearby, profits from weaving were declining. "The income from weaving gets smaller day by day," says a Lower Yangzi gazetteer for the Qianlong period (1736–96). Giving figures from the tax records, it compares the value of raw silk and of the equivalent weight of woven tabby over the two centuries up to the

---

[82] Zhang Lixiang 1983: 84.   [83] Chen Fu 1956: 21.

twelfth year of the Qianlong reign (1747): the value-added by weaving fell from 300–350 percent in the Jiajing reign (1522–66) to 150–200 percent in the Kangxi reign (1662–1722) and to a mere 55–110 percent in 1747.[84]

The decline in weaving profits also affected the organization of silk production in urban workshops. Fancy silk cloths were woven in what were known as "loom households," *jihu*. At the end of the Ming, an urban "loom household" owned its own loom or looms, and used either domestic labor or hired hands to spin and weave raw silk purchased on the market. Unlike rural landlord households, the urban loom-owners did not hire women.[85] Urban male weavers were highly specialized, but despite their valuable skills they had less security than their rural sisters who were hired by the year and fed whether there was weaving for them to do or not. The urban craftsmen were paid a wage only for the days they worked, and were employed only to work at their speciality. If there was no work for them, they starved:

There is a master who calculates the number of days and pays them accordingly; if there are additional tasks he may call in freelance workers, who assemble at the bridges waiting to be hired, satin workers at one bridge, gauze workers at another. Those who twist silk are called wheel-workers. Several dozens or a hundred may stand together in the Xianqi quarter craning their necks expectantly; after eating their congee they break up and go home. If the loom households lack work then this class has no way to make a living. The loom households provide the capital, the loom-worker the labor, and they both depend on each other for a steady living.[86]

As new centers developed in Fujian, Guangdong, and then Nanjing, and the silk trade became more competitive, the advantages of owning capital became more marked, and exploitation intensified. Employers played off ruined peasants looking for city work against experienced textile workers. While it was still possible to write convincingly of the interdependence of the loom-owners and their workers in the late Ming, during the Qing no worker imagined that the resources were equally

---

[84] Huzhou gazetteer (1578), *juan* 29, quoted in Chen 1958: 7; Xu Guangqi 1979: *juan* 31, quoted in Tong 1981: 231; Huzhou gazetteer (1758), *juan* 41, quoted in Tong 1981: 231.

[85] While Ming and Qing texts on rural subsistence silk production still have illustrations showing women involved in all the processes, the *Tiangong kaiwu* (Song 1637), which concentrates on the production of commodities, shows men not only weaving but also quilling or twisting silk. The significance of these illustrations is that the author, Song Yongxing, wished to emphasize the most advanced forms of technology in use at the time. He therefore devoted far more space to urban workshops than to household production of textiles. It is notable that he also includes the finishing processes like dyeing and calendering – which do not figure in the treatment of textiles in agricultural treatises.

[86] *Wanli shilu* (1573–1620), quoted in Chen 1958: 7.

pooled.[87] A memorial of 1734 speaks of a shift from daily wages to piece rates for hired weavers.[88] Meanwhile the loom-owners were displacing more and more of the burdens of production through the process of putting-out. Poor women were employed to wind the silk for workshops, but many silk merchants, instead of weaving silk on their own premises, hired out their looms to weaving families. In this way the owners did not have to deal with intransigent groups of male workers, and the work of the professional weavers was supplemented by that of their whole family, with men sitting at the loom while their womenfolk prepared and reeled the yarn.

The main rural contribution, still predominantly female, to fancy silks between the Song and the late Ming was the breeding of silkworms and reeling of raw silk. With the development of the new putting-out system, rural women were once again involved in the production of fancy cloth, but not as managers or skilled weavers, rather as auxiliary workers, reelers, and spinners, even within the context of family production. As the putting-out system developed in the late Ming, silk weaving over-flowed from Suzhou into surrounding villages like Shengze, many villages abandoned agriculture altogether, and everyone in the family worked together, with the men here again taking over from their wives at the loom: "Poor people all wove themselves, and had their offspring change the patterns, while the women's labor was insufficient to prepare the yarn and they reeled silk from morning to night. As soon as their sons and daughters were ten, they all toiled day and night to fill their bellies."[89]

The meaning of work

The late imperial ruling elite was deeply disturbed by prevailing condi-tions of production in agriculture and the textile industry and tried hard to alter them. By the late Ming we find a litany of complaints emerging

---

[87] Weavers were always a rebellious lot. During the Ming the loom-owners (who had to pay taxes on their looms and output) usually allied with the weavers against the state. By Qing times, the weavers rebelled not against the state but against the loom owners (see the paper on urban riots in the Ming and Qing by Tsing Yuan [1979], who also documents a series of riots by calenderers in Qing Suzhou). An early Qing memorial says that "the loom households of Suzhou used to hire many workers to weave ... and paid them a daily wage, and originally everyone agreed that both sides gained from this arrangement. But journeymen without training, who didn't know the work, were fined by their employers, which engendered great resentment. They grouped together into a union and called a strike for higher wages. This put the loom households out of work, and they sacked the weavers. Then loom owner He Junheng and others requested that a stone be engraved registering a perpetual ban on such strikes" (Tong 1981: 345).

[88] Tong 1981: 294.

[89] Wujiang gazetteer (1684?), *juan* 38, quoted in Tong 1981: 226–27.

about the degeneration of "work." Chinese literati and officials not only voiced traditional worries about the people, *min*, abandoning the fundamental occupation of farming, but also expressed anxieties about men performing women's work, and about women being without occupation. I would now like to probe a little deeper into the technological culture of late imperial China, to suggest what it was about the material world around them that so concerned the late imperial elite.

Let me start with the complaint of the writer Hu Juren (1434–84) that commercialization and the spread of artisan activities had turned weaving into a man's job.[90] Why did this matter? To understand the panic that seized late imperial intellectuals and officials when they saw men at the loom, women breaking clods in the fields, or farmers giving up their land to work as petty traders, we have to recognize that in their eyes the economic significance of work was at best secondary.

Confucian thought emphasized that morality was not a purely intellectual phenomenon but was rooted in bodily habit. Confucius himself attributed great moral importance to the study of *li*, a term which denoted both formal rituals and the everyday practices of etiquette and deportment. Confucius would not sit on a mat that was placed crooked; Zhu Xi, one of the founding fathers of the neo-Confucian school of the mid imperial period, in discussing the design of the family shrine and the practice of the major and minor rituals that took place in this sacralized space of everyday life, insisted on the moral significance of even minor details of rising and sitting, coming and going. James Watson has suggested that one reason why imperial Chinese elites were so successful in diffusing their values throughout society is that they paid little attention to orthodoxy as such, that is, to trying to inculcate correct ideas – instead, he says, they aimed for orthopraxy, the inculcation of correct practices, presuming that the corresponding values would be unconsciously absorbed in the process. This idea has most usually been explored in the field of ritual, but it can also be applied to deportment and to work.[91] To me it is quite convincing, and it helps explain the deep disquiet that educated Chinese felt when categories of work or of workers were mixed up.

In the Chinese statecraft tradition, work symbolized the embodiment of a social contract in which the ruler and his officials worked to ensure the welfare of the people, *min*, envisaged as peasant families. In return the male *min* worked in the fields to produce grain for their own food

---

[90] McDermott 1990: 30.
[91] Watson 1988; for a suggestive example of the importance of bodily practice in expressing orthodoxy, see Hevia (1994) on the refusal of Ambassador Macartney to perform the kowtow at the Qing court.

and for taxes, their wives produced the textiles that were used to clothe their families and the servants of the state. Agriculture was defined as the fundamental occupation, crafts and trade were considered at best secondary, at worst pernicious, since they drained labor from the fundamental occupations and encouraged extravagance. To farm and to weave were to fulfill one's obligations as a dutiful subject. According to Michel Cartier, the statement by the fourth-century BC Confucian philosopher Mencius, to the effect that those who work with their minds govern, while those who work with their bodies are governed, should not be taken to mean that laborers are naturally subordinate to thinkers, but rather as an expression of "the complementarity of human activities and the necessary solidarity of social groups"; "work was highly valued as a productive activity synonymous with civilization," and the art of ruling over this civilization was explored through technical metaphors drawn from carpentry, building, spinning, weaving, potting, and jade carving.[92]

At the same time work was ranked. The "basic" productive activity was agriculture, which like government was considered an essential form of labor. Other forms of labor than farming were considered of subsidiary dignity; even though houses, cloth, iron tools, and other craft products were indispensable everyday items, until relatively late in the imperial period craftsmen were considered "mean" people. "Working the land was the only economic activity that did not 'debase,' the activity that an educated man could and should take up whenever he was not studying or working in the service of the state. We can understand, then, why the best way to enable men to cultivate the civic virtues was to guarantee them access to land, and conversely, why it was to landowners that the reins of government were entrusted."[93]

This vision of a political-economic hierarchy in which grubbing in the mud for a bare subsistence was represented as morally superior to running a profitable manufacture can seldom have reflected the experiences or beliefs either of the people engaged in these different forms of work, or of the majority of the population. Nevertheless, until the later Ming permission to take the imperial examinations was restricted to the sons of peasants and of scholar-gentry families, and only in the eighteenth century was the "mean" (*jian*) status previously imposed upon craftsmen and their families abolished.[94] As Hill Gates puts it, the late

---

[92] See Cartier 1984: 278, 304 on the ideology of work, Keightley 1989 on political metaphors.

[93] Cartier 1984: 304.

[94] See Chen Shiqi 1958 on the status of craftsmen; Mann 1991 on the eighteenth-century abolition of mean status; Woodside and Elman 1994: 546 on the Ming opening of the examinations to merchants.

imperial state did all it could to maintain a "tributary mode of production" in the teeth of the consolidation on the ground of a "petty capitalist mode of production" that had radically transformed the social landscape and the rationalities of everyday survival.[95] One effective weapon in this struggle to maintain the values of a classical world order was the regulation of access to political power through the examinations. Another was the structuring of the tax system, which until the "New Whip" reforms of 1581 continued to predicate a subject population of subsistence farming couples. Neither remained workable by the late Ming. However statesmen still did not abandon their vision of a world order organized around a social contract between ruler and peasant subjects, but it seems as if they decided to shift the level at which they intervened, to essay social reform through the reform of working practices and gender relations.

The classic gender division of labor in China was encapsulated in the saying: "Men till, women weave" (*nangeng nüzhi*). *Min*, the people, was a gendered concept, implying peasant couples performing complementary work. The growing of food-grain and the production of textiles were considered equally fundamental in providing for the welfare of the common people and the strength of the state: this belief remained central to Chinese statecraft for more than two millennia, ever since it was first formulated by the political philosophers of the fifth century BC and institutionalized in the tax system. However, as I argued earlier, the efforts of later Chinese rulers to preserve a reasonably convincing and workable ideal of a *min* consisting of peasant families directly engaged with the state might well have been in vain were it not for the technical characteristics of wet-rice farming, and the constraints they exercise on the development of the means and relations of production. The structures of power and the nature of the social contract might have been transformed if the economic center of China had not shifted in medieval times from the millet-growing plains of the north to the southern rice regions. Yet intensive rice farming systems supported a diversified rural economy which in itself worried conventional Confucian thinkers, since it implied a lack of attention to the basic occupation of grain farming. And although China was producing more textiles than ever before, we see a stream of late imperial edicts and projects designed to increase female participation in weaving.[96]

[95] Gates 1989.
[96] For instance four of the five first Qing emperors commissioned and wrote inscriptions for imperial editions of the *Gengzhi tu*, and the Jiaqing emperor wrote poems for a work on domestic cotton production, the *Shouyi guangxun* (ed. Fang Guancheng), which was published in 1808. See also the collection of policy writings published as the *Huangchao jingshi wenbian*, mentioned in note 106.

It has been argued that the late imperial idealization of such female expressions of loyalty as widow chastity or the suicide of violated women was an expression of male anxiety and helplessness in the face of political turmoil that educated men projected on to women as the Ming crumbled and the alien Qing demanded their services.[97] Similarly, I believe, the late Ming and early Qing official obsession with bringing men back to farming, and returning women to the loom, is at least in part a projection on to the lower social classes of the elite's anxieties firstly about its failure to perform its proper role, and secondly about the extreme social mobility characteristic of the period, with its consequent dangers of disorder.[98]

Worries about women not weaving remind us that the material importance of cloth was only one dimension of its political significance and contribution to the social order. In Chinese thought clothing is what distinguishes humans from beasts, and among humans it distinguishes between the rulers and the ruled. "The noble wear sweeping robes, resplendent as mountain dragons they rule the empire; the humble wear coarse wool or hemp garments, in winter to protect them from the cold, in summer to shield their bodies."[99] The legendary Yellow Emperor invented proper clothing, replacing the skins of animals and the feathers of birds with silk and hemp, "making jackets in the image of Heaven." Of the silkworm the early Confucian philosopher Xun Zi says: "Its merit is to clothe and ornament everything under Heaven, to the ten thousandth generation. Thus rites and music are completed, noble and base are distinguished, the aged are nourished and the young reared."[100] In imperial China cloth was indispensable to every social ritual. Fine cloths were exchanged between families at the time of betrothal, and a bride entering her groom's family took with her a dowry often consisting largely of cloth that she herself had woven. The rituals of funerals and mourning required special clothing of coarse, undyed hemp. The ceremonials of marriage and burial both served to express the ties between individual families and the community or lineage reinforcing

---

[97] T'ien 1988, Carlitz 1994.

[98] Mann 1991 discusses the heavy emphasis on virtue and orthodoxy that tends to characterize periods of social mobility.

[99] Song Yingxing, *Tiangong kaiwu* (The exploitation of the works of nature) (Song 1637): 31. This work is a technical treatise written by Song Yingxing and first printed in 1637. Although it includes descriptions of peasant production of food and other basics, Song's main interest is in the most advanced and productive specialized commercial enterprises.

[100] *Huainanzi* (The Book of the Prince of Huainan, a compendium of natural philosophy compiled c. 120 BC), quoted in Kuhn 1988: 250; *Xun zi* (The Book of Master Xun, a philosophical treatise written c. 240 BC), ibid: 301.

or renegotiating the social order.[101] Clothing was the mark of civilization. Not only did it distinguish ranks and provide ornament, it was
linked to the reproduction of human society through descent, the care of
the old, the raising of children, and the proper distinction and complementarity between the sexes.

In the minds of the Chinese elite the material, social, and political
values of making cloth were indissociable. A woman's dignity and virtue
were continually sustained by her weaving or sericultural activities. The
symbolic importance of food grains and peasant men's role in their
production are equally clear. However we must also bear in mind that it
was not just the symbolic value of grain and of textiles that was at issue,
but the correct gender roles embodied in their production.

The canonical Confucian works like the "Book of Rites," *Liji*, stressed
that marriage was a partnership, in which husband and wife fulfilled
different but equally essential duties, complementary in every sphere
including that of work: "The wife is the fitting partner of her husband,
performing all the work with hemp and silk."[102] Furthermore the
canonical works insisted that of the five fundamental social relationships
– namely between prince and subject, father and son, husband and wife,
elder and younger brother, and friends – the most significant, the core of
social reproduction, was the bond between husband and wife. Marriage
joined families and produced offspring who were brought up as responsible members of society, each filling their appropriate role as subjects of
the state. The neo-Confucian doctrines formulated by the great philosophers of the Song dynasty and developed by philosophers and moralists
through the late imperial period, stressed that the social order of the
state formed a continuum with the conduct of family life. Women's
behavior was a matter of enduring political concern even though they
lived in seclusion from what we might think of as the public sphere. The
1712/13 preface to Lan Dingyuan's popular text *Women's Learning*
voices a typical opinion when it declares: "The basis of the government
of the empire lies in the habits of the people. The correctness of the
habits of the people depends on the orderly management of the family.
The Way (*dao*) for the orderly management of the family begins with
women." As early as Han times the female scholar Ban Zhao had
defined four attributes that all women should cultivate: womanly virtue,
womanly speech, womanly conduct, and womanly work.[103]

---

[101] Bray 1997, chapter 4.
[102] Quoted in Kuhn 1988: 20.
[103] Lan Dingyuan's *Nü xue*, quoted in Mann 1994: 23. On the history of the four
attributes and their use in late imperial didactic texts for women, see Handlin 1975;
Mann 1991; Mann 1994: 21 ff.

"Private" virtues were considered to underpin the "public" order in many ways, and for late imperial moralists women's weaving incorporated several levels of virtuous behavior. By spinning and weaving, women produced not only objects of value but also persons of virtue. Learning textile skills inculcated the fundamental female values of diligence, frugality, order, and self-discipline that characterized good wives and mothers. In early China little girls of gentle birth were taught to spin and weave from the age of eight or nine, when their brothers started learning to read and to carry arms. Long after elite households had turned to buying the cloth for their needs on the open market, patriarchs admonished their daughters to spin in order to learn respect for the hard work of their inferiors and to weave hemp to learn frugality. The moral value of personal involvement in spinning and weaving is clearly illustrated, for example, in the popular encyclopedia of 1607, *Bianyong xuehai junyu* [Seas of knowledge, mines of jade]. It contains a sequence of woodblock drawings modeled on the Song work *Gengzhi tu* [Agriculture and sericulture illustrated], that shows the women of a gentle household working in harmony to spin and weave patterned silks which, in the final tableau, they present to the grandparental couple so they can choose their clothes for the coming year. The evidence I have outlined above suggests that this is not a realistic depiction of contemporary life among the rural gentry (who by then would be more likely to buy patterned silks than to produce them at home), it is rather a parable of virtuous femininity and of the role of women's work in upholding the social order.[104]

When men started to perform peasant women's work, then, and when gentry women were no longer involved in spinning and weaving, the whole fabric of society seemed to be threatened. In Confucian terms this was a threat to the social order in part because basic production had fallen into the hands of artisans and merchants, but equally because it signaled a failure to distinguish properly between male and female work. Men weaving or women tilling the fields were deeply disquieting occurrences, because they were signs of a world turned upside down.

By the later Ming not only were peasant men to be seen taking over from their wives at the loom, there was also a growing class of well-off families whose women did little work of any kind. Most educated people in late imperial China viewed the middle-class lack of employment as a moral danger – but they also saw idleness where modern eyes would not

---

[104] See Mann 1991, McDermott 1990 for examples of the training value ascribed to textile work in late imperial gentry families. Stone-Ferrier 1989 offers an interesting parallel, showing the moral importance attributed to traditional gender divisions of labor in a period of social instability in Holland.

see it. Idleness did not always mean doing nothing, rather it meant not being engaged in proper work. And the sign of female idleness, in orthodox eyes, was that the women did not raise silkworms or weave textiles.

I gave the examples earlier of Lü Kun and Chen Hongmou's ill-fated attempts to train peasant women in sericultural skills. They are just two of numerous official attempts in the late Ming and early Qing to establish or revive a textile industry in poor regions where women no longer wove. Such women were described in the proposals for reform as being "without occupation" or some such expression – even though they were probably working hard all day long, and may well have been involved in farming tasks, handicrafts, or other economic activities as well as housekeeping and child rearing. But the only women's work worthy of that name in the eyes of the reforming officials was sericulture and weaving.

In regions that were not yet fully sinicized, teaching Chinese-style weaving skills was seen as a powerful method of enculturation. Susan Mann quotes a touching lament by an official posted to the Xiang region of Hubei, where the local women (who I presume were of some other ethnicity than Han) were shamelessly unfaithful to their husbands by Chinese standards. They thought nothing of marrying several times, nor did families in search of a bride mind this loose behavior.[105] The trigger to the official's concern was the sight of the women "breaking up clods of earth with a hoe." This shocked him deeply since such a confusion of gender categories indicated that "it would not be long before these same wives would be suing their husbands, and husbands their wives." Only sericulture, he felt, could save them. "They have no way to develop specialized work of their own and thereby affirm their commitment as faithful wives. The woman who has no work of her own should take up sericulture. Whether she comes from a gentry or a commoner household, a wife can personally tend silkworms in order to clothe her husband. When she sees that her own strength is sufficient to provide for her family's subsistence, her heart will be pure."[106]

Within the traditional Chinese heartland too, Qing statecraft writers

[105] This was a period when there were strong moral pressures on Han women to remain faithful to their husbands by refusing to remarry; however widows often came under severe pressure to marry again, not least because of legislation that allowed the in-laws to keep the dowry if the woman remarried. See T'ien 1988; Carlitz 1994.

[106] Mann 1992a: 87, quoting from a collection of essays on agricultural policy that comprise three chapters in the *Huangchao jingshi wenbian* [Collected essays on statecraft of the august dynasty], first published in 1826. "More than half of the forty-nine essays in these chapters refer to home weaving, and one entire chapter containing nineteen essays (*juan 37*) focuses exclusively on cotton and silk home handicraft industries" (ibid: 92, note 8).

believed that "those regions in China where 'women wove' were culturally and even morally superior to areas where women [did not]." Many tried to introduce the skills of advanced areas like the lower Yangzi to more backward areas where they held office, even though the local population would sometimes refuse to learn them.[107] One reason why local populations did not always welcome these attempts was precisely because they had developed alternative and more rewarding means for earning a livelihood, such as curing tea, making sugar, or producing handicrafts.[108] But these were not the type of women's work that late imperial officials were likely to encourage or promote, for they were activities that fell squarely under the orthodox category of craft, and were therefore – unlike textile production – considered not basic but subsidiary and commercial activities.

When officials wrote of the need to involve women in textile production, two reasons that feature prominently are: (i) that it will allow women to contribute to family income, and (ii) that it will help them meet tax obligations. The case of the women of Xiang indicates, however, that economic and moral effects were closely entwined. Although since 1581 women were no longer required to pay taxes directly in cloth they had woven, by making textiles they would regain their position as active subjects, fitting partners to their husbands, and responsible contributors to the state and to the social order.

On the issue of wives contributing to the family income, once more we must remember that late imperial officials did not evaluate such contributions according to modern criteria – nor did their understanding of the worth of such work necessarily coincide with that of most ordinary people of the period.[109] The term *li*[110] may be translated as "welfare," "benefit," "advantage" or "profit" depending on the context. I think I have shown convincingly in my account of the growth and changes in agriculture and the textile industry that by now the ubiquity of commercial competition meant that profits were a primary factor shaping the working patterns and survival strategies of the majority of the population. In this sense *li* represents a quantifiable attribute: one activity may generate higher profit margins than another. In the rhetoric of statecraft, however, the term *li* implies something more qualitative, more moral. The mandate of a responsible official is not to maximize revenues but to protect the welfare of the population

---

[107] Mann 1992a: 86.
[108] Mann 1992b: 249.
[109] I discuss this issue in Bray 1997: chapter 6.
[110] A different character from the *li* referred to earlier, which means "ritual" or "etiquette." On understandings of *li* as "profit" in the Ming, see Brook 1997.

under his care, to prevent famine and to ensure a level of modest prosperity sufficient to sustain respectable living without triggering instability.

On the question of profits and benefits, it is instructive to compare the ideas on *li* expressed in two agricultural works produced around the fall of the Ming. The first is the *Bu nongshu* [Expanded treatise on agriculture] (Zhang Lixiang 1983). It comprises a short treatise in the form of a farming calendar by one Master Shen, a small Huzhou landlord, composed in about 1640; and a section of additions completed in 1658 by Zhang Lixiang, a small landlord from the neighboring district of Tongxiang.[111] The second is the *Nongzheng quanshu* [Complete treatise on agricultural administration] (Xu Guangqi 1979) based on materials written between about 1607 and 1630 by the high official Xu Guangqi, edited and published posthumously in 1639 by Chen Zilong. Xu was from Shanghai, very close to Huzhou; although cotton rather than sericulture was the principal textile crop, from a general perspective farming conditions and levels of commercialization were very similar in the two districts. But the two works present a very different view of the economic goals of farming.

The *Bu nongshu* is representative of one important genre in Chinese writings on agriculture, those written by landlords for other landlords. This genre, which includes most of the original, personal material in the Chinese agricultural corpus, is perfectly secular and materialist, if not necessarily economically rational in the modern, capitalist sense.[112] The relationship between landowners and their laborers or tenants is presented as a practical one in which the interests of the landlords predominate; they think of their employees or dependants in terms of laborers, bondservants, or tenants, rather than as representatives of the sacred category of *min*. These authors were concerned with making ends meet, and with the exact calculations of prices and profits. As the passage quoted earlier from Master Shen on silk weaving indicates, they evaluated a woman's contribution to the family in precise monetary terms.[113]

---

[111] Shen and Zhang were both unusual for the time in that they were resident landlords actively involved in farming. In both the localities silk was described as of central importance, but ramie, fish-ponds, pigs, poultry, and goats are also described as profitable ventures, as well as domestic industries like brewing. Growing rice, it turns out, was more a labor of love than a source of profit.

[112] Other important or significant works in this genre include *Qimin yaoshu* [Essential techniques for the peasantry] written by Jia Sixie in about 535, *Nong shu* [Agricultural treatise] by Chen Fu of 1149 (Chen 1956), and the *Nongsang jing* [Classic of farming and sericulture] by the famous ghost-story writer Pu Songling (1640–1715) (Pu 1982).

[113] This does not mean that they were indifferent to the social and moral meanings of the contribution. On the contrary, Zhang stresses that a wife's earning capacity affects the

Although Xu Guangqi was also a landlord, one who in fact came to own much more land than Shen or Zhang ever possessed, and who depended heavily on the income from his estate to supplement his typically inadequate official salary, in his published writings on farming he always speaks with the voice of an official. The word *li*, which means value, profit or benefit, is used in both works, but Xu and Zhang imbue it with a very different meaning. Xu talks at the level of value or benefit, and noticeably avoids any concrete discussions of profit.

The administrative sections of the *Nongzheng quanshu* are full of quantitative details (elaborate calculations of the amounts of materials, the salaries, and labor costs required to run an irrigation or a land reclamation scheme), but when it comes to the financial details that would help a farmer decide which crop to choose in his particular circumstances, Xu is really not very helpful. He must have had detailed knowledge of prices and profit margins, not just in his native region of Shanghai but in the many parts of China where he had traveled. Yet in the *Nongzheng quanshu* this translates into such abstract phrases as: "Tea is a marvellous plant: growing it brings abundant profits, and drinking it brings mental lucidity. Above princes and nobles trade it, and below the populace cannot do without it; truly it is both a commodity that is part of the everyday life of the people, and an aid to the profits and revenues of the state."[114]

The *Nongzheng quanshu* represents a different genre of agricultural writing from the *Bu nongshu*, one composed in an official voice. Like the first genre, this one too aims to provide technical solutions for material problems. However the authors are officials writing for officials rather than landlords writing for landlords. Wholeheartedly espousing the Confucian understanding of the moral and political dimensions of farming work I mentioned earlier, they stress the need for the state to "encourage farming," and represent the targets of their programs of aid and instruction as an undifferentiated mass, the *min*, reiterating that its welfare is the sacred responsibility of the ruler as well as the foundation of a sound fiscality and a peaceful polity. The dialogue between state representatives and *min* is paramount.[115] The function of agriculture is as much ritual as material: in performing the actions of good farmers, the *min* embody the role of good subjects. The well-being that good agricultural practice and administration engendered was material first,

degree to which society will think of her as a partner to her husband; *Bu nongshu* (Zhang 1983): 148, 151.

[114] Xu Guangqi 1979: 1096–7.

[115] When landowners figure in such works they tend to be represented as disruptive elements in an essentially dualistic social contract between state and people.

but above all symbolic.[116] There is a quasi-mystical dimension in some important official writings on farming, in which what Pierre-Étienne Will calls "correct agriculture"[117] serves as a kind of fetish for producing a properly ordered society.

The *Nongzheng quanshu* is not mystical in form or content, and it was designed to tackle some extremely serious and urgent problems facing the late Ming state, including the fall in agricultural revenues occasioned by peasants leaving the land, and the consequent difficulties of adequately provisioning the army. Official concern about peasants driven by desperation or lured by gain into abandoning the "fundamental" occupation of farming for the "secondary" occupations of crafts and commerce had a pedigree dating back to the Warring States, a period of rapid urbanization and of corresponding growth in markets and in craft and commercial activities, which led politicians to ponder whether a state could hope to survive without tying all its peasantry to the land as tax-payers and reserve soldiers.

While the northern plains remained the heartlands of the Chinese state, officials most frequently complained that peasants were being dispossessed and driven off the land by large landowners – which is what we might expect given the technological characteristics of northern farming systems. By the Ming, officials and literati were less likely to blame landlords for the rural exodus than the higher profits to be gained in crafts and trade.[118] The danger lay not merely in farmers leaving the land; they were also prone to turn their land over from staple cereals to more profitable crops like sugar or cotton. One reason for official concern was that when farmers abandoned the production of subsistence crops and purchased food grains on the market for their own consumption any disturbance in the supply could easily lead to famine.[119] Another, a recurrent issue in the *Nongzheng quanshu*, was that agricultural diversification reduced the national surplus of staple grains available to the state – a concern that was particularly acute in the later Ming when coastal raids by "Japanese pirates," recurrent rebellions, and the threat of foreign invasion meant that military requirements for provisions were exceptionally high. Underlying all these

[116] This attitude is reflected in the organization of the imperially sponsored *Shoushi tongkao* [Compendium of works and days, 1743] in its long sections on "auspicious grains."

[117] Will 1994.

[118] Late Ming officials including Xu Guangqi gave due recognition to the fact that in those troubled times peasants also left their land because they were driven out by warfare, or because they were ruined by crop failures or natural disasters. The Manchu conquest ushered in a rather long period of civil peace and prosperity, and early Qing emperors and officials couched their anxieties about the abandonment of farming more exclusively in terms of the lure of more profitable activities.

[119] Will and Wong 1991.

concerns, I believe, was the anxiety about how the social order could be restored as long as the *min* were not behaving as true *min*, fulfilling the role of faithful subjects, tilling the land to grow the cereal crops that were the basis of the ordered state.

Viewed in isolation, late imperial official discourse about the balance between farming, commerce, and crafts can be understood as expressing justifiable economic concerns – and I certainly would not deny this element. But taken in the context of complaints about men at the loom, and about women without occupation, I think we must also see official comments on farming versus trade as part of a broader political-economic discourse about work and the social order.

By the standards of modern economics, the early Qing emperors were even more reactionary than the statesmen of the late Ming. They issued a series of edicts condemning the lust for profit that drove farmers to abandon the cultivation of food staples for commercial crops or to leave the land to work as artisans or traders in the towns, edicts that attempted to persuade farmers all over China to concentrate on the production of staple cereals and to develop the necessary resources for local self-sufficiency. Qing emperors and officials also promoted a series of policies to promulgate women's participation in weaving. As mentioned above, they sponsored numerous publications on farming and on domestic textile production, in all of which the element of ritual and symbolic efficacy was clearly expressed. Perhaps the ultimate expression of the symbolic instrumentality of farming and weaving came with the Qing emperors' revival of the court plowing and sericultural rituals. In a recreation of ceremonies that had been performed only intermittently after the Han dynasty, the emperor plowed a ritual furrow in his sacred field each spring, while the empress and her ladies retreated into special apartments to raise silkworms.[120]

At one level the Qing ruling class's preoccupation with re-creating a hard-working and frugal peasantry whose men plowed and women wove stemmed from their fears that the population had begun to outstrip natural resources.[121] But at another the edicts and campaigns were an attempt to forge anew the sacred Confucian social contract, the reciprocal bond of obligation between the rulers and the people (equated

---

[120] A detailed description of the Qing ceremonials, which were particularly lavish, is given in Mann 1992a: 80–81. Discussions of the range of sericultural rituals practiced in China, their historical variations and meanings are given in Kuhn 1988: 251ff and in Bray 1997: chapter 6.

[121] See the discussions in Will and Wong (1991) concerning the demographic concerns that arose after several decades of sustained peace, prosperity, and population growth that coincided with official recognition that the arable land frontier could no longer be indefinitely expanded.

with the peasantry) that underpinned the ordered state.[122] There were two reasons why the early Qing emperors, who in the eyes of many Chinese were barbarian upstarts, were so well served by such a strategy. The first was that the fall of the Ming was frequently blamed on a decline into luxurious living and consequent social promiscuity and moral decadence, and this ideological campaign was a means for the Qing rulers to distance themselves from Ming excess and commit themselves publicly to purity, moderation, and order (yet without the inconvenience of having themselves to live in austerity). The second was that it enabled the foreign Manchu emperors to declare their allegiance to the classic fundamentals of Confucianism by integrating themselves into the moral ruler–people dyad. They thus demonstrated their inherent worthiness to rule China here and now, while tying themselves into a native Chinese historical tradition. At the same time, it seems to me, for the Qing rulers the pair of "correct agriculture" and "women's weaving" were a fetish: if the people, *min*, could be persuaded to perform their proper work, then social order would be restored from below as well as from above.

A new materialism

In recent years the traditional history of pre-modern Chinese technology seems to have entered a period of decline. There have been few major new publications by technological historians, and – except for those studies that radically challenge or altogether reject conventional models (see below) – even fewer that offer new insights, whether on historical trends or on the overall technological culture of a particular period. One might even say that like its object of study the field is a "blocked system." The lack of vigor and novelty is not surprising, however. There is an inherent sterility in a working model that requires us to highlight in the vocabulary of a foreign culture only those terms that translate smoothly into our own language, and encourages us to cram into the

---

[122] This social contract was most directly expressed in the twice-monthly lectures on the *Sacred Edict* that Qing local magistrates were expected to organize in all the villages under their control. The *Sacred Edict* was issued by the Kangxi Emperor in 1670, when he was only sixteen years old, and in the ninth year of his reign. It consisted of sixteen maxims, each seven characters in length, and "was recognized as the most concise and authoritative statement of Confucian ideology" from its promulgation to the end of the dynasty (Mair 1985: 325). Maxims 4, 5, and 14 related to "correct agriculture" and its social goals: "Recognize the importance of husbandry and the culture of the mulberry tree, in order to ensure a sufficiency of clothing and food"; "show that you prize moderation and economy, in order to prevent the lavish waste of your means"; "fully remit your taxes, in order to prevent being pressed for payment" (ibid.: 325–26).

familiar mold of capitalist rationality complex symbolic systems in which material and moral elements were related quite differently.

As we well know, even in our current capitalist world the clash between the economic and the symbolic values attributed to certain products or activities can generate complex dilemmas in matters of technological choice. To take the example of agriculture, since it has featured so prominently in this essay, in the late-twentieth-century United States the Jeffersonian moral and political ideal of the family homestead continues to suffuse the rhetoric of state farming policies, even though less than 1 percent of the population is now involved in agricultural labor, and productive norms are imposed by giant international agribusinesses.[123] Meanwhile agricultural economists have argued for years that the rice-farming system of Japan, one of the most advanced capitalist economies, is hopelessly outdated and "inefficient," and that the heavy subsidies it enjoys are inequitable in a global free market. Even while Japanese economists and policymakers bow to this logic, the symbolism of native rice in Japan stands in the way of effective reform.

When a modern Japanese family sit round the supper table eating their bowls of Japanese-grown rice, they are not simply indulging a gastronomic preference for short-grained and slightly sticky Japonica rice over long-grained Indica rice from Thailand. They are eating and absorbing a tradition – in the sense of an invented and re-invented past. While the television beside the dining table pours out a stream of images of the here-and-now, of an urbanized, capitalist, and thoroughly internationalized Japan, each mouthful of rice offers communion with eternal and untainted Japanese values, with a rural world of simplicity and purity, inhabited by peasants tending tiny green farms in harmony with nature and ruled over by the emperor, descendant of the Sun Goddess, who plants and harvests rice himself each year in a special sacred plot. Simple peasant rice farmers are almost extinct in contemporary Japan, but the family rice farm lives on as a powerful symbol of national identity.[124]

There is no doubt that by standard economic criteria the production of Japanese rice is extremely inefficient – in terms of production costs,

---

[123] Tweeten *et al.* 1993.
[124] Most of Japan's remaining four million farm households work their farms part-time and derive the major part of their income from industrial or white-collar jobs. Moreover rice plays an ever-diminishing part in the Japanese national diet as Western-style foods like bread become popular. Despite strong opposition at home, at the final round of the Uruguay GATT negotiations in late 1993 Japan was obliged to open its doors, if only a crack, to rice imports. In March 1994 the Japanese government allowed foreign producers (from Australia, India, Thailand, and the United States) to exhibit rice for the first time at the annual food show in Tokyo.

labor productivity, over-use of chemicals, overinvestment in machinery, and consumer prices.[125] To this one could also add pollution of the rural environment. However, in political terms the smallholder technology of Japanese rice farming has been extremely efficient. The land-reform measures promulgated under American guidance after the war eradicated landlordism and distributed land to former tenants; furthermore, selling and renting of farm land became subject to very strict control. Farm support policies not only permitted farmers to modernize their methods and increase their incomes, they also supported the expansion of an internal market for Japan's manufacturing and service industries. Independent smallholder farming was firmly established as the basis of the rural economy. The average size of a rice farm in Japan today is less than 1 hectare, and many families continue to live on farms even though most of the members work in nearby cities. The proportion of the Japanese electorate registered as rural voters is extremely high for an industrial economy, and the Liberal Democratic Party, the ruling party in Japan from the end of the war, has been kept in power with only one short break in large part thanks to a loyal rural vote.[126]

The rice farmers and their families, the LDP, and the manufacturing and service sectors all benefit directly from this system of rice production. The benefits to the public at large are less obvious to outside eyes, but are nevertheless sufficiently appreciated within Japan for the rice protection lobby to be able to mobilize considerable popular support.[127]

[125] Almost all farmers own a full range of expensive machinery, and the average chemical use for rice is over 1 tonne per hectare, about ten times the US average. Such methods are made possible by heavy government subsidies. In 1977, a Japanese economist calculated that energy inputs in rice production amounted to three times the food energy of the rice itself. A 1987 comparison between the US and Japan showed that yields per hectare were the same (just over 6 tonnes), but rice production costs in Japan were over eleven times those in the US, farmgate rice prices were almost seven times as high, and as for labor productivity, while one US worker produced almost two and a half tonnes of rice in an hour, in Japan the figure was a mere 106 kg (Bray 1986: 57ff; 1994; Tweeten et al. 1993).

[126] The LDP was the single ruling party from the end of the war until 1993, participated in several of the subsequent short-lived coalitions, and regained its preeminent position in the elections of October 1996.

[127] "In questionnaires, more than seven out of 10 Japanese said they preferred domestic rice even at higher prices. But in blind tasting tests, six out of 10 could not tell the difference between Japanese and foreign Japonica" (*Guardian Weekly*, March 13, 1994). I visited Japan in October 1994 just after the rice harvest. In the food-hall basements of the big city department stores, which specialize in luxury (or at least top end of the market) foods, rice from up to a dozen well-known rice-producing localities was on sale at high prices. The only other products with comparable ranges of variety and provenance were tea, coffee, and wine – in fact the big notices announcing "the new rice is here!" reminded me of "le Beaujolais nouveau est arrivé!" campaigns. Meanwhile in less elegant streets the cheap take-away foodstalls were festooned in banners proclaiming that their dishes all used "100 per cent Japanese rice."

The modern parody of peasant rice farming provides the urban Japanese with a "tradition," an emotional and aesthetic refuge from rapid modernization and internationalization. Japanese rice is consumed not only as a food redolent of national essence, but also as a harmonious rural landscape, a week-end escape from the unnatural conditions of life in the modern city.[128] One could take the rosy-tinted public reading of this representation as what Michel de Certeau would call anti-discipline, a "reading in another key" whereby consumers of dominant representations subvert them and turn them to satisfying account. Yet at the same time it is the outcome of a highly successful political strategy of traditionalizing, of building modern national solidarity around an imagined past. The representation of Japan as a nation tied to its legendary roots by the labors of simple, thrifty, and patriotic rice farmers is one that has served Japanese nationalist causes well since before the turn of the century and still has immense popular appeal.[129] The economic efficiency of Japanese rice technology leaves much to be desired; its symbolic efficiency is remarkable.

There is no scientific method for making such jumps from the material to the mental, for linking artifacts to mentality or aesthetics to morals. When a historian or an archeologist attempts to reconstruct the technological cultures of a past society, she lays herself open to charges of speculation. Even where a social or cultural historian perceives a plausible fit with broader cultural patterns, interpretations of this nature often arouse hostility and suspicion among archeologists or historians of technology, many of whom believe that responsible scholarship should stick to functionalist explanations of the visible facts. Yet if we accept that people in past societies had different intentions and values from our own, we are also obliged to be critical even of straightforward functional interpretations, and of the selective interest that they imply. Naturally in the search for meaning and power we must not neglect the problem-solving dimension of technology. A piece of cloth will fall apart unless warp and weft interlock; a cooking-pot that is not watertight is useless. The mistake is to project our own values and hierarchies on to other societies. In an important sense, the characteristics of a particular

---

[128] In a presentation of the arguments for preserving small-scale rice farming in Japan today, the economist Kenji Ozawa propounds the environmental importance of paddy fields in preventing floods, and in maintaining a "traditional" Japanese landscape (1993). Yamaji and Ito also make much of the "cultural, emotional, and environmental factors" affecting whether or not Japan should open its rice markets (1993: 363). Ohnuki-Tierney (1993) discusses the role of rice in the construction of Japanese identity in much greater historical and anthropological depth than I have here.

[129] See Bray 1986: 214–16 for a brief account of the literature on "agrarian fundamentalism" in Japan. On the importance of rural imagery in the construction of tradition in Japan, see Goto 1993 and Ohnuki-Tierney 1993.

technology have to be accounted for in terms of choices – what are a society's tastes, its current needs and desires, and what technologies best fulfill them?[130]

To think both more realistically and more creatively about the meaning of technical choices, rather than reducing them to purely pragmatic considerations, let alone to capitalist rationality, we should re-embed technologies in their social and cultural context to see what agendas they served, or what conceptions of society they made possible.[131] The rationalities of modern social science, as of modern technological design, are historically limited: they presume a general preference for increased consumption, a progress from small to large scale, a so-called Cartesian separation of bodily habits and of aesthetics from moral experience.

Here I would like to mention some recent studies of pre-modern Chinese technology that break away entirely from conventional models, pointing the way to a new school of political or cultural history that would integrate technology with other forms of cultural expression, completely recasting its role in historical explanation. I have already mentioned the work of David Keightley on ancient China. Donald Wagner has argued that the normal model of historical progress from small- to large-scale production is reversed in the case of iron and steel production in pre-modern China, and that this technological logic relates to the particular character of the Chinese state. Lothar von Falkenhausen suggests that the extraordinarily accomplished techniques for casting bronze bells in ancient China are best understood in the context of a society which believed that the standardization of musical scales was an act of political and cosmological legitimation. Dieter Kuhn has carried out a social and political analysis of a society seen through

---

[130] "People unfamiliar with technology usually gravely understate the degrees of latitude and choice open to innovators as they seek to solve technical problems. More commonly, one sees a range of options, each with its tradeoffs, and it is far from obvious which, if any, is superior. In virtually every technical area, there is substantial latitude for choice" (Pfaffenberger 1992: 498). On the choices open to neolithic potters, see van der Leeuw 1993. On technological choice as a heuristic concept, see Wagner 1995 and Lemonnier 1993. The papers in Lemonnier (1993) study the interplay between material problem solving and cultural meaning as manifested in a range of technological choices, from neolithic potting to plans for a revolutionary subway system.

[131] See for example Keightley 1989 on how the componential structure of late neolithic Chinese ceramic styles necessitated an emphasis on precision, regularity and fit that seems to be reflected in the political structures of the early Chinese states. Wilson 1988 suggests that significant differences in social relations and values between hunter-gatherers and sedentary cultures can be attributed to the partitioning of space and consequent interruption of vision by walls and roofs.

the prism of its material culture in his study of the Song dynasty. Klaas Ruitenbeek's monograph on the *Lu Ban jing* [The carpenter's canon] shows how Confucian, magical and practical material discourses interwove in the key text that both builders and clients referred to when a house was to be built. Reevaluating a late Ming work on lacquer-ware, Craig Clunas warns us that what modern historians of technology have eagerly hailed as a technical document was in fact written not for producers but for consumers, thus calling into question how we approach a "technical" text. And in my own work I have explored how material technologies contributed to the shaping of gender and the reproduction of the social order in late imperial China. To be precise, I take three material technologies (domestic architecture, weaving, and techniques of fertility control) which defined late imperial femininity, to show that the historical shaping and interplay of these three "female" dimensions of material existence were absolutely central to the elaboration of Chinese civilization.[132]

I have argued here that the materialism of capitalist science, technology, and social sciences is an impoverished materialism that hinders rather than promotes insight into other world views. The retrojection of modern goals and values can only obscure our understanding of the relations among material, ideal, and social in other societies, or even in our own past. Currently the history of Western technology (like all the other social sciences) has taken a "cultural turn," seeking to decenter the "normal" material experiences and intellectual trajectories of the modern West. I hope I have suggested here that the study of non-Western histories can not only benefit from this critical approach, but also contribute to it.

For China alone, there exists a prodigious wealth of written, pictorial, and artifactual sources on past technologies, enough for many innovative studies of technology in the broader sense I have proposed, namely of material practices that construct social worlds. The resources for China are perhaps particularly rich because Confucian moral philosophy (as did Daoism and Chinese Buddhism) attributed great importance to the material and bodily dimensions of social identity and moral experience.[133] Some of these sources have not yet been perceived as relevant by historians of Chinese technology, some have been misread – like the little monograph on lacquer discussed by Clunas – because we presume that past societies attributed meanings in the way we do today.

---

[132] Keightley 1987, 1989; Wagner 1995; Falkenhausen 1994; Kuhn 1987; Ruitenbeek 1993; Clunas 1997; Bray 1997.
[133] For a discussion of the range of sources, see Bray 1997, Introduction.

But if we rethink technology as I have suggested, suddenly there is an abundance of new materials to work with – the possibilities are infinite. I hope that as a new history of Chinese, and of non-Western, technology flowers it will contribute to the new history of Western technology, suggesting fruitful new questions to ask of the material past.

6   The political economy of agrarian empire and its modern legacy

R. Bin Wong

The problems of explaining change in Chinese economic history

The difficulties of adapting explanations of economic change in European history to the Chinese experience have challenged some of the best specialists working on Chinese history throughout the twentieth century, as well as a number of equally gifted social theorists and comparativists. Many scholars have developed expectations for economic change in China based on readings of economic change in Europe because this is the better studied area. Indeed, until the last few decades, most general arguments about historical change in agrarian economies and the development of industrial economies had as their empirical base, either implicitly or explicitly, some assessment of European experiences of capitalism. When we take European developments as the norm, all other experiences appear to be abnormal. We begin to search for what went wrong in other parts of the world. This is especially the case for a civilization like China where improvements in agricultural production and handicrafts were joined to the spread of commercialization and urbanization beginning in the tenth century to create what one tradition of Japanese scholarship has labeled China's "modern age" (*kinsei*). The Japanese Marxist tradition, as we've seen in Timothy Brook's earlier chapter, disputes this assessment, but shares with interpretations of China's "modern" (by European standards) tenth-century economic development the challenge of explaining the absence of a European-like set of economic changes thereafter.

The failure to satisfy European expectations for economic change leads directly to the problem of "stagnation" (Ch. *tingzhi*, J. *teitai*) which proceeds from an assumption that something must be found to explain why change did not continue to occur. Economic change is assumed to be a kind of organic or natural phenomenon in both Marxist and non-Marxist lines of reasoning. Similar elements appear in both

210

Marxist and non-Marxist explanations of China's stymied economic development after the twelfth century.

The imperial state is singled out for a variety of faults; for John A. Hall it creates "institutional blockages to the market," while for Hong Huanchun it blocks the development of capitalism; for E. L. Jones, the Chinese state "undergoverns," while for Etienne Balasz scholar officials never allowed merchants to develop into a powerful social class.[1] The common denominator of the complaints about the Chinese state is its failure to implement policies like those pursued by European states. Another cluster of reasons for China's stymied economic development concerns social structure and organization. One strain of Marxist analysis stresses the relationship between particular social relations among owners of land and those who work the land. In European studies, the "Brenner debate" pitted Robert Brenner's arguments about the importance of agrarian social relations for the formation of capitalist property relations and subsequent development of production against accounts stressing such factors as demography and international trade.[2] In Chinese studies, restrictions on agricultural laborers' status are used to explain the failure of "capitalism" to develop.[3] Once again, Chinese practices fail to parallel those found in the successful European cases; they therefore can be used to suggest why Chinese economic changes did not simply follow a European trajectory.

Explanations of Chinese economic history that begin from a set of premises about what it was *not* face a serious analytical challenge. It is difficult to explain change when the object is to explain the absence of a particular pattern of change. Explanations of Chinese economic history as the failure to follow European patterns of change do not directly identify what patterns of change in Chinese economic history we should expect. Indeed, the failure to find European changes usually leads to a conclusion that no change of any significance took place, hence the easy appearance of stagnation. Since our notions of historical change generally are derived from European experiences, the categories for organizing significant information are also of European origin. Their "fit" for non-Western societies and cultures represents a general theoretical problem. For economic dynamics specifically, we rarely attempt to explain economic development without appeal to the rise of capitalism; this means we tend not to be aware of, let alone search for, dynamics of change that do not fit within a narrative of capitalist development.

[1] Hall 1985: 56; Hong 1983; Jones 1988: 141; Balasz 1964: 13–27.
[2] Ashton and Philpin 1985.
[3] Li, Wei, and Jing 1983.

Before considering what such a theoretical move leaves out, we should ponder briefly how difficult it is to pinpoint what it includes.

"Capitalism" is a vexing term because it is both basic and ill-defined. In perhaps its most generally accepted sense, it refers to the late twentieth-century global economic system in which sophisticated organizations and processes move capital, labor, and products around the world. "Capitalism" is also used to describe the economic system that emerged in early modern Europe. It is this early modern European capitalism that conventionally is considered to be the powerhouse behind the formation of a world economy in the ninteenth and twentieth centuries. Examining economic change in non-Western countries as they became part of this system forms the major alternative to considering non-Western deviations from patterns identified for European economic history. The danger of this general approach is to ignore the dynamics of economic activity that exist independently of and prior to the arrival of a powerful and significant European economic presence; this ignorance then becomes a basis for assuming that the relevant factors to explain economic change are all of foreign origin. Whereas looking at China's failures to trace European patterns of economic change obscures the dynamics of change in the Chinese case, a simple focus on European capitalism's incorporation of China (and other parts of the world) makes Chinese dynamics of economic change thoroughly reactive to European developments. This intellectual move by itself is no more satisfying than the search for what blocked European-style economic changes in China. It can in some formulations make Chinese intentions and efforts (except as reactions to Western stimuli) even less relevant than the "blockage" line of reasoning.

Before we go on to consider the dynamics of Chinese economic development, we must reach some understanding of early modern European capitalism. If we take a narrow and empirically specific definition of capitalism's traits, the only countries that fit easily are Holland and England. England is, of course, the frequent empirical referent for "capitalism's" various features, be these social relations of agricultural production, the formation of factories, the development of banking, etc. If we take a broader definition of capitalism, we can include those areas that between the sixteenth and nineteenth centuries became France, Germany, Italy, and Spain. These were countries lacking English or Dutch style agricultural capitalism and without the same financial institutions found in the two more "advanced" countries. But once we take a broader definition of "capitalism" and admit into its boundaries different kinds of European cases, it becomes difficult to make an analytical distinction between all the "real" European cases of capitalism in the early modern period and phenomena earlier in European history when merchants also pursued profits over great distances. More confusing yet, we can find instances in South as well as East Asia of some merchants operating on a scale and in the manner of "capitalist" merchants in early modern Europe. As soon as we try to define "capitalism" according to some set of traits, we either find ourselves with such a narrow definition that various parts of modern Europe we want to consider "capitalist" are not included or we fall into a simple abstract definition which at least some economic activity in numerous societies in world history can satisfy. Europe may be the hero or villain (depending on one's point of view) in the drama of world economic development and in the system created by changes beginning in roughly the sixteenth century which we conventionally call "capitalism." But it is difficult to assess "capitalism" unambiguously because it is easy to define capitalism in multiple fashions to serve a variety of purposes. This means that any effort to explain why China did not develop capitalism is aiming at a moving target. We end up with multiple reasons for why China did not develop "capitalism" because it is defined in a loose and contradictory way.

For present purposes let us accept that the rate and degree of economic change varied among European regions according in part to state policies and social structures. Let us also accept the reality that other parts of Eurasia enjoyed some measure of "capitalism." What matters for this chapter is that we develop a sense of European capitalism beginning in early modern times, not that all parts of Europe will share equally in capitalism's traits at any particular point in time or that the characteristics of the system will remain constant over time. But we will need a concrete and historical notion of European capitalism in order to have a set of changes in European political economy with which to contrast the dynamics in China.

Immanuel Wallerstein's analysis of the formation of a Europe-centered world-system provides a model of European capitalism with which we can compare Chinese experiences. His earlier chapter in this volume roots the genesis of the modern world-system in a conjuncture of four different crises around the fourteenth century – crises for European seigniors, European states, the Catholic Church, and the Mongols. All but the Mongols survived with their powers rejuvenated. By stressing these conjunctures, he avoids claims about a general superiority of European civilization reaching back into earlier centuries, a kind of explanation that he finds common among other comparative historians and social theorists. In this chapter, I will attempt to supplement Wallerstein's argument with an analysis of the dynamics in the Chinese

case, beginning with those dynamics of economic expansion and contraction I believe were shared across Eurasia.

If, as I argued earlier, it is difficult to imagine dynamics of economic
change in China that do not also occur in Europe, we would do well first
to explore whether or not there are some dynamics of economic change
common to both China and Europe that are separate from the logic of
European capitalism that we know did not shape China's political
economy. With a set of economic dynamics shared by Europe and
China we can then set out more sharply a contrast between European
capitalism and the political economy of agrarian empire in late imperial
China. Concrete historical contrasts between Chinese and European
political economies indicate some of the ways in which trajectories of
economic change are likely to be different. Once the similarities and
differences between Chinese and European political economies between
the sixteenth and eighteenth centuries have been sketched, we can then
consider the complex process through which these two trajectories of
economic change intersected in the formation of a world economic
system. As economic relations between China and the West grew more
substantial and complex in the nineteenth and twentieth centuries,
possibilities as well as constraints were formed.

I will argue that China and Europe shared very similar dynamics of
commercial expansion at the heart of which were processes analyzed by
Adam Smith in his book *The Wealth of Nations*. There were, of course,
many other differences – rural and urban social structures, roles of
kinship, and much more – but the differences I will stress in this chapter
center on the larger political context within which economic activities
took place. This focus complements Francesca Bray's discussion in the
previous chapter of different cultural contexts for defining and evalu-
ating technological activities. Just as Chinese and Europeans thought
about and pursued technological change in different ways, they also
conceived of political economy in quite distinct fashions rooted in
politically dissimilar situations. Europe's state-making dynamics un-
folded amidst territorial states expanding their powers in competition
with each other, while Chinese state formation and reproduction
focused upon creating and managing an agrarian empire seeking to
expand its territory and increase its population, confident that it was at
the center of the world, or at least that part of it that truly mattered.
When these two systems came into increasingly intense contact, China's
economic trajectory and also other aspects of its history became the
joint product of the dynamics China and Europe had shared, as well as
of the possibilities and problems introduced by their connection.
Chinese political economy in the twentieth century did not become a

replica of a European political economy of capitalism; nor did it simply become an appendage of a larger system, void of a logic and dynamics internal to the country and part of a longer trajectory of economic change. China's political economy of empire in late imperial times continued to shape China's post-imperial future in the twentieth century.[4]

Dynamics of economic expansion and contraction common to China and Europe

When we look concretely at patterns of economic activity in China we find a great diversity, not so very different in its range from the kinds of variation found in Europe between the tenth and eighteenth centuries. Amidst these variations some common trends appear, even if the timing and the spatial patterns are not exactly the same: (1) the spread of market exchange and long-distance commerce; (2) migrations, the clearance of new lands, and improvements of agricultural technology; (3) the expansion of rural industry.

Europe in 1500 already had well-established urban centers of trade. Italian traders had recovered from the devastating impact of the mid-fourteenth-century Black Death; in the north grain from Prussian Poland was exported to feed the cities of Flanders and the Low Countries. In the succeeding two centuries three related sets of marketing changes would take place: (1) the penetration of the countryside by large merchants and consequent multiplication of markets at which production from increasing numbers of people entered into large and long-distance trade flows; (2) the elaboration of long-distance marketing networks; (3) the formation of maritime trading circuits through which Europeans came to enjoy the benefits of silver, sugar, spices, coffee, and tea.

The creation of long-distance trade within commercializing regions of Europe brought forth new trading practices and commercial institutions designed to facilitate the patterns of exchange. These showed up clearly in both England and France in the grain trade which grew as the need to provide for swelling urban centers, especially London and Paris, increases. As Alan Everitt's detailed study of food supply marketing in England has shown, "open markets" or public market places of Tudor times were joined by "private markets," that is, corn chambers, warehouses, and inns located in provincial towns to serve wider areas as regional specialization in production began.[5] London in particular

---

[4] This essay draws on some of the arguments about economic change I make in Wong 1997.
[5] Everitt 1967.

required a larger development of private trade commensurate with its greater and growing population. For France, Usher's early twentieth-century work on grain marketing has shown how local and long-distance trade had been separated before the eighteenth century; the gap between town markets and the wholesale trade was bridged when merchants serving growing urban areas sought to increase their supplies beyond the levels previously mobilized. Penetrating beneath the town markets, merchants approached producers directly to bring their grain into the larger trading networks.[6]

Useful as the concept of market hierarchies is to understanding the development of commerce within European countries, the concept of market networks is more helpful to explain the development of long-distance trading systems. In the late medieval period the major node of Europe's long-distance commerce was a cluster of cities in northern Italy, with a secondary node among a set of cities in the Low Countries. The sixteenth and seventeenth centuries witnessed a shift from Genoa to Marseilles, Barcelona, Lisbon and Seville, and generally from southern to northwestern Europe – to Antwerp, Amsterdam, and finally London. The Atlantic came to displace the Mediterranean as the crucial European body of water.[7] With this shift came a larger set of changes in the scales and dynamics of European maritime commerce.

Europe's maritime trading networks were created by merchants and adventurers serving different governments.[8] The Spanish extracted New World silver, while the Portuguese and then the Dutch sought to control the lucrative trade in spices. The Dutch formed the Dutch East India Company to organize their maritime aspirations; the English did like-wise creating the English East India Company. Between 1500 and 1800, Europeans in Asia and the New World shifted from spices to drugs and stimulants – coffee, tea, and sugar. For sugar Europeans went beyond merely organizing lucrative trading arrangements, creating what Sidney Mintz has called "agro-industrial enterprises" in the Carribean and Brazil.[9] During the eighteenth century the English established them-selves as the paramount European power in Asia; with a base in India, English merchants took advantage of Indian cotton textiles which would become a mixed blessing in the late eighteenth and early nineteenth centuries as other English merchants began pushing English factory

---

[6] Usher 1913: 37–40.
[7] Hohenberg and Lees 1985: 161–65.
[8] My account is based on Furber 1976; Parry 1966; Tracy 1990, 1991; Wallerstein 1974, 1980.
[9] Mintz 1985: 61.

production of cotton textiles, ushering in the first phase of the Industrial Revolution.

Between 1500 and 1800 some of the same kinds of commercial expansion that took place in Europe also took place in China. G. William Skinner has analyzed marketing structures and urban hierarchies in late imperial and twentieth-century China, demonstrating the construction of marketing networks beginning in the countryside at periodic markets at which peasants from neighboring villages would buy and sell through higher-level marketing centers culminating in a regional city at the apex of one of what Skinner has called China's macroregions.[10] Commercialization penetrated to the village level and engaged peasants in cash cropping of many types. By value the most important commodity in long-distance domestic commerce was undoubtedly grain. Xu Dixin and Wu Chengming estimate that more than 40 percent of total long-distance Chinese trade in the eighteenth century was in grain.[11] Brought to market by both peasants and landlords, expanding grain commerce fed both urban dwellers and other peasants who specialized in either non-grain cash crops or textiles and were therefore unable any longer to grow their own food supplies. In the lower Yangzi region, peasants in some districts specialized in silk production which began with silkworm raising and moved through the spinning of thread to the weaving and finishing of cloth. High quality silks from the lower Yangzi enjoyed a market in many parts of the empire. Lower Yangzi peasants in other districts specialized in cotton cultivation, cotton yarn making, and cloth weaving. In other parts of China there were specialized crafts and crops like pottery, paper goods, certain teas, and fruits that commanded high prices across great distances, but much cash cropping and handicraft production was destined for commercial trade and personal consumption within its province of origin, including lower quality cotton textiles, vegetables, and simple implements.

At the larger market towns and cities, merchants were organized into guilds representing the products in which they specialized. Two major merchant groups came to occupy dominant positions across the empire. In the north the Shanxi merchants, who began their activities in the fifteenth century and expanded their wealth in the sixteenth century by supplying government troops in the northwest in return for the monopoly rights in salt distribution to the interior, were subsequently engaged in many kinds of business including the provision of commercial credit. In the central and southern portions of the empire, the Huizhou merchants established themselves in many marketing centers. In addi-

---

[10] Skinner 1977.   [11] Xu and Wu 1985: 251.

tion there were smaller regional merchant groups, from different parts of both north and south China, whose trading activities were usually related to buying goods for their home regions or selling products from these same areas. Accustomed to thinking in European terms, it is easy to think of China simply as another country with a domestic trade like that of France. But even allowing for the fact that the northwestern reaches of the empire were thinly settled, China's spatial scale of a densely settled population still dwarfed the situation in any European country. We are far better off thinking of Europe and China as broadly comparable spatial units. When we do so, part of Europe's international trade is no greater in geographical extent than China's domestic trade. Thus, it is not surprising that much of China's domestic trade took place within market hierarchies of a single province or two rather than across the entire empire.

When Europeans arrived in Southeast Asia intent upon expanding the reach of their trading operations, they discovered that Chinese merchants were already in many of the ports where they anticipated doing business. While the policies of European and Chinese states differed greatly in ways that will be addressed in the following section, the economic practices of Chinese and European merchants were broadly similar. Each competed with others for profits to be made from trade within Asian waters. As Europeans inserted themselves into Asian networks of exchange, division of routes and coordination became one pattern of connection.

In addition to similarities concerning commercial expansion, Eurasian populations also experienced comparable dynamics of population movement and agricultural expansion. Following the Black Death of the mid-fourteenth century, late medieval populations migrated to bring fertile lands back into use and to open lands previously uncultivated. With land abundantly available, there was little reason to stress raising land productivity instead of simply clearing additional land. But as populations recovered and densities grew, farmers faced increasing incentives to raise land productivity enhanced by demand for crops caused by urbanization. In China as well, population declines brought on by disease and the unrest attending dynastic transitions were followed by growing populations which provided incentives to clear new land and increase the productivity of land already under cultivation. In Europe, improvements centered on a combination of arable and livestock in which more intensive use of the land was achieved as strategies to maintain soil fertility advanced. In China, the extension of paddy agriculture, selection of higher yield seeds, and improvements in crop raising technologies all combined to raise land productivity.

Even more closely parallel were Chinese and European experiences with rural industry. Between the mid-sixteenth and mid-eighteenth centuries, much of Europe's industrial production took place in rural settings. The most common industry was textiles which became a rural cottage industry in many parts of Europe. Dubbed "proto-industrialization" by a number of scholars who see rural industrialization as a precursor to the Industrial Revolution of the late eighteenth and early nineteenth centuries, the spread of rural industry depended on the shift of rural labor out of agriculture and into handicrafts. This generally took place where labor was plentiful and therefore cheap. An areal specialization of production among those continuing to work the soil and those engaged in industry signaled an important form of division of labor.[12]

From the late fifteenth century, much of the expansion of industrial production in China took place in peasant households. Most important, as in Europe, were textiles. Home production of textiles was a venerable activity, but, in the late imperial period, increasing amounts of cloth were entering trading networks. Some coarse cloths were marketed for local and regional use only, while finer, more expensive weaves were produced by more highly skilled rural artisans and adorned the stratum of richer literati, landlords, and merchants living across a larger area. The center for Chinese silk and cotton textiles was the lower Yangzi region. There households specialized in the production of either cotton or silk, relying on grain markets to supply them with food for the several months each year when the grain they grew themselves was inadequate to feed them. While the lower Yangzi region was the pre-eminent textile producer of the empire, substantial textile production also developed in other parts of the empire. By the end of the eighteenth century, cotton was grown and textiles produced for commercial sale in most of China's provinces. An expanding commerce carried a wide range of products of handicraft industry over both long and short distances. The growth of rural industry in different parts of China involved areal specialization similar to that taking place in several parts of Europe.

Commercialization as the motor of growth, with its attendant clearance of land, technological improvements, and rural industrial expansion, was common to both China and Europe. The basic logic of this economic growth was presented by Adam Smith in his *The Wealth of Nations*. Smith highlighted productivity gains from division of labor and from specialization. By producing what they were best suited to produce and exchanging their products with others, people captured the benefits of comparative advantage at the market place. Division of labor was

[12] Rural industry was by no means limited to Europe and China; examples can be found in South Asia and in Japan as well (Perlin 1983, Saito 1985).

limited only by the extent of the market. As the market expanded, the opportunities for Smithan growth increased accordingly. A decentralized price system widened the scope for the market and extended the advantages accruing from the division of labor.[13] This expanding market economy, common to both ends of Eurasia, must be analytically distinguished from industrial capitalism. While the two may be *historically* connected in Europe, this contingent relationship need not be seen as a *logical* necessity anywhere.

In order to distinguish more sharply between the Smithian dynamics of commercial expansion common to many parts of Eurasia and "capitalism," which is a more limited phenomenon, consider Fernand Braudel's discussion of market economy and capitalism in his grand three-volume study of "civilization and material life." For Braudel, market economies exist wherever buyers and sellers get together to exchange goods at prices that both parties find sensible; he recognizes their presence in many parts of Eurasia. There are no mysteries about supply and demand because the transactions are usually conducted between people who both know the market situation well. Capitalism however is largely based, for Braudel, upon some combination of monopoly and force, and is distinctively European in origin and construction; capitalists are merchants who reap huge profits from their control over the supply of some scarce commodity; producer and consumer are usually distant from each other. Other scholars have argued for a kind of commercial capitalism in South Asia and yet others for a kind of incipient capitalism in China. Despite the terminological and empirical uncertainties surrounding the term "capitalism" reviewed earlier in this chapter, let us accept that a range of exchange relations spanning local market barter to overseas trade exists in the Eurasian world. Following Braudel, we can argue that when commerce covers especially long distances and a few merchants gain control over either supply or distribution (or both) for some highly desired commodity, commercial capitalism is at hand. The important distinction for present purposes is between a Braudelian commercial capitalism and the operation of Smithian dynamics of economic expansion which does not depend on the presence of a handful of powerful and wealthy merchants exerting their control over some precious products. Some type of commercial capitalism existed in most every part of Eurasia. Its importance, however, varied according to the fit between commercial capitalism and state making.

From 1500 to 1800, China and Europe generally shared similar

[13] Blaug 1985: 61.

dynamics of economic growth and were constrained by the same kinds of limits to growth. Smithian dynamics indicate similarities that serve as a base line against which to locate differences in the political economy of commercial capitalism and the political economy of agrarian empire that distinguish the Chinese and European cases from each other.

Political economies of agrarian empire and capitalism

European mercantilist states of the early modern period conceived themselves to be engaged in a competition with the governments and merchants of other European countries for wealth and power. This perspective led them to stress foreign trade and in particular the importance of amassing silver at the expense of other governments and merchants. In contrast to European governments, the Chinese government did not depend either economically or politically on the support of many rich merchants for its fiscal security or its political power and legitimacy. Foreign trade in particular and the merchants who engaged in it were simply not very important to dominant state concerns. Chinese political economy of agrarian empire and European political economy of mercantilist competition produced different priorities and promoted the development of different political and economic capacities. Chinese and European officials aimed for different goals, the Chinese to tax lightly and support the government without burdening the people, whose economic welfare was conceived to be basic to the state's political stability; merchants, especially the many of modest scale, had a socially useful function, but they had no political importance as a group. European governments aimed to amass ever larger resources to compete with each other in an era of aggressive state building and economic expansion; merchants, as basic members of urban elites, played an important political role as well as an economically crucial one.

The political context for Europe's development of capitalism was fundamentally different from the political context of China's late imperial economy. Commercial capitalism in Europe produced merchant houses of extraordinary wealth beginning in the sixteenth century. This in itself is not so very different from what happened in China where there were also sizeable merchant fortunes that were created, especially in the salt monopoly. What is, however, fundamentally different, are the relationships that emerge between European states and their rich merchant classes. Much of European commercial wealth was tapped by needy governments anxious to expand their revenue bases to meet the ever escalating expenses of war-making. Centralizing territorial states extracted revenues from growing European commerce. From the fourteenth through the eighteenth century, the Chinese government, in contrast, lightly taxed commerce, except for brief moments when extraordinary extractions took place.

Amidst the mercantilist competition among European merchants and their governments for wealth and power, maritime expansion played a role of particular importance. Both European merchants and their governments benefited from their many-stranded relationship, the former by gaining monopolies or other favorable conditions under which to amass fabulous profits, the latter by securing dearly desired revenues. The late imperial Chinese state did not develop the same kind of mutual dependence on rich merchants. Lacking the scale of fiscal difficulties encountered in Europe between the sixteenth and eighteenth centuries, Chinese officials had less reason to imagine new forms of finance, huge merchant loans and the concept of public as well as private debt. Not only did they have little dependence on mercantile wealth to support the state, they also feared the potentially disruptive consequences of both concentrations of wealth and the *pursuit* of such wealth. This opposition to what might have become a kind of commercial capitalism, had the government needed the merchants more and thus been supportive of them, does not mean that officials opposed markets and commerce more generally.

By 1500, the late imperial Chinese state possessed a complex tradition of policy options to shape economic activity, both to raise revenues and to achieve a stable social order. Official choices fluctuated. Two general approaches define the endpoints of possibilities. First, the state could choose activist and interventionist policies to control or direct economic activities; such efforts included the regulation of mining and the exchange of salt vouchers for grain shipments to troops in the northwest.[14] Second, the state could satisfy itself with monitoring private sector efforts and even informally delegate responsibility or it could depend on others to help achieve its goals; examples included market surveillance and reliance on elites for famine relief.[15] In between the extremes of direct state control and indirect monitoring lay all sorts of efforts to redirect, channel, or limit private sector economic practices. Amidst considerable variation in techniques there was basic agreement through the eighteenth century about the type of economy officials and literati sought to stabilize and expand. They supported an agrarian economy in

[14] Debates on mining policies during the Qing dynasty are detailed in the archival source materials collected by Qing specialists at People's University; see Zhongguo Renmin Daxue ed. 1983: 1–72. The same collection includes documents on state capitalization of major mining operations. On salt vouchers and grain shipments to the northwest during the Ming see Terada 1972: 80–119.

[15] Mann 1987, Will 1990.

which commerce had an important role. Some people emphasized commerce more; others stressed agriculture. But the differences were not crucial for they were not usually conceived as antithetical alternatives. Policy differences did not open up a large gap between competing visions of how to organize the material world. Commercial activity had come to occupy a recognized and accepted place in the agrarian economy, a position that some officials in earlier centuries already promoted. This did not mean that *all* merchant activities were equally acceptable. Nor did it mean that there were no disagreements about commerce and merchants, but the stereotypical notion of the late imperial Chinese government uniformly opposed to merchants and commerce is poorly supported empirically.

When trade moved goods from areas of low prices to those with high prices, market principles of supply and demand played a positive social function in Chinese official eyes. As the commodity most important to survival, the government took a special interest in the grain trade. Officials generally approved of long-distance shipments that moved grain from areas of surplus to those depending on commercial imports. But they were simultaneously against merchants holding grain off markets to drive up prices. They considered such hoarding to garner profits illegal and quite distinct from profits that came from moving grain from areas of surplus to those of deficit. A potential contradiction surfaced when merchants bought large sums of grain in surplus areas to export elsewhere. Such activities could be interpreted as hoarding, yet since the intent was not to sell the grain on the same market after prices rose, the activity was not really what officials were most concerned about.[16]

Officials generally favored market exchanges, except when shipments beyond an official's jurisdiction might cause hardship for his subject population. Officials understood the basic ideas of market supply and demand, consistent with Adam Smith's notions of how markets promote specialization and exchange. But at the same time they opposed the monopoly behavior of merchants who held grain off local markets to push prices upward. Government policies toward the food supply included, in the eighteenth century, the maintenance of more than one million tons of grain for sale and loans in the lean spring season and in years of especially poor harvest.[17] Subsistence issues made grain commerce of particular interest to the state. Where markets failed to adequately supply people, officials were more likely to take an active role. Government efforts at stabilizing grain distribution complemented

[16] Wong 1982.   [17] Will and Wong 1991.

elite efforts at making grain available at local levels. These efforts of both officials and elites to influence grain circulation flanked the efforts made by officials to promote expanded production through clearance of new lands and improved productivity of existing fields through better seed selection and water control. Grain was a special case because of its fundamental importance to survival. More generally, the late imperial government allowed trade to be carried on without much government oversight and with modest taxation.

In certain situations, however, officials departed from their support for markets and commerce with many buyers and sellers in favor of regulated exchange through a small number of merchants. First, the salt monopoly was a revenue maker for the state; licensing distribution made the state money and made a small number of merchants extremely wealthy. Second, foreign exchange was often regulated. Some foreign trade was framed within the tribute system which offered a political as well as economic rationale for exchanges between foreign governments and merchants. Other foreign trade was controlled because the goods desired were of strategic importance. Hence the tea and horse trade between northwest China and the steppe, for instance, was regulated because of the crucial importance of horses to the military and secondarily because revenue could be made on the tea sales. But when trade was neither foreign nor intended primarily as a revenue maker for the government, it was generally given free rein by the state, as long as officials believed that no small number of merchants were able to manipulate supplies and hence prices to the detriment of the consuming public at large.[18] Officials thereby supported commercial exchange without promoting concentrations of merchant wealth. The famous eleventh-century official Wang Anshi, a reformer responsible for promoting an activist set of government policies to raise revenues and order society, went so far as to help small-scale merchants with government credit to make them more competitive with large merchants. More generally, by late imperial times, officials simply cared that markets were running smoothly.

While they believed markets to be socially useful, late imperial officials did worry about people leaving the land and taking to the road in search of profit. There were two concerns at stake. First, there was a social concern that any people who were in perpetual or periodic movement were potentially dangerous to social order which was defined in terms of an ideal sedentary agrarian society in which men worked the fields and

---

[18] On salt, see Xu 1972 and Chen 1988; overseas foreign trade in the late imperial period is reviewed in detail by Li 1990 and Lin 1987. For the horse and tea trade and northwestern trade more generally, see Lin and Wang 1991.

women wove cloth and tended the home. Late Ming literature often counseled its readers against the dangers of men taking to the road for months or even years at a time.[19] Second, and more directly related to the economy, some official and elite writers despaired over what they perceived to be a growing taste for luxury and extravagance acquired by people who pursued profits from trade. The superior man was not swayed by the pursuit of advantage or profit; instead he was guided by his quest for Confucian virtues of benevolence and righteousness. The merchant pursuing profit (and not virtue) needed some external constraints on his behavior so that lust for luxury did not overcome Confucian sensibilities of restraint and moderation.[20] Confucian anxieties of officials and elites over the unbridled pursuit of profit qualified Chinese understandings of the market's social usefulness. Chinese officials recognized the virtues of market principles of supply and demand and yet abhorred the aggressive pursuit of wealth and prominent displays of extravagence. Within late imperial Chinese political economy, officials could comfortably promote market exchange and understand how an expanding commercial economy afforded peasants additional opportunities to make a living. But official support for a market economy with its benefits reaching the many peasants who bought and sold goods did not mean that the government therefore favored concentrations of wealth gained through market manipulation. Chinese official support for commerce did not mean promotion of a commercial capitalism like the one that developed in Europe.

Chinese political economy envisioned an agrarian commercial economy in which expansion came from opening new lands and improving productivity on already cultivated fields. Rural industry was clearly conceived as complementary to cash crops; giving women more work to do to supplement income from the fields was one way to keep the household economy going amidst population expansion. As Francesca Bray has stressed in the previous chapter on Chinese technology, a crucial goal of much state policy and official thinking was to bolster the

[19] One famous example of this sort of literature is "The Pearl Sewn Shirt" in which the opportunities for amorous misadventures depend upon husbands being away from home on commercial ventures. See Birch 1958: 37–96.

[20] As recent work by Lufrano (1997) and Brook (1998: 215–16) now suggests, Chinese Confucianism afforded resources for merchants to construct a positive view of their activities, not unlike the Osaka merchants studied by Tetsuo Najita (1987) who justified their activities in Confucian terms. But differences in social structure between the two countries, specifically the contrast between Japanese merchants who formed a social class distinct from warrior and noble elites and those in China who remained more closely tied to large landowners and officials, may have limited Chinese possibilities for a distinctly merchant vision of their Confucian social role to gain an independent basis from which to compete with the ideals expressed by agrarian and official elites.

economic viability and social cohesion of the family. Many of these families engaged in market exchange which enabled some of them to specialize in certain crops and crafts and on a larger spatial scale balanced supply and demand. Chinese political economy tied production and distribution together through its commitment to reducing or ameliorating relative inequalities and guaranteeing some absolute minimal standards for survival to Chinese families.

In general, the Chinese state (1) promoted agricultural production – opening new land, repairing and expanding water control in order to expand and stabilize production of both grains and cash crops; (2) influenced and occasionally regulated commercial distribution of some goods, most importantly grain, in order to achieve equity within local economies and balance across regions; and (3) encouraged migration to form new settlements so that populations and resource bases remained in relative balance. State efforts in these three general areas supported two distinct types of agrarian economy: (1) a series of small-scale self-sufficient economies reproduced across an expanding empire; (2) a complex large-scale interdependent economy to be monitored and if necessary managed by the state to achieve social stability. Increased production and regulated distribution could fit in either type of economy, while migration could create new small-scale economies or frontiers to be integrated economically in a larger society. The state promoted economic prosperity through both types of agrarian economy in order to gain the support of the people and thereby affirm its right and capacity to rule.

We can pose two images of social stability, the first based on the multiplication of healthy cells, the second on effective ties among diverse elements composing a complex compound. The first image in fact did not explicitly require a central government or even local government efforts in order to be promoted, nor did it exclude government efforts – it is a "fractal" vision in which the characteristics of social order appear the same at different spatial scales.[21] But the second image of social order did require far more of the state. Through its land reclamation policies, creation of a granary system, and movement of resources into frontier regions, the state made an active effort to develop those parts of the empire that private sector activities alone were not likely to change. In economically wealthy areas, the state worried far more about

---

[21] The term "fractal" was invented by the mathematician Benoit Mandelbrot to refer to the replication of certain irregular geometric patterns on different spatial scales with the degree of irregularity remaining constant. Thus, fractals look the same whether so tiny as to be viewed under a microscope or so large as to be visible only from an airplane. See Gleick 1987.

inequalities among rich and poor, as officials expected elites to help poorer people to survive and to help the state keep local order. The state promoted economic expansion in order to create the material conditions for a prosperous society which was the basis for a sound social order and political stability. The state's virtue was manifested by peasant security and well-being.

Political economy in medieval period Europe was generally conceived on a small spatial scale reflecting the small size of most political units. Political and religious leaders focused on the importance of markets providing goods without extreme price variations associated with the manipulations of wealthy merchants. The displacement of municipal administrations and regional aristocratic assemblies as the crucial arenas within which to decide economic matters by centralizing territorial states whose appetites for revenues dwarfed other concerns, were key political steps for constructing domestic markets. As small political units were increasingly challenged by rulers with territorial ambitions, larger-scale commercial networks developed which drew goods into broader spheres of circulation. Territorial states developed as larger market hierarchies were forged which penetrated the countryside and integrated many rural people and small town dwellers into commercial exchanges with large cities. This was a development distinct from and additional to the on-going exchange between major metropolises that had begun earlier. The older long-distance trade in luxuries that moved about the larger cities of Europe began to include items coming from beyond the European world. The merchants engaged in these forms of trade developed close relations with rulers in the political economy of mercantilism.

Mercantilism, the dominant philosophy of political economy in Europe between the late sixteenth and the early eighteenth century, posed a close relationship between power and wealth. In order for a state to become powerful, society had to become more wealthy. This was achieved through expanding economic production in rich core areas and extending trade across the country and especially beyond it to include other countries. Merchants and rulers shared a common interest in keeping wages and interest rates low, the land fully exploited, mining active, and fishing rights secured. Domestically, this meant promoting national production and economic unification. Internationally, a key goal was to build up a positive balance of trade which would increase the domestic money supply, money being essential for prosecuting wars. Analysts treated states like individuals or firms; success was measured by spending (importing) less than one's income (exports). Rulers conceived that one nation's commercial gain was to be achieved at another's loss. Thus, competition for wealth on a global scale became a component of state making on the European stage. European states promoted the production and commerce of their private entrepreneurs whose successes contributed to the consolidation and prosperity of national states in competition with each other. Foreign trade was a crucial battlefield.

Early modern maritime trade was often a risky business. A combination of natural misfortunes and man-made dangers threatened commercial voyages. Bad weather and poor winds could delay or destroy a vessel; pirates could do the same. While little could be done about the weather, the arming of ships to defend merchants against pirates was a key component in achieving economic success. The Mediterranean hegemony of the Venetians was based on their ability to protect merchants from predators. But the same military skills that helped protect could also be turned against other merchants. European rulers were anxious to protect their own merchants and pleased to gain spoils through plundering ships of other countries. What made maritime trade especially lucrative was monopoly control over some greatly desired good, like tea or pepper. Merchants who enjoyed monopoly privileges backed by armed force to keep out competitors could make great fortunes. The neo-classical economic norm of market competition among multiple buyers and sellers was empirically bounded by the two extremes of piracy and monopoly.

When Europeans went to Asia in the late fifteenth century, they came first as pirates and interlopers seeking to establish themselves forcibly in the Asian trading network. They achieved their greatest successes in the products and places where they could establish monopolies. In those commodities and trading ports where they did not enjoy military supremacy, they simply became new players in the game of Asian trade. Some analysts argue for important differences among European strategies to gain advantage in Asia; certainly there was a general shift from purely predatory actions to efforts to exact tribute and establish monopolies. But the underlying role of military force and coercion was a constant throughout; military power was as important to the European "discovery" of the world as it was to state-making competition within Europe.[22] While centralizing governments aimed to concentrate coercive powers domestically, they often allowed these powers to be held by chartered companies in Asia. The close connection between wealth and power in mercantilist logic appears in the variable division between public and private powers within Europe and overseas in Asia. The

[22] Parker 1988.

political economy of mercantilist empire created initially complementary
goals for states and merchants – states wanted a part of merchant profits
and merchants wanted state support to secure greater profits. Missing
from the mercantilist logic was any particular concern about the legitimacy of European political power in Asian settings. The Dutch faced
these problems in Southeast Asia in the first half of the eighteenth
century, but European rule in Asia more generally would not become a
serious problem until the nineteenth and especially the twentieth
century. What challenged the mercantilist logic by the late eighteenth
century were private traders, like the English private traders who undermined the monopoly power of the East India Company over trade with
China; private traders took advantage of the general framework set up
by the chartered companies to secure their own private profit. Adam
Smith's critique of mercantilism posed the "free market" economy of
private traders as the desirable alternative.

Domestically, the proponents of free markets had been waging a
battle to dismantle various medieval restrictions on trade during the
seventeenth and eighteenth centuries. One approach to these changes
stresses a shift from an active localist political paternalism in the market
place to an indifferent laissez-faire by the central government.[23] Another
approach highlights the role of the state in setting the ground rules and
affirming the individual property rights that gave people the security and
incentives to pursue their self-interest knowing that the fruits of their
efforts would be protected.[24] Yet other scholars have shown how the
market came to be seen as a benevolent influence, an arena in which
people's passions could be channeled to serve their interests in a
constructive manner.[25] From whatever vantage point one approaches
the changing political economy of early modern England and France
one can find new political principles at work. The national state made
an alliance with certain economic actors as individuals in order to
undercut the claims on resources and market control enacted by local
political authorities anxious to defend the interests of local groups.
Thus, the forging of a new political economy was enmeshed with issues
of the national state versus local authorities and with the issues of the
individual's rights and property. At broadly the same time as arguments
in favor of freer domestic commerce were being aired against the local
protectionism of what E. P. Thompson has called the "moral economy,"
arguments against monopoly control in overseas trade in favor of freer

---

[23] Thompson 1971.   [24] North 1981.
[25] See Hirschman 1977. Not all analysts, however, have stressed the positive features of
   markets. The uncertain political implications of free market ideology are traced in
   different ways in Macpherson 1962, Pocock 1985, and Appleby 1992.

movements by private traders were also being made. Reflecting distinct political and economic situations, the arguments against local protectionism and overseas monopoly came to share the intellectually powerful common denominator of free trade. After Adam Smith trumpeted the virtues of the market and the evils of mercantilism most persuasively, David Ricardo offered the further insight in the early nineteenth century that "comparative advantage" guaranteed that all parties to trade could gain from free market exchange even if one of the parties was uniformly less efficient and productive in any of the goods to be traded among them. Once it could be argued that everyone benefits from trade, irrespective of their initial endowments and skills, free trade made moral sense. The English government could disengage itself from overt manipulation of economic affairs.

At the same time as the English government could champion international free trade, English colonial administration grew. Flanked by growing colonial power, the free trade logic of England's industrializing economy proved inadequate to power economic connections between China and Britain. England relied on Indian opium imports into China to pay for its purchases of Chinese teas. England's nineteenth-century economic successes were not, therefore, simply achieved because of its Industrial Revolution, but resulted in part from the English government's continued capacity to set terms of exchange politically and economically, an ability begun by European powers under the political economy of mercantilism.

The European transformation of political economy, at the nexus of both political and economic changes, began with two rather distinct sets of changes joined by the centralizing state's role in each. First was the formation of national markets especially in England, France, and Holland. Second was the intrusion of European traders into Asian trading networks and the movement of European traders and settlers across the Atlantic to the New World. Territorial state interests drove Europe's support for the formation of national markets and the adventures of European merchants in Asia and the New World. The Chinese state acted from a different set of interests articulated through an ideology proclaiming the centrality of China's agrarian empire in a world order that embraced groups of people across the Inner Asian steppe and around the Southeast Asian archipelago. The collapse of this world order during the nineteenth century and its displacement by a European construction of political and economic relations helped to create a "modern" Chinese political economy. The new Chinese political economy grappled with categories of analysis that had not been previously conceived and methods of economic change that were pre-

viously unavailable. New economic possibilities predicated upon technologies brought in from abroad transformed Chinese ideas about both
the technology evaluated by Bray in the previous chapter and the
political economy addressed in this chapter. But these changes did not
simply and swiftly make the ideology or institutions of late imperial
Chinese political economy irrelevant to subsequent economic history.

Chinese political economy in the ninteenth and twentieth centuries

To stress the temporal arcs of Chinese and European political economy,
as I have done so far, minimizes the spatial dimensions of each, which is
the subject to which I now turn. Certainly commercial capitalism and
industrial capitalism forged a network of political and economic linkages
in Europe beginning in the sixteenth century. But it has proven all too
easy for scholars to read back from a late twentieth-century perspective
the nature of economic relationships in the past. What degrees of
integration characterized different spatial scales of the economy? The
sixteenth-century "world-system" linked a few seaports and their hinter-
lands across a grand maritime space, but created few economic linkages
within Asian societies at any distance from these ports. Varying degrees
of exchange and integration within different social and cultural universes
took place more or less independently of this maritime network. Thus,
Chinese domestic trade developed on a European spatial scale, but
much of it had little connection to overseas trade. In other places and at
later times, however, a stronger form of integration into maritime
networks could prove fatal to major economic activities, like that
experienced by South Asia where Asia's greatest textile producers were
destroyed by British cottons in the nineteenth century.[26] While Indian
cotton textile production was decimated, Chinese cotton textile production continued with both positive and negative impacts from international trade.

The European world-system has gone through important and dramatic changes which are portrayed in Immanuel Wallerstein's on-going
analysis of the world-system since 1450. I would stress four components
of change that matter to how we conceive the possible positions taken by
different parts of the world system. First, the patterns of capital flow
have changed as integration within the world-system has ebbed and
flowed over time. The institutions and technologies for moving capital
have made possible in the late twentieth century investment logics not

[26] Perlin 1983.

easy to imagine, let alone implement, in the late nineteenth century. Similarly, patterns of labor migration are another component of the world-system subject to changing institutional constraints. Like capital movements, these labor movements condition the kinds of linkages and positions that different parts of the world-system can achieve. A third source of variation is driven by technological change. The type of linkages present in the world-system at any point in time are made possible by technological capacities within the system. Changes in technology and the spread of technology create new possibilities as they displace older practices. Finally, organizational structures or institutions matter for they assemble capital, labor, and technologies; as the scales of production and distribution managed by firms change, the ways in which markets are institutionally constructed also change. For the Chinese case, the formation of new banking institutions in the 1920s and 1930s created opportunities for capital movements into and out of China that would have been more difficult to achieve in earlier decades. The temporal rhythms and spatial dimensions of the Chinese diaspora have been shifting features of the world-system. When we turn to the past two decades, the dissemination of industrial technology and the formation of joint-venture firms are simply two examples of the changes that alter how China can be integrated into the world-system.

Independent of the potential for the European world-system to incorporate China or some other non-Western country are the capacities and desires of these areas to engage or resist the world economy. During the late Qing dynasty, the government sought to strengthen the state through imitation of Western technologies – arsenals, steamships, and the like. The government accepted foreign loans, and officials beginning in the 1890s attempted to reform the government through the formation of new ministries and the abolition of old ones. These efforts notwithstanding, a fragile Qing government fell in 1911. China's political weaknesses during the next four decades were manifest in the absence of a central government with effective claims to national rule until 1927 and the end of such rule in 1937 when the Japanese invasion overran large stretches of territory. Chinese incorporation into the world economy proceeded amidst twentieth-century political uncertainties and as a modern industrial sector began to take shape.

No one challenges the basic fact that the modern industrial sector was growing in China. Estimates for the years 1914/1918 to 1933/1936 range from 7.7 to 8.8 percent annual growth rates for modern industry.[27] Growth followed from the adoption of new technologies and

[27] Rawski 1989: 272–74.

organizational practices from which great benefits could be derived. But even if industrial growth might have continued at a healthy rate, how this would have transformed the economy is uncertain.

A crucial cluster of simplifying assumptions in neo-classical economics assumes processes of change that in fact apply only to certain cases, namely those cases in which economic growth or development takes place. The gradual integration of factor and product markets is not a logically necessary phenomenon, but an empirical reality found in some places at certain junctures in history. There are any number of other instances in which these assumptions of change will not hold. The danger lies in assuming that economic growth is natural and that if it does not take place, there must be some arbitrary human actions (usually thought of as politics) that are interfering. By closely identifying a theoretical ideal with a "natural" state of affairs, economic theory loses its potential to explain how economic change is in fact historically created through the building of economic institutions. These institutions – both markets and firms – are what make it possible for economies to become integrated, to seize upon comparative advantage and the division of labor, to diffuse new technologies, and to move capital and labor to those projects yielding the highest returns. China in the 1930s was only beginning to develop many of these institutions. Much of China enjoyed the benefits of product markets for commodities produced in the countryside, but markets for capital and labor as well as for modern products were only beginning to be formed, and the firms to take fullest advantage of modern technologies and organizational structures were yet to be created. There were good reasons why it was difficult to create more integrated markets. Most obviously, transportation infrastructure outside of major waterways and railways was lacking. Republican era governments were not in a position to take a strong lead in developing infrastructure or promoting economic change.

At the same time, Western and Japanese economic powers were unable to assert dominance across all areas of production. They were most important in manufacturing, but even here, they accounted for less than 30 percent of manufacturing in China in 1933.[28] Great debates have raged over the healthy or negative impact of capitalism in twentieth-century China. But before we can assign such labels, more effort must go into measuring and assessing the impacts themselves. During the past decade, American scholarship has posed alternative perspectives on the relationship between urban industrialization and the rural economy in the twentieth century. On the one hand, Philip

[28] Rawski 1989: 74.

Huang's book on the lower Yangzi seems to suggest that urban industrialization did not have much impact on neighboring rural areas, while
Thomas Rawski's book on pre-war economic growth assumes a set of
smooth connections between urban and rural sectors so that improvements in urban China spelled improvements in rural China as well.[29]
Huang argues that rural areas surrounding Shanghai remained at a
subsistence standard of living in the twentieth century despite urban
industrialization, though he presents little data to substantiate his claim;
he sees economic development in the lower Yangzi countryside only
after 1978 when economic reforms facilitated the absorption of rural
labor into industries and labor productivity in agriculture rose at the
same time that industrial production expanded. He rejects "economic
dualism" for the earlier part of the twentieth century, yet his argument
resonates with the analysis of dual economies in other places made by
scholars who suggest that the absorption of surplus rural labor into
industrial production is a key bottleneck in many developing countries
with large agricultural populations.[30] Rawski's portrayal, in contrast to
Huang's, sees no barriers between urban and rural economic activities.
The basic argument begins with a modern manufacturing sector which
develops through increased investment in new forms of production,
supported by improved transport and communications and new financial and banking institutions.[31] A second component claims that many
kinds of traditional production and trade complemented modern developments, rather than being destroyed by the new forms; there was
integration among modern and traditional sectors and between urban
and rural sites of production and distribution.[32] Finally, Rawski argues
that the Chinese economy had achieved a "sustained expansion of
output per head" in the early twentieth century.[33] Rawski appeals to
Simon Kuznets' pioneering work on modern economic growth by
comparing Japanese growth rates with those he has estimated for China
to argue that China began modern economic growth because its rates
resemble those for Japan at a time it is recognized to have begun modern
growth.[34] Central to Kuznets' modern economic growth is a shift from

---

[29] Huang 1990; Rawski 1989.   [30] Huang 1990: 115–16.
[31] Rawski 1989: 65–238.
[32] Some of Rawksi's arguments depend on this integration. For instance, he estimates
agricultural growth by assuming that rising urban wages must mean that agricultural
wages were similarly rising; they in turn would not rise unless agricultural labor
productivity was also rising, and hence agricultural growth can be inferred from a rise
in urban labor wages (Rawski 1989: 299–321). If, however, differences persisted
between urban and rural wages, Rawski's arguments about agricultural growth would
lose some of their force.
[33] Rawski 1989: 344.
[34] Kuznets 1966; Rawski 1989: 336.

agriculture to industry with the application of expanding stocks of knowledge to push capital and labor productivity. Technology thus plays a key role in motoring advances fueled by continuous new investment. This may well characterize Japanese changes, but does it capture Chinese realities? The persistence of a large agricultural sector and a rural handicraft industrial sector presents a potential challenge to Rawski's assessment of modern economic growth. Rawski seeks to diminish the significance of this difficulty with his argument about the complementary nature of growth in modern and traditional sectors. Complementarity is crucial to his picture of a *generally* improving economic situation. But there are different reasons for growth in modern and traditional sectors. Growth in the modern sector comes from the application of considerable capital and new technologies that raise labor productivity. Improvements in traditional sectors are largely market induced. It is Smithian principles of market specialization that create advances and the ability of certain traditional activities to become integrated with modern ones, as is the case for handicraft weaving using machine-spun yarn, or to complement growing modern activities, like native banking and traditional transport. In most of these cases there is little clear advance in technology, levels of energy used or capital per worker. Thus, the possibilities for increased labor productivity remain limited. Accepting Rawski's demonstration of effective ties between modern and traditional sectors only underlines the profound difficulties the modern sector would have in transforming traditional activities to a higher level of productivity. That, of course, has proven the case since 1949 as well. More effective modern growth might have been expected to destroy traditional forms of output marked by limited technological change, capital use and labor productivity. Given the persistence of traditional forms of production, a logic for sustained modern growth leading to a transformation of the entire economy was not, in my opinion, clearly taking place in China before 1949.

At present we have no clear and systematic picture of the ways in which urban industrial changes were connected to and separate from economic activities in the countryside. It seems reasonable to expect that peasants in periurban areas did benefit from urban industrialization since demand for industrial raw materials and food supplies must both have risen. But complete integration of capital, labor, and product markets seems a bit far-fetched. The realities likely lie inbetween Huang's dismissal of important economic links channeling economic change beginning in the cities to the countryside and Rawski's assumption that markets were integrated. In contrast with European capitalist development in which the formation of large-scale markets was achieved by commercial capitalists and these markets were then used by industrial capitalists, a sophisticated market economy in China was constructed without a strong capitalist thrust; when twentieth-century industrial capitalists emerged in Chinese cities, they had little contact with the agrarian economy's vast commercial networks. How, and even if, urban capitalists would develop China's agrarian commercial economy was uncertain when the Japanese invaded in 1937.

Distinct from the issue of urban–rural relationships is the issue of spatial scale. Given China's great size, what are the appropriate units within which to envision economic change? What relations among these units seem most plausible? In Rawski's effort to examine national aggregates, the lower Yangzi region looms large. For modern industry, Rawski's estimates that together with Manchuria, Shanghai accounted for two-thirds of China's industrial output with only one-seventh of the country's population in 1933.[35] Rawski stresses in his conclusion the regional locus of economic growth. Since changes in the lower Yangzi and Manchuria drive Rawski's estimated per capita output increase of 1.2–1.3 percent annually and per capita consumption increase of 0.5 percent annually, this means "other regions experienced below average, and possibly negative, growth."[36]

Of course, economic development must start somewhere. We can underestimate its presence in China by thinking in conventional national terms. China dwarfs in size any particular European country; many of China's provinces are themselves larger than smaller European countries. To make more meaningful comparisons we might want to look at regions of China and compare them with European countries. Were we to do so, China's most advanced regions might look little different in their growth profiles from European regions. European industrialization also took place at specific geographical locations. As Sidney Pollard says, "The industrial revolution jumped, as it were, from one industrial region to another, though in a general direction outward from the North-West, while the country inbetween remained to be industrialized, or at least modernized, much later, if at all."[37] By 1914 Europe was economically integrated. Those areas that had been largely ignored by the initial spurts of industrial change became more firmly tied to flows of capital, goods, and services. Europe's more backward regions remained less prosperous than the advanced areas, but they were nevertheless linked. The process of integration has proceeded slowly however. It should not then perhaps surprise us that for twentieth-century China, the connections between the advanced regions of Shanghai and Man-

[35] Rawski 1989: 73.   [36] Rawski 1989: 271.   [37] Pollard 1981: 45.

churia to the rest of China remain unclear. The formation of a modern industrial sector suggests that at least part of the economy was moving beyond Smithian dynamics of expansion, even as classical fears of a population and resource crisis in agriculture were echoed in the pronouncements of twentieth-century Chinese and foreign observers. But the uncertain linkages between modern industrial and traditional agricultural sectors make the impact of twentieth-century industrial change difficult to assess. What needs to be determined is whether or not the economic linkages among different regions and within them were adequate to judge whether there was an integrated economy, a network of loosely connected economies, or an economy segmented into separate spheres bearing traits of a dual economy.

Since we conventionally think of modern economic growth in national terms, we ignore regional variations and implicitly assume that market integration will at some point coordinate allocation and production decisions across the country and that economic differences that exist under these circumstances are caused by rational decisions. These are major simplifying assumptions that explain away developments that are historically contingent. If firms lack information on the costs of materials in some areas or lack the ability to respond to such information even when they do have it, market integration is limited at best. At present we need to learn more about credit, labor, and product markets in pre-war China. While urban-based credit networks through modern banking clearly existed, it remains unclear how systematically, if at all, urban credit was integrated with rural credit. Similarly for labor, migration patterns were limited and labor markets limited in their spatial dimensions, but the degree to which these institutional limitations created disparities in regional economic performance in the Republican period have not yet been analyzed. Certainly, striking regional differences between standards of living in China's remote northwest or southwest and in the lower Yangzi region, Canton, or Manchuria are known to exist. But expecting these differences to disappear "naturally" over time had the Republican period economy's development not been interrupted by the Japanese invasion remains a heroic assumption. In fact, integration could mean an increased concentration of resources in core areas rather than the diminishing of economic differences.[38]

Economic integration deserves more direct and careful analysis.

---

[38] Kenneth Pomeranz's work on a portion of inland North China between 1853 and 1937 argues for a shift of resources from peripheries to cores (Pomeranz 1993). Ming-te Pan's research on credit markets in the Qing and Republican periods suggests that funds previously available for rural credit increasingly were drawn into urban financial networks (Pan 1994).

Market integration is a key feature of Smithian growth and becomes a dimension of economies which experience growth for other reasons as well. Without market integration it is hard for new technologies, innovative organization, or increased investment to have much effect. Recent research on Qing dynasty grain markets often shows related price movements on distant markets, testimony to the role of markets in the eighteenth and nineteenth centuries.[39] These findings are important to the study of twentieth-century changes for two reasons. First, they remind us that markets were hardly new in Republican China and that arguments about their increased importance must create some reasonable baseline from which to begin assertions about increased marketing. Second, price movements in grain markets by themselves cannot tell us about other product markets or the factor markets for land, capital, and labor. Exploring how closely these factor markets were integrated will help us better assess the possibilities for economic growth in the 1920s and 1930s.[40]

Institutions matter because economic growth only happens when human efforts are channeled through effective organizations. Moreover, the institutions necessary for one kind of growth need not be present for another; Smithian growth based upon division of labor and a comparative advantage rationale does not necessarily require the kinds of skills that technological change, for instance, demands; nor will Smithian economic expansion guarantee that technological change, organizational innovation, or capital accumulation will necessarily occur. In an economy as large as China's we should expect an uneven spread of institutions across the country both among regions – a Gansu compared to a Guangdong – and within them – a Wuhan and the Han River highlands. Thus, the kinds of growth possible in some areas will likely not be possible everywhere.

Market institutions have promoted commercial exchange since the

---

[39] Rawski and Li 1992.

[40] For their parts Loren Brandt and Thomas Rawski either assume or assert with spotty evidence a neo-classical world in which wage rates equilibrate across sectors, labor and capital move easily across urban and rural sectors to achieve optimal returns, and integration if not present in particular area is expected to develop in the future (Brandt 1989: 106–37; Rawski 1989: 285–329). Huang, to the contrary, essentially argues that Chinese land, labor and credit markets fell far short of neo-classical ideals that he assumes to be at work in England (Huang 1990: 93–114). Only a concrete comparison of economic institutions, however, could demonstrate how similar and different real–world cases truly are. Kenneth Pomeranz's work on Shandong analyzes credit markets in a manner that helps to establish a baseline for assessing economic possibilities based on changes in credit markets. His careful reconstruction of the institutional structure of Shandong credit markets is an exemplary alternative to the diametrically opposed lines of reasoning Brandt and Rawski on one side and Huang on the other employ to address the general issue of economic institutions and economic growth (Pomeranz 1993: 27–68).

Song dynasty. These markets were diffused across ever greater areas in the Ming and Qing periods. Republican-period changes made them work even better, but the basic dynamics were present in many parts of urban and rural China for centuries. Not so for other sources of growth which in European experiences were components of capitalism. Modern banking and finance were primarily urban phenomena, the creation of new factories was largely an urban phenomenon, new communication networks mainly linked urban centers, and so on. Even those skeptical of significant modern economic growth in Republican China agree that urban economic change did take place. What we have yet to determine carefully across a series of case studies is how this growth was tied to economic change in the countryside. Nor have we sorted out the intentions and impacts of Republican period governments upon urban and agrarian economies across core and peripheral regions.

In contrast to our uncertainties about the political economy in the first half of the twentieth century, the political economy of the agrarian empire in Qing China has become reasonably clear. The government achieved economic integration through mobilizing and moving resources into border regions only marginally connected by markets. The government also invested more in promoting production in such areas. This kind of compensatory or complementary integration in which the roles of officials and merchant elites were defined by the spatial structure of Chinese agrarian political economy diminished in the nineteenth century as the central Qing state was increasingly occupied with foreign affairs. No grand structure came to replace the eighteenth-century edifice before 1949.

After the founding of the People's Republic of China, the country largely cut off its connections with outsiders; after 1960 the ties with the USSR were also virtually severed. The world-system had little significance for Chinese blueprints for developing the economy. Despite the radical shift in ideology and the fundamental expansion of bureaucratic capacity, much of the post-1949 state's political economy, especially regarding issues tied to the countryside and food supplies, resonated with those of the Qing dynasty.[41] In cities, there was a new political economy of industrialization based on Soviet socialist principles of capital mobilization and investment in heavy industry. Not only institutionally separate from the rural agrarian economy, this political economy was ideologically and institutionally divorced from the world-system. But the industrialization drive was not so very different from earlier government efforts, as either the post-1949 government or many Western treatments of the

[41] Wong 1988.

post-1949 economy either state or imply. The new government had several immediate traditions of political economy to draw upon in principle and practice. All of the governments active in wartime China – the Japanese, the Nationalists and the Communists – had taken control over at least some production, and in both Nationalist and Communist controlled areas they also regulated distribution. In principle, however, none of these experiences was most important to the Communists after 1949. Instead, the Chinese created a five-year economic plan modeled on Soviet experiences of industrialization with a stress on developing a heavy industrial base. In fact, the logic of state-run heavy industries resonated strongly with the approach of the previous Nationalist government. Japanese efforts to control heavy industrial production in their areas provided a second example of how governments went about controlling the economy. When these experiences are combined with the Communists' own efforts at managing poor and backward agrarian economies, there seems to have been little room to imagine anything less than a major state effort to mount a strong controlling role over the economy. The new government embarked upon efforts to expand the heavy industrial base begun by the Nationalists and to stabilize the light industrial base in private hands which they gradually socialized over the first seven years of Communist rule. Though not consciously admitted, Chinese government commitment to creating an industrial base broadly distributed through the country followed on efforts by the Nationalist government to establish an industrial sector in the southwest during the war. The Nationalist effort, of course, was driven by wartime losses of territory, while the Communist plan was conceived for the entire country. Communist policies also represented the unacknowledged application of a logic promoting geographically widespread economic development that had been used by the Qing government with respect to the agrarian economy two centuries earlier. Both the techniques and significance of socialist industrial development differed from the Qing political economy of agrarian empire, but the logic of creating comparable economic activities across the entire country was a common theme. Much as Qing dynasty political economy pushed for agrarian prosperity across a vast empire, Communist political economy promoted industrialization across an equally large agrarian country.

The post-1978 reforms have reintroduced a market economy and increasing ties with a world capitalist economy that encourages us to put what may be a socialist interlude in the longer perspective of Chinese market economy and world capitalism in the nineteenth and twentieth centuries. The pre-war Chinese economy possessed both a vital agrarian commercial economy, the basic institutions of which had existed for several centuries, and a growing industrial economy constructed by native and foreign capitalists. Growth certainly took place in the industrial capitalist economy and some growth appears to have taken place in some parts of the agrarian commercial economy. These market and capitalist economies each continued to retain their own distinct identities, even if they became increasingly connected. In Europe the relationship between the two had always been closer. Commercial capitalism played a far more significant role in creating a market economy in early modern Europe. Industrial capitalism in turn was built upon market hierarchies that integrated economic regions and commercially connected major cities.

The nineteenth-century European economy experienced increasing integration. First, there were multiple forms of market integration through which growing volumes of capital, labor, and finished goods passed within national borders and across them. Second, there was an increasing integration of commercial capitalism and the market economy, which had developed somewhat independently of each other in earlier centuries. What powered their closer connection were the demands and desires of industrialization that transformed commercial capitalism into industrial capitalism. Industry devoured resources and labor with a power and passion unimagined in earlier times. The industrial revolution created a new set of ways for capitalism and the market economy to become joined. Only in the second half of the nineteenth century did a "modern" economy clearly emerge in much of Europe. The nineteenth-century European linkages between market economy and capitalism were not swiftly repeated in many other parts of the world, North America and Japan being the obvious exceptions. The confluence of a market economy driven by Smithian dynamics, a largely independent dynamic of technological change leading to an energy revolution, and a commercial capitalism came together to form a nineteenth-century industrial capitalism. In China, market economy and capitalism were not so tightly connected. After 1949, their relationship was, at least for a while, broken entirely as the Communist state resolutely rejected capitalism but found it periodically acceptable to use various types of commerce.[42] Since the economic reforms beginning in 1978, market institutions have been increasingly developed both domestically and for international trade.

Conventional Western assessments of the market economy and capitalism in the contemporary world posit markets as a basic component of the larger institutional structures of capitalism. Communist assessments

[42] Solinger 1984.

in both the former Soviet Union and China have generally accepted this identification. But where Western analyses promote the virtues of markets and capitalism, Russian and Chinese economic policies generally avoided what they considered dangerous vices until less than two decades ago. For their part, late imperial Chinese thinkers could distinguish between the beneficial impacts of markets allocating products and services according to supply and demand and the manipulative power of rich merchants who made huge profits by controlling prices, one basic component of capitalism. Confucian ideology supported markets and decried scheming merchants. Though post-1949 Chinese leaders have not consciously called upon this Confucian distinction, they have proven more able to promote market exchange than their Russian Communist counterparts.

Chinese policymakers and theorists have repeatedly asserted a basic distinction between a commodity or market economy and capitalism, a distinction most Western analysts find forced and hollow.[43] Yet Fernand Braudel made just this distinction for an earlier period of European history. Can we be sure it does not apply at all to recent Chinese changes? Consider the similarities of Confucian and Communist views on political economy. Late imperial ideology accepted markets and understood how they could promote economic welfare. The same ideology also aimed to control degrees of inequality and guarantee minimal subsistence to all. But late imperial Chinese ideology never completely accepted the profit motive; virtue always lay beyond pursuit of material advantage. Communist ideology has also had difficulties accepting the pursuit of profit. Like Confucian understandings, Communist visions aimed to reduce inequality and provide for the material security of everyone in society. With these similarities, perhaps it is not so surprising that both argue for the virtues of markets and yet do not support capitalism. But, even if this distinction between market economy and capitalism can be made, the recent double rejection of at least some Confucian and Communist sensibilities leads to the question of what will guide future Chinese understandings of economic change. Various Western notions of economics are filling the partial vacuum, but it is by no means clear that they will succeed in displacing all remaining

---

[43] Chinese works have considered the nature of China's socialist commodity economy since the founding of the People's Republic in 1949; see Zhang, Zhang, and Wu 1979 for a collection of essays and bibliography on commodity production and pricing under socialism written in the 1950s, 1960s and 1970s. A major subject in the early years of the reform era was commodity circulation; see the collection of views on the issue in *Zhongguo shehui kexueyuan* 1980. More recent works have addressed China's commercial geography (e.g., Zhang, Tao, Dai and Ke 1988).

Confucian and Communist Chinese ideas about economic change. Future directions of Chinese political economy remain open.

Chinese official efforts to argue a distinction between capitalism and the market economy they are constructing seem increasingly difficult to sustain as the linkages between China's economy and the world capitalist economy embrace the movements of capital, labor and goods produced with more advanced technologies, often in factories employing Western labor management techniques which are part of larger complex firms. Many observers, both Chinese and foreign, have been acutely aware of the unbridled pursuit of economic gain supplying the driving force for popular participation in "modernization." Gone are both the Confucian and the Communist sensibilities that previously guided the search for material gain and security. China has become a society in which the passionate pursuit of profit has come to color and shape social behavior more generally. How different, then, is China's situation from that of other parts of the world-system? Certainly, much of China's integration into the world-system includes the promotion of sensibilities and desires found elsewhere in the world. But it is too easy to imagine that this integration was inevitable and to believe that Maoist isolation was an aberration.

In general, we tend to believe that the path to the present was a necessary and natural one since it was in fact taken. This view conflates explanations of what has happened with a logic that "predicts" what has already happened as necessary. But many large events and processes did not have to take the particular shapes that they have. In natural history, it is perhaps easier to understand that the Grand Canyon did not necessarily have to come into existence, but its existence can be explained as a historical process. Similarly, Mao Zedong's vision of social revolution did not have to emerge, but it can be explained. Once major events do occur, however, they influence the probabilities of what will happen in the future. History is, in other words, path-dependent. What has happened before does influence what happens later, even if there is never a tight causal chain according to which we can predict the future. Despite the confident proclamations that the world is converging economically and politically with the collapse of communism in Eastern Europe and Russia and the dramatic reforms in China, multiple possibilities continue to persist.

Imagining China's possible futures simply on the basis of its present conditions suggests, at least implicitly, that the past no longer matters. A quarter of a century ago, when knowledge of less-developed countries was more limited than it is today, it was quite common for development theorists to propose recipes for economic change that they believed could work anywhere. In order to explain the failures of an earlier optimism, some scholars now scrutinize more closely the conditions under which development strategies are difficult to implement. Joining structuralist critiques of organizational confusion in less-developed countries are recommendations from the "new political economy," which seeks to clarify property rights and delineate material incentives in order to mobilize people's efforts to create economic change. Missing from many of these considerations are discussions of what is not simply possible but what is desirable. What kinds of material improvement count more than others? What are the tradeoffs between more cars and more pollution? How do we judge the relative merits of concentrating resources in relatively advanced areas with higher returns to capital and labor and dispersing resources to develop infrastructure in poorer peripheral areas? Once we begin to confront these kinds of questions, history matters and abstract notions of "rationality" become inadequate. Yet the ways in which we conventionally think about history discourages us from recognizing its relevance to these questions.

Timothy Brook's chapter in this volume explains the manner in which the Chinese "pre-modern" has been conceived in terms of its relationship to the "modern," the characteristics of which are derived from European historical experiences. The characteristics of the "pre-modern" are read retrospectively from a definition of what they are not, namely "modern." But the Chinese case, unlike the European, does not encourage, at least before the late twentieth century, an analysis of the trajectory of the "pre-modern" forward to the "modern." Instead we are confronted with its failures. As I mentioned at the beginning of this chapter, we focus on "what went wrong." Scholars seek to explain why what should have happened did not. Analysts of contemporary China, especially the Chinese themselves, reject the past because they see it as the source of China's problems. An iconoclastic rejection of "tradition" as the weight that prevents China's present from lifting off into the future has been a view shared by many Chinese intellectuals since the May Fourth period beginning in 1919. A totalistic rejection of the past limits the capacity of observers to perceive the present. As Chinese intellectuals discover post-modern vantage points on their society, they face a danger of becoming further crippled analytically. The basic and positive power of post-modern analyses liberates the intellectual from an unthinking dependence on categories that are themselves freighted with the intent to subordinate and order the world to serve the interests of others. But unless this liberation leads to the discovery of alternative modes of analysis and understanding, its intellectual power merely destroys; it does not create.

When coupled with the Chinese rejection of the past, there is little left with which to contemplate the future.

One way to escape this crisis is to turn back to history and to consider the particular conditions explaining major processes of reproduction and transformation. Immanuel Wallerstein's chapter does just this for the conditions leading to the formation of Europe's world system. A similar effort must be mounted to explain China's reproduction and transformation from the tenth century forward. This chapter and the previous one propose some crucial ways in which the political economy of an agrarian empire in China led to a distinctive social, political and economic formation. They further suggest that the dynamics of this political economy matter to our understanding of China's later trajectory when, in the nineteenth and twentieth centuries, China collided with the European world-system on a scale and to a degree dwarfing its contacts with foreigners in earlier centuries. The late nineteenth-century shift to concern with foreigners and the search for wealth and power diminished attention given to the political economy of an agrarian empire, but as the twentieth-century revolution would show, issues of the countryside remain basic to the construction of a viable political economy. Since 1949 the challenge of transforming the descendants of an agrarian empire into the citizens of an industrialized society has remained a basic focus of political concern.

If we continue to subscribe to economic histories that subordinate the "pre-modern" to the "modern" and to explain failures as a set of absences identified by developmentalist analyses that claim to specify the necessary conditions for growth but that derive conceptually from an abstract theoretical vantage point, we will continue to find that the resulting analyses lack much contact, let alone overlap, with actual possibilities. Yet there should be more than a simple hinge point as we move from questions of how an economy has developed to considerations of how it might change in the future. There is in fact a common terrain created by joining the two together, but it is so poorly understood that we will need far more exploration. The territory spanning the late-imperial past, the Western imperialist past, and the succession of presents composed of elements of these two kinds of past can be mapped more closely in the future to yield a better understanding of Chinese history and bolster hopes for consciously creating a desirable Chinese future.

Bibliography

Abu-Lughod, Janet. 1989. *Before European Hegemony: The World System A.D. 1250–1350.* New York: Oxford University Press.

Adas, Michael. 1989. *Machines as the Measure of Men: Science, Technology, and Ideologies of Western Domination.* Ithaca: Cornell University Press.

Alexander, Jennifer and Paul Alexander. 1982. "Shared Poverty as Ideology: Agrarian Relationships in Colonial Java." *Man* 17:4, 597–619.

Amin, Samir. 1976. *Unequal Development,* trans. Brian Pearce. New York: Monthly Review.

Anderson, Perry. 1974a. *Lineages of the Absolutist State.* London: New Left Books.

1974b. *Passages from Antiquity to Feudalism.* London: New Left Books.

Andreev, M. G. 1929. "Institut rabstva v Kitae." *Problemyi Kitaya* 1: 228–306.

Anon. 1984. *Die Werke von Karl Marx und Friedrich Engels in China: Katalog und Auswahlbibliographie.* Trier: Karl-Marx-Haus.

Appadurai, Arjun (ed.). 1986. *The Social Life of Things: Commodities in Cultural Perspective.* Cambridge: Cambridge University Press.

Appleby, Joyce. 1992. *Liberalism and Republicanism in the Historical Imagination.* Cambridge, Mass.: Harvard University Press.

Appleton, William. 1951. *A Cycle of Cathay: The Chinese Vogue in England during the Seventeenth and Eighteenth Centuries.* New York: Columbia University Press.

Ashton, T. H. and C. H. E. Philpin (eds.). 1985. *The Brenner Debate.* Cambridge: Cambridge University Press.

Bacon, Francis. 1905. *Philosophical Works.* London: Routledge.

Baechler, Jean, John Hall, and Michael Mann (eds.). 1988. *Europe and the Rise of Capitalism.* Oxford: Blackwell.

Bai Gang. 1984. *Zhongguo fengjian changqi yanxu wenti lunzhan de youlai yu fazhan* [The origins and development of the controversy over the question of the prolongation of the period of feudal society in China]. Beijing: Zhongguo Shehui Kexue Chubanshe.

Bailey, Anne M. and Josep R. Llobera (eds.). 1981. *The Asiatic Mode of Production: Science and Politics.* London: Routledge and Kegan Paul.

Balazs, Etienne. 1964. *Chinese Civilization and Bureaucracy: Variations on a Theme.* New Haven: Yale University Press.

Baltrusaitis, Jurgès. 1960. *Reveils et prodiges: Le gothique fantastique.* Paris.

Barber, John. 1981. *Soviet Historians in Crisis, 1928–1932.* London: Macmillan.

Barkan, Elazar. 1992. *The Retreat of Scientific Racism: Changing Concepts of Race in Britain and the United States between the World Wars.* Cambridge: Cambridge University Press.

Barlow, Tani. 1993. "Colonialism's Career in Postwar China Studies." *Positions* 1:1, 224–67.

Barros, João de. 1563. *Terceira Decada da Asia de Ioam de Barros: Dos feytos que os Portugueses fizeram no descobrimento e conquista dos mares e terras do Oriente.* Lisboa: Ioãm de Parreira.

Barthold, V. V. 1947. *La découverte de l'Asie: Histoire de l'orientalisme en Europe et en Russie*, trans. B. Nikitine from 2nd Russian edn. (Leningrad, 1925). Paris: Payot.

Baudier, Michel. 1624. *Histoire de la cour du roi de la Chine.* Paris.

Bayle, Pierre. 1686a. *Commentaire philosophique sur ces paroles de Jésus-Christ "Contrain-les d'entrer"; où l'on prouve par plusieurs raisons demonstratives qu'il n'y a rien de plus abominable que de faire des conversions par contrainte.* Rotterdam.

1686b. *Ce que c'est que la France tout catholique sous le règne de Louis le Grand.* Rotterdam.

Bayly, C.A. 1986. "The Origins of Swadeshi (home industry): Cloth and Indian Society." In *The Social Life of Things: Commodities in Cultural Perspective*, ed. Arjun Appadurai. Cambridge: Cambridge University Press, pp. 285–321.

Beasley, W. G. and E. G. Pulleyblank (eds.). 1961. *Historians of China and Japan.* London: Oxford University Press.

Behring, Siegfried (ed.). 1959. "Lenin über China." *Zeitschrift für Geschichtswissenschaft* 7: 18–58.

Berg, Maxine. 1986. *The Age of Manufactures 1700–1820.* New York: Oxford University Press.

Berger, Willy Richard. 1990. *China-Bild und China-Mode im Europa der Aufklärung.* Köln/Wien: Böhlau.

Bergesen, Albert. 1995. "Let's Be Frank about World History." In *Civilizations and World Systems: Studying World-Historical Change*, ed. Stephen K. Sanderson. London: Sage, pp. 193–205.

Bernal, Martin. 1987a. *Black Athena: The Afro-Asiatic Roots of Greece*, vol. I: *The Fabrication of Ancient Greece, 1785–1985.* London: Free Association Press.

1987b. "First Land, then Sea: Thoughts about the Social Formation of the Mediterranean and Greece." In *Geography in Historical Perspective*, ed. E. Genovese and L. Hochberg. Oxford: Blackwell.

Bernier, François. 1671. *The History of the Late Revolution of the Empire of the Great Mogol: together with The most considerable Passages for 5 years following in that Empire, to which is added A Letter to Lord Colbert touching the extent of Indostan; the Circulation of Gold and Silver of the World, to discharge it self there; as also the Riches, Forces and Justice of the same: and the Principal Cause of the Decay of the States of Asia.* London.

1688. "Extrait de diverses pièces envoyées pour étrennes par M. Bernier à Mme. de la Sablière; Introduction à la lecture de Confucius" (8 June 1688). *Journal des savans* 16: 25–40.

1914. *Travels in the Mogul Empire A.D. 1656–1668*, trans. A. Constable; ed. V. A. Smith and H. Milford. Oxford: Oxford University Press.

248   *Bibliography*

Binns, Elliott. 1934. *The History of the Decline and Fall of the Medieval Papacy.*
London: Methuen.
Birch, Cyril (ed.). 1958. *Stories from a Ming Collection.* New York: Grove Press.
Blaug, Mark. 1985. *Economic Theory in Retrospect.* Cambridge: Cambridge
University Press.
Bloch, Marc. 1976. *Les caractères originaux de l'histoire rurale française,* 2 vols.
New. edn. Paris: Armand Colin.
Blue, Gregory. 1988. "Traditional China in Western Social Thought: An
Historical Inquiry, with Special Reference to Contributions from Montes-
quieu to Max Weber." Ph.D. diss., Cambridge University.
    1989. "Chinese History and Soviet Marxism in the Early Stalin Period."
Paper presented to the conference on "The Dynamics of Oriental Socie-
ties," Needham Research Institute, Cambridge.
    1999. "Gobineau on China: Race Theory, the Yellow Peril, and the Critique
of Modernity." *Journal of World History* 10:1.
Bodde, Derk. 1950. *Tolstoy and China.* Princeton: Princeton University Press.
    1991. *Chinese Thought, Society and Science: The Intellectual and Social Back-
ground of Science and Technology in Pre-Modern China.* Honolulu: University
of Hawaii Press.
Bodin, Jean. 1579. *La république.* 4th edn. Paris.
Bois, Guy. 1976. *Crise du féodalisme.* Paris: Presses de la fondation nationale des
sciences politiques.
    1985. "Against the Neo-Malthusian Orthodoxy." In *The Brenner Debate,* ed.
T. H. Ashton and C. H. E. Philpin. Cambridge: Cambridge University
Press, pp. 107–18.
    1989. *La mutation de l'an mil: Lournand, village méconnais de l'antiquité au
féodalisme.* Paris: Fayard.
Bolingbroke, Henry St. John. 1841. *Works.* Philadelphia.
Bond, C. Hubert. 1894. "Observations on a Chinese Brain." *Brain, A Journal of
Neurology* 17: 37–49.
Boserup, Ester. 1981. *Population and Technological Change: A Study of Long-Term
Trends.* Chicago: University of Chicago Press.
Boswell, James. 1887. *Life of Johnson,* ed. G. B. Hill. 3 vols. New York.
Botero, Giovanni. 1630. *Relations of the Most Famous Kingdoms and Common-
wealths throwout the World: Discoursing of their Situations, Religions, Lan-
guages, Manners, Customes, Strengths, Greatnesse and Policies,* trans.
R. Johnson. London.
Boulanger, Nicolas. N.d.[1761]. *Recherches sur l'origine du despotisme oriental.* N.p.
Bourdieu, Pierre. 1977. *Outline of a Theory of Practice.* Cambridge: Cambridge
University Press.
Bouvet, Joachim. 1697. *Portrait historique de l'Empereur de la Chine.* Paris.
Boxer, C. R. (ed.). 1953. *South China in the 16th Century.* London: Hakluyt Society.
    1961. "Some Aspects of Western Historical Writing on the Far East,
1500–1800." In *Historians of China and Japan,* ed. W. G. Beasley and E. G.
Pulleyblank. London: Oxford University Press.
    1968. *Fidalgos in the Far East, 1550–1770.* Oxford: Oxford University Press.
    1981. *João de Barros, Portuguese Humanist and Historian of Asia.* New Delhi:
Concept.

Brandt, C., B. Schwartz, and J. K. Fairbank (eds.). 1952. *A Documentary History of Chinese Communism*. Cambridge, Mass.: Harvard University Press.

Brandt, Loren. 1989. *Commercialization and Agricultural Development: Central and Eastern China, 1870–1939*. Cambridge: Cambridge University Press.

Braudel, Fernand. 1972–73. *The Mediterranean and the Mediterranean World in the Age of Philip II*, trans. S. Reynolds. 2 vols. London: Collins.

1979. *Civilisation matérielle, économie et capitalisme, XVe-XVIIIe siècle*. 3 vols. Paris: Armand Colin.

1981. *The Structures of Everyday Life*, vol. I of *Civilization and Capitalism, 15th–18th Century*. New York: Harper and Row. Translation of Braudel 1979.

1982. *The Wheels of Commerce*. New York: Harper and Row.

1984. *The Perspective of the World*. New York: Harper and Row.

Bray, Francesca. 1979. "The Green Revolution: A New Perspective." *Modern Asian Studies* 13: 4, 681–88.

1984. *Science and Civilisation in China*, vol. VI, pt. 2: *Agriculture*. Cambridge: Cambridge University Press.

1986. *The Rice Economies: Technology and Development in Asian Societies*. Oxford: Blackwell. Berkeley: University of California Press.

1994. "Le travail féminin dans la Chine impériale: sur l'élaboration de nouveaux motifs dans le tissu social" (tr. P.E. Will). *Annales: histoire, sciences sociales* 49:4 (July-August), 783–816.

1997. *Technology and Gender: Fabrics of Power in Late Imperial China*. Berkeley: University of California Press.

Brecht, Bertolt. 1953. *Der gute Mensch von Sezuan parabielstük*. Berlin: Suhrkamp.

Brenner, Robert. 1985a. "Agrarian Class Structure and Economic Development in Pre-Industrial Europe." In *The Brenner Debate*, ed. T. H. Ashton and C. H. E. Philpin. Cambridge: Cambridge University Press, pp. 10–63.

1985b. "The Agrarian Roots of European Capitalism." In *The Brenner Debate*, ed. T. H. Ashton and C. H. E. Philpin. Cambridge: Cambridge University Press, pp. 213–327.

Brook, Timothy. 1981. "The Merchant Network in Sixteenth Century China: A Discussion and Translation of Chang Han's *On Merchants*." *Journal of the Economic and Social History of the Orient* 24:2, 165–212.

1993. *Praying for Power: Buddhism and the Formation of Gentry Society in Late-Ming China*. Cambridge, Mass.: Council on East Asian Studies, Harvard University.

1995. "Weber, Mencius, and the History of Chinese Capitalism." *Asian Perspective* 19:1, 79–97.

1996. "The Sinology of Joseph Needham." *Modern China* 22:3, 340–48.

1997. "Profit and Righteousness in Chinese Economic Culture." In *Culture and Economy: The Shaping of Capitalism in Eastern Asia*, ed. Timothy Brook and Hy V. Luong. Ann Arbor: University of Michigan Press, pp. 27–44.

1998. *The Confusions of Pleasure: Commerce and Culture in Ming China*. Berkeley: University of California Press.

Brook Timothy (ed.). 1989. *The Asiatic Mode of Production in China*. Armonk, NY: M. E. Sharpe.

Brucker, P.J. 1919. *La Compagnie de Jésus*. Beauchesne.

Brunetière, Ferdinand. 1906. "L'Orient dans la littérature française" (review of P. Martino). *Revue des deux mondes* 35: 693–707.

Buckle, Henry Thomas. 1908. *History of Civilisation in England*. First published 1857–61. London: Longmans Green.

Budde, Hendrik *et al.* (eds.). 1985. *Europa und die Kaiser von China*. Frankfurt: Insel Verlag.

Budgell, Eustace. 1731. *A Letter to Cleomanes King of Sparta*. London.

Bukharin, Nikolai. N.d. [1921]. *Teoriya istoricheckogo materializma*. 2nd edn. Moscow: Gosizdat.

   1925. *Historical Materialism: A System of Sociology*, trans. from the 3rd Russian edn of 1921. New York: International Publishers.

Byres, T. J. 1991. "The Agrarian Question and Differing Forms of Capitalist Agrarian Transition: An Essay with Reference to Asia." In *Rural Transformations in Asia*, ed. Jan Breman and Sudipto Mundle. Delhi: Oxford University Press.

Cain, P. J. and A. G. Hopkins. 1993. *British Imperialism: Innovation and Expansion, 1688–1914*. London: Longmans.

Cameron, Nigel. 1970. *Barbarians and Mandarins: Thirteen Centuries of Western Travellers in China*. Tokyo: Weatherhill.

Caprasse, Jean. 1974. *Les formes de la propriété foncière dans la société féodale Chinoise: une controverse entre historiens chinois, 1954–1963*. Louvain: University of Louvain.

Carlitz, Katherine. 1994. "Desire, Danger, and the Body: Stories of Women's Virtue in Late Ming China." In *Engendering China: Women, Culture and the State*, ed. Christina K. Gilmartin, Gail Hershatter, Lisa Rofel, and Tyrene White. Cambridge, Mass.: Harvard University Press, pp. 101–24.

Cartier, Michel. 1984. "Travail et idéologie dans la Chine antique." In *Le travail et ses représentations*, ed. Michel Cartier. Paris: Editions des archives contemporaines, pp. 275–304.

Cary, George. 1956. *The Medieval Alexander*, ed. D. J. A. Ross. Cambridge: Cambridge University Press.

Centre de Recherches Interdisciplinaires de Chantilly. 1980. *Actes du colloque international de sinologie: la mission française de Pékin aux XVIIe et XVIIIe siècles*. Cathasia, Paris: Les Belles Lettres.

Chamberlain, Houston Stewart. 1911. *The Foundations of the Nineteenth Century*, trans. J. Lees; introduction by Lord Redesdale. 2 vols. New York/London: J.Lane/Bodley Head.

Chambers, William. 1757. *Designs of Chinese Buildings, Furniture, Dresses, Machines and Utensils ... To which is annexed a Description of their Temples, Houses, Gardens, etc.* Introduction by Samuel Johnson. London.

   1772. *A Dissertation on Oriental Gardening by Sir William Chambers, Controller-General of Her Majesty's Works ... To which is annexed an Explanatory Discourse, by Tan Chet-qua, of Quang-Chew-Fu*. London

Chang, Y. Z. 1947. "China and English Civil Service Reform." *American Historical Review* 42: 539–44.

Chao Kang. 1977. *The Development of Cotton Textile Production in China*. Cambridge, Mass.: Harvard University Press.

Chatterjee, Partha. 1986. *Nationalist Thought and the Colonial World: A Derivative Discourse?* Tokyo: United Nations University.

Chaudhuri, N.C. 1974. *Scholar Extraordinary: The Life of Professor the Rt. Hon. Friedrich Max Müller P.C.* London: Chatto and Windus.

Cheek, Timothy. 1984. "The Fading of Wild Lilies: Wang Shih-Wei and Mao Tse-Tung's Yenan Talks in the First CPC Rectification Movement." *Australian Journal of Chinese Affairs* 11: 25–58.

Chen Feng. 1988. *Qingdai yanzheng yu yanshui* [The Qing-dynasty salt administration and salt tax]. Kaifeng: Zhougzhou Guji Chubanshe.

Chen Fu. 1956. *Nong shu* [Agricultural treatise]. Beijing: Zhonghua Shuju. Original dated 1149.

Chen, Jerome. 1979. *China and the West: Society and Culture, 1815–1937.* London: Hutchinson.

Chen Qiyou (ed.). 1974. *Han Fei zi jishi* [Annotated works of Han Fei]. Shanghai: Shanghai Renmin Chubanshe.

Chen Shiqi. 1958. *Mingdai guanshougongye de yanjiu* [A study of official handicraft production during the Ming dynasty]. Wuhan: Renmin Chubanshe.

Chen, Shou-Yi. 1928. "The Influence of China on English Culture during the Eighteenth Century." Ph.D. diss., University of Chicago.

    1935–36. "John Webb: A Forgotten Page in the Early History of Sinology in Europe." *Chinese Social and Political Science Review* 19:3, 295–330.

Chen, Weiji (ed.). 1992. *History of Textile Technology of China.* New York: Science Press.

Cheong, W. E. 1978. *Mandarins and Merchants: Jardine, Matheson and Co., a China Agency of the Early 19th Century.* Scandinavian Inst. of Asian Studies Monograph Series, no. 26. London: Curzon.

Chi, Madeline and Iriye Akira (eds.). 1980. *The Chinese and the Japanese: Essays in Political and Cultural Interaction.* Princeton: Princeton University Press.

Churchill, Awnsham and John Churchill (eds.). 1704. *A Collection of Voyages and Travels, Some now first Printed from Original Manuscripts, Others Translated out of Foreign Languages, and Now first Publish'd in English.* 4 vols. London.

Clifford, James. 1988. *The Predicament of Culture: Twentieth-Century Ethnography, Literature, and Art.* Cambridge, Mass.: Harvard University Press.

Clunas, Craig. 1997. "Luxury Knowledge: The *Xiushilu* [Records of Lacquering] of 1625." *Techniques et culture* 29: 27–41.

Cockburn, Cynthia and Susan Ormrod. 1993. *Gender and Technology in the Making.* London: Sage Publications.

Cohen, J. M. (ed. and trans.). 1969. *The Four Voyages of Christopher Columbus, Being his own log-book, letters and dispatches, with connecting narrative drawn from the Life of the Admiral by his son Hernando Colon and other contemporary historians.* Harmondsworth: Penguin.

Cohen, Paul A. 1978. "Christian Missions and their Impact to 1900." *Cambridge History of China* 10: 545–612.

    1984. *Discovering History in China: American Historical Research on the Recent Chinese Past.* New York: Columbia University Press.

Collani, Claudia von. 1981. *Die Figuristen in der Chinamission.* Frankfurt: Lang.

Collis, Maurice. 1941. *The Great Within.* New York: Books for Libraries Press.

Comte, Auguste. 1698. *Cours de Philosophie Positive.* 2nd edn. 6 vols. Paris: Corbeil.

Condorcet (M. J. A. N. Caritat), Marquis de. 1988. *Esquisse d'un tableau historique des progrès de l'esprit humain.* First published 1795. Paris: Flammarion.

Cooper, Michael. 1974. *Rodrigues the Interpreter.* New York/Tokyo: Weatherhill.

Cordier, Henri. 1920. *Histoire générale de la Chine et de ses relations avec les pays étrangers depuis les temps les plus anciens jusqu'à la chute de la dynastie Mandchoue.* 4 vols. Paris.

   1924. *Biblioteca Sinica: Dictionnaire bibliographique des ouvrages relatifs à l'empire chinois.* 2nd edn. 4 vols. Paris: Guilmoto. Author index: New York: Columbia University Libraries, 1953.

Cortesao, Armando (ed. and trans.). 1944. *The Suma Oriental of Tom, Pires: An account of the East, from the Red Sea to Japan, written in Malacca and India in 1512–1515 and The Book of Francisco Rodrigues: Rutter of a voyage in the Red Sea, nautical rules, almanack and maps, written and drawn in the East before 1515.* 2 vols. London: Hakluyt Society.

Costin, W. C. 1937. *Great Britain and China, 1833–1860.* London: Oxford University Press.

Cowan, Ruth Schwartz. 1983. *More Work for Mother: The Ironies of Household Technology from the Open Hearth to the Microwave.* New York: Basic Books.

Cranmer-Byng, J. L. (ed.). 1957–58. "Lord Macartney's Embassy to Peking in 1793 from Official Chinese Documents." *Journal of the Oriental Society of Hong Kong* 4:1–2, 117–87.

   1962. *An Embassy to China, Being the Journal kept by Lord Macartney during his Embassy to the Emperor Ch'ien-lung 1793–1794.* London: Longmans.

Crookshank, Francis Graham. 1931. *The Mongol in Our Midst: A Study of Man and His Three Faces.* 3rd edn. London: Kegan Paul, Trench Trubner and Co.

Croot, Patricia and David Parker. 1985. "Agrarian Class Structure and the Development of Capitalism: France and England Compared." In *The Brenner Debate,* ed. T. H. Ashton and C. H. E. Philpin. Cambridge: Cambridge University Press.

Cross, F. L. and E. A. Livingstone. 1974. *The Oxford Dictionary of the Christian Church.* 2nd ed. Oxford: Oxford University Press.

Cummins, J. S. 1978. "Two Missionary Methods in China: Mendicants and Jesuits." *Archivo ibero-americano* 38:149–152, 33–108.

Cummins, J. S. (ed. and trans.). 1962. *The Travels and Controversies of Friar Domingo Navarette 1618–1686.* London: Cambridge University Press/ Hakluyt Society.

Curtin, Philip. 1964. *The Image of Africa: British Ideals and Action, 1780–1850.* Madison: University of Wisconsin Press.

Daffino, Paolo. 1957. "La Cina nel giudizio di G. B. Vico." *Cina* 3, 1–17.

Dai Angang. 1985. "Jindai Zhongguo xinshi nongken qiye shulüe" [Modern Chinese agricultural reclamation companies]. *Zhongguo nongshi* 1: 14–21.

Daire, Eugen (ed.). 1843. *Économistes-financiers du XVIIIe siècle.* Paris: Guillaume.

Daniel, Norman. 1979. *The Arabs and Mediaeval Europe*. 2nd edn. London/ Beirut: Longman/Librairie du Liban.

Daniels, Christian. 1996. "Agro-Industries: Sugarcane Technology." In *Science and Civilisation in China* VI.3, *Agro-Industries and Forestry*, by Christian Daniels and Nicholas Menzies. Cambridge: Cambridge University Press.

Dapper, Olfert. 1676. *Naukeurige beschrijving der Afrikaenische gewesten van Egypten, Barbaryen, Lybien, Biledulgerid, Negroslant . . . (Tesamen met) Naukeurige beschrijvinge der Afrikaenische Eilanden*. Amsterdam: Jacob van Meurs. English trans. by John Ogilby, 1670; German trans., 1670; French trans., 1686.

Darwin, Charles. 1881. *The Descent of Man, and Selection in Relation to Sex*. 2nd edn. London: Murray.

Davis, John Frances. 1845. *The Chinese: A General Description of China and its Inhabitants*. 2nd edn. 3 vols.

Davis, Mike. 1990. *City of Quartz*. New York: Vintage Books.

Dawson, Raymond. 1967. *The Chinese Chameleon: An Analysis of European Conceptions of Chinese Civilisation*. London: Oxford University Press.

de Bary, W. Theodore (ed.). 1975. *The Unfolding of Neo-Confucianism*. New York: Columbia University Press.

de Bary, W. Theodore, Wing-tsit Chan and Chester Tan (eds.). 1960. *Sources of Chinese Tradition*. 2 vols. New York: Columbia University Press.

de Mailla, J.A.M. de Moyriac, trans. 1777–1785. *Histoire générale de la Chine, ou Annales de cette Empire, traduites du Tong Kien Kang Mu*, ed. Grosier and le Roux des Hautesrayes. 13 vols. Paris: Pierres and Clousier.

De Pauw, Cornelius. 1774. *Recherches philosophiques sur les Égyptiens et les Chinois*. 2nd edn. Amsterdam/Leiden: Ulam and Murray.

1788. *Recherches philosophiques sur les Grècs*. 2 vols. Berlin: Decker.

De Quincey, Thomas. 1885. *Confessions of an English Opium-Eater*, ed. R. A. Garnett. London.

Debon, Günther and Adrian Hsia (eds.). 1985. *Goethe und China: China und Goethe: Bericht der Heidelberger Symposions*. Bern: Lang.

Decournoy, Jacques. 1970. *Péril Jaune, Peur Blanche*. Paris: Grasset.

Defoe, Daniel. 1840–3. *Works*, ed. William Hazlitt. 3 vols. London.

1868. *The Life and Adventures of Robinson Crusoe*, ed. with an introduction by Henry Kingsley. London: Macmillan.

Degras, Jane (ed.). 1956–59. *The Communist International, 1919–1943*. 3 vols. Oxford: Oxford University Press.

Delvèze, Michel. 1970. *L'Europe et le monde à la fin du XVIIIe siècle*. Paris: Albin Michel.

Deng Chumin. 1942. *Zhongguo shehuishi jiaocheng* [A course on the history of Chinese society]. Guilin: Wenhua Gongying.

Deng, Gang. 1993. *Development versus Stagnation: Technological Continuity and Agricultural Progress in Pre-modern China*. Westport: Greenwood Press.

Deng Tuo. 1979. *Lun Zhongguo lishi de jige wenti* [On some questions concerning Chinese history]. Enlarged from 1959 edn. Beijing: Sanlian.

Dermigny, Louis. 1964a. *La Chine et l'Occident: le commerce à Canton au XVIIIe siècle, 1719–1833*. 3 vols. Paris: S.E.V.P.E.N.

1964b. *Les mémoires de Charles de Constant sur le commerce à la Chine*. Paris: S.E.V.P.E.N.

Desrosiers, Sophie. 1994. "La soierie méditerannéenne." *Revue du Musée des Arts et Métiers* 7: 51–58.

Diderot, Denis. 1771. *Les bijoux indiscrets*. 2 vols. Paris: Cazin.

Diderot, Denis and Jean Le Rond D'Alembert (eds.). 1751–80. *Encyclopédie, ou Dictionnaire raisonné des arts, des sciences, et des métiers, par une société de gens de lettres*. 17 vols. Paris and Amsterdam.

Dirlik, Arif. 1978. *Revolution and History: Origins of Marxist Historiography in China, 1919–1937*. Berkeley: University California Press.

Dobb, Maurice. 1946. *Studies in the Development of Capitalism*. London: Routledge and Kegan Paul.

1976. "From Feudalism to Capitalism." In *The Transition from Feudalism to Capitalism*, ed. Rodney Hilton. London: New Left Books, pp. 165–69.

Dockès, Pierre. 1982. *Medieval Slavery and Liberation*. Chicago: University of Chicago Press.

Dower, John. 1986. *War without Mercy: Race and Power in the Pacific War*. London: Faber and Faber.

Draper, Hal. 1977. *Karl Marx's Theory of Revolution*, vol. I: *State and Bureaucracy*. New York: Monthly Review Press.

Drew, K. F. and F. S. Lear (eds.). 1963. *Perspectives in Medieval History*. Chicago: University of Chicago Press.

Duara, Prasenjit. 1993. "Bifurcating Linear History: Nation and Histories in China and India." *Positions* 1:3, 779–804.

Dubrovskii, Sergei Mitrofanovitch. 1929. *K voprosu o sushchosti "aziatskogo" sposoba proizvodstva, feodalizma, krepostnichestva i torgovogo kapitalizma*. [On the essence of the Asiatic mode of production, feudalism, serfdom and commercial capitalism]. Moscow: Izdan. Nauch. Assotsiatsii Vostokovedeniia.

Du Halde, Jean-Baptiste. 1735. *Description géographique, historique, chronologique, politique de l'empire de la Chine et de la Tartarie Chinoise*. Paris.

1736. *The General History of China, Containing a Geographical, Historical, Chronological, Political and Physical Description of the Empire of China, Chinese-Tartary, Corea, and Tibet, Including an Exact and Particular Account of their Customs, Manners, Ceremonies, Religion, Arts and Sciences*, trans. Richard Brookes. London: Watts.

1741. *The General History of China, Containing a Geographical, Historical, Chronological, Political and Physical Description of the Empire of China, Chinese-Tartary*. 4 vols. London: Watts.

Dunn, S. L. 1982. *The Fall and Rise of the Asiatic Mode of Production*. London: Routledge and Kegan Paul.

Durbin, Paul T. (ed.). 1984. *A Guide to the Culture of Science, Technology, and Medicine*. New York: Free Press. First published 1980.

Edmunds, Cifford, Jr. 1982. "Politics and Historiography after the Great Leap: The Case of Chien Po-Tsan." In *Chinese Communist Politics: Selected Studies*, ed. F. Gilbert Chan and Harlan Jenks. Hong Kong: Asian Research Service, pp. 79–124.

Elias, Norbert. 1985 [1933]. *La société de cour* ["Die höfische Gesellschaft"], trans. Pierre Kamnitzer and Jeanne Etoré, preface by Roger Chartier. Paris: Calmann-Lévy.

Ellis, William (trans.). 1912. *The Politics of Aristotle, or a Treatise on Government.* Introduction by A. D. Lindsay. London: Dent.

Elman, Benjamin and Alexander Woodside (eds.). 1994. *Education and Society in Late Imperial China, 1600–1900.* Berkeley: University of California Press.

Elson, R. E. 1978. "The Cultivation System and 'Agricultural Involution'." CSEAS Working Paper no. 14, Monash University.

Elster, Jon. 1975. *Leibniz et la formation de l'ésprit capitaliste.* Paris: Aubier Montaigne.

Elvin, Mark. 1973. *The Pattern of the Chinese Past.* Stanford: Stanford University Press.

Engels, Friedrich. 1884. *The Origin of the Family, Private Property, and the State.*

Étiemble. n.d. [1959–61] . *L'Orient philosophique au XVIIIe siècle* (Cours de Sorbonne [mimeographed]). 3 pts. Paris: Centre de Documentation Universitaire.

1964. *Connaissons-nous la Chine?* Paris: Gallimard.

1966. *Les Jésuites en Chine: la querrelle des rites.* Paris: Archives.

1976. *Quarante années de mon maoisme. 1934–1974.* Paris: Gallimard.

1988–89. *L'Europe Chinoise.* 2 vols. Paris: Gallimard.

Everitt, Alan. 1967. "The Marketing of Agricultural Produce." In *The Agrarian History of England and Wales*, ed. Joan Thirsk, 4: 466–592.

Falkenhausen, Lothar von. 1994. *Suspended Music: Chime Bells in the Culture of Bronze Age China.* Berkeley: University of California Press.

Fan, Tsen-Chung. 1945. *Dr Johnson and Chinese Culture.* London: The China Society.

1949. "Chinese Fables and Anti-Walpole Journalism." *Review of English Studies* 25: 141–51.

Fan Wenlan. 1942–43. *Zhongguo tongshi jianbian* [A concise comprehensive history of China]. 3 vols. Yan'an.

Fan Wenlan. 1945. *Zhongguo jindai shi* [A history of modern China]. Yan'an

Fang Guancheng. 1765. *Mianhua tu* [Illustrations of cotton planting and manufacture].

1808. *Shouyi guangxun* [Expanded instructions on procuring clothing]. Revised edition of the *Mianhua tu*, in *Zhongguo gudai banhua congkan* [Series of ancient Chinese illustrated books], vol. IV. Beijing: Zhonghua Shuju.

Ferguson, Adam. 1966. *An Essay on the History of Civil Society 1767*, ed. D. Forbes. Edinburgh: Edinburgh University Press.

Feuerwerker, Albert. 1958. "From 'Feudalism' to 'Capitalism' in Recent Historical Writing from Mainland China." *Journal of Asian Studies* 18 (November): 107–16.

1968. "Chinese History in Marxian Dress." In *History in Communist China*, ed. Albert Feuerwerker. Cambridge, Mass.: MIT Press, pp. 14–44.

Fogel, Joshua A. 1984. *Politics and Sinology: The Case of Naito Konan. 1866–1934.* Cambridge, Mass.: Council on East Asian Studies, Harvard University.

1988. "The Debates over the Asiatic Mode of Production in Soviet Russia, China, and Japan." *American Historical Review* 93:1, 56–79.

Fossier, Robert. 1983. "La grande épreuve." In *Le moyen age 3: le temps des crises, 1250–1520*, ed. R. Fossier. Paris: Armand Colin, pp. 55–118.

Frank, Andre Gunder. 1991. "Transitional Ideological Modes: Feudalism, Capitalism, Socialism." *Critique of Anthropology* 11:2, 171–88.

1995. "The Modern World System Revisited: Rereading Braudel and Wallerstein." In *Civilizations and World Systems: Studying World-Historical Change*, ed. Stephen K. Sanderson. London: Sage, pp. 163–92.

1998. *ReOrient: Global Economy in the Asian Age*. Berkeley: University of California Press.

Franke, Otto. 1903. *Die Rechtsverhaltnisse am Grundeigentum in China*. Leipzig: Dieterich'sche Verlagsbuchhandlung.

Freedman, Maurice. 1979. *The Study of Chinese Society*, ed. G. William Skinner. Stanford: Stanford University Press.

Friedmann, Harriet. 1990. "Family Wheat Farms and Third World Diets: A Paradoxical Relationship Between Unwaged and Waged Labor." In *Work Without Wages: Comparative Studies of Domestic Labor and Self-Employment*, ed. Jane L. Collins and Martha Gimenez. New York: SUNY Press, pp. 193–213.

Fu Yiling. 1982. *Ming-Qing shehui jingji shi lunwen ji* [Essays on the socio-economy of the Ming-Qing period]. Beijing: Beijing Renmin Chubanshe.

Fu Zhufu. 1980. *Zhongguo jingji shi luncong* [Essays on the history of the Chinese economy]. 2 vols. Beijing: Sanlian.

1983. "Zai lun zibenzhuyi mengya" [Further discussion of the sprouts of capitalism]. *Shehui kexue zhanxian* 1: 129–40.

Fuchs, Walter. 1943. *Der Jesuiten-Atlas der Kanghsi Zeit*. Beijing: Fu-Jen University.

Fueter, Eduard. 1914. *Histoire de l'historiographie moderne*, trans. E. Jeanmaire. Paris.

Fujii Hiroshi. 1953–1954. "Shin'an shōnin no kenkyō" [A study of the Xin'an merchants]. *Tōyō gakuhō* 36:1, 1–44; 2, 32–60; 3, 65–118; 4, 115–45.

Fukuyama, Francis. 1992. *The End of History and the Last Man*. Toronto: Maxwell Macmillan.

Fukuzawa, Yukichi. 1966. *The Autobiography of Yukichi Fukuzawa*. New York: Columbia University Press.

Furber, Holden. 1976. *Rival Empires of Trade to the Orient, 1600–1800*. Minneapolis: University of Minnesota Press.

Ganelius, T. (ed.). 1986. *Progress in Science and Its Social Conditions*. Oxford: Pergamon, for the Nobel Foundation.

Gates, Hill. 1989. "The Commoditization of Chinese Women." *Signs* 14:4, 799–832.

Geertz, Clifford. 1963. *Agricultural Involution: The Process of Ecological Change in Indonesia*. Berkeley: University of California Press.

Gellner, Ernest. 1988. "Introduction" to *Europe and the Rise of Capitalism*, ed. Jean Baechler, John Hall, and Michael Mann. Oxford: Blackwell, pp. 1–5.

Génicot, Leopold. 1966. "Crisis: From the Middle Ages to Modern Times." In *Cambridge Economic History of Europe*, vol. I: *The Agrarian Life of the Middle Ages*, ed. M. M. Postan. 2nd edn. Cambridge: Cambridge University Press.

Genovese, E. and L. Hochberg (eds.). 1987. *Geography in Historical Perspective.* Oxford: Blackwell.

Giedion, Siegfried. 1948. *Mechanization Takes Command: A Contribution to Anonymous History.* New York: Oxford University Press.

Gilchrist, John. 1969. *The Church and Economic Activity in the Middle Ages.* London: Macmillan.

Gille, Bertrand. 1978. "Les systèmes bloqués." In *Histoire des techniques,* ed. Bertrand Gille. Paris: Encyclopédie de la Pléiade, pp. 441–507.

Gillispie, Charles Coulston (ed.). 1970–80. *Dictionary of Scientific Biography.* 16 vols. New York: Scribner's.

Gimpel, Jean, 1983. *The Industrial Revolution of the Middle Ages.* New York: Grove Press.

Gleick, James. 1987. *Chaos: Making a New Science.* New York: Viking.

Gobineau, Arthur, Comte de. 1970. *Selected Political Writing,* ed. M. Biddiss. London: Cape.

1983. *Oeuvres,* ed. J. Gaulmeir *et al.* Paris: Gallimard.

Godes, Mikhail (ed.). 1931. *Discussiya ob aziatskom sposobe proizvodstva.* Leningrad/ Moscow: Gosizdat.

Goldsmith, Oliver. 1762. *The Citizen of the World; or Letters from a Chinese Philosopher, residing in London, to his Friends in the East.* London: J. Newbery.

Gollwitzer, Heinz. 1962. *Die gelbe Gefahr: Geschichte eines Schlagworts; Studium zum imperialistischen Denken.* Göttingen: Vanderhoek und Ruprecht.

Goody, Esther N. 1982. "Introduction." In *From Craft to Industry: The Ethnography of Proto-Industrial Cloth Production,* ed. Esther N. Goody. Cambridge: Cambridge University Press, pp. 1–37.

Goto, Junko and Naraomi Imamura. 1993. "Japanese Agriculture: Characteristics, Institutions, and Policies." In *Japanese and American Agriculture: Tradition and Progress in Conflict,* ed. Luther Tweeten *et al.* Boulder: Westview Press, pp. 11–29.

Gould, Stephen Jay. 1981. *The Mismeasure of Man.* Harmondsworth: Penguin.

Greenberg, Dolores. 1990. "Energy, Power, and Perceptions of Social Change in the Early Nineteenth Century." *American Historical Review* 95 (June): 693–714.

Grinevich, P. 1935. "K voprosam istorii kitaiskogo feodalizma." *Problemyi Kitaya* 14: 186–271.

Grove, Linda and Christian Daniels (eds.). 1984. *State and Society in China: Japanese Perspectives on Ming-Qing Social and Economic History.* Tokyo: Tokyo University Press.

Gu Yanwu. 1984. *Rizhi lu jishi* [Record of knowledge gained day by day, with collected commentaries], ed. Pan Lei, 1834. Repr. Shanghai: Shanghai Guji Chubanshe.

Guenée, Bernard. 1971. "Y a-t-il un état des XIVe et XVe siècles?" *Annales* 26:2, 399–406.

Guerreau, Alain. 1980. *Le féodalité: un horizon théorique.* Paris: Le Sycomore.

de Guignes, Charles Louis Joseph. 1808. *Voyages à Peking, Manille et l'Ile de France faits dans l'intervalle des années 1784 à 1801.* 3 vols. Paris: Imprimerie Impériale.

de Guignes, Joseph. 1760. *Mémoire dans lequel on prouve, que la nation chinoise est une colonie Égyptienne.* (A paper read to the Académie des Inscriptions et Belles-Lettres, Nov. 14, 1758). Paris: Desaint and Saillant.

Guo Moruo. 1930. *Zhongguo gudai shehui yanjiu* [Studies in ancient Chinese society]. Shanghai.

1955. *Zhongguo gudai shehui yanjiu* [Studies in ancient Chinese society]. Rev. edn. Beijing: Zhonghua Shuju.

Guo Wentao *et al.* 1986. *Zhongguo chuantong nongye yu xiandai nongye* [Chinese agriculture, traditional and modern]. Beijing: Nongye Chubanshe.

Guo Wentao. 1988. *Zhongguo nongye keji fazhan shilüe* [A brief history of the scientific and technological development of Chinese agriculture]. Beijing: Nongye Chubanshe.

Guy, Basil. 1963. *The French Image of China Before and After Voltaire* (Studies in Voltaire and the 18th Century, no. 21, ed. T. Besterman). Geneva: Institut et Musée Voltaire.

Hall, A. R. 1963. "Merton Revisited, or, Science and Society in the Seventeenth Century." *History of Science* 2:1.

Hall, John. 1965. "Changing Conceptions of the Modernization of Japan." In *Changing Japanese Attitudes toward Modernization*, ed. Marius Jansen. Princeton: Princeton University Press.

Hall, John A. 1985. *Powers and Liberties: The Causes and Consequences of the Rise of the West.* London: Blackwell.

1988. "States and Societies: The Miracle in Comparative Perspective." In *Europe and the Rise of Capitalism*, ed. Jean Baechler, John Hall, and Michael Mann. Oxford: Blackwell, pp. 119–37.

Hamashita Takeshi. 1989. *Chōgoku kindai keizaishi kenkyō* (Studies in the modern economic history of China). Tokyo: Institute of Oriental Culture, University of Tokyo.

Hamrin, Carol. 1986. "Yang Xianzhen: Upholding Orthodox Leninist Theory." In *China's Establishment Intellectuals*, ed. Carol Hamrin and Timothy Cheek. Armonk, NY: M. E. Sharpe, pp. 51–91.

Handlin, Joanna F. 1975. "Lü Kun's New Audience: The Influence of Women's Literacy on Sixteenth-Century Thought." In *Women in Chinese Society*, ed. Margery Wolf and Roxane Witke. Stanford: Stanford University Press, pp. 13–38.

Harrison, James P. 1969. *The Communists and Chinese Peasant Rebellions: A Study in the Rewriting of Chinese History.* New York: Atheneum.

Hase, Johan. 1743. *Historiae universalis politicae.* Nuremburg.

Hashikawa, Bunso. 1980. "Japanese Perspectives on Asia: From Dissociation to Coprosperity." In *The Chinese and the Japanese: Essays in Political and Cultural Interaction*, ed. Madeline Chi and Akira Iriye. Princeton: Princeton University Press, pp. 328–55.

Haudricourt, A. G. 1962. "Domestication des animaux, culture des plantes, et traitement d'autrui." *L'Homme* 40.

Hay, Denys. 1959. "Geographical Abstractions and the Historian." *Historical Studies* 2: 1.

Hayami, Akira. 1990. "Preface." In *Economic and Demographic Development in Rice Producing Societies*, ed. Akira Hayami and Yoshihiro Tsubouchi. Leuven: Leuven University Press, pp. 1–5.

Hayden, Dolores. 1986. *Redesigning the American Dream: The Futures of Housing, Work and Family Life*. New York: Norton.

He Changqun. 1964. *Han-Tang jian fengjian tudi suoyouzhi xingshi yanjiu* [Studies in the forms of feudal landownership from the Han to Tang dynasties]. Shanghai: Renmin Chubanshe.

He Ganzhi. 1939. *Zhongguo shehui xingzhi wenti lunzhan* [The controversy over the nature of Chinese society]. Chongqing: Shenghuo.

Hegel, G. W. F. 1956. *The Philosophy of History*, trans. J. Sibree. New York: Dover.

Hentsch, Thierry. 1988. *L'Orient imaginaire: la vision politique occidentale de l'Est Méditerranéen*. Paris: Minuit.

Herder, J. G. 1800. *Outlines of a Philosophy of History of Mankind*, trans. T. Churchill. London.

Hevia, James L. 1994. "Sovereignty and Subject: Constituting Relations of Power in Qing Guest Ritual." In *Body, Subject, and Power in China*, ed. Angela Zito and Toni Barlow. Chicago: University of Chicago Press, pp. 181–200.

1995. *Cherishing Men from Afar: Qing Guest Ritual and the Macartney Embassy of 1793*. Durham: Duke University Press.

Hilton, Rodney. 1975. "A Crisis of Feudalism." In *The Brenner Debate*, ed. T. H. Aston and C. H. E. Philpin. Cambridge: Cambridge University Press, pp. 119–37.

1985. *Class Conflict and the Crisis of Feudalism*. London: Hambledon Press.

Hilton, Rodney (ed.). 1976. *The Transition from Feudalism to Capitalism*. London: New Left Books.

Hindess, Barry and Paul Hirst. 1975. *Pre-Capitalist Modes of Production*. London: Routledge and Kegan Paul.

Hirschman, Albert O. 1977. *The Passions and the Interests: Political Arguments for Capitalism before its Triumph*. Princeton: Princeton University Press.

Ho, Ping-Ti. 1963. *The Ladder of Success in Imperial China: Aspects of Social Mobility, 1368–1911*. New York: Columbia University Press

Hobsbawm, Eric. 1976. "From Feudalism to Capitalism." In *The Transition from Feudalism to Capitalism*, ed. Rodney Hilton. London: New Left Books, pp. 159–164.

Hohenberg, Paul and Lynn Lees. 1985. *The Making of Urban Europe, 1000–1950*. Cambridge, Mass.: Harvard University Press.

Hong Huanchun. 1983. *Ming Qing fengjian zhuanzhi zhengquan dui zibenzhuyi mengya de zuai* [Obstacles to the development of incipient capitalism posed by the Ming Qing feudal autocracy]. Nanjing: Nanjing Daxue.

Honour, Hugh. 1961. *Chinoiserie: The Vision of Cathay*. New York: Dutton.

Horsman, Reginald. 1981. *Race and Manifest Destiny: The Origins of American Radical Anglo-Saxonism*. Cambridge, Mass.: Harvard University Press.

Hoston, Germaine A. 1986. *Marxism and the Crisis of Development in Prewar Japan*. Princeton: Princeton University Press.

Hou Wailu. 1955. *Zhongguo gudai shehui shilun* [Essays on the history of China's ancient society]. Rev. edn. Beijing: Renmin Chubanshe. First published 1946.

Hsia, Adrian. 1974. *Hermann Hesse und China: Darstellung, Materialen und Interpretation*. Frankfurt: Suhrkamp.

Hsia, Adrian (ed.). 1985. *Deutsche Denker über China*. Frankfurt: Insel.

Hsü, Cho-yun. 1980. *Han Agriculture: The Formation of the Early Chinese Agrarian Economy*. Seattle: University of Washington Press.

Hu Peizhao and Lin Pu. 1985. *Zibenlun zai Zhongguo de chuanbo* [The dissemination of *Das Kapital* in China]. Jinan: Shandong Renmin Chubanshe.

Hu Shi. 1919. *Zhongguo zhexueshi dagang* [An outline of the history of Chinese philosophy]. Shanghai: Shangwu Yinshuguan.

    1922. *The Development of the Logical Method in Ancient China*. Shanghai: Oriental Book Co.

    1934. *The Chinese Renaissance*. Chicago: Chicago University Press.

Hu Zhongda. 1989. "The Asiatic Mode of Production and the Theory of Five Modes of Production." In *The Asiatic Mode of Production in China*, ed. Timothy Brook. Armonk, NY: M.E. Sharpe, pp. 164–75.

Huang, Philip C. C. 1985. *The Peasant Economy and Social Change in North China*. Stanford: Stanford University Press.

    1990. *The Peasant Family and Rural Development in the Yangzi Delta, 1350–1988*. Stanford: Stanford University Press.

Huang, Ray. 1974. *Taxation and Governmental Finance in Sixteenth-Century Ming China*. Cambridge: Cambridge University Press.

    1988. *China: A Macro-History*. Armonk, NY: M.E. Sharpe.

Huang Yiping and Zhang Min. 1988. "Jindai zaoqi nongye kenzhi gongsi jianlun" [Agricultural reclamation companies in the modern period]. *Huadong shifan daxue xuebao* 3: 65–72.

Hudson, G. F. 1931. *Europe and China: A Survey of their Relations from the Earliest Times to 1800*. London: Arnold.

Huff, Toby. 1993. *The Rise of Modern Science: Islam, China, and the West*. Cambridge: Cambridge University Press.

Humboldt, Wilhelm von. 1906. "Lettre à Monsieur Abel-Rémusat, sur la nature des formes grammaticales en général, et sur le génie de la langue Chinoise en particulier." *Gesammelte Schriften*, vol. 5. Berlin: Behr, pp. 254–308.

Hume, David. 1854. *The Philosphical Works of David Hume*. 4 vols. Boston/ Edinburgh: Little, Brown/A. and C. Black.

Huxley, Julian and A. C. Haddon. 1935. *We Europeans: A Study of the Racial Problem*, with a chapter on "Europe Overseas" by A. M. Carr-Saunders. London: Cape.

Hyndman, H. M. 1919. *The Awakening of Asia*. London: Cassell.

Impey, Oliver. 1977. *Chinoiserie: The Impact of Oriental Styles on Western Art and Decoration*. London: Oxford University Press.

Intorcetta, Prosperus, Christianus Herdtrich, Franciscus de Rougemont, and Philippus Couplet (eds.). 1867. *Confucius Sinarum Philosophus, sive Scientia Sinensis, latine exposita ... Adjecta est tabula chronologica sinicae monarchiae ab huius exordio ad haec usque tempora*. Paris: Horthemels.

Iolk, E. S. 1930. "K voprasam ob osnovakh obshchestvennogo stroya drevnego Kitaya." *Problemyi Kitaya* 2: 87–135.

Isaacs, Harold. 1980. *Scratches on Our Minds: American Views of China and India.* White Plains: M. E. Sharpe.

Jacobs, Margaret. 1976. *The Newtonians and the English Revolution.* Hassocks, Sussex: Harvester.

Jian Bozan. 1944. *Zhongguo shigang* [An outline of Chinese history]. Chongqing: Wushi Niandai.

1954. "Guan yu Liang Han de guan si nuli wenti" [On the question of state-owned and private slaves in the Han dynasties]. *Lishi yanjiu* 4: 1–24.

1957. "Chūgoku-shi no jidai kubun no mondai ni tsuite" [On the question of periodizing Chinese history]. In *Chūgoku-shi no jidai kubun* [The periodization of Chinese history], ed. Suzuki Jun and Nishijima Sadao. Tokyo: Tōkyō Daigaku Shuppansha, pp. 3–30.

Johnson, David, Andrew J. Nathan, and Evelyn S. Rawski (eds.). 1985. *Popular Culture in Late Imperial China.* Berkeley: University of California Press.

Johsua, Issac. 1988. *La face cachée du Moyen Age.* Montreuil: La Brèche-PEC.

Jones, E.L. 1981. *The European Miracle: Environments, Economies and Geopolitics in the History of Europe and Asia.* Cambridge: Cambridge University Press.

1987. *The European Miracle.* 2nd edn. Cambridge: Cambridge University Press.

1988. *Growth Recurring: Economic Change in World History.* Oxford: Clarendon Press.

Jones, William. 1799. *The Works of Sir William Jones,* ed. Lord Teignmouth. 6 vols.

Justi, J. H. G. von. 1762. *Vergleichung des Europäischen mit den Asiatischen und andern vermeintlich Barbarischen Regierungen.* Berlin.

Kahn, Ely Jacques, Jr. 1976. *The China Hands: America's Foreign Service Officers and What Befell Them.* Harmondsworth: Penguin.

Kahn, Joel S. 1980. *Minangkabau Social Formations: Indonesian Peasants in the World Economy.* Cambridge: Cambridge University Press.

Kammerer, Albert. 1944. *La découverte de la Chine par les Portugais au XVIème siècle et la cartographie des Portugais; avec des notes de toponymie chinoise par Paul Pelliot.* Leiden: Brill.

Kasaba, Resat. 1993. "Treaties and Friendships: British Imperialism, the Ottoman Empire, and China in the Nineteenth Century." *Journal of World History* 4:2 (Fall): 215–42.

Kawakatsu, Heita. 1994. "Historical Background." Introduction to *Japanese Industrialization and the Asian Economy,* ed. A. J. H. Latham and Heita Kawakatsu. London: Routledge, pp. 4–8.

Ke Changji. 1989. "Ancient Chinese Society and the Asiatic Mode of Production." In *The Asiatic Mode of Production in China,* ed. Timothy Brook. Armonk, NY: M.E. Sharpe, pp. 47–64.

Keightley, David N. 1987. "Archaeology and Mentality: The Making of China." *Representations* 18 (Spring): 91–128.

1989. "Craft and Culture: Metaphors of Governance in Early China." *Proceedings of the Second International Conference on Sinology.* Taipei: Academia Sinica.

Kiernan, E. Victor G. 1969. *The Lords of Human Kind: Black Man, Yellow Man and White Man in an Age of Empire*. Boston: Little, Brown.

1972. *The Lords of Human Kind. Black Man, Yellow Man and White Man in an Age of Empire*. 2nd edn. Harmondsworth: Penguin.

Kircher, Athanasius. 1667. *China Monumentis qua Sacris qua Profanis Illustrata*. Amsterdam.

Knowles, David and Dimitri Oblensky. 1968. *The Christian Centuries: A New History of the Catholic Church*, vol. II: *The Middle Ages*. New York: McGraw-Hill.

Knox, Robert. 1862. *The Races of Man: A Philosophical Inquiry into the Influence of Race over the Destinies of Nations*. 2nd edn. London.

Kokin, M. and G. Papayan. 1930. *"Tszing-tyan": agrarnyii stroi drevnego Kitaya*. Preface by L. Mad'iar. Leningrad: Izdanie Leningradskogo Vostochnogo Instituta imeni A.S. Enukidze.

Kors, Alan Charles. 1990. *Atheism in France*. Princeton: Princeton University Press.

Kovalev, S.I. 1934. "O nekotoryikh problemakh rabovladel'cheskoi formatsii." *Problemyi istorii dokapitalisticheskikh obshchestv* 2: 70–80.

Krader, Lawrence. 1975. *The Asiatic Mode of Production: Sources, Development and Critique in the Writings of Karl Marx*. Assen: Van Gorcum.

Krader, Lawrence (ed. and trans.). 1974. *The Ethnological Notebooks of Karl Marx (Studies of Morgan, Phear, Maine, Lubbock)*. 2nd edn. Assen: Van Gorcum.

Kriedte, Peter. 1983. *Peasants, Landlords and Merchant Capitalists*. Cambridge: Cambridge University Press.

Kroeber, Alfred L. 1957. *Style and Civilizations*. Ithaca: Cornell University Press.

Ku Chieh-kang [Gu Jiegang]. 1931. *The Autobiography of a Chinese Historian*, trans. Arthur Hummel. Leiden: E. J. Brill.

Kuhn, Dieter. 1976. "Die Darstellung des *Keng-chih-t'u.*" *Zeitschrift der Deutschen Morgenländischen Gesellschaft* 126:2, 336–67.

1977. *Die Webstühle des Tzu-jen I-chih aus der Yuan-Zeit*. Wiesbaden: Franz Steiner.

1987. *Die Song-Dynastie (960 bis 1279): eine neue Gesellschaft im Spiegel ihrer Kultur*. Weinheim: Acta Humaniorum VCH.

1988. *Science and Civilisation in China*, vol. V, part 9. *Textile Technology*, I: *Spinning and Reeling*. Cambridge: Cambridge University Press.

Kuhn, Dieter. Forthcoming. *Science and Civilisation in China*, vol. V, part 10. *Textile Technology*, II: *Weaving*. Cambridge: Cambridge University Press.

Kuznets, Simon. 1966. *Modern Economic Growth: Rate, Structure, and Spread*. New Haven: Yale University Press.

Lach, Donald F. (tr.). 1957. *Preface to Leibniz "Novissima Sinica": Commentary, Translation, Text*. Honolulu: University of Hawaii Press.

1965. *Asia in the Making of Europe*, vol. I. Chicago: University of Chicago Press.

1970. *Asia in the Making of Europe*, vol. II, pt. 1. Chicago: University of Chicago Press.

1977. *Asia in the Making of Europe*, vol. II, pt. 2: The Literary Arts. Chicago: University of Chicago Press.

Lamouroux, Christian. 1995. "Politique rizicole et déséquilibres régionaux: la région du Jiang-Huai (VIIIe-XIe siècles)." *Journal of the Social and Economic History of the Orient* 85: 145–84.

1995. "Crise politique et développement rizicole en Chine: la région du Jiang-Huai (VIIIe-XIe siècles)." *Bulletin de l'Ecole Française d'Extrême-Orient* 85: 145–84.

le Comte, Louis. 1696. *Nouveaux mémoires sur l'état présent de la Chine*. Paris.

1698. *Memoirs and Observations made in the late Journey through the Empire of China*. Translation of le Comte 1696. London.

Lemonnier, Pierre. 1992. *Elements for an Anthropology of Technology*. Ann Arbor: Museum of Anthropology, University of Michigan.

Lemonnier, Pierre (ed.). 1993. *Technological Choices: Transformation in Material Cultures Since the Neolithic*. London: Routledge.

Lenglet-Dufrenoys, Nicolas. 1772. *Méthode pour étudier l'histoire avec un catalogue des principaux historiens et de remarques sur la bonté de leurs ouvrages et sur le choix des meilleurs éditions*. Paris.

Lesser, Alexander. 1985. *History, Evolution, and the Concept of Culture: Selected Papers by Alexander Lesser*, ed. Sidney W. Mintz. Cambridge: Cambridge University Press.

Levenson, Joseph. 1967. *European Expansion and the Counter-Example of Asia, 1300–1600*. Englewood Cliffs, NJ: Prentice-Hall.

1968. *Confucian China and its Modern Fate: A Trilogy*. Berkeley: University of California Press.

Lévy-Bruhl, Lucien. 1910. *Les fonctions mentales dans les sociétés inférieures*. Paris: Alcan.

1926. *How Natives Think*. London: Allen and Unwin.

Li Bozhong. 1984a. "Ming Qing shiqi Jiangnan shuidao shengchan jiyue chengdu de tigao – Ming Qing Jiangnan nongye jingji fazhan tedian tantao zhi yi" [The rise in paddy productivity in Ming-Qing period Jiangnan: a study of the economic development of Ming-Qing period Jiangnan agriculture]. *Zhongguo nongshi* 1: 24–37.

1984b. "Ming Qing Jiangnan gongnongye shengchan zhong de ranliao wenti" [Fuel problems in Jiangnan industry and agriculture during the Ming and Qing dynasties]. *Zhongguo shehui jingjishi yanjiu* 4: 34–49.

Li Bozhong. 1990. *Tangdai Jiangnan nongye de fazhan* [Agricultural development in Tang Jiangnan]. Beijing: Nongye Chubanshe.

Li Dazhao [pseud. Li Shouchang]. 1926. *Shixue yaolun* [Essentials of historical study]. 2nd edn. Shanghai: Shangwu Yinshuguan.

Li Guohao, Zhang Mengwen and Cao Tianqin (eds.). 1982. *Explorations in the History of Science and Technology in China*. Shanghai: Chinese Classics Publishing House.

Li Hua. 1986. "Qingdai Shandong shangren shulüe" [Qing-dynasty Shandong merchants]. *Pinglun xuekan* 3:2, 133–60.

Li Ji. 1936. *Zhongguo shehuishi lunzhan pipan* [Critique of the Chinese social history controversy]. Rev. edn. Shanghai: Shenzhou Guoguang She.

Li Jinming. 1990. *Mingdai haiwai maoyishi* [A history of Ming maritime trade]. Beijing: Zhongguo Shehui Kexueyuan.

Li Shu. 1985. "On the Making of History and Other Problems." *Social Sciences in China* 1: 51–63.

Li Wenzhi. 1981. "Lun Zhongguo dizhu jingjizhi yu nongye zibenzhuyi mengya" [The Chinese landlord economy and incipient capitalism in agriculture]. *Zhongguo shehui kexue* 7: 143–60.

Li Wenzhi, Wei Jinyu, and Jing Junjian. 1983. *Ming-Qing shidai de nongye zibenzhuyi mengya wenti* [The question of the sprouts of agrarian capitalism in the Ming-Qing period]. Beijing: Zhongguo Shehui Kexue Chubanshe.

Liang Qichao [Liang Ch'i-ch'ao]. 1959. *Intellectual Trends in the Ching Period*, trans. Immanuel Hsü. Cambridge, Mass.: Harvard University Press.

   1901. *Zhongguo shixue lun* [On Chinese historiography].

   1922. *Zhongguo lishi yanjiu fa* [Research methodology for Chinese history].

Lin Bishu. 1988. "Makesi Weibo lishi fangfalun piping" [A critique of Max Weber's historical methodology]. *Shixue lilun* 2: 172–83.

Lin Ganquan, Tian Renlong, and Li Zude. 1982. *Zhongguo gudaishi fenqi taolun wushi nian, 1929–1979.* [Fifty years' discussion on the periodization of ancient Chinese society, 1929–1979]. Shanghai: Renmin Chubanshe.

Lin Ganquan and Ye Guisheng. 1985. "Yin Da." (Biography of Yin Da). In *Zhongguo shixuejia pingzhuan* [Critical biographies of Chinese historians], ed. Chen Qingquan. Kaifeng: Zhongzhou Guji Chubanshe.

Lin Renchuan. 1987. *Mingmo Qingchu siren haishang maoyi* [Late-Ming and early-Qing private maritime trade]. Shanghai: Huadong shifan daxue chubanshe.

Lin Yonggui and Wang Xi. 1991. *Qingdai Xibei minzu maoyishi* [A history of northwest trade in the Qing]. Beijing: Zhongyang Minzu Xueyuan.

Liu, Lydia, 1993. "Translingual Practice: The Discourse of Individualism between China and the West." *Positions* 1:1, 160–93.

Liu Yongcheng, 1979. "Lun Zhongguo zibenzhuyi mengya de lishi qianti" [On the historical preconditions of the sprouts of capitalism in China]. *Zhongguo shi yanjiu* 2: 32–46.

Liu Yongcheng and He Zhiqing. 1982. "Lüelun Zhongguo fengjian jingji jiegou" [Brief comments on the economic structure of Chinese feudalism]. *Zhongguo shi yanjiu* 1: 1–14.

Loehr, G. R. 1976. "L'artiste Jean-Denis Attiret et l'influence exercée par sa description des jardins impériaux." In *Actes du colloque international de sinologie: la mission française de Pékin aux XVIIe et XVIIIe siècles*. Paris: Les Belles Lettres.

Lowe, Donald M. 1966. *The Function of "China" in Marx, Lenin, and Mao*. Berkeley: University of California Press.

Lu Xun. 1973. *Re feng* [Hot winds]. In *Lu Xun quanji* [The collected works of Lu Xun], vol. 2. Shanghai: Renmin Chubanshe. First published 1925.

Lü Zhenyu. 1943. *Zhongguo yuanshi shehui shi* [A history of China's primitive society]. Guilin: Gengyun Chubanshe. First published 1934 under the title *Shiqian qi Zhongguo shehui yanjiu*.

   1954. *Zhongguo shehuishi zhu wenti* [Some questions concerning the history of Chinese society]. Rev. edn. Shanghai: Huadong Renmin Chubanshe.

Lufrano, Richard. 1997. *Honorable Merchants: Commerce and Self-Cultivation in Late Imperial China*. Honolulu: University of Hawaii Press.

Lundbaek, Knud. 1982. "China in Transcultural Communication Research." *Social Science Information* 21:6, 887–99.

Lust, John. 1987. *Western Books on China Published Up To 1850 in the Library of the School of Oriental and African Studies, University of London: A Descriptive Catalogue.* London: Bamboo.

Lyell, Charles. 1830–33. *Principles of Geology: Being an Attempt to Explain the Former Changes of the Earth's Surface by Reference to Causes Now in Operation.* London: John Murray.

Ma Xin. 1989. "The Theory of Marx's 'Four Modes of Production'." In *The Asiatic Mode of Production in China,* ed. Timothy Brook. Armonk, NY: M.E. Sharpe, pp. 176–83.

Macfarlane, Alan. 1977. *Origins of English Individualism.* Oxford: Basil Blackwell.

1987. *The Culture of Capitalism.* Oxford: Basil Blackwell.

Mackerras, Colin. 1989. *Western Images of China.* Hong Kong/Oxford: Oxford University Press.

Macpherson, C. B. 1962. *The Political Theory of Possessive Individualism: Hobbes to Locke.* Oxford: Oxford University Press.

Mad'iar, L. I. 1928. *Ekonomika sel'skogo khozyaistva v Kitae* [China's rural economy]. Moscow/Leningrad: Gosizdat.

1930a. *Ocherki po Ekonomika Kitaya* [An outline of the Chinese economy]. Moscow.

1930b. "Predislovie" (Preface) to *"Tszing-tyan": Agrarnyii Stroi Drevnego Kitaya,* ed. M. Kokin and G. Papayan. Leningrad: Izdanie Leningradskogo Vostochnogo Instituta imeni A.S. Enukidze, pp. i–lxxiv.

1930c. *Zhongguo nongcun jingji yanjiu* [Studies on China's rural economy]. Shanghai: Shenzhou Guoguang She. Translation of Mad'iar 1928.

1933. *Zhongguo jingji dagang* [General outline of the Chinese economy]. Shanghai: Xin Shengming, trans. of Mad'iar. 1930a.

Mair, Victor H. 1985. "Language and Ideology in the Written Popularizations of the *Sacred Edict*." In *Popular Culture in Late Imperial China,* ed. David Johnson *et al.* Berkeley: University of California Press, pp. 325–59.

Mann, Michael. 1986. *The Sources of Social Power,* vol I: *A History of Power from the Beginning to 1760 A.D.* Cambridge: Cambridge University Press

1988. "European Development: Approaching a Historical Explanation." In *Europe and the Rise of Capitalism,* ed. Jean Baechler, John Hall, and Michael Mann. Oxford: Blackwell, pp. 6–19.

Mann Susan. 1987. *Local Merchants and the Chinese Bureaucracy, 1750–1950.* Stanford: Stanford University Press.

1991. "Grooming a Daughter for Marriage: Brides and Wives in the Mid-Ch'ing period." In Watson and Ebrey 1991, pp. 204–30.

1992a. "Household Handicrafts and State Policy in Qing Times." In *To Achieve Security and Wealth: The Qing Imperial State and the Economy 1644–1911,* ed. Jane Kate Leonard and John R. Watt. Ithaca: Cornell University East Asia Program, pp. 75–95.

1992b. "Women's Work in the Ningbo Area, 1900–1936." In *Economic Growth in Prewar China,* ed. Thomas Rawski and Lillian Li. Berkeley: University of California Press, pp. 243–70.

1994. "The Education of Daughters in the Mid-Ch'ing Period." In *Education and Society in Late Imperial China, 1600–1900,* ed. Benjamin Elman and Alexander Woodside. Berkeley: University of California Press, pp. 19–49.

Mao Zedong [Mao Tse-tung]. 1965. *Selected Works of Mao Tse-tung*, vol. 2. Peking: Foreign Languages Press.

Markham, Clements (ed. and trans.). 1893. *The Journal of Christopher Columbus (During his First Voyage, 1492–1493), and Documents Relating to the Voyages of John Cabot and Gaspar Corte Real*. London: Hakluyt Society.

Marshall, P. J. and Glyndwr Williams. 1982. *The Great Map of Mankind*. London: J. M. Dent.

Marx, Karl. 1954–1959. *Capital. A Critical Analysis of Capitalist Production*. 3 vols. Moscow: Progress, and London: Lawrence & Wishart.

　1965. *Pre-Capitalist Economic Formations*, ed. Eric Hobsbawm. New York: International Publishers.

　1971. *A Contribution to the Critique of Political Economy*. London: Lawrence and Wishart.

　1972. "The British Rule in India." In *On Colonialism: Articles from the "New York Tribune" and Other Writings*, by Karl Marx and Friedrich Engels. New York: International Publishers, pp. 35–41.

　1973. *Grundrisse: Foundations of a Critique of Political Economy*, trans. M. Nichlaus. Harmondsworth: Penguin/NLB.

　1975. *Capital: A Critical Analysis of Capitalist Production*, ed. Friedrich Engels. 3 vols. New York: International Publishers.

Marx, Karl and Friedrich Engels. 1970. *The German Ideology*. New York: International Publishers.

Mason, Mary Gertrude. 1939. *Western Conceptions of China and the Chinese, 1840–1876*. Durham NC: Seeman Printing Co.

Mauss, Marcel. 1979 [1935]. "Les techniques du corps." In his *Sociology and Psychology*. London: Routledge and Kegan Paul.

Maverick, Lewis A. 1946. *China, a Model for Europe*. San Antonio, Texas: Paul Anderson Co.

Max Müller, Friedrich. 1866. *Lectures on the Science of Language*. London: Longmans, Green and Co.

McGough, J., ed. *Fei Hsiao-t'ung: The Dilemma of a Chinese Intellectual*. White Plains, NY: M. E. Sharpe.

McDermott, Joseph P. 1990. "The Chinese Domestic Bursar." *Ajia bunka kenkyū* [Studies in Asian culture], 15–32.

McNeill, William. 1982. *The Pursuit of Power Technology, Armed Force and Society since A.D. 1000*. Chicago: University of Chicago Press.

McVey, Ruth. 1992. *Southeast Asian Capitalists*. Ithaca: Southeast Asia Program, Cornell University.

Meisner, Maurice. 1967. *Li Ta-Chao and the Origins of Chinese Marxism*. Cambridge, Mass.: Harvard University Press.

Mendoza, Juan Gonzalez de. 1585. *Historia de las Cosas mas notables, Ritos y Costumbres del Gran Reyno de la China*. Rome.

Meng Qi, ed. 1847. *Nongsang jiyao* [Fundamentals of agriculture and sericulture]. Compiled 1273. Palace edition, Beijing.

Merrington, John. 1976. "Town and Country in the Transition to Capitalism." In *The Transition fron Feudalism to Capitalism*, ed. Rodney Hilton. London: New Left Books, pp. 170–95.

Metzger, Thomas A. 1977. *Escape from Predicament*. New York: Columbia University Press.

Miles, James. 1996. *The Legacy of Tiananmen: China in Disarray*. Ann Arbor: University of Michigan Press.

Mill, James. 1817. *History of British India*. 3 vols. London.

Mill, John Stuart. 1872a. *Utilitarianism, On Liberty and Considerations on Representative Government*, ed. H. B. Acton. London: Dent.

1872b. *Principles of Political Economy with Some of Their Applications to Social Philosophy*. London: Longmans, Green, Reader, and Dyer.

Miller, Stuart C. 1969. *The Unwelcome Immigrant: The American Image of the Chinese, 1785–1882*. Berkeley: University California Press.

Min, Tu-Ki. 1989. *National Polity and Local Power: The Transformation of Late Imperial China*, ed. Philip A. Kuhn and Timothy Brook. Cambridge, Mass.: Council on East Asian Studies, Harvard University.

Mintz, Sidney. 1985. *Sweetness and Power: The Place of Sugar in Modern History*. New York: Viking.

Mitcham, Carl. 1984. "Philosophy of Technology." In *A Guide to the Culture of Science, Technology, and Medicine*, ed. Paul T. Durbin. New York: Free Press, pp. 282–363.

Mitzman, Arthur. 1970. *The Iron Cage: An Historical Interpretation of Max Weber*. New York: Knopf.

Miyakawa, Hisayuki. 1955. "An Outline of the Naito Hypothesis and its Effects in Japanese Studies of China." *Far Eastern Quarterly* 14:4, 533–53.

Mokyr, Joel. 1990. *The Lever of Riches: Technological Creativity and Economic Progress*. New York: Oxford University Press.

Mommsen, Wolfgang. 1984. *Max Weber and German Politics, 1890–1920*. Chicago: University Chicago Press.

Montagu, Ashley. 1979. *Man's Most Dangerous Myth: The Fallacy of Race*. Cleveland and New York: Meridien.

Montaigne, Michel de. 1979. *Essais*. Introduction by A. Micha. 3 vols. Paris: Flammarion.

Montesquieu. 1922. *De l'esprit des lois, avec des notes de Voltaire, etc.* 2 vols. Paris: Garnier.

1949. *The Spirit of the Laws*, trans. Thomas Nugent, with an introduction by Franz Neumann. New York: Hafner.

1973. *Persian Letters*. Harmondsworth: Penguin.

Moore, Richard H. 1990. *Japanese Agriculture: Patterns of Rural Development*. Boulder: Westview Press.

Morgan, Lewis Henry. 1877. *Ancient Society: Researches in the Lines of Human Progress from Savagery through Barbarism to Civilisation*. New York: Holt.

Mori, Masao. 1980. "The Gentry in the Ming: An Outline of the Relations between the Shih-ta-fu and Local Society." *Acta Asiatica* 38: 31–53.

Moritani Katsumi. 1936. *Zhongguo shehui jingji shigang* [A socioeconomic history of China], trans. Wang Yudun. Shanghai: Shenghuo. Trans. of *Shina shakai keizai shi*, first published 1934.

Morse, Hosea Ballou. 1910–18. *The International Relations of the Chinese Empire*. 3 vols. London: Longmans Green.

1921. *The Trade and Administration of China*. Shanghai: Kelly and Walsh.

1926–29. *The Chronicles of the East India Company Trading to China, 1635–1843*. 5 vols. Cambridge, Mass./Oxford: Harvard University Press/ Oxford University Press.

1932. *The Guilds of China, with an account of the Guild Merchant or Co-Hong of Canton*. 2nd edn. Shanghai: Kelly and Walsh.

Mukhia, Harbans. 1981. "Was There Feudalism in Indian History?" *Journal of Peasant Studies* 8:3, 273–310.

Müller, F. Max. *See* Max Müller, F.

Mumford, Lewis. 1934. *Technics and Civilization*. New York: Harcourt Brace.

1964. *The Myth of the Machine, II: The Pentagon of Power*. New York: Harcourt, Brace, Jovanovich.

1967, 1970. *The Myth of the Machine*. Vol. I: *Technics and Human Development*; Vol. II: *The Pentagon of Power*. New York: Harcourt Brace Jovanovich.

Mungello, David E. 1977. *Leibniz and Confucianism: The Search for Accord*. Honolulu: University of Hawaii Press.

1985. *Curious Land: Jesuit Accommodation and the Origins of Sinology*. Wiesbaden: Steiner.

Najita, Tetsuo. 1987. *Visions of Virtue in Tokugawa Japan: The Kaitokudo Merchant Academy of Osaka*. Chicago: University of Chicago Press.

Navarette, Domingo Fernandez. 1676. *Tratados historicos, politicos, ethicos, y religiosas de la monarchia de China*. Madrid.

Needham, Joseph. 1954. *Science and Civilisation in China*, vol. I. Cambridge: Cambridge University Press.

1956. *Science and Civilisation in China*, vol. II. Cambridge: Cambridge University Press.

1959. *Science and Civilisation in China*, vol. III: *Mathematics, and the Sciences of the Heavens and the Earth*. With Wang Ling. Cambridge: Cambridge University Press.

1965. *Science and Civilisation in China*, vol. IV, part 2: *Mechanical Engineering*. With Wang Ling. Cambridge: Cambridge University Press.

1969. *The Grand Titration: Science and Society in East and West*. Toronto: University of Toronto Press.

1971. *Science and Civilisation in China*, vol. IV, pt. 3: *Civil Engineering and Nautics*. With Wang Ling and Lu Gwei-Djen. Cambridge Cambridge University Press.

1986. *Science and Civilisation in China*, vol. VI, pt. 1: *Botany*. With Lu Gwei-Djen and Huang Hsing-tsung. Cambridge: Cambridge University Press.

Needham, Joseph and Ray Huang, 1974. "The Nature of Chinese Society: A Technical Interpretation." *Journal of Oriental Studies* (Hong Kong University Press) 12: 1–2, 1–16.

Needham, Joseph and Dorothy Needham. 1948. *Science Outpost*. London: Pilot Press.

Niida Noboru. 1981. *Chūgoku hōseishi kenkyū: dorei nōdo hō, kazoku sonraku hō* [Studies in Chinese legal history: slave and serf law, family and village law]. Tokyo: Tōkyō Daigaku Shuppansha.

Nikiforov, V. N. 1970. *Sovetskie istoriki o problemakh Kitaya*. Moscow: Nauka.

Ning Ke and Zou Zhaochen. 1984. "Shixue lilun" [Historiographical theory]. *Zhongguo lishixue nianjian* [China history studies annual], pp. 19–27.

Nishijima Sadao. 1957. "Chūgoku kodai shakai no kōzōteki tokushi ni kansuru mondaiten" [Questions regarding the special structural character of ancient Chinese society]. In *Chūgoku-shi no jidai kubun* [The periodization of Chinese history], ed. Suzuki Jun and Nishijima Sadao Tokyo: Tōkyō Daigaku Shuppansha, pp. 175–208.

—— 1984. "The Formation of the Early Chinese Cotton Industry." Trans. in *State and Society in China: Japanese Perspectives on Ming-Qing Social and Economic History*, ed. Linda Grove and Christian Daniels. Tokyo: Tokyo University Press, pp. 17–77.

North, Douglass C. 1981. *Structure and Change in Economic History*. New York: Norton.

—— 1990. *Institutions, Institutional Change and Economic Performance*. Cambridge: Cambridge University Press.

Nott, J. C. and G. R. Gliddon. 1854. *Types of Mankind: or, Ethnological Researches, based upon the ancient monuments, paintings, sculptures, and crania of races*. Philadelphia: Lippincott, Grambo & Co.; London: Trübner.

Nuccio, Oscar. 1983. "Medieval and Italian Sources of Economic Rationalism." *Rivista de Politica Economica: Selected Papers* 17: 69–131.

Ohnuki-Tierney, Emiko. 1993. *Rice as Self: Japanese Identities through Time*. Princeton: Princeton University Press.

Olender, Maurice (ed.). 1981. *Pour Léon Poliakov: Le racisme: mythes et science*. Paris: Complexe.

Olson, Lawrence. 1992. *Ambivalent Moderns: Portraits of Japanese Cultural Identity*. Savage, Maryland: Towman and Littlefield.

Osipov, P. I. 1935. "O rabstve v drevnem obshchestve Kitaya." *Problemyi istorii dokapitalisticheskikh obshchestv* 7–8: 134–59.

Ozawa, Kenji. 1993. "A New Phase for Rice in Japan: Production, Marketing, and Policy Issues." In *Japanese and American Agriculture: Tradition and Progress in Conflict*, ed. Luther Tweeten *et al.* Boulder: Westview Press, pp. 367–75.

Pacey, Arnold. 1990. *Technology in World Civilization: A Thousand-Year History*. Cambridge, Mass.: MIT Press.

Pan Jixing (ed.). 1989. *Tiangong kaiwu jiaozhu ji yanjiu* [Critical edition and researches on the *Tiangong kaiwu*]. Chengdu: Ba-Shu Shushe.

Pan, Ming-te. 1994. "The Rural Credit Market and Peasant Economy in China, 1600–1949." Ph.D. diss., University of California, Irvine.

Pan Ruxuan. 1979. "Fan Wenlan" [Biography of Fan Wen-Lan]. *Zhongguo shi yanjiu xingtai* 11: 14–16.

Pang Zhuoheng. 1981. "Zhong xi fengjian zhuanzhi zhidu bijiao yanjiu" [Comparative study of Chinese and Western systems of feudal autocracy]. *Lishi yanjiu* 2: 3–13.

Parker, Geoffrey. 1988. *The Military Revolution: Military Innovation and the Rise of the West, 1500–1800*. Cambridge: Cambridge University Press.

Parry, J. H. 1966. *The Establishment of European Hegemony, 1415–1715: Trade and Exploration in the Age of the Renaissance*. 3rd edn. New York: Harper and Row.

Parsons, Talcott. 1971. *The Systems of Modern Societies*. Englewood Cliffs, NJ: Prentice-Hall.

Pellicani, Luciano. 1988. *Saggio sulla genesi del capitalismo: alle origini della modernita*. Milan: SugarCo Ediz.

Perkins, Dwight H. 1969. *Agricultural Development in China, 1368–1968*. Chicago: Aldine.

Perlin, Frank. 1983. "Proto-industrialization and Pre-colonial South Asia." *Past and Present* 98: 30–95.

Perroy, Eouard. 1949. "A l'origine d'une économie contractée: les crises du XIVe siècle." *Annales* 4: 2, 167–82.

Pfaffenberger, Bryan. 1992. "Social Anthropology of Technology." *Annual Review of Anthropology* 21: 491–516.

Pinot, Virgile. 1932. *La Chine et la formation de l'esprit philosophique en France, 1640–1740*. Paris: Geuthner.

Pocock, J. G. A. 1985. *Virtue, Commerce, and History: Essays on Political Thought and History, Chiefly in the Eighteenth Century*. Cambridge: Cambridge University Press.

Polanyi, Karl. 1957 *The Great Transformation: The Political and Economic Origins of our Time*. Boston: Beacon Press.

Pollard, Sidney. 1981. *Peaceful Conquest: The Industrialization of Europe, 1760–1970*. Oxford: Oxford University Press.

Pomeranz, Kenneth. 1993. *The Making of a Hinterland: State, Society, and Economy in Inland North China, 1853–1937*. Berkeley: University of California Press.

Postel, Guillaume. 1543. *De Orbis Terrae Concordia*. Basel: Oporin.

1575. *Des Histoires Orientales et principalement des Turkes ou Turchiques et Schitiques ou Tartaresques et autres qui en sont descendus*. 3rd edn.

Pretot, Étienne de. 1753. *Analyse chronologique de l'histoire universelle, depuis le commencement du monde, jusqu'à l'empire de Charlemagne*. Paris.

Prigozhin, A. G. (ed.). 1934. *Karl Marks i problemyi istorii dokapitalisticheskikh formatsii: Sbornik k pyatidesyatiletiyu so dnya smerti Karla Marksa*. Moscow/Leningrad: Ogiz, Gosudarstvennoe sotsial'no-ekonomicheskoe izdatel'stvo.

Pu Songling. 1982. *Nongsang jing jiaozhu* [A critical edition of the *Nongsang jing*], ed. Li Changnian. Beijing: Nongye Chubanshe.

Pulleyblank, Edwin. 1958. "The Origins and Nature of Chattel Slavery." *Journal of the Economic and Social History of the Orient* 1:2.

Pursell, Carroll. 1984. "History of Technology." In *A Guide to the Culture of Science, Technology, and Medicine*, ed. Paul T. Durbin. New York: Free Press, pp. 70–120.

1995. *The Machine in America: A Social History of Technology*. Baltimore: Johns Hopkins Press.

Pusey, James. 1983. *China and Charles Darwin*. Cambridge, Mass.: Council on East Asian Studies, Harvard University.

Quesnay, François. 1768. *Physiocratie, ou constitution naturelle du gouvernement le plus avantageux au genre humaine*, ed. Pierre Samuel Dupont de Nemours. Leyden: Merlin.

1965. *Oeuvres économiques et philosophiques*, ed. A. Oncken. Aalen: Scientia. First pub. 1888.

Rawski, Thomas G. 1989. *Economic Growth in Prewar China*. Berkeley: University of California Press.

Rawski, Thomas G. and Lillian M. Li (eds.). 1992. *Chinese History in Economic Perspective*. Berkeley: University of California.

Reichwein, Adolf. 1925. *China and Europe: Intellectual and Artistic Contacts in the Eighteenth Century*. London: Kegan Paul, Trench, Trubner. Repr. Routledge and Kegan Paul, 1968.

Rémusat, J. P. A. 1825a. *Mélanges Asiatiques, ou choix de morceaux critiques et de mémoires relatifs aux religions, aux sciences, aux coutumes, à l'histoire et à la géographie des nations orientales*. 2 vols. Paris: Dondey-Dupré.

1825b. *Nouveaux mélanges Asiatiques, ou receuil des morceaux critiques et de mémoires relatifs aux réligions, aux sciences, aux coutumes, à l'histoire et à la géographie des nations orientales*. 2 vols. Paris: Schubart et Heideloff.

Renaudot, Eusibius [Eusèbe]. 1733. *Dissertation on the Chinese Learning*. London.

Rong Sheng. 1979. "Zhi you nongmin zhanzheng cai shi fengian shehui fazhan de zhenzheng dongli ma?" [Is peasant war the only true impetus for the development of feudal society?]. *Lishi yanjiu* 4: 49–56.

Rose, Ernst. 1951. "China as a Symbol of Reaction in Germany, 1830–1880." *Comparative Literature* 3: 57–76.

Rousseau, J. J. 1971. *Discours sur les sciences et les arts: discours sur l'origine de l'inégalité*. Paris: Garnier-Flammarion.

Rowbotham, Arnold H. 1942. *Missionary and Mandarin: The Jesuits at the Court of China*. Berkeley: University California Press.

Rowe, William. 1984. *Hankow: Commerce and Society in a Chinese City, 1796–1889*. Stanford: Stanford University Press.

Roy, Patricia. 1989. *A White Man's Province. British Columbia Politicians and Chinese and Japanese Immigrants, 1858–1914*. Vancouver: University of British Columbia Press.

Rozman, Gilbert. 1973. *Urban Networks in Ch'ing China and Tokugawa Japan*. Princeton: Princeton University Press.

Ruitenbeek, Klaas. 1993. *Carpentry and Building in Late Imperial China: A Study of the Fifteenth-Century Carpenter's Manual Lu Banjing*. Leiden: E.J. Brill.

Rule, Paul. 1986. *K'ung-tzu or Confucius? The Jesuit Interpretation of Confucianism*. Sydney/London: Allen & Unwin.

Sabban, Françoise. 1994. "L'industrie sucrière, le moulin à sucre et les relations sino-portugaises aux XIVe-XVIIIe siècles." *Annales: Histoires, Sciences Sociales* 49, 4: 817–62.

Sachs, Wolfgang. 1992. *For Love of the Automobile: Looking Back into the History of our Desires*. Trans. Don Reneau. Berkeley: University of California Press.

Saeki Yūichi. 1957. "Nihon no Min-Shin jidai kenkyū ni okeru shōhin seizan hyōka o megutte" [On the evaluation of commodity production in Japanese studies of the Ming-Qing Period]. In *Chūgoku-shi no jidai kubun* [The periodization of Chinese history], ed. Suzuki Jun and Nishijima Sadao. Tokyo: Tōkyō Daigaku Shuppansha, pp. 253–321.

Safarov, G. 1928. *Klassyi i klassovaya bor'ba v kitaiskoi istorii*. Moscow/Leningrad: Gosizdat.

Said, Edward. 1978. *Orientalism*. New York: Vintage.

Saitō Osamu. 1985. *Puroto kōgyōka no jidai* [The age of protoindustrialization]. Tokyo: Nihon Hyōronsha.

Sandnemyer, E.C. 1973. *The Anti-Chinese Movement in California*. Chicago: University of Illinois Press.

Sawer, Marian. 1977. *Marxism and the Question of the Asiatic Mode of Production*. The Hague: Martinus Nijhoff.

Saxton, Alexander. 1971. *The Indispensible Enemy: Labor and the Anti-Chinese Movement in California*. Berkeley: University California Press.

Schneider, Laurence. 1971. *Ku Chieh-Kang and China's New History: Nationalism and the Quest for Alternative Traditions*. Berkeley: University California Press.

Schneider, Jane. 1987. "The Anthropology of Cloth." *Annual Review of Anthropology* 16: 409–48.

Schneider, Jane and Annette B. Weiner. 1989. "Introduction." In *Cloth and Human Experience*, ed. Weiner and Schneider. Washington: Smithsonian Institution Press, pp. 1–29.

Schumpeter, Joseph A. 1939. *Business Cycles: A Theoretical, Historical, and Statistical Analysis of the Capitalist Process*. New York: McGraw-Hill.

——— 1954. *History of Economic Analysis*. Oxford: Oxford University Press.

Schwartz, Benjamin. 1954. "A Marxist Controversy on China." *Far Eastern Quarterly* 13:2, 143–53.

——— 1964. *In Search of Wealth and Power: Yen Fu and the West*. Cambridge, Mass.: Harvard University Press.

Scott, Joan Wallach. 1989. "History in Crisis? The Others' Side of the Story." *American Historical Review* 94: 680–92.

Sélincourt, Aubrey de, trans. 1979. *Herodotus, The Histories*. Harmondsworth: Penguin.

Semedo, Alvarez. 1642. *Imperio de la China*. Madrid.

Shelley, Percy Bysshe. 1970. *Poetical Works*, ed. T. Hutchinson and G. M. Matthews. London: Oxford University Press.

Shiva, Vandana. 1991. *The Violence of the Green Revolution: Third World Agriculture, Ecology and Politics*. London: Zed Press.

Shuckford, Samuel. 1728. *The Sacred and Profane History of the World Connected, from the Creation of the World to the Dissolution of the Assyrian Empire*. London.

Silhouette, Étienne. 1729. *Idée générale du gouvernement et de la morale des Chinois, et réponse à trois critiques*. Paris.

——— 1764. *La balance chinoise*. London.

Simon, Renée. 1940. "Henri de Boulainvilliers: Historien, politicien, philosophe, astrologue, 1658–1722." Ph.D. diss., Faculté des Lettres de Lille.

Sirén, Osvald. 1950. *China and the Gardens of Europe in the 18th Century*. New York: Ronald Press.

Skinner, G. William (ed.). 1977. *The City in Late Imperial China*. Stanford: Stanford University Press.

Sladkovskii, M. I. 1966. *History of Economic Relations Between Russia and China*, trans. M. Roublev. Jerusalem: Israel Programme for Scientific Translations.

Slicher van Bath, B. H. 1977. "Agriculture in the Vital Revolution." In *Cambridge Economic History of Europe*, vol. 5 : *The Economic Organization of Early*

Modern Europe, ed. V. E. E. Rich and C. H. Wilson. Cambridge: Cambridge University Press.

Smith, Adam. 1893. *An Inquiry into the Nature and Causes of the Wealth of Nations*. London: Routledge.

1937. *An Inquiry into the Nature and Causes of the Wealth of Nations*. New York: Random House.

Smith, Paul J. 1991. *Taxing Heaven's Storehouse: Horses, Bureaucrats and the Destruction of the Sichuan Tea Industry*. Cambridge, Mass.: Harvard-Yenching Institute.

Smith, R.E.F. and David Christian. 1984. *Bread and Salt: A Social and Economic History of Food and Drink in Russia*. Cambridge: Cambridge University Press.

Smith, Thomas C. 1959. *The Agrarian Origins of Modern Japan*. Stanford: Stanford Univeristy Press.

Solinger, Dorothy. 1984. *Chinese Business under Socialism*. Berkeley: University of California Press.

Song Min. 1989. "The Scientific Validity of the Concept of the Asiatic Mode of Production." In *The Asiatic Mode of Production in China*, ed. Timothy Brook. Armonk, NY: M. E. Sharpe, pp. 149–56.

Song Yingxing. 1637. *Tiangong kaiwu* [The exploitation of the works of nature]. References are to the 1771 ed., reproduced as *Jiaozheng tiangong kaiwu*, ed. Yang Jialuo. Taibei: Shijie, 1962. Trans. as Sung 1966.

Soranzo, Giovanni. 1930. *Il Papato, l'Europa cristiana e i Tartari: un seculo di penetrazione occidentale in Asia*. Milano: Università Cattolica del Sacro Cuore, Serie Quinta, Scienze Storiche, vol. XII.

Spence, Jonathan D. 1977. *Emperor of China: Self-Portrait of K'ang-Hsi*. Harmondsworth: Penguin.

1980. *To Change China: Western Advisers in China*. Harmondsworth: Penguin.

1990. *The Search for Modern China*. London: Hutchinson.

Spencer, Herbert. 1937. *First Principles*. 6th edn. London: Watts.

Spengler, Oswald. 1928. *The Decline of the West: Perspectives of World History*, trans. C.F. Atkinson. 2 vols. London: Allen and Unwin.

Stalin, Joseph. 1974. *On the Opposition*. Peking: Foreign Languages Press.

Staudenmeier, John M. 1985. *Technology's Storytellers: Reweaving the Human Fabric*. Cambridge, Mass.: MIT Press.

1990. "Recent Trends in the History of Technology." *American Historical Review* 95: 715–25.

Staunton, George Thomas (ed. and trans.). 1810. *Ta Tsing Leu Lée; being the fundamental laws, and a selection from the supplementary statutes, of the penal code of China*. London: Caddell and Davies.

Stone-Ferrier, Linda. 1989. "Spun Virtue, the Lacework of Folly, and the World Wound Upside-Down: Seventeenth-Century Dutch Depictions of Female Handwork." In *Cloth and Human Experience*, ed. Weiner and Schneider. Washington: Smithsonian Institution Press, pp. 215–42.

Strayer, Joseph R. 1955. *Western Europe in the Middle Ages: A Short History*. New York: Appleton-Century-Crofts.

1970. *On the Medieval Origins of the Modern State*. Princeton: Princeton University Press.

Sung Ying-Hsing (trans. E-Tu Zen Sun and Shiou-Chuan Sun). 1966. *T'ien-kung K'ai-wu: Chinese Technology in the Seventeenth Century*. University Park and London: Pennsylvania State University Press.

Sweezy, Paul. 1976a. "A Critique." In *The Transition from Feudalism to Capitalism*, ed. Rodney Hilton. London: New Left Books, pp. 33–56.

    1976b. "A Rejoinder." In *The Transition from Feudalism to Capitalism*, ed. Rodney Hilton. London: New Left Books, pp. 101–05.

Taguchi Ukichi. 1887. *Shina kaika shoshi* [A short history of Chinese civilization], vol. I. Tokyo.

Takahashi, Kohachiro. 1976. "A Contribution to the Discussion." In *The Transition from Feudalism to Capitalism*, ed. Rodney Hilton. London: New Left Books, pp. 68–97.

Takeuchi Yoshimi. 1980. "Kindai no chōkoku" [Overcoming the modern]. First published 1959. Reprinted in *Takeuchi Yoshimi zenshu* [Complete works of Takeuchi Yoshimi] 8: 3–67. Tokyo: Chikuma Shobō.

Tam, Yue-Him. 1980. "An Intellectual's Response to Western Intrusion: Naitō Konan's View of Republican China." In *The Chinese and the Japanese: Essays in Political and Cultural Interaction*, ed. Madeline Chi and Iriye Akira. Princeton: Princeton University Press.

Tan Chung. 1978. *China and the Brave New World: A Study of the Origins of the Opium War, 1840–42*. Bombay: Allied Publishers.

Tanaka Masatoshi. 1957. "Chūgoku rekishikai ni okeru 'shihonshugi no myōga' kenkyū" [Research on the sprouts of capitalism in Chinese history]. In *Chūgoku-shi no jidai kubun* [The periodization of Chinese history], ed. Suzuki Jun and Nishijima Sadao. Tokyo: Tōkyō Daigaku Shuppansha, pp. 219–52.

    1984. "Rural Handicraft in Jiangnan in the Sixteenth and Seventeenth Centuries." Trans. in *State and Society in China: Japanese Perspectives on Ming-Qing Social and Economic History*, ed. Linda Grove and Christian Daniels. Tokyo: Tokyo University Press, pp. 79–100.

Tanaka, Stefan. 1993. *Japan's Orient: Rendering Pasts into History*. Berkeley: University of California Press.

    1994. "Imaging History: Inscribing Belief in the Nation." *Journal of Asian Studies* 53:1, 24–44.

Tang, Xiaobing. 1996. *Global Space and the Nationalist Discourse of Modernity: The Historical Thinking of Liang Qichao*. Stanford: Stanford University Press.

Tanigawa Michio. 1985. *Medieval Chinese Society and the Local "Community,"* trans. Joshua A. Fogel. Berkeley: University California Press.

    1987. "Problems Concerning the Japanese Periodisation of Chinese History," trans. Joshua A. Fogel. *Journal of Asian History* 21:2, 150–68.

Tao Xisheng. 1933. *Zhongguo shehui zhi shi de fenxi* [Analysis of the history of Chinese society]. Shanghai: Xinshengming Shuju. First published 1929.

    1944. *Zhongguo shehui shi* [A history of Chinese society]. Chongqing: Wenfeng Chubanshe.

Tatlow, Antony. 1973. *Brechts chinesische Gedichte*. Frankfurt: Suhrkamp.

Tawney, R. H. 1966. *Land and Labor in China*. Boston: Beacon. First published 1932.

Tedder, Henry R. (ed.). 1910. *Descriptive Sociology; or Groups of Sociological Facts, Classified and Arranged by Herbert Spencer*. (Compiled and abstracted upon the plan organized by Herbert Spencer by E. T. C. Werner) London: Williams & Norgate.

Temple, William. 1720. *Works*. 2 vols. London: A. Churchill.

Teng, Ssu-yü. 1943. "Chinese Influence on the Western Examination System." *Harvard Journal of Asiatic Studies* 7:4, 267–312.

1949. "Chinese Historiography in the Last Fifty Years." *Far Eastern Quarterly* 8:2, 131–56.

Terada Takanobu. 1972. *Sansei shōnin no kenkyū* [Studies on Shanxi merchants]. Kyoto: Dōhōsha.

Thompson, E. P. 1971. "The Moral Economy of the English Crowd in the Eighteenth Century." *Past and Present* 50: 76–136.

Thompson, R. A. 1978. "The Yellow Peril 1890–1940." Ph.D. diss., University Wisconsin, 1957. Reprint. New York: Arno Press.

Thorne, Christopher. 1978. *Allies of a Kind: The United States, Britain, and the War Against Japan, 1941–1945*. London: Hamish Hamilton.

Tian Changwu. 1989. "You guan nuli zhi shehui xingtai de yixie wenti" [Some questions concerning the slave social formation]. *Shexue lilun* 1: 55–63.

Tian Jujian. 1983. "Zhongguo fengjian shehui changqi yanxu taolun de youlai he fazhan" [The origin and development of the discussion on the prolongation of Chinese feudal society]. In *Jianguo yilai shixue lilun wenti taolun juyao* [Essentials of the debates over questions of historical theory since 1949], ed. *Lishi yanjiu* bianjibu [Editorial board of *Lishi yanjiu*]. Jinan: Qi-Lu Shushe, pp. 166–202.

Tian Renlong. 1981. "Jianguo yilai Yaxiya shengchan fangshi wenti taolun zongshu" [A survey of the debates on the question of the Asiatic mode of production since 1949]. *Zhongguo shi yanjiu* 3: 147–59.

T'ien, Ju-k'ang. 1988. *Male Anxiety and Female Chastity: A Comparative Study of Ethical Values in Ming-Ch'ing Times*. Leiden: Brill.

Tilly, Charles. 1983. "Flows of Capital and Forms of Industry in Europe, 1500–1900." *Theory and Society* 12:1 (January), 123–43.

Tindal, Matthew. 1730. *Christianity as Old as Creation: or the Gospel, a republication of the Religion of Nature*. London.

Tōa kenkyūjo [East Asia Institute] (ed.). 1939. *Shina keizai hihan* [Critiques of the Chinese economy], vol. I. Tokyo: Tōa Kenkyūjo.

Tocqueville, Alexis de. 1974. *The Ancien Régime and the French Revolution*, trans. Stuart Gilbert. London: Collins/Fontana.

Tong Shuye. 1981. *Zhongguo shougongye shangye fazhan shi* [A history of the development of handicrafts and commerce in China]. Jinan: Qi-Lu Shushe.

Torr, Dana (ed.). 1951. *Marx on China, 1853–1860: Articles from the "New York Daily Tribune."* London: Lawrence and Wishart.

Tracy, James D. (ed.). 1990. *The Rise of Merchant Empires: Long-Distance Trade in the Early Modern World, 1350–1750*. Cambridge: Cambridge University Press.

(ed.). 1991. *The Political Economy of Merchant Empires*. Cambridge: Cambridge University Press.

Treadgold, Donald. W. 1973. *The West in Russia and China: Religious and Secular Thought in Modern Times*. Vol. I: Russia, 1472–1917; vol. II: China, 1582–1949. Cambridge: Cambridge University Press.

Trigault, Nicolas. 1615. *De Christiana Expeditione apud Sinas.* Augsburg.

Trotsky, Leon. 1966. *Problems of the Chinese Revolution,* with appendices by Zinoviev, Vuyovitch, Nassunov, and others, trans. M. Shachtman, introduction by B. Schwartz. New York: Paragon.

Tsing, Yuan. 1979. "Urban Riots and Disturbances." In *From Ming to Ch'ing: Conquest, Region, and Continuity in Seventeenth-Century China,* ed. Jonathan D. Spence and John E. Wills, Jr. New Haven: Yale University Press.

Tweeten, Luther, Cynthia L. Dishon, and Wen S. Chern, Naraomi Imamura, and Masaru Morishima (eds.). 1993. *Japanese and American Agriculture: Tradition and Progress in Conflict.* Boulder: Westview Press.

Ulmen, G. L. 1978. *The Science of Society: Toward an Understanding of the Life and Work of Karl August Wittfogel.* The Hague: Mouton.

Unger, Roberto. 1987 *Plasticity into Power: Comparative-Historical Studies on the Institutional Conditions of Economic and Military Success.* Cambridge: Cambridge University Press.

Usher, A. P. 1913. *The History of the Grain Trade in France.* Cambridge, Mass.: Harvard University Press.

Van Braam Houckgeest, André Everard. 1797. *Voyage de l'ambassade de la compagnie des Indes orientales hollandaises, vers l'empereur de la Chine, en 1794–1795.* 2 vols. Philadelphia.

——— 1798. *An Authentic Account of the Embassy of the Dutch East-India Company, to the Court of the Emperor of China, in the Years 1794–1795.* 2 vols. London.

van der Leeuw, Sander. 1993. "Giving the Potter a Choice: Conceptual Aspects of Pottery Techniques." In *Technological Choices: Transformation in Material Cultures Since the Neolithic,* ed. Pierre Lemonnier. London: Routledge, pp. 238–88.

Van Kley, Edwin J. 1971. "Europe's 'Discovery' of China and the Writing of World History." *American Historical Review* 76: 358–85.

Varga, Yevgeni. 1928. "Osnovyie problemyi kitaiskoi revolutsii." *Bolshevik,* no. 8

——— 1968. "The Asiatic Mode of Production." In Y. Varga, *Political Economic Problems of Capitalism,* trans. D. Danemanis. Moscow: Progress.

Vauban, Sebastian le Prestre de. 1698. *Projet d'une dîme royale, suivie de deux écrits financiers.* In Daire (ed.) 1843.

Vera, Domenico. 1989. "Del servus al servus quasi colonus: una altra transició?" *L'Avenç* 131 (Nov.): 32–37.

Vincent of Beauvais. 1474. *Speculum historiale.* Vol. III of *Speculum Mundi.* Augsburg.

——— 1515. *Den Spieghel historael.* Antwerp.

Vinh, Sinh. 1986. "Meiji Japan and its International Environment: Fukuzawa Yukichi's Views of Asia." *Kindai Nihon kenkyū* 3:113–61.

Vissering, W. 1877. *On Chinese Currrency: Coin and Paper Money.* Leiden: Brill.

Volin, M. 1929. Introduction to M. G. Andreev, "Institut rabstva v Kitae." *Problemyi Kitaya* 1: 206–28.

Voltaire. 1877–85. *Oeuvres complètes,* ed. L. Moland. 52 vols. Paris: Garnier.

——— 1963. *Essai sur les moeurs et l'esprit des nations et sur les principaux faits de l'histoire depuis Charlemagne jusqu'à Louis XIII,* ed. R. Pomeau. 2 vols. Paris: Garnier.

Wagner, Donald B. 1985. *Dabieshan: Traditional Chinese Iron Production Techniques Practised in Southern Henan in the Twentieth Century.* London: Curzon Press.

1993. *Iron and Steel in Ancient China.* Leiden: Brill.

1995. "The Traditional Chinese Iron Industry and its Modern Fate." *Chinese Science* 12: 136–59.

Wakeman, Frederic Jr. 1978. "The Canton Trade and the Opium War." *Cambridge History of China* 10: 163–212.

Waley, P. J. and D. P. Waley (eds.). 1956. *The Reason of State* and *The Greatness of Cities* by Giovanni Botero, trans. R. Peterson. New Haven: Yale University Press.

Wallerstein, Immanuel. 1974. *The Modern World-System*, vol. I: *Capitalist Agriculture and the Origins of the European World-Economy in the Sixteenth Century.* New York: Academic Press.

1980. *The Modern World-System*, vol. II: *Mercantilism and the Consolidation of the European World-Economy, 1600–1750.* New York: Academic Press.

1984. "Long Waves in History." *Review* 7:4.

1989. *The Modern World-System: The Second Era of Great Expansion in the Capitalist World-Economy, 1730–1840s.* New York: Academic Press.

Walpole, Horace. 1903–25. *The Letters of Horace Walpole, 4th Earl of Oxford*, ed. Mrs. Pagel Toynbee. 19 vols. London: Oxford University Press.

Wang Dunshu and Yu Ko. 1989. "Further Comments on the 'Asiatic Mode of Production'." In *The Asiatic Mode of Production in China*, ed. Timothy Brook. Armonk, NY: M. E. Sharpe, pp. 118–35.

Wang Hongjun. 1980. "Zhongguo cong xianjin dao luohou de sanbai nian" [The three centuries when China went from advanced to backward]. *Zhongguo shi yanjiu* 1: 20–28.

Wang Sizhi, Du Wenkai, and Wang Rufeng. 1955. "Guanyu Han shehui xingzhi wenti de tantao" [Queries on the question of the nature of Han society]. *Lishi yanjiu* 1.

Wang Yanan. 1957. *Zhongguo banfengjian banzhimindi jingji xingtai yanjiu* [Studies on the semi-feudal semi-colonial economic formation of China]. Beijing: Renmin Chubanshe.

1981. *Zhongguo guanliao zhengzhi yanjiu* [Studies in China's bureaucratic politics]. Beijing: Zhongguo Shehui Kexue Chubanshe. Originally pub. Shanghai: Shidai Wenhua, 1948.

Wang Zhen. 1313. *Nong shu* [Agricultural treatise], ed. Wang Yuhu. Beijing: Nongye Chubanshe, 1981.

Wang Zhongluo. 1957. *Guanyu Zhongguo nuli shehui de wajie ji fengjian guanxi de xingcheng wenti* [On the question of the dissolution of slave society in China and the formation of feudal relations]. Wuhan: Hubei Renmin Chubanshe.

1985. "Zhongguo fengjian shehui de tedian" [The characteristics of Chinese feudal society]. *Lishi yanjiu* 1: 6–10.

Waring, Marilyn. 1988. *If Women Counted: A New Feminist Economics.* New York: Harper Collins.

Watanabe, Hiroshi. 1983. *Marco Polo Bibliography.* Tokyo: Tōyō Bunko.

Watson, Burton. 1962. *Early Chinese Literature.* New York: Columbia University Press.

(trans). 1964. *Han Fei Tzu: The Basic Writings*. New York: Columbia University Press.

Watson, James L. 1988. "The Structure of Chinese Funerary Rites: Elementary Forms, Ritual Sequence, and the Primacy of Performance." In *Death Ritual in Late Imperial and Modern China*, ed. James L. Watson and Evelyn Rawski. Berkeley: University of California Press, pp. 3–19.

Watson, James L. and Evelyn S. Rawski (eds.). 1988. *Death Ritual in Late Imperial and Modern China*. Berkeley: University of California Press.

Webb, John. 1667. *An Historical Essay Endeavouring a Probability that the Language of the Empire of China is the Primitive Language*. London.

Weber, Max. 1947. *Protestantische Ethik und der Geist des Kapitalismus*. Tubingen: J. C. B. Mohr.

1951. *The Religion of China: Confucianism and Taoism*, trans. and ed. H. H. Gerth. Glencoe: Free Press.

1958. *The Protestant Ethic and the Spirit of Capitalism*. New York: Charles Scribner's.

1971. *Gesammelte Politische Schriften*, 3rd edn, ed. J. Winckelmann. Tübingen: J. C. B. Mohr (Paul Siebeck).

1976. *The Agrarian Sociology of Ancient Civilisations*, trans. R. I. Frank. London: New Left Books.

1978. *Economy and Society: An Outline of Interpretive Sociology*, ed. Guenther Roth and Claus Wittich. 2 vols. Berkeley: University of California Press.

1984. *General Economic History*, trans. F. H. Knight. New Brunswick/ London: Transaction.

Wei Yingqi. 1941. *Zhongguo shixue shi* [A history of Chinese historiography]. 2 vols. Changsha: Shangwu Yinshuguan.

Weiner, Annette B. and Jane Schneider (eds.). 1989. *Cloth and Human Experience*. Washington: Smithsonian Institution Press.

Weiss, Johannes. 1986. *Weber and the Marxist World*. London: Routledge and Kegan Paul.

Wen Jize. 1942. "Douzheng riji" [A diary of struggle]. *Jiefang ribao* [Liberation Daily], 28 June.

Werskey, Gary. 1974. *The Visible College: A Collective Biography of British Scientists and Socialists of the 1930s*. London: Allen Lane.

Wesley, John. 1909–16. *The Journal of John Wesley*. 8 vols. London: Kelly.

White, Lynn, Jr. 1975. "The Study of Medieval Technology, 1924–1974: Personal Reflections." *Technology and Culture* 16 (October): 519–30.

1984. "Symposium on Joseph Needham and *Science and Civilisation in China*." *Isis* 75: 172–79.

Whitehead, Cynthia R. 1984. "The Optics of Imperialism: British Images, Actions, and Interests in China, 1793–1840." B.A. thesis, Harvard and Radcliffe Colleges.

Wickham, Chris. 1984. "The Other Transition: From the Ancient World to Feudalism." *Past and Present* 103: 3–36.

Widmer, Eric. 1976. *The Russian Ecclesiastical Mission in Peking during the 18th Century*. Foreword by J. K. Fairbank. Cambridge Mass.: East Asian Research Center, Harvard University.

Wilhelm, Richard (trans.). 1969. *I Ching, or the Book of Changes*. Princeton: Princeton University Press.

Will, Pierre-Étienne. 1990. *Bureaucracy and Famine in Eighteenth-Century China*. Stanford: Stanford University Press.

  1991. "Of Silk and Potatoes: Efforts at Improving Agriculture in Eighteenth-Century China." Paper given at Cornell University, East Asia Program.

  1994. "Développement quantitatif et développement qualitatif en Chine à la fin de l'époque impériale." *Annales: histoire, sciences sociales* 49: 4 (July–August), 863–902.

Will, Pierre-Étienne and R. Bin Wong, with James Lee. 1991. *Nourish the People: The State Civilian Granary System in China, 1650–1850*. Ann Arbor: University of Michigan Press.

Williams, Raymond. 1983. *Keywords: A Vocabulary of Culture and Society*. Rev. edn. London: Fontana.

Williams, Samuel Wells. 1848, 1857. *The Middle Kingdom*. 2 vols. 4th edn. New York: C. Scribner's.

Williams, William Appleton. 1980. *Empire as a Way of Life*. New York: Oxford University Press.

Wills, J. E., Jr. 1974. *Pepper, Guns and Parleys: The Dutch East India Company and China, 1662–1681*. Cambridge, Mass.: Harvard University Press.

  1984. *Embassies and Illusions: Dutch and Portuguese Envoys to K'ang-hsi, 1666–1687*. Cambridge, Mass.: Council on East Asian Studies, Harvard University.

Wilson, Peter J. 1988. *The Domestication of the Human Species*. New Haven: Yale University Press.

Winckelmann, J. J. 1766. *Histoire de l'art chez les anciens*. 2 vols. Amsterdam.

  1850. *The History of Ancient Art among the Greeks*, trans. G. H. Lodge. London: Chapman.

Wittfogel, Karl A. 1931. *Wirtschaft und Gesellschaft Chinas: Versuch der wissenschaftlichen Analyse einer grossen asiatischen Agrargesellschaft*. Leipzig: C. L. Hirschfeld.

  1935. "The Foundations and Stages of Chinese Economic History." *Zeitschrift für Sozialforschung Jahrgang* 4:1, 26–60.

  1957. *Oriental Despotism: A Comparative Study in Total Power*. New Haven: Yale University Press.

  1978. *China und die osteurasische Kavallerie-Revolution*. Wiesbaden: Harrassowitz.

Wolf, Eric. 1982. *Europe and the People without History*. Berkeley: University of California Press.

Wolf, Margery and Roxane Witke (eds.). 1975. *Women in Chinese Society*. Stanford: Stanford University Press.

Wolff, Christian. 1726. *Oratio de Sinarum Philosophia Practica*. Halle.

Wong, R. Bin. 1982. "Food Riots in the Qing Dynasty." *Journal of Asian Studies* 41: 4, 767–88.

  1988. "Naguèrre et aujourd'hui: réflexions sur l'État et l'économie en Chine." *Études chinoises* 7: 1, 7–28.

  1997. *China Transformed: Historical Change and the Limits of European Experience*. Ithaca: Cornell University Press.

Woodside, Alexander and Benjamin E. Elman. 1994. "Afterword." In *Education and Society in Late Imperial China, 1600–1900*, ed. Benjamin E. Elman and Alexander Woodside. Berkeley: University of California Press, pp. 525–60.

Wotton, William. 1694. *Reflections on Ancient and Modern Learning*. London.

Wright, Tim. 1984. *Coal Mining in China's Economy and Society, 1895–1937*. Cambridge: Cambridge University Press.

Wrigley, Edward Anthony. 1988. *Continuity, Chance and Change: The Character of the Industrial Revolution in England*. Cambridge: Cambridge University Press.

1989. "The Limits to Growth: Malthus and the Classical Economists." In *Population and Resources in Western Intellectual Traditions*, ed. Michael S. Teitelbaum and Jay M. Winter. Cambridge: Cambridge University Press.

Wu Dakun. 1989. "Some Questions concerning Research on the Asiatic Mode of Production." In *The Asiatic Mode of Production in China*, ed. Timothy Brook. Armonk, NY: M. E. Sharpe, pp. 35–46.

Wu Jing. 1978. *Zhenguan zhengyao* [Policy essentials from the Zhenguan era]. Shanghai: Shanghai Guji Chubanshe.

Xu Dixin and Wu Chengming (ed.). 1985. *Zhongguo zibenzhuyi de mengya* [Incipient Chinese capitalism], vol. I of *Zhongguo zibenzhuyi fazhan shi* [A history of the development of Chinese capitalism]. Beijing: Renmin Chubanshe.

Xu Guangqi. 1979. *Nongzheng quanshu* [Complete treatise on agricultural management], ed. Shi Shenghan. 3 vols. Shanghai: Shanghai Guji Chubanshe.

Xu Hong. 1972. *Qingdai Lianghuai yanchang de yanjiu* [Studies on the Qing-dynasty Lianghuai salt yard]. Taibei: Taiwan daxue lishi yanjiusuo.

Yamaji, Susumu and Shoichi Ito. 1993. "The Political Economy of Rice in Japan." In *Japanese and American Agriculture: Tradition and Progress in Conflict*, ed. Luther Tweeten *et al.* Boulder: Westview Press, pp. 349–65.

Yamane Yukio. 1980. "Postwar Japanese Studies on Ming History." *Acta Asiatica* 38: 93–123.

Yates, Frances A. 1964. *Giordano Bruno and the Hermetic Tradition*. London: Routledge and Kegan Paul.

1972. *The Rosicrucian Enlightenment*. London: Routledge and Kegan Paul.

Ye Guisheng and Liu Maolin. 1983. "Zhongguo shehuishi lunzhan yu Makesizhuyi lishixue de xingcheng" [The Chinese social history controversy and the formation of Marxist historiography]. *Zhongguo shi yanjiu* 1: 3–16.

Yin Da. 1969. "Bixu ba shixue geming jinxing dao di" [We must carry the historiographical revolution through to the end]. *Jian Bozan pipan wenti huibian* [A collection of materials regarding the question of the criticism of Jian Bozan]. Hong Kong: O.K. Newspaper Agency.

Yin Da (ed.). 1987. *Zhongguo zhexue fazhan shi* [A history of the development of Chinese philosophy]. Kaifeng: Zhongzhou Guji Chubanshe.

Yoshihara, Kunio. 1988. *The Rise of Ersatz Capitalism in South-East Asia*. Singapore: Oxford University Press.

Yü, Ying-shih. 1987. *Shi yu Zhongguo wenhua* [The literati and Chinese culture]. Shanghai: Renmin Chubanshe.

1993. "The Radicalization of China in the Twentieth Century." *Daedalus* 122:2.

Yule, Henry and Henry Cordier (eds. and trans.). 1903–1920. *The Book of Ser Marco Polo the Venetian Concerning the Kingdoms and Marvels of the East.* 3rd edn. Reprinted in 2 volumes, 1975. London: J. Murray.

  1915. *Cathay and the Way Thither, Being a Collection of Medieval Notices of China.* 4 vols. London: Hakluyt Society.

Zhang Lixiang. 1983. *Bu nongshu jiaoshi* [Supplemented treatise on agriculture, annotated], ed. Chen Huanli and Wang Dacan. Beijing: Nongye Chubanshe.

Zhang Shichu. 1986. "The Comparative Study of East and West Cultures in China in Recent Years." *Social Sciences in China* 3: 35–48.

Zhang Wengui, Tao Guangliang, Dai Juanping, and Ke Xiaodan. 1988. *Zhongguo shangye dili* [China's commercial geography]. Beijing: Zhongguo Caizheng Jingji Chubanshe.

Zhang Wenmin, Zhang Zhuoyuan, and Wu Jinglian. 1979. *Jianguo yilai shehui-zhuyi shangpin shengchan he jiazhi guilü lunwen xuan* [Selected articles on socialist commodity production and the law of value since 1949]. 2 vols. Shanghai: Shanghai Renmin Chubanshe.

Zhao Lisheng. 1984. *Zhongguo tudi zhidu shi* [A history of Chinese land systems]. Jinan: Qi-Lu Shushe.

  1989. "The Well-Field System in Relation to the Asiatic Mode of Production." In *The Asiatic Mode of Production in China,* ed. Timothy Brook. Armonk, NY: M. E. Sharpe, pp. 65–84.

Zhongguo Renmin Daxue [China People's University] (ed.). 1983. *Qingdai de kuangye* [Qing dynasty mining]. 2 vols. Beijing: Zhonghua Shuju.

Zhou Gucheng. 1935. *Zhongguo shehui zhi jiegou* [The structure of Chinese society]. 4th edn. Shanghai: Xin Shengming. First published 1930.

  1940. *Zhongguo tongshi* [A history of China]. Shanghai: Kaiming.

  1980. "Ancient Feudalism." *Social Sciences in China* 3: 83–102.

Zhu Jiazhen. 1989. "Some Questions Concerning Research on the Theory of the Asiatic Mode of Production." In *The Asiatic Mode of Production in China,* ed. Timothy Brook. Armonk, NY: M. E. Sharpe, pp. 104–17.

Zhu Weizheng. 1987. *Zou chu zhongshiji* [Coming out of the middle ages]. Shanghai: Renmin Chubanshe.

  1990. *Coming Out of the Middle Ages,* trans. Ruth Hayhoe. Partial translation of Zhu Weizheng 1987. Armonk, NY: M. E. Sharpe.

Index

Printed in the United Kingdom
by Lightning Source UK Ltd.
104609UKS00001B/107